AS Business Studies

Richard Thompson
Denry Machin

Published by HarperCollins*Publishers* Limited
77–85 Fulham Palace Road
Hammersmith
London
W6 8JB

www.**Collins**Education.com On-line Support for Schools and Colleges

© HarperCollins *Publishers* Limited 2003
First published 2003

Reprinted 10 9 8 7 6 5 4 3 2

ISBN 0 00 715120 9

British Cataloguing in Publication Data
A cataloguing record for this publication is available from
the British Library

Almost all the case studies in this book are factual.
However, in some cases the persons, locations and subjects
are fictitious and the accompanying images are for
aesthetic purposes only. They are not intended to represent
or identify any existing person, location or subject. The
publishers cannot accept any responsibility for any consequences resulting from this use, except as expressly
provided by law.

Series commissioned by Graham Bradbury
Design by Derek Lee
Cover by Phil Barker
Cover picture by Corbis
Pictures researched by Thelma Gilbert
Artwork by Jerry Fowler
Index by Marie Lorimer
Project managed by Kay Wright
Edited by Mike March
Production by Hilary Quantrill
Printed and bound in Hong Kong by Printing Express Ltd.

www.**fire**and**water**.co.uk The book lover's website

Dedications

For Sara, Joanna, William, Emily, Merry and Ron
Richard Thompson

For Sally
Denry Machin

Acknowledgements

The authors and publishers would like to thank Colin
Malone at McCann-Erikson for his contribution to Unit
11, Promotion.

The publishers would like to thank the following for
permission to reproduce photographs (T = top, B =
bottom, L = left, R = right and C = centre).

The Accessory People 25; **Ace Photo Library** 68, 83, 86,
89, 96, 186, 209; **Advertising Archives** 37T, 37CL, 37CR,
48, 62, 75, 276; **Alamy Images** 7, 70, 135; **BBC** 188;
Auto Express 245; **BMW/Mini** 55, 60B, 106, 228;
Camera Press Ltd 158; **Caterham's** 52; **Corbis** 33, 97,
124, 155T, 157, 187, 190, 254; **Cummins Inc.** 193;
Demon Tweeks 182B; **The Document Company Xerox**
232; **easyJet** 30, 128; **egg.com** 182T; **Elizabeth Whiting**
263BL; **Empics Ltd** 44, 109; **Financial Times** 165;
Haribo 116BL; **Henry Halstead** 236; **Lister Petter** 114;
Louis Vuitton 69; **Marks & Spencer** 78CL, 88L&R;
McDonald's 28; **Millennium Experience Company** 90;
Nike 36; **Nokia** 58; **Office of Fair Trading** 257;
PA Photos 243; **Photofusion** 250, © Paul Balesare, 259,
© Robert Brook, 268; **Pickfords** 263TR; **Popperfoto** 244,
246, 247, 269, © Charles Platiau, 208, © Thierry Roge
Reuters 282, © NATS Reuters 297; **Rex Features** 98,
116TL&TR, 195, 217, 277TR, 288, © Action Press 155B,
© Elizabeth Welch 164, © Mark Pain 172, © Ken McKay
173T, © Jonathan Player 173B, © Business Collection,
215, © Rex Rysted/Timepix, 240; **Robert Harding**/Scott
Thode, 224; **Roger Scruton** 16, 53, 60T, 67, 79, 80, 112,
116BR, 123, 138, 204L, 204R, 221, 233, 263TL, 263BR;
Ronald Grant Archive/Walt Disney Co 141; 160;
Ryanair 127; **Sainsbury's** 37; **Stove's** 236B; **Sunday
Times**/Noel Watson 170; **Unilever Plc** 277BL; **University
of Alberta** 156L; **Virgin** 9, 34TL, 74; **Yamaha** 218

Contents

The AQA Examiner speaks to the Candidate

John Dymott, Principal Examiner AQA
Director of Studies Farnham College

The AQA specification enables you to study business in an integrated context. You will study internal business functional areas, such as marketing and operations management, the context of business objectives and strategies, and the external environment in which businesses operate.

Assessment method

AQA AS Business Studies is assessed using three units. Each examination lasts one hour and consists of a written paper.

- **Unit 1** (Marketing and Accounting & Finance) is two compulsory data-response questions.
- **Unit 2** (People & Operations) is based on a pre-released case study.
- **Unit 3** (External Influences and Objectives & Strategy) uses the same pre-released case study as unit 2.

There is no coursework within AQA AS Business Studies (though this book can be used to assist with coursework titles that are likely to have arisen – for example, should Next plc open another branch in Aldershot?).

What the examiners are looking for – how to get a good grade

AQA Business Studies rewards candidates for the highest skill-level demonstrated in each answer. There are four main assessment skills.

- **Level 1:** knowledge and understanding. Marks will be gained by an explanation of business terminology showing good understanding.
- **Level 2:** application. The point or points made in the answer should be applied to the context of the case or the data-response.
- **Level 3:** analysis. Points made should analyse the set question using relevant theory. Analysis is about depth and this could be gained by following a line of argument in a paragraph.
- **Level 4:** evaluation. Evaluation is about showing judgment, either in the text or in conclusion.

Using this book and handy hints for the examination

There are three critical tools that will help you to obtain a high grade – the notes taken in class, a copy of the specification and your textbook. This textbook is excellent as it covers the whole specification in a lively way. Whether or not you have undertaken a Business Studies course before, you will benefit from its clear layout.

The data-response paper

The AQA AS Business Studies Unit 1 examination consists of one data-response paper with two questions, one on marketing, and one on finance and accounts. The stimulus material may comprise written, numerical or graphical data – largely drawn from newspapers and other real-world sources, such as magazines. The 'Exam practice' feature in this book, at the end of each unit, provides first-class preparation. The questions are styled in a similar way to the AQA unit one examination paper – starting with a short definition-type question and finishing with a high-mark question, which requires the higher-order skills of evaluation and analysis.

The pre-released case studies

The papers for units two and three are based on a pre-released case study. Pre-releasing the case study reduces the reading time during the examination, enabling you to get the feel of the case study. The same case study is used for both papers and it will include data that you can study – for example, a table of economic indicators. This textbook, and your notes, can help you prepare to use this data. It is important to be aware of the implications of the type of business presented in the case study – its legal structure, the type of product or service it produces, the objectives of its owners and the role of external constraints.

Matching chart – AQA specification

AQA Unit 1: Marketing and Accounting & Finance

Topic		Units in this book
10.1	Market analysis	5, 6, 7
10.2	Marketing strategy	8
10.3	Marketing planning	9, 10, 11, 12
10.4	Costs and breakeven analysis	13, 14
10.5	Cash flow and sources of finance	15, 17
10.6	Budgeting	16
10.7	Cost and profit centres	16

AQA Unit 2: People and Operations Management

11.1	Management structure and organisation	22
11.2	Motivation and leadership	24, 25, 26
11.3	Human resource management	27, 28
11.4	Productive efficiency	30, 31, 32
11.5	Controlling operations	34, 35
11.6	Lean production	36

AQA Unit 3: External influences and Objectives & strategy

12.1	The market and competition	37, 38
12.1	Macro economic issues e.g. inflation, business cycle, exchange rates, unemployment	40, 41, 42
12.2	Government constraints UK and EU law	37, 39
12.3	Social and other constraints, including business ethics and technological change	43, 44
12.4	Starting a small firm	1, 2, 4
12.5	Business objectives	3
12.6	Business strategy – including SWOT analysis	3

For a fuller version of this message, go to www.**Collins**Education.com/ASBusinessStudies/AQA

The Edexcel Examiner speaks to the Candidate

Brian Ellis, a Chief Examiner for Edexcel
Business Studies teacher and trainer

THE parts of a Business Studies course are like interlocking blocks – more like Lego than a jigsaw, because they can be joined in different ways and in different sequences. If you work through this book, you will have covered all the 'blocks' in the Edexcel AS Business Studies course.

Assessment method
The three Edexcel exam units are each one-hour long, and all three share a pre-released case study on which questions will be based.

What the examiners are looking for – how to get a good grade
Business Studies entails far more than simply learning facts to regurgitate in exams. Edexcel AS Business Studies assesses four skill levels:

- **Level 1**: knowledge and understanding
- **Level 2**: application of ideas to situations
- **Level 3**: analysis explanations building ideas logically
- **Level 4**: evaluation or judgment.

Using this book and handy hints for the examination
This book will be a valuable aid to your skills development. Its frequent and lively use of examples helps to clarify ideas and shows you how they are applied. It is packed with analysis and practice and, importantly, it shows you how to evaluate. Very often, there isn't just one right answer to evaluation questions. What matters is your ability to apply the idea to the situation given, your ability to analyse by logical steps and your readiness to conclude with a judgment supported by your analysis. (Some detective work on the numbers and the situation may be required before you can make a judgment.)

Business success is as much about managing risks carefully as about having bright ideas. The same is true in exams. The brightest students often do less well than those who approach the exam carefully and plan to minimise the risks of things going wrong. The difference between good and bad performance is often down to blunders that throw marks away. The candidates who go wrong often make similar mistakes:

- **Getting the words right.** Build explanations step by step. Pay special attention to link words and to subject jargon terms; for example, you pay the **price**, not the **cost**. Finish with a clear conclusion. Only a small mark is allocated for the quality of written communication, but some language skills are really important. To analyse successfully, you need to use link words such as **if, therefore, but** and **because** as precisely as possible – just as this textbook does.
- **Understanding and interpreting your business knowledge.** Simply repeating notes or a book's contents fails to impress. You must show that you understand what you've learnt. Link ideas to the evidence.
- **Using facts.** Look beyond the bare facts to what use the information will be, and what problems it helps to solve. Having the pre-released case-study material to hand as you revise should prompt some useful ideas.

- **Using numbers.** Numbers count in Business Studies. We don't want complicated sums (even with calculators). We do want to know you've understood the concept – what matters is the point that numbers make, what do they tell us?
- **Time management pays.** It is important to use most of your time where there are the most marks. Look at the total marks for the paper against the time available. If there are 120 marks on a one-hour paper, you have two marks to earn per minute. Edexcel uses structured questions that tend to start with small parts and build up to bigger sections with more marks.
- **Read the question carefully.** What is the question asking for? Don't rush into answers. Command words are particularly important as they tell you which skills are required. 'Define' is self-evident. 'Explain' or 'analyse' is asking for more in-depth consideration of the issues surrounding a topic. 'Assess', 'critically examine', 'evaluate', 'to what extent' and even 'discuss' want supported judgment. If you don't reach a conclusion or give an opinion, you cannot earn the evaluation marks (though there are always some marks for the other skills). **Reaching a conclusion is far more important than mentioning every possible relevant point.**
- **Plan your answer.** For the sections with most marks, jot your thoughts down and see how they fit together. Planning helps you to stay on track and to remember to finish with a conclusion.

If the paper seems tough, it might mean that you can see complications that weaker students miss. Keep going, even if one answer is weak you can still attain high grades.

Matching chart – Edexcel specification
The 'core' units are the major ones you must cover. Those marked 'extension' are useful, but not essential, at this stage as they will broaden your understanding and start your thinking for the A2 course.

Edexcel Unit 1 [6121]:
Business structures, objectives and external influences

Topic	Units in this book	
	Core	Extension
Business structures	1–3	4
Business objectives	22–26	27–29
External influences	37–43	44

Edexcel Unit 2 [6122]:
Marketing and Production

Marketing	5–12	
Production	30–36	
30–36		

Edexcel Unit 3 [6123]:
Financial management

	13–20	21

The OCR Examiner speaks to the Candidate

Steve Challoner, Principal Examiner (OCR)
Head of Business Studies (Bromsgrove School)

THE OCR specification brings together the functional areas of business with a consideration of the nature of business and the external environment within which it operates.

Assessment method

OCR AS Business Studies is assessed using three units:

- Unit 2871 (Businesses, Their Objectives and Environment) is a written paper based on a pre-released case study. There are five questions, and the examination lasts one hour.
- Unit 2872 (Business Decisions) is a data-response paper based on information seen on the day of the examination. There are four questions, and the paper lasts forty-five minutes.
- Unit 2873 (Business Behaviour) is another pre-released case study. There are four questions, and the paper lasts seventy-five minutes (an hour and a quarter).

There is no coursework within OCR AS Business Studies (though the book can be used to assist with much of the content that forms the basis for the business project at A2).

What the examiners are looking for – how to get a good grade

OCR Business Studies rewards candidates for the highest skill-level demonstrated in each answer. There are four levels:

- **Level 1:** knowledge and understanding
- **Level 2:** application – using the information in terms of the organisation presented in the question
- **Level 3:** analysis – taking the information and turning it into evidence for the arguments presented
- **Level 4:** evaluation – making 'value judgements' about the response presented.

Analysis and evaluation should be the target in as many answers as possible.

Using this book, revision and examination hints

A good textbook, such as this one, offers a safety net. It offers opportunities for revision, a clear set of notes, and plenty of 'practice' questions. To be awarded high marks you must relate your answers to the specific firms highlighted in the question. More successful candidates are those who develop knowledge to answer the specific question in relation to **that firm, in that situation, at that time**. Simply demonstrating you have lots of knowledge will only gain you top marks at the lower grades.

The examination is a stressful situation and requires careful planning. This book enables you to use a variety of techniques for revision. Pay particular attention to the flow diagrams, sections that highlight benefits or drawbacks of advantages and disadvantages and the case study questions. 'Stop and think' helps you consider wider issues.

If you are taking the three papers in one session you will need to adapt to the demands of the papers within a three-hour time period. **Remember careful planning**.

The pre-released case studies

Two of the papers can be considered well in advance of the day. Avoid predicting actual questions, but be aware of the issues that could arise. Study the papers carefully, look for clues about what has happened to the firm in the study, and consider how this impacts on future decisions. The focus of the first paper (2871) will be the external environment. The firm used will be one where the external influences are of greater significance than normal. The 2001 and 2002 papers, for example, used a building society and a holiday firm.

The other pre-released paper (2873) will focus on the functional areas. Expect one question on each of Marketing, Accounting & Finance, People, and Operations Management. The four middle sections of this book prepare you well for this, but remember to revise the topics in relation to the firm in the pre-released case study. The examiner will expect you to demonstrate the higher skills of evaluation in each answer. A calculation is also possible.

The data-response paper

This is relatively short (45 minutes), but is often considered the toughest test. Some candidates feel that it is difficult to prepare for this paper. You need to react quickly to the presented data and to consider the type of questions asked. Responding to the data presented is the only route to higher marks. Establish what you can about the chosen firm, or firms and use as much of this as you can in your answers. You will need to deal with specific business calculations. These can relate to several aspects of the course including price elasticity of demand, cash flow forecasts, payback periods, and breakeven. **Prepare carefully for this**. State all assumptions, and show your working. It is essential to have a working calculator that you know how to use.

Matching chart – OCR specification

OCR 2871 Businesses, Their Objectives and Environment

Topic	Units in this book
The nature of business	1, 3, 4, 17
Classification of business	1, 2, 31
Objectives	3, 4
Objectives and strategy	3
External influences	37, 38, 39, 41, 42
Other influences	37, 39, 43, 44

OCR 2872 Business Decisions and 2873 Business Behaviour

Marketing:	The market	5, 7
	Market research	6
	Marketing planning	8
	Four Ps	9, 10, 11, 12
Accounting and finance:	Budgets	16
	Cash flow	15
	Costs	14
	Investment decisions	21
	Final accounts	13, 18, 19, 20
People in organisations:	Human resource planning	27, 28, 39
	Motivation and leadership	24, 25, 26
	Management structure	22
Operations management:	Operational efficiency	30, 31, 32
	Organising production	33, 36
	Quality	35
	Stock Control	34

For a fuller version of this message, go to www.**Collins**Education.com/ASBusinessStudies/OCR

Section 1 Business objectives and strategy

What is the point of business?

Who owns a business?

What are SMART objectives?

What is a franchise?

How do I do a SWOT analysis?

How is a business run?

Why start your own business?

What is business?

The nature of business

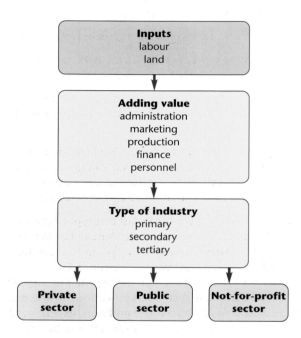

Inputs
labour
land

↓

Adding value
administration
marketing
production
finance
personnel

↓

Type of industry
primary
secondary
tertiary

↓

| Private sector | Public sector | Not-for-profit sector |

1 What is a business?

What do Coca Cola, a local hairdresser, your school or college and Oxfam all have in common?

They are all businesses. A **business** is an organisation that uses resources to create a good (an item) or a service for its customers. Many, like Coca Cola, make and sell goods in order to earn a profit for their owners. Others, such as schools, are seeking to provide a quality service for a particular group. What they all have in common is the way they combine different inputs to meet the needs of their customers.

A business needs a variety of inputs to produce their good or service:

- sources of finance – the money to set up the business and keep it running

- labour – the skills and efforts of the workforce and management

- equipment – the 'physical capital' needed to manufacture a good or help to deliver a service such as tools, vehicles or computers

- premises – a suitable site for the business to make and sell its product

- materials – the raw materials or components used to provide the basic parts for products

- business flair – the ideas and risk-taking of a businessperson, often known as an **entrepreneur**.

Using these inputs, businesses provide products (a product means either a good or a service) that meet people's needs and wants. People's basic *needs* are what they must have for survival – food and drink, shelter and warmth. *Wants* cover a huge range of products. Here the opportunities for business are endless – from fashion to entertainment and from relaxation to travel.

2 Adding value

By combining inputs to produce a good or service that customers want, a business aims to create a product that is worth more than the total cost of the inputs. This is known as **adding value**. By creating willingness, in the mind of the consumer, to pay more for a product than the total cost of the inputs, the business is able to make a profit – the selling price is higher than the cost of production.

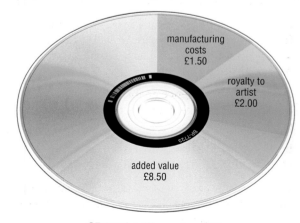

manufacturing costs £1.50

royalty to artist £2.00

added value £8.50

CD total selling price: £12

Figure 1.1 The value added in CD production and sales

Figure 1.1 illustrates the value that is added in making and selling a CD. You can see that manufacturing costs are only small and even after royalty payments to the artist, the added value is significant. However, this is not all profit for the music company, which must cover its overheads, the costs of marketing and the retailer's share of the profits.

A business can seek to add value in a variety of ways:

- **Design.** Developing new technology or adding new design features to make their product unique. James Dyson's 'dual cyclone' technology allowed Dyson vacuum cleaners to be sold at a price well above the costs of production.

- **Production.** Achieving quality and efficiency in production creates added value. Quality will help ensure a higher price for the output, while efficiency helps to cut the costs of the inputs. The gap between the two is added value.

- **Marketing.** Finding ways of increasing the customer's willingness to pay can be done through clever marketing – creating an image that makes the product more desirable. People are often willing to pay quite a bit more for a branded product, such as Gap clothing.

3 Specialisation

One business cannot hope to meet the wide range of needs and wants of every consumer. So most businesses focus on producing a very limited range of goods or services; for example, Kellogg's focus on food products, and on breakfast cereals in particular, while HSBC provide banking and financial services.

This focus on a limited range of products is called **specialisation**. Businesses tend to specialise because:

- It allows them to focus on a product in which they have an expertise. Most small businesses, such as a hairdresser, are based around the particular skills of the owner.

- Practice and experience enables the business to become more efficient and more organised in producing the product.

- It allows them to use specialist equipment that is ideal for making one type of product.

- The business can employ workers skilled in that area of production and develop their expertise to make them specialists.

- It helps them to understand what consumers want from that product. Research and experience over time allows the business to predict what its customers want, giving the business a real edge over its rivals.

- It builds an image in the mind of the consumer that could help the business add value and retain customer loyalty. Stretching this image to a new type of product could be a disaster – would you eat Pedigree Chum Chocolate?

However, there are drawbacks to specialisation:

- It limits the business to just one market, which limits the opportunities to make profits.

- If this one market faces a fall in demand, the business will have no other products from which to make a profit.

- If workers have to concentrate on just one task they are likely to become bored and demotivated. This could lead to slower production, poorer quality or more workers leaving the business.

Not all businesses specialise in just one type of product area. Richard Branson's company Virgin has become famous for offering new types of goods and services. This is known as diversifying (see Figure 1.2).

Branson believes he can challenge the big companies that dominate each market without losing the image of the Virgin brand. The problems experienced in running Virgin Trains have shown this to be a risky strategy that can damage the whole company if it goes wrong.

Figure 1.2 Virgin is well known for offering a wide range of products

The stages of business activity

Businesses that specialise rely on other businesses to:

- supply them with the materials or parts needed to make their product

- be their customers, buying their product in order to make another

- provide support services that help the business in its production process.

As a result, different business activities are closely linked to each other. These activities can be grouped into three stages of production.

- **Primary production** is the initial stage when raw materials are extracted from land or sea ready to be used by other industries. For example, forestry provides timber that is used in the production of a whole range of other goods.

- **Secondary production** transforms these raw materials into a finished product. Car production, for example, involves a variety of secondary businesses producing the parts that are needed for final assembly.

- **Tertiary production** is about providing services to consumers or to other businesses. Transport and retailing of finished products is within the tertiary sector, as are the tourism and leisure industries.

Identify which stage or stages of production the following businesses are in:
- an insurance company
- Shell (multinational energy providers)
- a double glazing manufacturer
- an auto electrician
- Eidos (computer games publisher)
- Nike (sportswear)

 Business functions

All businesses carry out similar roles to organise the business and make sure that it runs effectively. These functions include:

- **Marketing**. Finding out what consumers want, planning how to meet these needs in a way that will produce a profit, determining the product's ideal features and the best ways to promote, sell and distribute it.

1 **Production.** The business plans the best ways of making the good or delivering the service. It focuses on ensuring high quality while using resources efficiently.

- **Finance.** It is essential to keep track of money coming in and going out of the business, and to ensure that there is always enough cash to meet outgoings. Keeping accurate records of costs and revenues is vital to meet the demands of the Inland Revenue and of the law.

- **Personnel.** This includes managing the workforce to ensure it is well organised, skilled and motivated, recruiting and selecting the right people, organising training and finding ways to keep the workforce happy and hard working.

- **Administration.** Effective administration ensures smooth operation and cooperation within and between departments. It includes the paperwork and communication needed to link departments, suppliers and customers.

6 **Sectors of business activity**

A business can be grouped into one of three sectors, according to its ownership.

- **The private sector** refers to businesses owned by individuals or shareholders. In the UK, most businesses are in the private sector. They range from small local businesses, such as a plumber or architect, to large businesses that operate across the country and throughout the world, such as British Airways. The main objective of private sector businesses is to make profit as a reward for the risk taken by the investors (shareholders).

- **The public sector** includes any organisation owned or funded by government. These can be:

Activity

Investigate the activities of a charity of your choice. Consider the following issues:
- What are its aims? Who or what is it set up to help?
- What is its main source of income?
- Are commercial activities used to boost revenue?
- Does it successfully meet its aims?

Want to know more?

www.shelter.co.uk or
www.oxfam.co.uk

– public corporations, such as the Royal Mail, that sell a good or service
– public services provided through taxation, such as the National Health Service
– organisations run by local authorities, such as leisure centres or refuse collection.

The aims of these organisations differ from those in the private sector. Achieving a profit is likely to be much less important than providing a value-for-money service that meets the needs of the population.

● **The 'not-for-profit' sector** comprises voluntary organisations such as:

– charities seeking to raise funds and campaign for the needs of particular groups, such as Oxfam which campaigns to support the world's poor
– self-help groups, such as a local playgroup, where parents help fund and run a service for their own children
– pressure groups seeking to persuade government or business to listen to their views, such as Greenpeace's environmental issues campaigns.

While these organisations may have some different objectives from private and public sector businesses, they all have 'customers' to reach and an idea to 'sell'. They will, therefore, operate in a very similar way to other businesses.

For example ...

Reaching new heights

Dave Fox set up Foxes Scaffold in 1985. The firm supplies scaffold to business and, occasionally, to retail customers. The most lucrative contracts are those with the big building firms – often involving supplying the scaffolding for a new housing estate development. The firm purchases scaffold direct from the manufacturer and then alters the basic scaffold to suit customers' needs.

1 From the evidence in the case, suggest which stage of production Foxes Scaffold operates in. **[1]**
2 Which stage of production do building companies operate in? **[1]**
3 Which sector of business (public or private) do you think Dave operates in? **[1]**
4 Using Foxes Scaffold as an example, explain the concept of added value. **[3]**
5 Explain the importance of each of the main business functions to Foxes Scaffold. **[6]**
Total 12 marks

 Privatisation

Over the last 20 years, many government-owned organisations have been sold to the private sector. This is known as **privatisation**. The Government sold a range of nationalised industries, including electricity, water and telecommunications, to individuals who became shareholders in the new companies. More recently, the railways and the air traffic control service were fully or partly privatised.

The benefits of privatisation were that:

● Businesses would be more efficient and responsive to the wishes of consumers because they were aiming to make a profit.

● More companies would be able to compete in the market. This encourages companies to cut costs and improve quality, both of which should be good for the consumer.

● Operating in the private sector, would enable the industries to raise more funds for investment both to improve the quality of service and to make it profitable.

A number of major drawbacks have been apparent:

● In the private sector, the prime aim of these businesses is to make a profit, not simply to provide a public service. This has sometimes led to higher prices or the closure of valuable, but loss-making services.

● The benefits of efficiency and quality have not always been seen. This has been the case in the railway industry, where it is almost impossible to create real competition.

● Without direct control over these businesses, the Government is less able to ensure that a quality service is run in the interests of the general public.

The current policy of the Labour Government is to develop *Public–Private Partnerships*. These seek to combine private finance and expertise with public sector ownership. In the area of health, for example, the NHS is encouraged to buy private treatment for patients on lengthy waiting lists.

STOP & THINK

In what ways are all businesses similar? And in what ways are there crucial differences? Why?

The nature of business: summary

KEY TERMS

Business – an organisation that uses resources to create a good or a service for its customers.

Entrepreneur – an individual with a business idea willing to invest their own money and take risks to make a profit.

Adding value – the ways in which a business creates a product that is worth more than the cost of the inputs that made it.

Specialisation – the way in which businesses focus on producing a limited range of products, or in which workers are given a limited range of tasks to carry out.

Primary production – businesses involved in the extraction of raw materials from land or sea.

Secondary production – businesses involved in turning raw materials into finished products.

Tertiary production – businesses that provide a service to consumers or to other businesses.

Private sector – those businesses owned by individuals or by shareholders.

Public sector – organisations owned or financed by central or local government.

Summary questions

1 State **three** business inputs? Give an example of how each is used within business.
2 Distinguish between wants and needs.
   What is meant by specialisation in business?
3 Outline **two** benefits and two drawbacks of specialisation.
4 List **six** businesses in your local area and categorise each into the primary, secondary or tertiary sectors.
5 Explain the role and importance of **two** business functions.
6 Why do the aims of the private and public sectors differ?
7 Explain, using an example, the purpose of 'not-for-profit' organisations.
8 Explain **two** advantages and two drawbacks of 'privatisation'

Not-for-profit sector – charities, pressure groups or political parties that have objectives other than making a profit.

Privatisation – the sale of public sector organisations to the private sector.

Doing your business in public

The Iron Lady, Margaret Thatcher, was Prime Minister from 1979 to 1990. She left a legacy of privatisation. By 1990, one in four of the population owned shares in the 40 or so former state-owned businesses that had been privatised.

British Gas, British Steel and British Telecom all moved into private ownership. As Figure 1.3 shows, their subsequent performance bettered that of

Figure 1.3 Privatisation portfolio

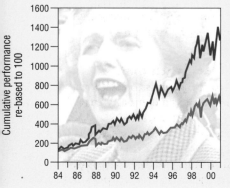

Cumulative performance re-based to 100

84 86 88 90 92 94 96 98 00

Portfolio: Cable & Wireless, Nycomed Amersham, Associated British Ports, Enterprise Oil, British Telecom, BG Group, British Airways, Rolls Royce, BAA, Corus Group, United Utilities.

—— Portfolio

—— FTSE100

Source: ING Bearings

the benchmark FTSE 100. Yet many customers complained of poor service, rising prices and unhelpful company representatives. Alongside this the 'fat cat' pay packages paid to company executives drew much criticism.

Railtrack hit trouble in 2002 when it was put into administration. The chaos of the railways has been blamed on Railtrack's privatisation, with some experts arguing it should have remained under state control. Rail companies, such as Virgin Rail, have found their own plans for investment to improve train services hampered by the poor state of the rail network.

Despite this, many herald privatisation a great success and even the Labour Party, once very much against privatisation, launched a policy of Public–Private Partnerships. The Iron Lady's legacy lives on.

Source: *The Guardian*
22 November 2000

Exam practice

1 Explain what is meant by privatisation. **[2]**
2 In what sector of industry would you place Railtrack? **[2]**
3 What are Public–Private Partnerships? **[3]**
4 Explain how a rail operator might attempt to add value to its products. **[6]**
5 What might be the advantages and potential drawbacks of selling Royal Mail to the private sector? **[12]**

Total 25 marks

2 Business ownership

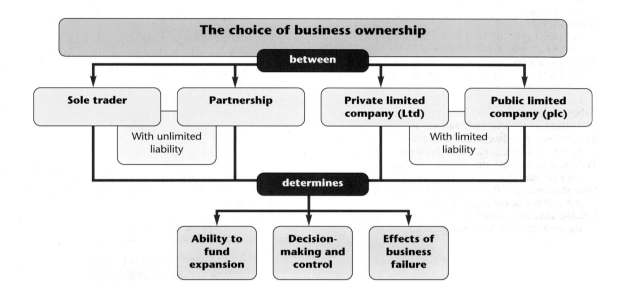

1 The choice

WH Smith, Marks & Spencer, Sainsbury's – are big businesses now but, as their names suggest, they all began with the ideas and efforts of just one or two business owners. Trace the history of any large business and you are likely to find key moments when ownership and organisation changed. You will see in this unit how choosing the right type of ownership at the right time can be crucial to the success of a business.

In the private sector of the economy, businesses are owned by individuals not the government. There are four main types of business organisation within the private sector:

- sole traders
- partnerships
- private limited companies (Ltd)
- public limited companies (plc)

2 Limited liability

In choosing the ideal type of ownership, the first decision is what legal status to give the business.

- **Unincorporated businesses with unlimited liability.** Unincorporated businesses tend to be small organisations and include sole traders and partnerships. The law does not see these businesses as being separate from their owners. This means that, if the business runs into financial trouble and cannot pay the money it owes, the owners are responsible for paying the debts. This is known as having **unlimited liability**.

- **Incorporated businesses with limited liability.** The alternative option is to *incorporate* the business by setting it up as a company that, in the eyes of the law, is separate from the business owners. Incorporated businesses are known as *limited companies* because they have **limited liability**. This means that the owners do not have to pay off any debts using their personal finances – all they would lose is the money they had originally invested in the business. If there were not enough money left in the business to pay all those to whom it owes money (its creditors), the debts would go unpaid. There are two types of limited company – a private limited company (Ltd) – and a public limited company (plc).

3 Sole traders

A sole trader is a business owned by just one person. There are more sole trader businesses in the UK than any other type of business. The single owner of the business has full control over decision-making and receives all the business profits, although there may be a number of other employees working for the business. The popularity of the sole trader as a form of business ownership is largely down to its simplicity.

> ### Guru's views
> 'The key to success is to exploit the advantages of being a sole trader and yet to take seriously the disadvantages.'
>
> *Business Bureau-uk*

4 Partnerships

A partnership is the joint ownership of a business by more than one owner. These joint owners will each:

- contribute their own financial capital to the business
- share the responsibility for decision-making and control
- share the business profits

A partnership, like a sole trader, has unlimited liability and so the personal finances of partners could be taken to pay off business debts. The workload and profits are shared between the partners, though not necessarily equally. The partners can draw up a Deed of Partnership when they set up the business. In this they can state:

- what share of the profits each partner receives
- the role each partner can play in decision-making
- rules and procedures for solving disagreements between partners.

The Deed of Partnership is a legal document that can help to prevent disputes over who is entitled to what. It is not required by law, but without it there is an assumption that all profits will be shared equally.

Being a sole trader

Advantages

- **Easy to set up the business** – few forms to complete, allowing the business to be set up swiftly and cheaply.
- **Complete control** – the single owner makes all decisions about running the business. This allows the business to adapt quickly to customers' needs. Many sole traders find the independence of self-employment crucial to job satisfaction.
- **Keep all the profit** – with no other owners, the sole trader won't have to share business profits or discuss with others how they should be used.
- **Personal service** – a business owned and run by the same person, the sole trader, can get to know customers well and ensure their needs are met. This quality of personal service can be an excellent tool for gaining customers and keeping them loyal.
- **Privacy** – the business's financial information does not have to be published (except to the Inland Revenue for tax purposes).

Disadvantages

- **Unlimited liability** – if the business fails debts must be paid by the owner, personal possessions may be at risk.
- **Shortage of finance** – the owner's savings may be the only source of financial capital. A bank loan may be difficult to get if the business idea is a risky one. Shortage of finance may prevent expansion.
- **Pressure of responsibility** – running your own business can involve long hours, stress and difficulty during times of illness.
- **Lack of expertise** – sole traders usually have an area of expertise that led them to set up the business; but they are unlikely to have all the skills needed to manage a business successfully.
- **Lack of continuity** – because the business is not legally separate from the owner, if the owner retires or dies the business must be *wound up* (closed down).

Partnerships

Advantages

- **Extra financial capital** – with more than one business owner contributing finance, the business has more capital with which to grow.
- **Additional skills** – partners may bring different skills to the business, allowing each to specialise in their own area of expertise.
- **Shared workload** – the running of the business and the decision-making is shared between the business owners.

Disadvantages

- **Unlimited liability** – the personal possessions of partners are at risk in the event of business failure.
- **Shared profit** – the downside of having partners to share the workload is that the profit has to be shared out as well!
- **Disagreements** – having more than one person making decisions can lead to conflict.
- **Shortage of capital** – although there may be more financial capital, the amount available is still limited to the owners' contributions and what can be borrowed from a bank.

STOP & THINK

Partnerships are a common type of business ownership for a variety of professional services – such as dentists, solicitors or accountants. Why do you think it is a particularly suitable form of ownership for these types of businesses?

5 Limited companies

The alternative to being a sole trader or partnership is to set up a limited company. A limited company has a separate legal identity from its owners and so brings the protection of limited liability. Capital is invested in a limited company through the purchase of shares. A share is a part ownership of a business. The business owners are therefore known as **shareholders**.

Shareholders have a right to share in decision-making and in profits. The more shares owned by a shareholder the greater their power in decision-making and the greater their share of the profits. A board of directors, headed by a chairperson is elected by shareholders to carry out the day-to-day running of a limited company.

Setting up a limited company

Setting up a limited company (see Figure 2.1) involves following the formal process of incorporation by registering the business with the Registrar of Companies.

Private limited companies

A private limited company (Ltd) is the smaller of the two types of limited company. It is suitable for a new business start-up or for an existing sole trader or partnership seeking the benefits of limited liability. The shares it issues cannot be advertised for sale or traded on the stock market. This is why it is a *private* limited company – any transfer of shares must be done privately and with the agreement of all shareholders. Many Ltds are family businesses, with the family members being directors and shareholders.

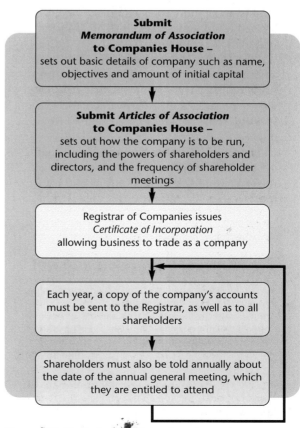

Submit
Memorandum of Association
to Companies House –
sets out basic details of company such as name, objectives and amount of initial capital

↓

Submit *Articles of Association*
to Companies House –
sets out how the company is to be run, including the powers of shareholders and directors, and the frequency of shareholder meetings

↓

Registrar of Companies issues
Certificate of Incorporation
allowing business to trade as a company

↓

Each year, a copy of the company's accounts must be sent to the Registrar, as well as to all shareholders

↓

Shareholders must also be told annually about the date of the annual general meeting, which they are entitled to attend

Figure 2.1 Limited company legal requirements

For example ...

Limited options

Mark Sprink and Jason Shuttleworth had no doubts about how their company would be formed when they set up FixIT, an IT systems maintenance company.

Both former software engineers, they were advised to become a limited company. Although they were confident that their idea would be successful, they wanted the extra security that private limited status would offer.

Like many business start-ups, they bought a £100 limited company off the shelf, got their solicitor to set up the venture and began trading.

1 What initials represent private limited companies? **[1]**
2 Why does limited status provide extra security? **[3]**
3 Give **two** reasons why FixIT might prefer private to public limited status. **[4]**
4 What advantages would setting up as a partnership have offered over limited status? **[4]**
5 Some small businesses may be nervous when supplying limited companies with goods on credit. Why might this be the case? **[3]**

Total 15 marks

Private limited companies

Advantages

- **Limited liability** – the key benefit over a sole trader or partnership. If the business fails, shareholders lose only the value of their share capital.
- **Sources of finance** – the security of limited liability makes it easier to attract investors and so raise finance.
- **Continuity** – the separate legal identity of the business means that it continues to exist even if one of the owners dies.

Disadvantages

- **Legal requirements** – the added burden of legal duties (see figure 2.1) takes time and money.
- **Loss of privacy** – the need to declare business accounts to Companies House means that anyone (including competitors) can find out about a company's financial position.
- **Limited growth** – the restriction of share capital to a maximum of £50,000, and the inability to sell shares to the public, limits the opportunities to raise finance and expand.

Public limited companies

A public limited company (plc) is a much larger type of company that must have at least £50,000 of share capital and which has its shares traded on the stock market. The majority of the big and famous High Street names are either plcs or are owned by plcs. When a company decides to become a plc it must be **floated** on the Stock Exchange. This involves publishing a prospectus to advertise the company to potential shareholders and can be an expensive process. Once a plc has a listing on the Stock Market, any member of the general public can buy and sell shares in the company.

Activity

Using a copy of the Yellow Pages or the internet, find five examples of each of the four types of business ownership.

Public limited companies

Advantages

- **Sources of finance** – the key benefit compared to a Ltd. Enormous potential to raise large amounts of capital as shares can be advertised to the general public, and bought and sold with ease.

- **Expansion** – the capital available to a plc allows it to expand and benefit from the increased business size and market power.

- **Credibility** – plc status is likely to give the business more credibility with lenders, suppliers and customers.

Disadvantages

- **Costs** – initial flotation on the stock market is expensive, as are the requirements to publish detailed accounts and to keep large numbers of shareholders informed each year.

- **Loss of control** – by selling shares on the stock market, the original owners' control of the company can be lost. Other individuals or businesses could take major shareholdings in a plc and maybe influence key decisions even launching a takeover.

- **Business size** – the growth of a plc could lead to problems, such as a lack of flexibility or loss of personal touch with customers or employees.

Divorce of ownership and control

This can introduce a divide between those who own the company (the shareholders) and those who are controlling it on a day-to-day basis (the board of directors). This *divorce* (separation) of ownership and control can have important effects on the business. Decisions could be taken that meet the needs of the directors – for example, greater financial bonuses – but are not in the best interest of the business owners. Shareholders can, in theory, use their power at the annual general meeting to overrule or remove directors, but these meetings occur only once a year and are often poorly attended.

 ## The effects of business ownership

The important effects that business ownership has on the way businesses operate and develop include:

- **The ability to expand** – a successful business might want to grow and limited company status will allow this to happen.

- **Who is in control** – from the sole trader, where a single owner is in complete control of decision-making, to a plc, where shareholders play a limited role in decision-making, business ownership determines who is in charge.

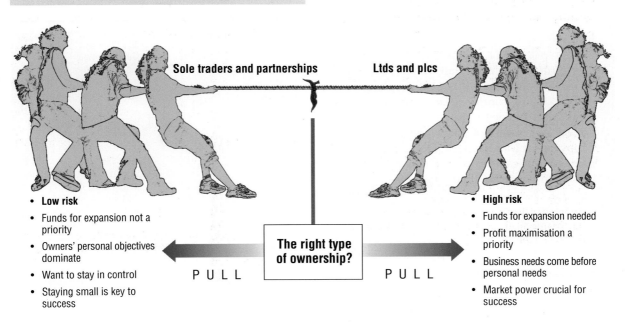

Sole traders and partnerships

Ltds and plcs

- **Low risk**
- Funds for expansion not a priority
- Owners' personal objectives dominate
- Want to stay in control
- Staying small is key to success

The right type of ownership?

P U L L   P U L L

- **High risk**
- Funds for expansion needed
- Profit maximisation a priority
- Business needs come before personal needs
- Market power crucial for success

Figure 2.2 The business ownership tug-of-war

● **The effects of business failure** – for a sole trader or partnership, business failure can mean personal ruin. The owners of a failed limited company, on the other hand, could be back in business with a new company almost instantly. These consequences of limited liability, however, also mean that anyone who is owed money (a *creditor*) by a failed limited company may never be paid.

STOP & THINK

Why do you think small businesses are so popular? Given the advantages of larger plcs, how do small businesses manage to survive?

Business ownership: summary

KEY TERMS

Unincorporated business – a business that is not legally separate from its owner (sole traders and partnerships).

Unlimited liability – where the business owner can lose personal wealth to pay off business debts.

Incorporated business – an organisation with a separate legal identity from its owner (a limited company).

Limited liability – where a business owner can only lose the amount of money invested into the business if it fails, not their personal wealth.

Shareholders – the joint owners of a limited company, whose investment entitles them to vote on major decisions and take a share of the profit.

Flotation – becoming a plc by issuing shares for general sale on the stock market.

Summary questions

1 Why might an entrepreneur choose to set up as a sole trader rather than a partnership?
2 What are the main advantages of a partnership?
3 What is limited liability?
4 Why might a growing partnership wish to incorporate?
5 Compare and contrast public limited ownership and private limited ownership.
6 Compare the options available to sole traders and plcs for raising finance.
7 In choosing a type of ownership, identify **three** considerations that need to be made.

Exam practice

Growing up

Business expansion is perhaps one of the most difficult challenges facing entrepreneurs today. Many businesses stay small for a reason – they find it very difficult to grow. Many small business managers fear the divorce of ownership and control that expansion often brings and lack the management skills to control a large organisation. Restricted finance is also a significant barrier to growth, particularly where owners are reluctant to borrow large sums or to share ownership. The small business owner is often happy as just that, preferring to stay small and to operate well within their management capabilities. No wonder then that 93 per cent of all UK businesses employ fewer than 20 people.

Some businesses do, however, show spectacular growth. Amazon.com and Microsoft are both companies initially started by a handful of people and operated from home out of garages. They are both now market leaders, having grown rapidly over very short periods of time.

Another example is Cisco Systems, set up in 1984, by two university professors. It now operates in over sixty-seven countries and employs 38,000 people worldwide.

1 Explain what is meant by 'divorce of ownership and control'. **[3]**
2 Describe **two** disadvantages that businesses choosing to stay small might face? **[4]**
3 Identify and explain **two** benefits that businesses might gain from increased size. **[4]**
4 Why do unincorporated businesses often face difficulties gaining finance? **[8]**
5 'Expansion is crucial to business survival'. To what extent do you agree with this statement? **[7]**
Total 26 marks

3 Business strategy

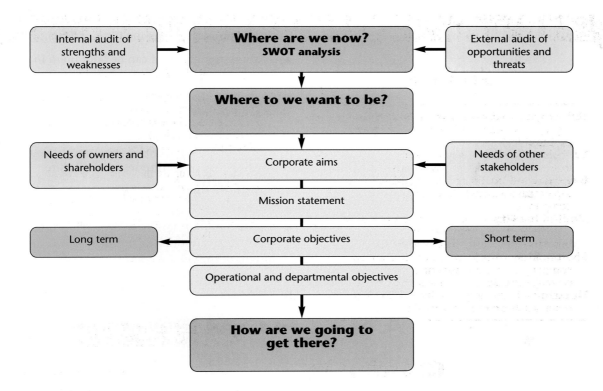

In order to plan effectively for the future, businesses must consider three key questions:

- **Where they are now?** Understanding its strengths and weaknesses, and the opportunities and threats that face it.

- **Where do they want to be?** Setting goals and objectives for the future.

- **How they are going to get there?** Planning a strategy of how to achieve these goals.

For many large businesses this will be a formal and ongoing process, while for many smaller businesses it may be no more than ideas in the mind of the entrepreneur. Planning ahead, however, is crucial if a business is to have realistic goals and know how to achieve them. A firm must find a fit between its capabilities, what its customers demand and what its competitors are doing.

 Where are we now? SWOT analysis

Understanding the present situation of the business is the starting point for any business strategy. A **SWOT analysis** is one method a business can use to help understand where it is now in its market and in comparison to its competitors. SWOT stands for:

- Strengths (of the organisation)

- Weaknesses (of the organisation)

- Opportunities (in the external environment)

- Threats (in the external environment).

Strengths and weaknesses lie in the reputation and resources of an organisation. To identify these strengths and weaknesses a business will need to carry out an internal audit. This could be done by a

OUTSIDE THE BUSINESS
INSIDE THE BUSINESS
STRENGTHS
WEAKNESSES
OPPORTUNITIES
THREATS
+
–

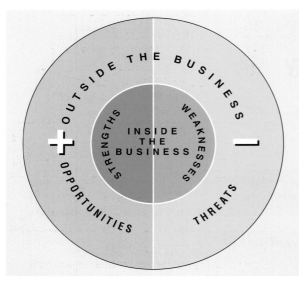

Figure 3.1 SWOT analysis

business's own managers and employees, or by management consultants.

An external audit can be carried out to consider the opportunities and threats in the business's external environment. Opportunities are those factors in its external environment that are likely to benefit a business in the future, while threats are likely to cause problems or limit success. The external environment includes:

- The competition, trends and conditions in the markets.
- The wider political, economic, social and technological conditions in the country as a whole.

As Figure 3.1 shows, SWOT analysis can be of great value to a business in helping it to understand:

- existing strengths that can be built upon in the future.
- weaknesses that need to be turned into strengths to achieve greater success
- trends in the market, and how these present challenges that need to be overcome or could open up new opportunities for the future.

The value of the analysis, though, depends on a number of factors:

- Has the internal audit been carried out honestly and objectively, drawing on the expertise and insight of the employees?

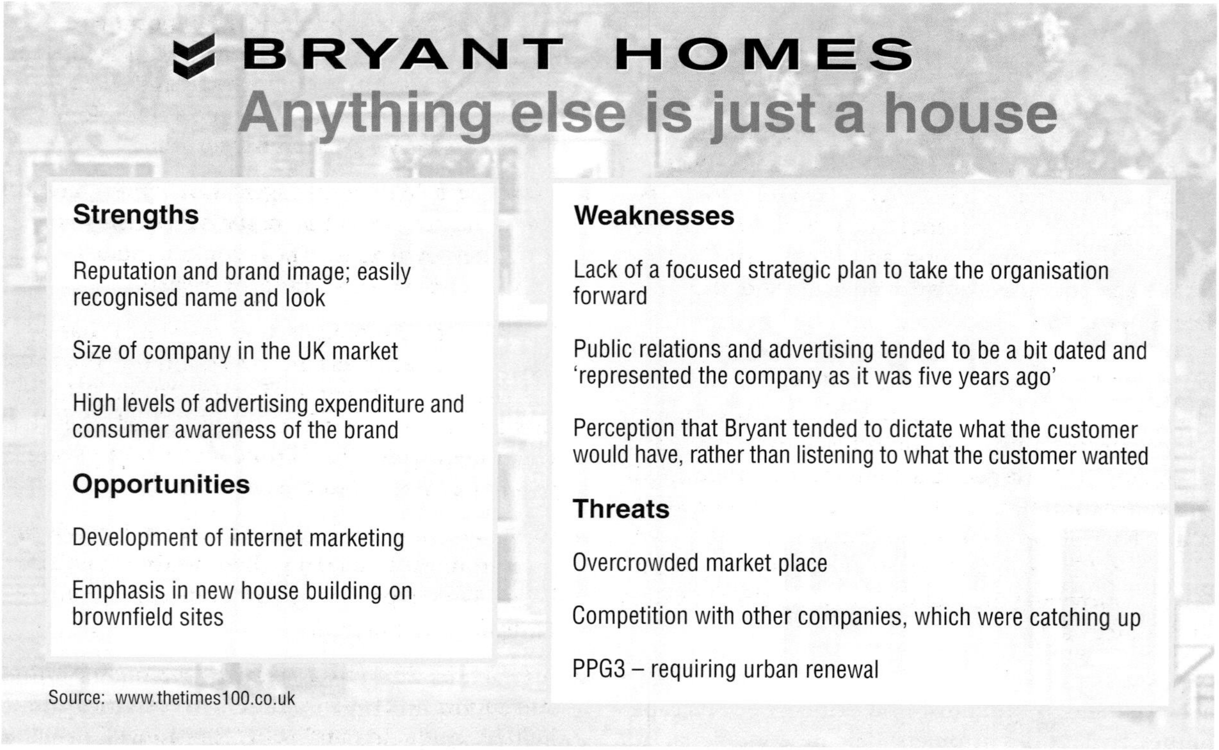

BRYANT HOMES
Anything else is just a house
Strengths
Reputation and brand image; easily recognised name and look
Size of company in the UK market
High levels of advertising expenditure and consumer awareness of the brand
Opportunities
Development of internet marketing
Emphasis in new house building on brownfield sites
Weaknesses
Lack of a focused strategic plan to take the organisation forward
Public relations and advertising tended to be a bit dated and 'represented the company as it was five years ago'
Perception that Bryant tended to dictate what the customer would have, rather than listening to what the customer wanted
Threats
Overcrowded market place
Competition with other companies, which were catching up
PPG3 – requiring urban renewal
Source: www.thetimes100.co.uk

Figure 3.2 Bryant Homes SWOT analysis

- Has the business been compared against the best in the industry?

- Has the external audit drawn on sufficient evidence about the future environment, not just the present?

- Have the results of the SWOT analysis been fully communicated to employees and used to develop future strategy?

This final point is crucial – if the SWOT analysis is not used throughout the business as a starting point for meaningful strategic planning, it will have been a wasted exercise.

Activity

Prepare a SWOT analysis for an organisation that you know well. You might wish to use IT to prepare your analysis and present your results to the rest of your group.

S | W

O | T

---

2 Where do we want to be? – Mission, aims and objectives

At the heart of every business is its purpose, its reason for existence. It is this that drives it forward and gives it direction. Phil Knight, Chairman of Nike, sees Nike's reason for existence as a way to 'enhance people's lives through sport and fitness' and to keep 'the magic of sports alive' (Naomi Klein, *No Logo*, Flamingo, 2000).

For many small businesses these goals may never be precisely formed or written down – they may simply be the ideas or values of an entrepreneur. Larger organisations, on the other hand, may go to great lengths to define and communicate their goals. In every business, though, it is these basic **corporate aims** that determine its plans and actions.

Figure 3.3 illustrates the importance of corporate aims, as providing the foundation on which objectives and strategy are built.

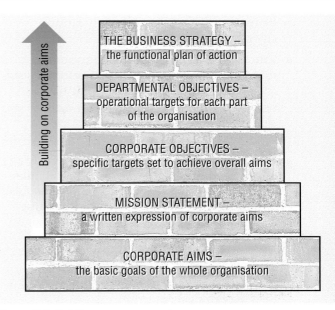

Building on corporate aims

THE BUSINESS STRATEGY – the functional plan of action

DEPARTMENTAL OBJECTIVES – operational targets for each part of the organisation

CORPORATE OBJECTIVES – specific targets set to achieve overall aims

MISSION STATEMENT – a written expression of corporate aims

CORPORATE AIMS – the basic goals of the whole organisation

Figure 3.3 Building on corporate aims

Corporate aims and stakeholders

The basic goals of an organisation depend on which group of people it is seeking to serve. These different groups (known as **stakeholders**) may include:

- **Owners and shareholders.** If the business seeks first and foremost to meet the needs of owners and shareholders, its goal must be to maximise returns to these owners. This is likely to involve a focus on profits, growth and share prices, creating what has become known for larger companies as 'shareholder value'.

- **Managers.** Where managers, not owners, are in day-to-day control of an organisation they may have their own goals. These could include maximising personal status or wealth.

- **Employees.** An organisation may feel it has a duty to look after its employees and this may be a key element of its corporate aims. Virgin Atlantic Airways states as one if its business goals that it seeks '*to recognise, develop and motivate employees so that they reach their full potential*'.

- **Customers.** Every business's success depends on its customers; so meeting their needs is crucial. Disneyland expresses its corporate aim as simply to '*make people happy*'.

- **Suppliers.** Building a positive relationship with its suppliers may be a central aim for a business. Reliability, quality and value-for-money from a supplier helps a business to achieve success, but there is much a business can do to ensure these criteria are built over time.

- **The local community.** Giving something back to the local community is often more than just a good public relations exercise – some businesses see it as central to their existence. A business may aim to conserve or improve the local environment or meet the needs of local residents.

- **Government and society.** A business may aim to be a good citizen, meeting its responsibilities to government and to society. This could involve setting high standards in its conduct, meeting legal requirements and promoting development. Public sector organisations, such as the NHS, place public service before any other goal. Some private sector businesses, such as the Body Shop, also place their responsibility to society ahead of their duty to shareholders.

Conflicting aims

The needs of different stakeholders are likely to be competing, and often conflicting. If a business aims above all else to serve the interests of shareholders, it may seek profit at the expense of employees or the environment. 'Giving back to the local community' or rewarding employees could mean lower profits, at least in the short-term. Where aims conflict, a business must decide its priorities and identify which of its stakeholders it is most important to serve.

Common aims

Meeting the needs of different stakeholders can be achieved through a number of common aims. Business success and growth can benefit a range of groups, providing returns to shareholders, status to managers, security to employees and employment for the local community. Focusing on customers' needs is an aim that will help achieve this success. High standards of behaviour in dealings with suppliers, government and the community build a positive image for the business.

Mission statements

In recent years, many organisations have expressed their corporate aims in the form of a **mission statement**. Often short and snappy, these statements seek to sum up the ultimate goal of the business (see Figure 3.4). They have been likened to the business equivalent of a modern-day coat of arms – creating an image of what the organisation stands for.

For example ...

Stake & Chips

The day of the relocation was hectic. Bits of computers were everywhere and you could hardly move for boxes. Staff, all dressed in 'scruffs', were carrying boxes to the various vans hired to move the company to its new offices 50 miles away.

The move had been agreed six months ago. Paragon plc, a pottery manufacturer, under pressure from shareholders to cut costs and improve profit margins, had been faced with some tough decisions. Competition in the market was fierce; most businesses in the industry had already moved production facilities to South East Asia and now had significant cost advantages over Paragon. Paragon's Managing Director had avoided the inevitable for as long as possible, 'we have a duty to our staff, the local community and to the UK to remain here' she argued 12 months ago. But, under increasing pressure from shareholders the company moved production to Vietnam and the factory and offices were sold to a housing developer.

The majority of staff were made redundant; a small number would manage the company from offices 50 miles from the original UK factory. The local newsagent and chip shop owner, who had supplied the staff with refreshments for over 20 years, although obviously upset by the move came out to wish everybody well.

1 What is a stakeholder?   [2]
2 Identify as many direct stakeholders from this case study as possible.   [3]
3 Identify **one** indirect stakeholder.   [1]
4 Using the information in this case study, highlight why managers' responsibilities to different stakeholders are often in conflict.   [6]

Total 12 marks

Figure 3.4 Examples of mission statements

Business objectives

Objectives are the measurable targets that a business seeks to achieve in order to fulfil its overall aims. These objectives are valuable because they:

● focus managers and employees on what the business needs to achieve

● set a time-period for their achievement

● provide a measure of business performance

● can motivate managers and employees

● co-ordinate the actions of different parts of a business.

Good objectives should be SMART:

SPECIFIC

MEASURABLE

ACHIEVABLE

REALISTIC

TIME-SPECIFIC

The point of writing a mission statement is to communicate the aim of the business to stakeholders – notably employees and customers. The hope is that it will inspire and unite employees behind the business purpose, helping to motivate them to achieve the business aim. Customers, it is hoped, will also be impressed and remain loyal to a business they believe has their best interests at heart. It is not surprising then that most mission statements focus on values, beliefs and non-financial goals rather than stating they seek to maximise profits!

Many business leaders, however, are critical of mission statements believing that they add little or nothing to the success of a business. They are seen as no more than a slick public relations exercise, convincing no one. All too often they are neither communicated effectively nor turned into action. Where the reality differs from the theory, the mission statement will quickly become irrelevant.

Guru's views

'A good mission statement gives workers a reason to get out of bed'

Bill Beaver, The Industrial Society

'A mission statement is no substitute for proper leadership. What's the point of having one if people won't bother to read it?'

Sir John Hall, Property Developer

Short-term versus long-term objectives

Different timescales can be set for objectives for different reasons.

Short-term objectives (typically for the year ahead) can provide a powerful focus for business achievement. By linking targets to reward, employees can be motivated to achieve short-term objectives. These objectives are also particularly suited to the annual process of financial reporting and review. Some businesses are accused of focusing too much on short-term goals at the expense of long-term aims.

Long-term objectives (over a year) are set to provide direction for the business in pursuit of its overall goals. These are important in showing where short-term plans are heading and how they are to be developed.

Setting objectives

The precise objectives set by a business will depend on a number of factors:

● **Corporate aims** – most importantly the overall goals of the business will shape its specific objectives. As discussed before, this depends on which stakeholders a business is seeking to please. Figure 3.5 illustrates the objectives that might be

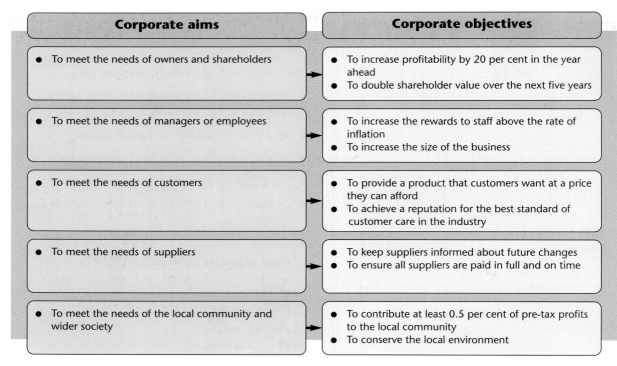

Corporate aims	**Corporate objectives**
• To meet the needs of owners and shareholders	• To increase profitability by 20 per cent in the year ahead • To double shareholder value over the next five years
• To meet the needs of managers or employees	• To increase the rewards to staff above the rate of inflation • To increase the size of the business
• To meet the needs of customers	• To provide a product that customers want at a price they can afford • To achieve a reputation for the best standard of customer care in the industry
• To meet the needs of suppliers	• To keep suppliers informed about future changes • To ensure all suppliers are paid in full and on time
• To meet the needs of the local community and wider society	• To contribute at least 0.5 per cent of pre-tax profits to the local community • To conserve the local environment

Figure 3.5 Corporate aims and objectives

set to meet the needs of different groups of stakeholders.

- **The SWOT analysis** – what the business wants to achieve depends in part on its current strengths and weaknesses, and future opportunities and threats. It may target core strengths and seek to build on them, or try to turn weaknesses into strengths.

- **Business ownership** – public sector businesses are more likely to target improvements in public service, rather than profitability. Even within the private sector, many sole traders and partnerships may put personal or employee objectives before profit.

Operational objectives

From its corporate objectives, a business sets specific targets for each of its departments, areas or products. These are designed to ensure that all aspects of the business have clear goals to work towards, and against which their success can be measured.

3 How are we going to get there? – Business strategy

The final link in the chain is the plan of action through which the business will achieve its aims and objectives. This strategy will be set at a number of levels, mirroring the levels of objectives described above:

- **At a whole business level**, the corporate strategy will be set to identify how the overall business objectives are to be achieved. Corporate strategies may focus on building market share, developing new products or diversifying into new markets.

- **At an area (or 'divisional') level** and then at **a departmental level**, specific tactics will be developed to achieve set objectives.

- Even **at an individual level**, a plan of action can be set to identify how an employee could develop to meet set objectives.

Business strategy: summary

KEY TERMS

SWOT analysis – an assessment of the current strengths and weaknesses of an organisation, together with the opportunities and threats facing it from outside.

Corporate aims – the overall goals of the business as a whole.

Stakeholders – those groups who have an interest ('stake') in the running and success of the business.

Mission statement – a written expression of a business's corporate aims.

Objectives – the specific and measurable targets set to achieve the overall aims.

Business strategy – the plan of action to achieve a business's aims and objectives.

Summary questions

1   What is a stakeholder?
2   Identify **three** stakeholders in your school or college.
3   What is 'short-termism'? How might it affect business decision-making?
4   Distinguish between operational and tactical objectives.
5   Identify and explain **two** reasons why a business might draw up a mission statement.
6   How might the objectives of a plc differ from those of a sole trader?
7   What is SWOT analysis used for?
8   Draw a suitable diagram to represent the flow of corporate strategy and objectives through the organisational hierarchy from senior management to an individual worker.
9   How valuable is a mission statement to an organisation?

Exam practice

Mobile mania

Six years ago, Nasa Khan, now in his early thirties, started The Accessory People, which wholesales mobile-phone fascias, earpieces and protective covers. It is now the top mobile-accessories business in Europe, made a profit of £250,000 in 2000 and has plans to expand into Asia.

Khan puts his success down, in part, to careful planning and clear objectives. His clear vision of where he wanted the business to go and his dedication to detailed planning have been key success factors. He feels that, as all staff share a common vision, grounded in a mission statement, developing and planning for long-term growth has been easier. He says that he sets realistic goals rather than those that look good on paper. Plans are made and refined quarterly. Progress towards objectives is closely monitored and new realistic, but ambitious, targets are set regularly.

Source: *The Sunday Times*, 14 April 2002

Nasa Khan, founder of The Accessory People

1   What is a mission statement?   **[2]**
2   Distinguish between long-term objectives and tactical goals.   **[4]**
3   Using the evidence in this case study, discuss the importance of clear long-term business objectives.   **[7]**
4   'The only objectives that really matter in modern firms are financial ones'. To what extent do you agree with this statement?   **[12]**

Total 25 marks

4 Setting up a business

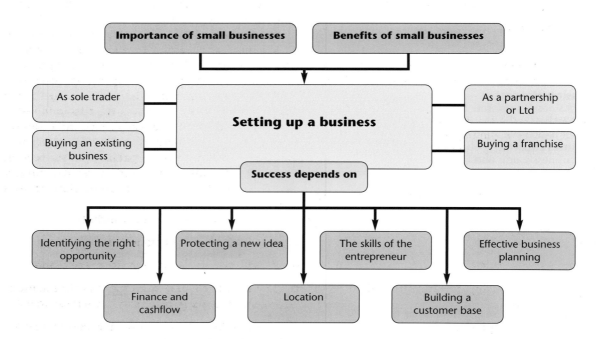

1 The importance of small business

Tomorrow's big business is today's small business. Every day new businesses are set up and some of them will grow to become household names. The origins of Richard Branson's Virgin empire began when he was still at school with the launch of a student magazine. The magazine didn't make his fortune, but out of this came his idea to sell cheap records by mail order through the magazine. Virgin Records was born and the rest is history.

In the UK today, two-thirds of all businesses are owned and run by one person, and over two and a half million people work for themselves. The small business sector is a major source of employment and wealth creation.

2 The benefits of small business

Small businesses are not just the seedlings for tomorrow's big business. There will always be small businesses and many will stay small because they bring a unique range of benefits:

- **Responding to the needs of local consumers** – providing local services, such as plumbers or decorators. By staying small, a business is able to spot gaps in the market, and be flexible enough to meet changing customer needs.

- **Providing a high standard of personal service** – individual and personal attention to customers can help build a loyal customer base.

- **Keeping costs low** – *overheads* can be kept down with smaller premises and lower bills. This allows small businesses to keep prices low for consumers while still making profits.

- **Meeting the needs of larger businesses** – many small businesses exist to provide service to larger businesses, such as transport or maintenance.

Why start your own business?

The benefits of running a small business are numerous, but the motivation to set one up is often driven by personal circumstances, such as:

- **Redundancy** – the need to find employment combined with the funds from redundancy payment provide the ideal opportunity.

- **Dissatisfaction or boredom** with working for someone else's business.

- **Profit** – an opportunity to make your own profit rather than being paid a wage by someone else is a great motivator!

- **Invention** – a new product idea may be developed and setting up a business may be the best way to produce and sell it.

 Setting up in business: the options

Having made the decision to set up a business, there are four main options:

1. Set up as a sole trader.

2. Establish a partnership or private limited company (Ltd).

3. Buy an existing business.

4. Become a franchisee.

Setting up a new business as a sole trader (see Unit 2) is a particularly attractive option. It is unique in that it offers complete independence to make decisions and the reward of keeping all the profit. It allows an entrepreneur to use their own ideas, develop their own products or pursue their own hobbies through the business. However, it brings limitations and burdens that lead many sole trader businesses to fail in their first year.

If a new business is to be jointly set up with others, it will need to be established either as a partnership or as a private limited company. This can bring additional specialist skills to develop the expertise of the business, additional managers to share the workload and additional finance to fund expansion. However, this option loses some of the attractive features of setting up as a sole trader – decisions and profits must be shared and some independence will be lost.

Some entrepreneurs buy an existing business rather than start their own. This involves purchasing a business as a *going concern*, or a *buy out* of the company they work for. A buyout is when the managers or workforce of a company buy the business from the existing owners or shareholders. **Management buyouts** became increasingly popular during the 1990s when many larger companies were selling off or closing down parts of their business. The success of buyouts seems to be the incentive it offers managers and workers to run the business efficiently in order to make a profit.

The final option in some ways represents not setting up your own business at all. Buying a franchise is paying for the right to sell the products of another company. Becoming a franchisee (the person buying these rights) is a way of reducing the risk of business failure by using the tried and tested ideas and products of an already successful business. The franchisor (the business selling the rights to a franchisee) will provide a package of services in return for an initial fee and a regular royalty payment (usually based on a proportion of sales revenue).

A franchise package typically includes:

- use of the company's brand name and image

- advertising campaigns to promote the brand

- materials and equipment for the franchisee to use in production or ready-made goods or services to sell

- training – initially to start the business and later to successfully manage it

- an exclusive area in which to sell, especially in the case of *dealer franchises* such as car retailers or petrol stations.

The benefits of buying a franchise as a method of starting up in business are:

- **Greater chance of success** – only around 6 per cent of franchises fail in the first two years, compared to up to 50 per cent of other types of new business.

- **Reputation and customer loyalty** – a successful franchisor probably already has a reputation that ensures a loyal customer base. This should help to ensure a steady and more certain level of sales than a brand new business could hope for.

- **Experience and knowledge** – of the franchisor in running a successful business are shared with the franchisee, so reducing the scope for mistakes. The support of training and research provided by the franchisor could give the business a competitive edge.

However, there are a number of potential drawbacks to franchising:

- **Financial costs** – the initial fee and ongoing royalty payments are a financial drain that a sole trader would avoid.

- **Loss of independence** – as a franchisee, you are not entirely your own boss with the franchisor making key decisions about location, marketing, employment and so on.

- **Dependence on the success of the franchisor** – if the franchisor's support is poor or their brand fails, there is little that the franchisee can do to make their business a success.

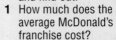

Activity

Visit www.mcdonalds.co.uk and find out:
1 How much does the average McDonald's franchise cost?
2 How many McDonald's franchises are there in the UK?
3 What assistance does McDonald's give the franchisee?
4 What requirements are made of the franchisee?

Want to know more?

www.franchisebusiness.co.uk or www.franinfo.co.uk.

 The requirements for success

New business start-ups are not a quick and easy route to fame and fortune! They bring with them a whole range of practical problems and risks. Success can never be guaranteed and luck may play a crucial role in the ultimate success or failure of a business. Yet a number of key ingredients for success can be identified.

- **Identifying the right opportunity.** Perhaps the most important ingredient for success is identifying the right market to enter. An innovative product or business idea is an excellent starting-point and yet, on average, 80 per cent of new products fail. Why? In many

cases it is because the business does not fully understand the market it is entering: the needs and wants of consumers and the strengths and weaknesses of competitors. Careful market research is therefore essential (see unit 6) and yet a new business will only have a small budget for research and promotion. It will need to use a range of low-cost primary and secondary research methods to find answers to key questions. These are shown in Figure 4.1

Protecting the business idea

If a business develops an innovative product idea it could become a valuable asset in the years ahead and therefore needs protection. A **patent** ensures that the

Figure 4.1 Market research on a small budget

Primary research	Secondary research
Approaching local business people to find out more about the area and its potential.	Look up competitors in the Yellow Pages or local newspapers.
Conducting in-depth interviews with a small group of consumers to identify what really matters to them.	Obtain competitors' brochures and price lists by post, from exhibitions or from the internet.
Observing competitor products – their packaging, prices and promotions.	Find trends and developments in the market through trade publications, such as *The Grocer*.
Pedestrian and traffic-flow counts to identify the most desirable location for passing trade.	Local business link organisations or banks provide free information about specific product markets.
Discuss consumers' preferences, new products and trends in the market with suppliers or retailers.	Government facts and figures about society and the economy are available on the internet or from local libraries. These help a new business identify the threats and opportunities it faces from its external environment.

business is the only one allowed to make the new product, or use a particular production process, for up to 20 years. To be awarded a patent, the business will need to prove that its product is its own, distinctive and original work. Certain names and symbols can also be registered as **trademarks**.

A **copyright** is the equivalent protection offered to authors, artists and composers. Patents, trademarks and copyrights offer important protection for a new business, giving it the right to reap the rewards for its innovation. However, to enforce the patent or copyright would need expensive court action – something a small business is unlikely to be able to afford.

The skills of the entrepreneur

The success of a new business will rest to a great extent on the personal skills of the entrepreneur. It is they who must plan, manage and lead the business forward. There is no unique set of characteristics that make a successful entrepreneur, but they are likely to bring the following qualities to the business:

- a strong desire to succeed
- hard-work and energy
- ideas and creativity
- organisation and leadership skills
- ability to get on with and motivate others.

STOP & THINK

Why do you think each of these qualities is so important to the success of a new business?

Effective business planning

However good the business idea and however skilled the entrepreneur, without effective business planning a new business will quickly lose its way. A well-researched **business plan** that is regularly reviewed and updated can undoubtedly make the difference between success and failure.

A business plan is a document that sets out how the business will operate and what it hopes to achieve. Figure 4.2 illustrates the usual content of a business plan.

A business plan is an essential business tool, providing the framework within which a business can develop. It brings a number of benefits:

- **Providing focus and direction** for the ideas that lie behind the new business venture. The business plan forces an entrepreneur to consider all the key aspects of running the business, and whether it has a good chance of success.

- **Testing the viability** of the business proposal through financial forecasts that show whether the business has a good chance of success before

THE BUSINESS PLAN

1 Introduction
a basic business details
b the type of legal ownership
c the goals of the business

2 The business idea
a the product/service to be provided
b summary of its key selling points

3 Management and personnel
a the roles of managers
b the experience and skills of the workforce

4 The marketing plan
a market analysis showing level of demand
b who customers are and what they want
c the strengths and weaknesses of competitors
d the marketing mix – product, price, promotion and place

5 The production plan
a the methods and stages of production
b the premises and equipment needed
c ways of ensuring quality

6 The financial plan
a sources of finance required
b profit forecast / break-even analysis
c cash-flow forecast

Figure 4.2 The business plan

committing any money. Potential problems can be identified at an early stage and action taken to avoid them.

- **Convincing potential investors** or lenders such as the high street banks that this is a business idea they should be willing to support.

- **Planning and reviewing the business strategy** through the targets and forecasts in the plan provides a way of measuring the actual performance of the business over time.

Guru's views

'It is not the plan that is important, it's the planning.'

Dr Graeme Edwards

Finance

A significant practical problem for a new business is raising sufficient initial finance to successfully launch the business. Even with a convincing business plan, the risk attached to new business start-ups make potential investors very wary of committing their funds.

A new business requires finance for two main purposes:

- **purchase** of premises and equipment

- **working capital** – the cash needed to keep the business working, pay bills and so on in its early months of trading.

Many new businesses underestimate the importance of raising finance for working capital and quickly find themselves short of cash when revenues are slow to come in. The result is a **cash-flow crisis** (see unit 15).

The potential sources of finance open to a new business are explained in Unit 17.

Location

Many new businesses depend on the right location for their success. Manufacturing businesses need to balance accessibility to suppliers with closeness to their market. For retailers and other service-based businesses, location at the heart of their market is the key to maximising sales.

Most new small businesses do not have sufficient finance to fund an ideal location. Their priority is to keep start-up costs down and overheads low, but in doing so they may be stuck with a location that makes it very difficult for them to succeed.

For example ...

The Big Idea?

Alan Catto gets some curious looks from people who see him talking to his key ring. But for Catto, a serial entrepreneur, using voice recorders is just one of the methods he uses to keep track of ideas for new businesses.

Finding successful ideas is not easy though, Catto estimates that fewer than 20 of the 400 ideas he has had over the past decade have come to anything. He recommends sticking to what you know; ideas based on the market knowledge that entrepreneurs already have are often the most successful.

Stelios Haji-Ioannou (pictured), founder of easyJet, suggests taking a trip abroad as a source of business ideas. The idea for easyJet came from his experiences with Southwest Airlines, a budget

America carrier. *Boom* magazine (sent free to 50,000 British millionaires) was another idea borrowed from America.

Source: The Sunday Times, 7 April 2002

Want to know more?

www.bplans.com

1 Suggest **three** factors that might determine whether a business idea will be successful or not. **[3]**
2 Suggest why ideas 'based on what you already know' might be more likely to be successful. **[4]**

3 In the absence of a good idea, franchising offers entrepreneurs a way of starting up a business. Discuss the pros and cons of this approach. **[8]**

Total 15 marks

Building a customer base

Unless an entrepreneur has bought an existing business or a franchise, he faces the immediate problem of building a customer base. The launch of the business may secure initial interest, but the key to success lies in developing customer loyalty and ensuring repeat purchases. This can be done by:

- Convincing the target market that the business offers a product that is distinctive, value-for-money and meets their needs.

- Providing a high standard of customer care and service.

- Building a reputation through word of mouth and effective promotion.

Setting up a business: summary

KEY TERMS

Management buyout – the purchase of a business by its existing management team.

Patent – a government grant of ownership rights to a person or business assuring sole rights to make, use and sell a new invention or manufacturing process for a limited period.

Trademarks – names or symbols used by businesses to represent a particular good or service that they provide, and to distinguish it from competing manufacturers.

Copyright – the legal right provided by Act of Parliament to produce copies and to control an original literary, musical or artistic work for a specified time.

Business plan – a document that sets out how the business will operate and what it hopes to achieve.

Cash-flow crisis – when more money is going out of the business than is coming in, despite monies being owed to the business.

Summary questions

1 Identify **two** personality characteristics that an entrepreneur might have?
2 Explain **two** sources of competitive advantage that small businesses have.
3 Give **three** reasons why people set up their own businesses.
4 What help do banks provide to new business start-ups?
5 What help might the Government provide to start-ups?
6 State **three** items that would appear in a business plan.
7 Explain the importance of business plans for start-up companies.
8 Explain **three** problems a start-up is likely to face.
9 Contrast the issues facing a business setting up in the tertiary sector with those faced by starting businesses in the secondary sector.

Exam practice

Starting this week?

There is a good reason why many people do not like the first day of the working week. It brings 'Monday blues' and it is often when the dreams of self-employment (and perhaps the prospect of not bothering with Monday's) resurface.

Over the last few years the Government has made it much easier for entrepreneurs' dreams to be turned into reality. The Government now gives more cash to start-ups, has cut small-company taxes and has reduced red tape.

Self-employment sounds tempting. You pay less tax, for example. But starting a business comes with a health warning. The hours can be punishing – 70 a week is common. You might think you are your own boss but, at the end of the day, it is the customer who is really king. When every customer counts, you can't afford to let them down.

But the prospects for those looking to make the leap are better than ever, according to Barclays. Its figures show that more than two-thirds of all start-ups succeed and the number is rising every year.

Source: *The Sunday Times*, 7 April 2002

1 Define the term entrepreneur. **[2]**
2 State **four** advantages of being self-employed. **[4]**
3 Suggest and explain **two** reasons why the government might wish to encourage small business start-ups. **[6]**
4 Examine the reasons why a third of small business start-ups fail. **[8]**
5 Evaluate whether the long-term success of small business start-ups is primarily based on having a 'good idea'. **[10]**
Total 30 marks

Getting the grade: Objectives and strategy

AN understanding of business objectives and strategy underpins all other business studies knowledge.

Many of the topics covered in these units may not be assessed directly in the exam (though you will still need to revise the material and understand any key terms). Rather, the examiner will require you to demonstrate that you understand *how* business size, structure and strategy might influence a business's response to particular situations.

The material covered throughout this section should shape your answers to all questions. Some key things to think about include:

Type of business

The size of the business, the stage of production it operates in, whether it is private, public or not-for-profit and the type of ownership, all have an important effect on business operations. Above all, these factors affect a business's overall aims and objectives, and it is this that influences how a business acts. You need to consider the particular mix of elements that shapes the business presented in the exam, for example:

- Is it large or small?
- How will this affect its actions?
- What industry does it operate in?
- How does this affect your answer?

Strategy does not always equal success

Having a good business plan will not *always* lead to success. Clear strategy and objectives *may* contribute towards success *but* will not guarantee it. First, the strategy itself needs to be right. The plan may be perfect, but the direction may be wrong – 'rearranging the deck chairs on the Titanic'. Second, you need to get the implementation right (putting the strategy in place). It is this that separates great businesses from mediocre ones. Microsoft's success is, in part, due to its ability to combine strategic planning with superior implementation – getting the right thing right.

Also remember that not all organisations will have the time, or feel the need, to set down missions, aims, objectives and strategies. For many small businesses, there will be little formal planning. However, the entrepreneur may have a clear strategy in mind, which will be visible in the actions of the business. In contrast, many larger organisations with elaborate and expensive planning may struggle in communicating their goals or in putting them into practice effectively.

Take a risk

Risk management is a key business issue, but don't make the mistake of thinking that all risk is bad. After all, profit is the reward for risk. Just because a business decision is risky doesn't mean it should be avoided. The risk should be considered and measured against potential returns:

- Is the return worth the risk?
- What is this business's attitude to risk?
- Does the situation require risk?

SWOT it?

SWOT (**s**trengths, **w**eaknesses, **o**pportunities and **t**hreats) is a good starting point for analysis of business issues, especially if your exam board (AQA & OCR) uses a pre-released case study. However, you are unlikely to be asked to complete a SWOT analysis in an examination, and should not approach questions from a rigid SWOT perspective. Like all business tools, SWOT should be used to help you understand the situation the business faces, but not as a solution in itself. SWOT analysis may suggest issues needing further analysis and may prompt you to ask questions, but it does not provide the answers – for you or for the business!

You are the boss

Above all you need to think big. Don't get hung up on small details. The examiner will not be asking you to recite all you know about limited liability or any other business concept. Imagine *you* were faced with the case study situation, what would you do? Tackle the case study from a manager's point of view. You need to take an overview of the whole company and consider the impact of your decisions on all business functions (finance, people, marketing and so on). Take a few key issues and analyse them fully.

Be critical

Consider the impact and validity of your answers. Will they definitely work (almost certainly not)? Who will be affected? How? What factors might be needed for success? What future changes, internally or externally, might affect success? Remember the key to top grades is analysis and evaluation applied to the context.

The best way to develop these skills and to understand business strategy and objectives is to keep up-to-date with real business issues. Read a business newspaper at least once a week during the course. Relate theory to practice, and consider the issues above as they affect the businesses you are reading about. Why did they react like that? Why that decision? Why that aim?

Section 2

Marketing

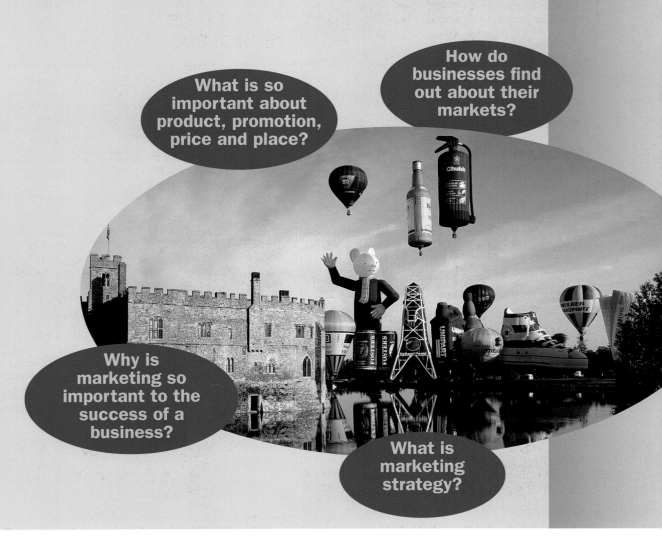

What is so important about product, promotion, price and place?

How do businesses find out about their markets?

Why is marketing so important to the success of a business?

What is marketing strategy?

5 What is marketing?

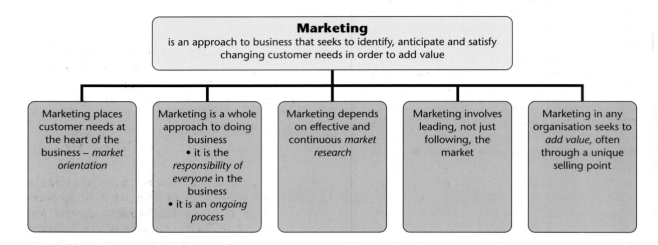

> **Marketing**
> is an approach to business that seeks to identify, anticipate and satisfy changing customer needs in order to add value

- Marketing places customer needs at the heart of the business – *market orientation*
- Marketing is a whole approach to doing business
  - it is the *responsibility of everyone* in the business
  - it is an *ongoing process*
- Marketing depends on effective and continuous *market research*
- Marketing involves leading, not just following, the market
- Marketing in any organisation seeks to *add value*, often through a unique selling point

1 What is marketing?

The key to the success of any business is to satisfy the needs of its customers. Satisfying customers attracts more custom and keeps existing customers loyal, allowing the business to expand and be profitable. If the business fails to satisfy customers, it will not survive because its customers will turn to the competition. Essentially **marketing** is about identifying, anticipating and satisfying customer demands.

There are many different ways of defining marketing, as shown in Figure 5.1

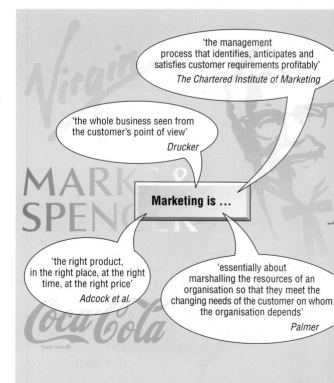

Marketing is …

'the management process that identifies, anticipates and satisfies customer requirements profitably'
The Chartered Institute of Marketing

'the whole business seen from the customer's point of view'
Drucker

'the right product, in the right place, at the right time, at the right price'
Adcock et al.

'essentially about marshalling the resources of an organisation so that they meet the changing needs of the customer on whom the organisation depends'
Palmer

STOP & THINK

Which of the definitions in Figure 5.1 captures the real essence of marketing? Why?

Figure 5.1 Some famous definitions of marketing

The principles of marketing

The rest of this unit deals with the five basic principles of marketing.

1   Marketing is a whole approach to doing business

Marketing is not just about promoting and selling a product, nor can it be the responsibility of just one department. Rather it is about the focus of the whole business and, therefore, the responsibility of everyone in it. Drucker's definition of marketing emphasises that, from a customer's point of view, all that matters is whether the business's product meets their needs. This makes marketing 'the key business function' and all aspects of a business must focus on it. There will always be a role for a separate marketing department to conduct research, communicate with customers and contribute to new product development and pricing decisions. Marketing thinking, though, needs to exist throughout the business. Marketing is also more than just a one-off action, such as an advertising campaign. It is an ongoing process of researching, planning, implementing and reviewing strategies to meet customers' needs. Disney came to realise that their business was more than just making and promoting films. It was about a whole concept of childhood imagination that stretched into the leisure and retail industries. Their ongoing development of merchandise and theme parks has become a total approach to meeting customer needs and fulfilling their mission, 'to make people happy'.

2   Marketing places customer needs at the heart of the business

Above all else, marketing is about being customer-driven. This is known as **market-orientation**. A market-orientated business begins by asking what consumers want when they buy a product, and then seeks to develop products to meet these needs. Decisions about product design, pricing, promotion and distribution will be based on market analysis to ensure that what the business offers is what the consumer wants. Coca Cola's development of new flavours, such as Cherry Coke or Lemon Diet Coke, is a response to the changing wants of different groups of consumers. The benefits of a 'market-orientated' approach are clear:

- A new product will be more likely to succeed because it has been *based on what consumers want*.

- *Customer loyalty* can be built up by ensuring customer needs and wants are satisfied.

- A business can gain a **competitive advantage** over its rivals by targeting and meeting the needs of a specific group of consumers.

- *Changes in the market* and the needs of customers can be anticipated, allowing the business to be the first to react.

> ### Guru's views
> 'Figure out what is desirable and make that what you deliver; or figure out what you can deliver and make that desirable. But remember, the former is a lot easier than the latter'.
>
> *Sergio Zyman*
> *(Coca-Cola's former Chief Marketing Officer)*

As well as understanding what consumers want, a business also needs to consider what competitors offer, and what its own strengths and weaknesses are. Seeking to find an overlap between what consumers want and a business's distinctive strengths is known as **asset-led marketing**, it ensures a business makes the best use of its reputation and expertise. Virgin, for example, has sought to do this by identifying consumer needs in markets where its own image of youth and simplicity will prove attractive: mobile phones, cola and insurance.

The alternative approach is to be **product-orientated**. This focuses on creating the product before considering the views of consumers. The business invents, innovates and improves methods of production. Once the product is developed, the business seeks ways to promote and sell it. Contact with the consumer comes only at the end of the development process. By this stage, the product-orientated business is relying on consumers wanting the product.

A product-orientated approach therefore brings a number of dangers:

- The risk of failure is greater – the product has been developed without the knowledge that it will meet customer needs.

- The product may not offer a unique selling point (see page 29) – consumers are likely to turn to competitors' products.

- The business may be myopic (short-sighted) – it is unable to spot changing needs and the threat of new competition.

However, product-orientated businesses do not necessarily fail. Indeed, many of the most successful products in the last hundred years have come through product innovation, not market analysis. The television, the CD player, and the mobile phone all owe their existence to invention and product development. Some products, such as 3M's 'Post-It' note, have even been discovered by accident!

In hi-tech, leading-edge industries – such as pharmaceuticals and electronics – consumers may not yet be aware of what is possible and so invention and technical development will always be the priority. In reality, even the most product-orientated modern business will have half an eye on the market and the needs of potential customers. The exact mixture of the two will depend on the nature of the product, the business itself and the market in which it operates.

For example ...

Just do it

'For years we thought of ourselves as a product-orientated company, meaning we put all of our emphasis on designing and manufacturing the product. But now we understand that the most important thing we do is market the product. We've come around to saying that Nike is a market-orientated company, and the product is our most important marketing tool.'

Nike CEO, Phil Knight

Source: Naomi Klein, *No Logo*, Flamingo (2001)

1 Identify and explain **two** advantages of market-orientation.   **[4]**
2 Suggest **two** reasons why a market-orientated approach might not be successful.   **[2]**
3 In what ways might Nike have changed its business practices when it shifted focus from product-orientation to market-orientation?   **[6]**

Total 12 marks

3 Marketing depends on effective and continuous market research

To satisfy the needs of its customers, a market-orientated business depends on market research to identify these needs. Market research also allows a business to anticipate future needs by spotting market trends. Patrick Barwise, of the London Business School, identifies four key tasks for marketing personnel to fulfil through research and analysis:

● To develop a detailed understanding of current customers.

● To develop a deep understanding of today's competitors.

● To understand how the market may change and develop in the future.

● To use all this knowledge to shape a marketing strategy that meets the organisations' objectives.

The roles and methods of market research are considered in more detail in Unit 6.

4 Marketing involves leading, not just following, the market

Successful marketing must anticipate future market trends, enabling a business to be the first to meet a new or previously unrealised consumer need. By being proactive rather than reactive, a business can achieve much greater success. It is estimated that being the first to enter a new market (known as 'first-mover advantage') can double a product's profitability. Kellogg's and Heinz have both gained a reputation as market leaders by being first into the market – 'the original and the best'!

Sometimes this approach requires the business to 'see out of the box', to take risks by acting against market trends and doing the opposite to its competitors. When Müller saw all its competitors launching yoghurts in smaller pots, it launched a product in a bigger pot, 'Fruit Corner'. Its thinking established the product as a market leader.

5   Marketing seeks to add value through a unique selling point

Unit 1 explained that *adding value* is the route to business success. To add value is to be able to sell a product for more than it cost to make, thus producing profit for the business. Marketing is a crucial tool for achieving added value as it creates consumer willingness to pay for a product that satisfies their needs. This willingness to pay may be well in excess of the cost of production – the marketing has been effective in delivering a product and an image that consumers want. Nike trainers are a classic example.

It is not enough, though, for a business just to meet customer needs. It must gain a competitive advantage by meeting these needs better than its rivals do. To achieve this, a business must identify its **unique selling point (USP)** – a feature of the product, its image or price that is different from, and superior to, the competition. For Haagen-Dazs it is an image of sensual luxury, for Asda it is affordability. What is crucial is that the chosen USP is:

- important to consumers

- a genuine strength of the business

- consistent with being profitable.

A successful USP enables consumers to identify the main reason why they should purchase a specific brand, and will also encourage them to do so. The USP must be supported and developed through a consistent marketing strategy. The role of the marketing mix – product, price, promotion and place – in achieving this will be developed in Units 9 to 12. What is crucial is that all aspects of the marketing mix are used together to build a coherent brand image.

The success of Stella Artois has been built on a USP of quality, supported by a high price and a promotional slogan of 'reassuringly expensive'! Sainsbury's recent revival in its 'grocery war' with Tesco has been based on a consistent promotion of the values of quality and choice, rather than using price-cutting to win back customers.

Jamie Oliver endorses the Sainsbury's image of providing quality products

What is marketing: summary

KEY TERMS

Marketing – an approach to business that seeks to identify, anticipate and satisfy changing customer needs in order to add value.

Market-orientated – a business that is customer-driven, finding out what customers want before making decisions about product, price or promotion.

Asset-led marketing – an approach to marketing that bases a product's appeal not just on what the customer wants, but also on what the company's existing strengths are.

Product-orientated – a business that focuses on creating a product or developing a production process rather than on the needs of the customer.

Unique selling point – a feature of the product, its image, its price, its promotion or its distribution that is different from and superior to the competition.

Competitive advantage – the ability to offer consumers something different from, or superior to, the market competition.

Summary questions

1 What is 'marketing'?
2 List **four** activities that marketing might involve.
3 Distinguish between market and product orientation.
4 Explain, using examples, **two** benefits of market orientation.
5 Explain the risks involved with product orientation.
6 Give **two** examples of how marketing adds value.
7 What is meant by the term 'first mover advantage'? Why is being 'first mover' considered an advantage?
8 Define the term 'unique selling point' and give **two** examples

Exam practice

Marketing – everybody's at it

Everybody's at it. You are bombarded by it every day. You are probably bombarded with it at school or college and could even be witnessing it right now. Marketing is, perhaps, the most public face of business. We live in a branded world. Most things that can be advertised have been. Coca-Cola ranks as one of the world's most well known phrases – such is the power of marketing.

Not surprisingly then, even not-for-profit organisations have had to get in on the act. In the modern business climate not-for-profit organisations have to be self-sufficient. No longer can they rely solely on donations. Not-for-profit organisations are selling goods and services that further their causes as well as bringing in additional revenue. The art of doing that successfully involves marketing. The promotion of membership, goodwill in the community, services and opportunities for volunteers now attracts a considerable marketing budget in many not-for-profit organisations. Greenpeace not only attempts to protect the environment, but also, in order to support this cause, successfully markets a wide range of related merchandise. Does your school or college have an open day? Most probably – even education is firmly onboard the marketing bandwagon.

Source: www.nonprofits.org

1 Define marketing.   [2]
2 State and explain **two** reasons why marketing has become so important to business.   [4]
3 Explain, in relation to marketing, the concept of adding value. Give an example of how a not-for-profit organisation might seek to add value.   [4]
4 Explain the possible benefits a not-for-profit organisation might gain from a market-orientated approach.   [6]
5 Evaluate the relative importance of marketing to not-for-profit organisations compared to profit making commercial organisations.   [12]
Total 28 marks

6 Market research

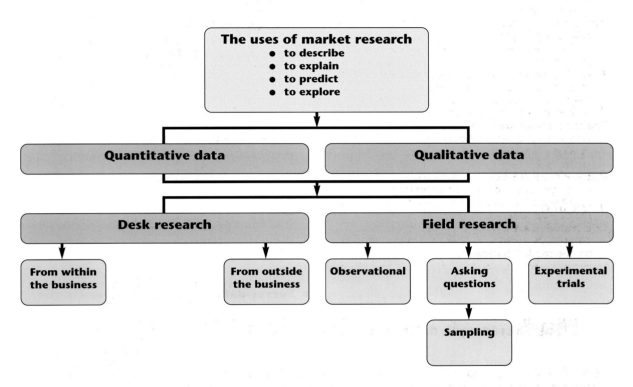

The uses of market research
- to describe
- to explain
- to predict
- to explore

Quantitative data | Qualitative data

Desk research | Field research

From within the business | From outside the business | Observational | Asking questions | Experimental trials

Sampling

 1   What is market research?

Market research is the process of collecting and interpreting data about customers and competitors. This research is the key both to understanding the needs of customers and to making more reliable business decisions.

New and existing businesses use market research to investigate:

- **market size and trends**
    - number of customers and whether their spending is growing
    - potential size of the market
    - actual and potential sales and market share

- **market segments**
    - actual and potential customers
    - the needs, habits and lifestyles of different groups of consumers

- **customer preferences**
    - what customers want from the product
    - what price they are prepared to pay
    - what methods of promotion will be most effective
    - how customers wish to buy the product

- **competition**
    - who are the main competitors
    - what is the market share of these competitors
    - strengths and weaknesses of each competitor

2   The importance of market research

By understanding more about their market, a firm can make decisions focused on their customers' needs. Market research allows a firm both to stay in touch with the market and with what customers want. It could help a firm to anticipate future needs or trends and so be the first to react to a profitable new opportunity.

Market research is used for different reasons at different times. Four main reasons can be identified:

- **To describe** – *who* the business' customers and competitors are and *what* is happening in its market. For example, gathering data that allows a firm to conclude its market share is falling over time.

- **To explain** – *why* trends occur. Having identified a fall in market share, for example, a firm will want to find out why customers prefer the competition.

- **To predict** – *what might happen next.* If a firm experiences a fall in market share, they need to look closely at what other changes may occur in the market, how these will affect the trend and what the firm's share of the market is likely to be in the future.

- **To explore** – *how consumers might react* to new ideas and use this knowledge to make key marketing decisions. To halt the slide in market share, the firm may consider launching a new product and will want to test consumer reaction before doing so.

Types of research data

There are two different types of information that market research can generate:

- **Quantitative data** is information acquired from a large group of respondents showing numbers, proportions or trends within a market, such as how many people buy a particular product. This is particularly useful when a firm is using research *to describe* its market. The quantity of data makes it accurate and representative of the whole market. Analysis of statistics helps a firm to understand its market. However, on its own, quantitative data is unlikely to help explain *why* the market is as it is. To understand *why*, qualitative data is needed.

- **Qualitative data** is information gathered from a small group of people, using in-depth discussions and interviews to *explore* their attitudes. This gives detailed information about the reasons *why* consumers act as they do. The information provides an opportunity to respond more fully to customers' ideas. However, the few who are

interviewed may not be representative of the whole market. Data is also more difficult to quantify and analyse and, therefore, conclusions will be less scientific than with quantitative research. In addition, gathering qualitative data may be an expensive task as interviewers need to be trained, and interviews can be lengthy.

4   Desk research

Desk research is the process of gathering information that has already been collected or published. This type of information is known as **secondary data**.

Secondary data may exist within the business in the form of:

- **Sales records** – identifying trends in sales over time or sales patterns around the country.

- **Customer information** – there may be customer records of purchases, or what their future needs might be. The use of EPOS (electronic point of sale) and loyalty cards allows many large retailers to identify customers' shopping habits and to use this information to target promotions.

- **Survey data** – the results of previous market research surveys may still be of value.

There will also be external sources from where existing, valuable information can be gained. The growth of the internet has made an immense volume of secondary information easily accessible to firms. Such sources include:

- **Commercial data** – organisations such as Mintel or the Economist Intelligence Unit specialise in gathering market research data about a wide range of markets. Their reports can be purchased to provide detailed, up-to-date information about a specific market.

- **Government data** – government departments collect and publish a wide variety of information about all aspects of the economy and society. The Office of National Statistics produces up-to-date data about social, economic and labour market trends, whilst the Census of Population provides a valuable snapshot of the country every 10 years.

- **Information about competitors** – examining rivals' websites reveals much about their products and prices. Competitors' annual reports and accounts can help to build up a valuable picture of their strategy.

For example ...

Men Are So Average

Percentage of men in employment	80%
Average man's weekly gross pay	£452
Number of hours the average man works	44 per week
Average man's lunch	Sandwich
Average man's holiday entitlement	24 days per year
Top reasons why average man is looking for new work	Unsatisfactory pay;wants shorter hours; unsatisfactory commute to work; threat of redundancy.

Average man's gross earnings by age (per week)

Age	(£s)
16–24	274
25–34	416
35–44	492
45–54	505
55–64	437
65+	408

Source: *Men's Health* magazine survey, March 2002

1 If a company were to use this information, would it be classified as primary or secondary data? **[1]**
2 Calculate the *annual* gross pay of 'average man' (ignore age). **[1]**
3 Calculate the hourly wage rate of 'average man' (ignore age). **[1]**
4 Explain the problems with using 'averaged' data such as this. **[3]**

5 Why might a firm choose to use secondary rather than primary research? **[5]**

Total 11 marks

Want to know more?

www.menshealth.co.uk

- **Other publications** – local libraries, Business Link or high street banks help by providing access to a wide variety of other secondary sources, such as market profiles or journal articles.

Desk research can gather large quantities of data without great expense. Extracting useful information, however, can be difficult and time-consuming – whilst the data itself may be neither reliable nor up-to-date!

5 Field research

Field research involves gathering new and original, first-hand information or **primary data**. Field research can be carried out through observation, experimentation, surveys and interviews.

Observation

Observation involves, among other things, watching consumers as they shop, measuring pedestrian flows in a town centre or looking at how rival products are packaged and displayed. Market researchers try to draw conclusions about shoppers from observing their behaviour – such as where they go when they enter a store, or how long they spend selecting a

product from the shelves. This information can be used to improve store and shelf layout or point-of-sale promotions. In itself, though, observation of consumer behaviour cannot answer questions about why customers act in certain ways.

Experimentation

A crucial stage in the development and launch of a new product is to assess the reaction of potential consumers. It is vital to test and experiment with new product ideas. Manufacturing companies may build a prototype for testing and showing to prospective customers. This will be an essential part of the development and marketing process.

Consumer panels are groups of consumers who are asked to give their opinions on ideas or products over a period of time. They may be used by marketers to comment on a range of product ideas or samples. Alternatively, a product may be launched in a small part of the market – such as a region or just a few stores in a chain– in order to see how consumers react to it. This is known as test marketing.

Experimentation and testing may seem like an additional cost or time delay, but without it a much greater loss of time and money may be suffered if a new product proves unsuccessful in the market.

Surveys

Questionnaires can be used to ask pre-set questions of a large number of people. Before carrying out a questionnaire-based survey, a business must decide:

- **Objectives for the survey – what it is trying to find out?** A business is better able to collect the data it needs if the objectives are clear. Some objectives may be:

    - to *describe* the current habits of customers
    - to *explain* why they act as they do
    - to help *predict* future trends in the market
    - to *explore* how customers might react to a new product.

- **How to write the questionnaire to gain this information.** In order to get data that is accurate and unbiased, careful attention must be paid to the way questions are phrased:

    - the meaning of each question must be clear– the way the question is worded must not lead the respondent towards a particular answer
    - a balance must be struck between *closed questions*, which offer a limited choice of pre-set responses, and *open questions*, which allow respondents to offer their own views. Closed questions make it easier to collate and analyse data, while open questions allow for a more detailed insight.

- **The most effective method of carrying out the survey.** Surveys may be face-to-face, by telephone or by post.

    - *Face-to-face surveys* allow an interviewer to explain questions that the respondent doesn't understand, but introduce the possibility of bias in the way the interviewer presents the questions.
    - *Telephone surveys* are quicker and cheaper than face-to-face surveys, but may generate resentment among customers.
    - *Postal surveys* rely on customers completing and returning the questionnaire. It is a cheap method that may avoid interviewer bias, but suffers from low response rates.

- **How many people to question?** To question every actual and potential customer would be both expensive and time-consuming. To avoid this problem, a sample is chosen. A **sample** is a smaller group selected from a larger total group. However, the sample should be large enough to provide data that is reliable and representative of the attitudes and characteristics of the total population. The more people who are asked, the

greater the *degree of confidence* the business can have in the accuracy of the results. If everyone in the population were asked, there would be a 100 per cent confidence level. If a sample can provide a 95 per cent confidence level, the results can be considered statistically reliable. There is a small margin of error, but nothing that makes the results unusable.

- **Sampling: who to question?** If a business questions a sample of consumers, it must select a group of people representative of the whole population. Businesses will approach this in different ways. (See Figure 6.1 for sampling methods.)

Interviews

To gain more detailed, qualitative information from a smaller group of people, personal interviewing will be much more useful than a survey. In a personal interview, the interviewer spends longer with each respondent, asking them a wide range of questions and exploring their responses more deeply. The interview is often led by the customer's (interviewee's) comments and will not necessarily follow set questions. The interviewer must be well trained, and the information gained must be properly recorded and analysed.

The results will not be statistically representative of the whole population because of the small sample size. However, when carried out professionally, this method may generate information that *explains* and *explores* issues far more effectively than any other market research method.

Activity

What methods of primary research would you use to collect information about the following products? Justify your choices.

The Products
- A new alcopop drink
- A handheld computer (PDA)
- Breakfast cereals
- Portable MP3 players

Think about ...
a The method you would use and how you would you carry this out.
b What type of person you might ask.
c Why you would ask those particular people.

Want to know more?

www.mad.co.uk

Sampling methods

- **Random sampling** involves selecting individuals in such a way that anyone in the total population has an equal chance of being chosen. To achieve a truly random sample involves careful planning, otherwise the location or time of day could lead to an unrepresentative sample. For example, a random survey outside a secondary school at 3.30 p.m. may lead to an over-representation of teenagers! A systematic method of random sampling, such as choosing every 100th name from a census list, is more likely to be successful. Small random samples are more likely to be unrepresentative as they probably won't include all types of people.

- **Stratified random sampling** is use when a business is specifically interested in the views of a particular **market segment**, such as females in their 20s. The business first selects its market segment, the types of people it wants to include in its sample, then within this group, it chooses people at random in the way described above.

- **Quota sampling** involves identifying the exact sample proportions that the business wants to draw from each market segment. This may be done to build a sample that reflects the proportions of different groups within the total population. For example, if 60 per cent of Cola drinkers are male, 60 per cent of the sample questioned should be male. If half of that 60 per cent is under 25, the final sample selected should also reflect this. As long as the original information was accurate, this method has the benefit of producing a sample that reflects the make up of the market.

- **Cluster sampling** draws a random sample from a single, specific area to gain a snapshot of customer opinion in that area. It is most useful when the cluster is reasonably typical of the customer type in which the business is interested, and if that is their only area of interest. However, it is unlikely that the sample will be in any way representative of wider markets.

Figure 6.1 Methods of sampling potential consumers

6   How essential is market research?

Careful market research underpins almost all product launches, and yet 90 per cent of all new products end in failure. Market research is not the simple route to success. While its findings can prove of great benefit, it cannot provide scientific evidence on which to base business decisions. Human behaviour is unpredictable and no amount of research can overcome this. Figure 6.2 shows the key benefits of carrying out research and many of the drawbacks.

Market research

Benefits

- Helps to identify the wants and needs of customers
- Allows the business to design and vary its *marketing mix* (product, price, place and promotion) to target the needs of different market segments
- Enables a swifter response to changes in customer needs, allowing the business to stay a step ahead of its competitors
- Research into existing competition allows a business to spot a 'gap in the market' that it can profitably fill
- A new product can be developed and launched with greater confidence in its future success
- The wasted expense of failed products or promotions can be reduced or eliminated

Drawbacks

- Without clear objectives, research may produce irrelevant information or leave important questions unanswered
- The sample may be unrepresentative of the total population due to a small sample size, bias in the method of choosing respondents or poorly constructed questions
- Even with a carefully constructed sample, the results cannot provide 100 per cent accuracy – if the business relies on the results costly mistakes may be made
- Respondents may provide answers they think the interviewer wants to hear rather than their true views
- Secondary data is often out-of-date while primary data can be expensive to collect and analyse

Figure 6.2 The benefits and drawbacks of market research

Market research: summary

KEY TERMS

Market research – the process of collecting and interpreting data about customers and competitors.

Quantitative data – data from a large group (quantity) of respondents showing numbers, proportions or trends within a market, such as how many people buy a particular product.

Qualitative data – information gathered from a small group of people, using detailed discussions and interviews (quality information) to explore the attitudes of consumers in depth.

Desk research – the process of gathering secondary data.

Secondary data – information that has already been collected or published.

Field research – the process of gathering primary data, using observation, experimentation or asking questions.

Primary data – information collected first-hand, that did not previously exist.

Sample – a smaller group selected from a larger total in order to be representative of the attitudes and characteristics of the total population.

Summary questions

1   What is market research?
2   Explain the **four** different types of question that market research can seek answers to, giving an example of each.
3   What is the difference between quantitative and qualitative data?
4   Give **three** examples of secondary data that may exist:
  a within the business
  b outside the business.
5   What is primary data?
6   Explain why observation and experimentation can be useful types of field research.
7   What does a business need to consider before conducting a survey.
8   Explain what is meant by the phrase '95 per cent confidence level'.
9   What is the difference between random sampling and quota sampling?
10 State **three** benefits and **three** drawbacks of market research.

Football fan facts

The cosmopolitan face of the English Premier League – demonstrated by the presence of foreign players and foreign coaches – is, according to surveys, not always represented on the terraces.

Market research reveals that football is still watched mainly by white males, and fans continue to be concerned about the way they are treated by clubs as well as the standard of facilities in football grounds.

The annual Football Association Premier League Fans Survey (2002) paints a picture of a game with a distinct north-south divide, but which is attracting more wealthy fans – spending on average £1089 on following their team.

The survey also reveals that:

● 61 per cent of Tottenham Hotspur season tickets holders are social class AB, the highest in the premiership
● 22 per cent of fans said their club was one of the most important things in their life
● 64 per cent of fans have satellite or cable television so that they can watch football
● The average fan spends £131 on club merchandise each year

Source: *The Guardian* 27 February 2002

Exam practice

1   Define the term market research.   **[2]**
2   Explain what 'social class AB' means.   **[4]**
3   Examine **two** reasons why firms of all types should be cautious when interpreting the results of secondary research.   **[6]**
4   Examine the benefit footballs clubs might gain from having detailed information such as this about their fans.   **[8]**
5   'Market research is the key to successful marketing'. Discuss this statement.   **[10]**
Total 30 marks

7 Market segmentation

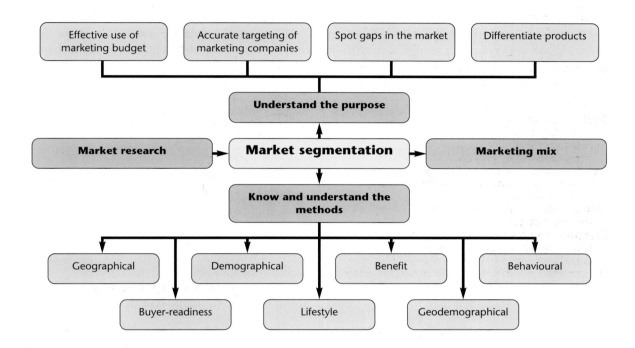

 What is market segmentation?

Market segmentation involves the division of larger markets into small clearly identifiable sections. So, for example, the energy drink market is one segment of the much larger drinks market. Producers might use market segmentation to identify people with similar needs and characteristics, aiming an energy drink directly at clubbers rather than all energy drink consumers for instance.

 The purpose of market segmentation

Very few goods are truly **mass-market** products. In most markets, at least to some degree, products are **differentiated**. A business that tries to make a product that is all things to all people will probably fail. Similarly, trying to advertise a product to everybody and hoping that a few will buy it is also likely to

fail. Segmenting larger markets helps businesses to differentiate their products and to market them effectively. **Segmentation** might also help a business to identify small (often very profitable) **niche markets** (see unit 8).

Defining customers – target markets

Through market research, businesses try to discover a huge range of information about customers (and potential customers). They might find out things such as:

- what TV programmes they watch
- what magazines they read
- how much they earn
- where they do their shopping
- who does the shopping
- what products they use and why they use them.

45

This information can then be used to develop products and marketing strategies that appeal directly to specific consumer groups. Actors and actresses used in TV adverts are specifically chosen because they represent (or will appeal to) the market segment that the advertisement is aimed at. For example, the market segment interested in the BMW Mini is young, fun loving and in search of something a little different – promotional strategy will reflect this and the people used in advertisements will be of a similar age to the target customers.

Knowing and understanding market segments, or **target markets**, makes marketing activities more likely to succeed.

Market mapping

Once a business understands both its own specific market segment and the broader segment in which it operates, it is possible to create a market map. A market map uses key product differentiation features to position each product on a map to create a visual representation of a particular market. Figure 7.1 shows how Cadbury's segmented the chocolate market according to price and type of chocolate snack; from light snack through to filling snack, before it launched its Fuse bar. Cadbury's identified a gap in the 'gutfill' segment of the market (a heavy, filling and reasonably priced bar). It identified the characteristics of target customers in this segment and launched the Fuse, aimed at people 'on the go' needing a quick and filling snack.

Market mapping can be used to watch for 'brand creep' – this occurs when a brand's image is changing in the minds of consumers. The maps also allow businesses to monitor and examine the position of competing brands. Marketing departments might decide to re-launch a brand, repackage it or even to reposition it.

Market share

Market share is the percentage of total sales a firm achieves in a market (see Figure 7.2). It is an important measure of business success. Businesses constantly try to increase their market share. As shown, market segmentation can help – allowing marketing departments to work more effectively, hopefully leading to increased sales and improved market share.

By identifying segments where the company has a strong reputation, marketers can use this reputation

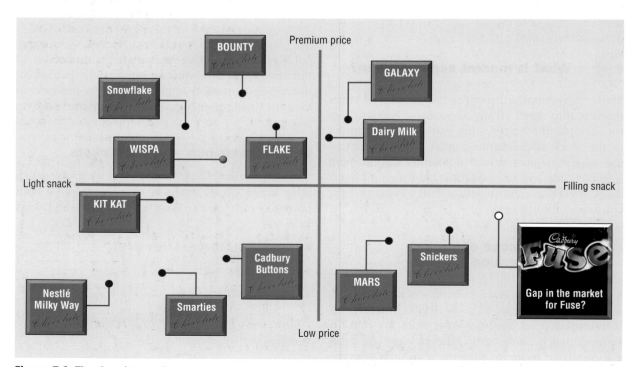

Figure 7.1 The chocolate market map

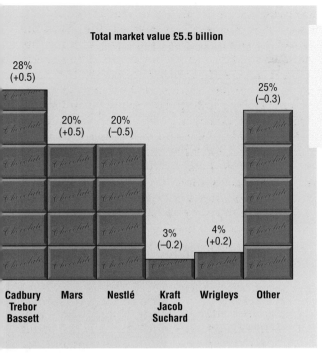

Total market value £5.5 billion

Figure 7.2 Market share of leading confectionery manufacturers, 2001

Source: www.cadbury.co.uk

It is important to distinguish between market share and **market growth**. Market share refers to the proportion of the market held by one company and market growth refers to the whole market. So, for example, the total confectionary market was worth £5.5 billion in 2001, having grown by 1 per cent in 2000. Cadbury's has a 28 per cent share of this total market.

3 Ways of segmenting the market

Businesses use many different criteria to segment markets, such as:

- **Geographical segmentation** which is concerned with identifying consumers according to the area where they live. This could be fairly broad – for example, Waitrose supermarkets are located predominantly in the south of England. Or, it may be quite specific – many insurance companies target customers according to crime rates in their locality.

- **Demographical segmentation** which is the broadest of all segmentation methods and includes a wide range of different criteria (see examples in Figure 7.3). Markets may also be segmented according to social class groupings (socio-demographic segmentation). Figure 7.4 shows one way that this is done within the UK. Products can then be aimed at specific groupings, such as ABs or DEs. (For example, hair salons such as Toni & Guy are aimed at ABs).

- **Benefit segmentation** which may be used by organisations such as car companies to develop a range of products. The market is segmented

to move into other market segments where they have less presence. They know their customers' habits, hobbies, likes and dislikes so, why not try and sell other products to them? *FHM* magazine, for instance, knew its readers were style conscious and expanded its presence in the magazine segment by launching *FHM Collections* (a fashion magazine).

Type	Example
Age	Nightclubs aimed at over 21s
Gender	Hair products aimed at females
Ethnic group	Food products aimed at different religious groups (for example, kosher or halal meat)
Income	Credit cards aimed at people earning over certain amounts.
Family characteristics	Products such as replacement furniture and foreign holidays aimed at 'empty nesters' (middle-aged parents whose children have left home)
Education	Courses aimed at those with few qualifications
Occupation	Magazines, such as *The Grocer* or *Management Today*, aimed at specific professions

Figure 7.3 Examples of demographic market segmentation

Group	Social Status	Description
A	Upper middle class	Higher managerial, administrative or professional (doctors, solicitors, company directors)
B	Middle class	Middle management, administrative or professional (teachers, nurses, managers)
C^1	Lower middle class	Supervisory, clerical or junior management (shop assistants, clerks, police officers)
C^2	Skilled working class	Skilled manual workers (electricians, service engineers, technicians)
D	Working class	Semi and unskilled manual workers (farm hands, labourers)
E	The poorest in society	State pensioners, casual workers, unemployed

Source: Institute of Practitioners in Advertising

Figure 7.4 Social class groupings

STOP & THINK

Is social class a good way to segment markets? Do you think occupation truly determines social class? Will all people in similar occupations purchase similar products?

according to the benefit consumers seek from the product. For example, some people will be interested in safety, others in load space or performance. Hence, car companies develop ranges of products to appeal to these different segments (five-door, sports, estate and so on) and usually promote the product in different ways to the different groups.

- **Behavioural segmentation** which involves segmenting consumers according to different behaviours. A supermarket might use its loyalty card scheme to track the spending habits of customers and identify that, for example, most over-50s tend to shop on Mondays. Having identified this, it may run special promotions every Monday to attract even more over-50s and to encourage them to spend a greater amount in the store.

- **Buyer-readiness segmentation** which divides consumers according to how ready they are to buy a product.

- **Lifestyle segmentation** is based on how the opinions interests, hobbies and activities of individuals affect spending habits. For example, 'experiencers' are considered to be young, frequently engaged in physical or social activities and avid consumers of new products.

Activity

Identify which types of segmentation are used by *Max Power* magazine in the statement below. 'Our typical reader is male, aged 15–24, drives a GTI (and if he doesn't he wishes he did) and his car is his life. He is interested in modifying cars, up to 15-years-old, he can live anywhere in the country and is predominately B/C1/C2/D. He spends his time working on his car, buys on strength of brand and is highly image-conscious'.

Source: from *British Rates And Data*, June 1997

Want to know more?

www.brad.co.uk

- **Geodemographic segmentation** which is perhaps the most powerful of all the segmentation types. It combines both geographic and demographic data to build a detailed picture of different localities. The data can be used to pinpoint the best location for a new store or to identify where a mailshot might be most effective. A brief example of the type of information geodemographics can provide is given in Figure 7.5.

Most businesses, as the *Max Power* example in the above activity shows, use a combination of methods to accurately describe their market segments.

4   Summary

Segmentation is an essential part of the marketing process, it allows businesses to:

- use marketing budgets effectively

- target marketing campaigns accurately

- spot gaps in the market and identify new opportunities

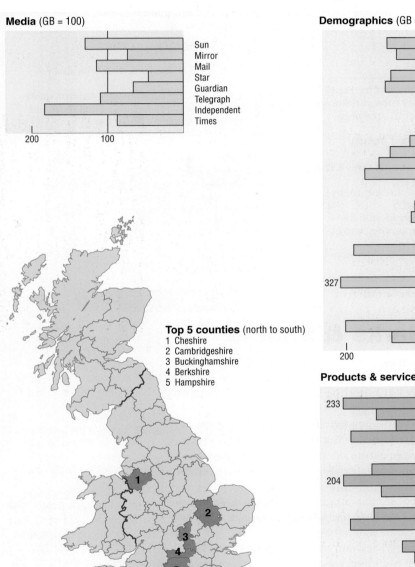

Media (GB = 100)

Sun
Mirror
Mail
Star
Guardian
Telegraph
Independent
Times

200   100

Top 5 counties (north to south)
1 Cheshire
2 Cambridgeshire
3 Buckinghamshire
4 Berkshire
5 Hampshire

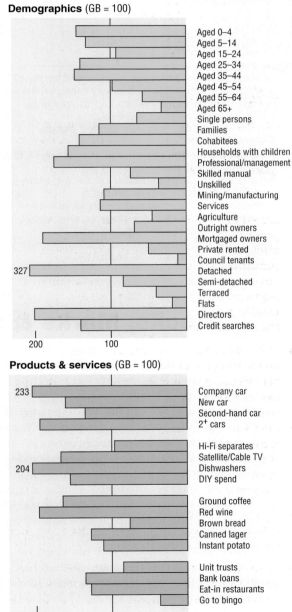

Demographics (GB = 100)

Aged 0–4
Aged 5–14
Aged 15–24
Aged 25–34
Aged 35–44
Aged 45–54
Aged 55–64
Aged 65+
Single persons
Families
Cohabitees
Households with children
Professional/management
Skilled manual
Unskilled
Mining/manufacturing
Services
Agriculture
Outright owners
Mortgaged owners
Private rented
Council tenants
327   Detached
Semi-detached
Terraced
Flats
Directors
Credit searches

200   100

Products & services (GB = 100)

233   Company car
New car
Second-hand car
2⁺ cars

Hi-Fi separates
Satellite/Cable TV
204   Dishwashers
DIY spend

Ground coffee
Red wine
Brown bread
Canned lager
Instant potato

Unit trusts
Bank loans
Eat-in restaurants
Go to bingo

200   100

Figure 7.5 Information about 'rising materialists' provided by geodemographic segmentation

Source: MOSAIC Data (produced by Credit Control Nottingham, 1987)

- differentiate products from those of competitors (allowing higher prices to be charged).

The basic foundation of marketing success – know your customer – is an integral part of segmentation. Segmentation involves clearly defining who these customers are and developing a detailed understanding of their needs, which, as we have seen, is essential to marketing success.

Activity

Produce a segmentation statement (like the one in the *Max Power* activity) for each of the following products:
1 *Vogue* magazine
2 Red Bull
3 The *Financial Times*

Market segmentation: summary

KEY TERMS

Differentiated – products are different to those offered by competitors; this may mean adding or altering features for the product to appeal to specific segments.

Market segment – a clearly defined market section.

Market share – the percentage of total sales a firm achieves in a market

Mass market – a large market containing many customers buying similar products

Niche market – a small and clearly identifiable segment of a market; for example, the market for expensive home audio equipment.

Target market – the particular market segment at which a business aims its product(s).

Summary questions

1 Describe, using an example, what is meant by a market segment.
2 What is meant by geodemographic segmentation?
3 State and explain **three** methods a firm might use to segment its market.
4 Outline the key advantages of market segmentation.
5 Segmentation is especially important in niche marketing. Explain why this is the case.
6 Suggest how marketing might be used to make a product appeal to social grouping DEs
7 Give **two** examples of markets that might be segmented by age.

Exam practice

Becks, Marks & Sparks

Marks & Spencer now produce a range of clothing 'inspired by' David Beckham. It is all about credibility; to 6–14 year old boys Beckham is a footballing god, above that age he is still a sporting hero, but more importantly, he's a style icon.

Above the age of 14, the youth market for clothing becomes very fashion- and label-conscious. Brand image is a key differentiator. The link with Beckham, with his name appearing on the label and as part of the design, should help Marks & Spencer appeal to this increasingly affluent market segment.

Marks & Spencer attempted similar strategies (though without the famous name associated) with its Per Una and Autograph ranges. Both were designed to appeal to specific female market segments.

Marks & Spencer will be hoping Beckham can do for them what he did for Brylcream. The product, with his 'help', was rebranded and now appeals to a much younger market segment than had previously been the case. It would appear that he can create as much magic in marketing as he can on the soccer pitch.

Source: *The Daily Telegraph* 28 February 2002

1 Define the term 'market segment'. **[2]**
2 Explain, using an example, what is meant by the phrase: 'Brand image is a key differentiator'. **[4]**
3 Examine the benefits Marks & Spencer might gain from aiming key ranges at specific market segments. **[6]**
4 Marks & Spencer has traditionally spent relatively little on advertising compared to competitors. Analyse possible reasons for this strategy. **[8]**
5 To what extent can association with a 'famous name' ensure the success of a brand? **[10]**
Total 30 marks

8 Marketing: objectives and strategy

1 Marketing objectives

Overall marketing strategy will be expressed through a range of marketing objectives, which might include:

- increase market share
- increase product awareness or brand recognition
- increase product usage
- expand into new market segments
- develop new products.

2 What determines strategy?

A wide range of factors influence a business's marketing strategy and objectives. These include:

- **Corporate objectives**. Most importantly, marketing objectives must directly reflect overall

corporate objectives. Orange may have the corporate objective to increase its total global sales revenue; this might translate as a set of marketing objectives relating to awareness of Orange products in different countries.

- **People.** In smaller businesses, marketing objectives might simply be based on the owner's 'hunches'. Strategy might also be based on the amount of risk individuals within a business are willing to face.

- **The market.** Highly competitive markets demand flexible marketing strategies. Music companies, for example, constantly adjust their strategies to cope with new music trends and new music formats, such as MP3.

- **Competition.** One of the most important determinants of marketing strategy is, perhaps, competition. Businesses constantly seek to attain or maintain market leadership and will introduce strategies accordingly – a price cut or special offer by the market leader just as a competing product is about to be launched might help to maintain market position.

- **Finance.** Marketing can be very expensive. The amount of money a business can afford to spend on marketing will usually determine its marketing strategy.

- **Type of product.** Industrial goods are likely to require different marketing strategies to consumer goods. Industrial markets are often characterised by small numbers of buyers and sellers, and products can often be very specialised. Increasing market share may well be difficult, therefore a business might concentrate on cost reductions or developing new products in related markets (for example, Rolls Royce's entry into the marine engine market).

 ## 3   Marketing strategies

The mantra *'high volume – low price versus low volume – high price'* is a basic business principle. This may seem a little simplistic, but it is a good starting point for considering marketing strategies. Businesses must choose their strategy based on one of these two market positions and so determine all other aspects of their marketing strategy.

Niche marketing

Niche marketing (also known as focused marketing) involves selling goods to small, clearly identifiable segments of a market. Niche markets are usually characterised by:

- premium priced products – good potential for profitability

- small sales volumes

- highly differentiated products

- high skills base – difficult for large competitors to easily replicate these skills.

Examples of niche markets include the market for specialist sports cars, such as the Caterham Lotus Super 7, or the market for tailor-made clothing.

Choosing to pursue a niche marketing strategy has a significant effect on the type of marketing activities undertaken. Promotion will be very specific, the product needs to be clearly differentiated and the outlets it is sold in must reflect its image.

Mass marketing

In contrast to niche marketing, **mass marketing** aims for high sales volume at the expense of low prices. Mass markets are characterised by:

- low prices

- undifferentiated products

- a wide range of sales outlets and wide availability

- extensive promotion

- high sales volume.

Mass-market products include items such as sugar, salt, fruit and vegetables.

If a business sells a truly undifferentiated product, then it may pursue a strategy of **cost leadership**. This is where the business seeks to be the lowest-priced seller in the market (supermarkets such as CostCo and Aldi are examples). The problem with this strategy is that there is only room for one cost leader in a market – if a business is not the cheapest then it must offer some form of differentiation to attract customers. Prices may be forced so low that it is difficult to make a profit. (American farmers growing potatoes to sell to fast-food chains face this problem.)

The Caterham Lotus Super 7, a niche market product

For example ...

All over the place

Most, if not all of you, have heard of FCUK. Most major high streets now have a branch of French Connection, and the company's adverts can be seen on billboards across the country. This was not true just a few years ago. French Connection was a small retailer, with an exclusive image, very few outlets and premium prices – a classic example of niche marketing. The launch of the FCUK slogan was part of the company's aggressive strategy to move into the mass market – a strategy that has clearly worked.

1 Discuss the issues that French Connection may have faced as it moved from a niche to a mass-market position. **Total 10 marks**

Differentiated marketing

Cost leadership is difficult to achieve and can result in low profitability so most businesses differentiate their products – that is, they offer customers something different or superior to what the competition offers. Even milk is differentiated with different treatments – pasteurised, filtered, semi-skimmed and so on – which helps milk producers to compete. A business can reasonably justify charging a higher price for a differentiated product.

Some products rely on perceived (how customers see the product) differentiation rather than actual tangible (physical) differences. For example, a branded shirt may be identical to an unbranded one in quality (it may even have been made in the same factory!), but the presence of a well-known logo and brand name helps to differentiate the branded shirt and justify a higher price.

Competitive strategies

Marketing strategy is also determined by a business's competitive environment. Intel is the **market leader** in microchip production, but AMD has, over recent years, challenged that dominance. The threat from AMD necessitated that Intel defend its market share. Research into new, faster chips increased and a host of new, faster microchips flooded the market as AMD and Intel tried to keep up with each other.

AMD, as a **market challenger**, pursued a strategy of directly attacking Intel's leadership position. AMD microchips claim to be faster than Intel's, and are significantly cheaper; a fact that they promoted heavily.

A 'me-too' strategy might be used where a **market follower** copies the strategy of the market leaders in an attempt to benefit from their success. This often happens in fast growing markets as companies attempt to quickly jump on the bandwagon of success.

4 Marketing tools

In order to decide which marketing strategies are most suitable and least risky, businesses can use marketing models to consider and analyse strategies.

Porter's Generic Strategies

The strategies previously discussed in this chapter are often represented in a matrix (see figure 8.1) known as Porter's Generic Strategies. Porter believes that a business can use any competitive advantage it holds to shape pricing strategy. For example, a business with a low cost base and efficient production may be able to exploit the advantage of offering low prices (as easyJet does). This combined with the competitive

		Competitive advantage	
		Low cost	Higher cost
Competitive scope	Broad	Overall cost leadership	Differentiation
	Narrow	Cost focus	Differentiation focus leadership

Figure 8.1 Porter's Generic Strategies
Source: Porter M. E., *Competitive Strategy* (New York Free Press, 1980)

Activity

Using a blank matrix for Porter's Generic Strategies, try to identify the competitive position and marketing strategy of some major companies in the airline industry:

- easyJet
- Emirates
- Virgin Atlantic
- Quantas
- MyTravel
- Ryanair

- British Airways
- Iberia
- BMI Baby
- British Midlands
- SAS
- BA – Concorde

scope of a business (niche or mass-market) can then be used to suggest the type of marketing strategy a business may follow.

Ansoff's Matrix

The risk inherent in different marketing strategies has been represented in what is known as Ansoff's Matrix. This considers whether a business is entering a new market and/or developing new products and shows the risk involved (see Figure 8.2).

- **Market penetration** – existing products are sold to existing customers. This might involve promoting the product, repositioning the brand or encouraging increased usage (Kellogg's has advertised Cornflakes as *'good to eat at any time of the day'*). (Low risk.)

- **Market development** – existing products are sold in a new market. This means that the product remains the same, but it is marketed to a new audience. (Medium risk.)

- **Product development** – a new product is marketed to existing customers. New product

offerings are developed to replace existing ones. For example, mobile phone companies constantly develop new phones and then attempt to get existing customers to upgrade. (Medium risk.)

- **Diversification** – this carries the most risk. The business launches a new product into a new market. For example, Virgin's diversification into rail transport was a particularly risky strategy. (High risk.)

Competitive advantage

Competitive advantage, in terms of cost, may allow a firm to charge lower prices. This might be achieved through lower labour costs or through more efficient production methods (see unit 30). easyjet based its business model on the competitive advantage it held over its larger rivals of having a much lower cost base.

A superior brand, a high quality product, excellent customer service or superior distribution, among many other things, are all examples of other types of **competitive advantage** that can be exploited through marketing. Dell Computers, for instance, has an enviable reputation for both quality and service. These competitive advantages give Dell an edge in the market and help to shape its marketing strategy.

 The marketing plan

Marketing plans are vital to marketing success. They help to focus the mind of companies and marketing teams on the process of marketing. As with corporate plans they involve a consideration of:

- Where are we now?
- Where do we want to go?
- How are we going to get there?
- How will we know when we are there?

Where are we now?

Finding out the current market position of a business involves a marketing audit. This might involve:

- analysing Political, Economic, Social, Technical, Legal and Environmental factors that might affect marketing strategy. (PEST/LE analysis)

- considering the marketing plans and campaigns of competitors

Figure 8.2 Ansoff's Matrix

- conducting a SWOT analysis

- examining current and future demand and market trends

- analysing current marketing campaigns.

Where do we want to go?

This stage involves considering corporate objectives and overall marketing strategy as discussed throughout this unit.

How are we going to get there?

To determine how the company is to achieve its marketing objectives, the operational tactics must be laid out in detail. The marketing plan must clearly define the target market segment and describe how the **marketing mix** (see units 9–12) will be used to achieve the marketing objectives. The marketing budget required to implement these tactics must also be considered.

How will we know when we are there?

This is the measurement or evaluation stage. Not only must the business consider whether its marketing objectives have been met, but also if the marketing process has stayed within its predefined budget. The success of the tactics themselves must also be measured. In this way the business can build up a picture of the type of marketing activities that work for its products. For example, a radio advertisement may have generated lots of sales, whereas newspaper advertisements may have proven unpopular.

As with all business plans, once a marketing plan is drawn up it must be constantly monitored and reviewed. Some objectives may not be met, others may need reviewing – marketing planning is an ongoing process, evaluation of results must feedback into the planning process and be used in future marketing audits. Figure 8.3 represents this process.

Guru's views
'All business plans should be seen as signposts and not as destinations.'

Unknown

Activity

The launch of the BMW Mini was a great success. The car was well received by critics and consumers. BMW plans to launch a Mini Cabriolet in the near future.

Produce a marketing plan for the launch of the Mini Cabriolet. Consider the following:

- What marketing objectives might you (BMW) have?
- Who might your target market be?
- What promotional methods might you use?
- What message will you use in promotions?
- How will your car be distributed and sold?
- What pricing strategy should you use?

Want to know more?

www.mini.co.uk

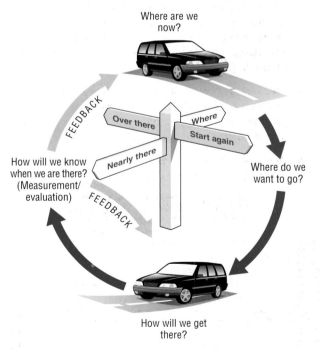

Figure 8.3 The marketing cycle

Marketing objectives and strategy: summary

KEY TERMS

Cost leadership – achieving competitive advantage through a lower cost base allowing a firm to successfully compete on price (potentially offering the lowest prices in a market).

Market leader – the business with the greatest share of a market.

Market challenger – often the focus of marketing strategy is on the challenge element, attempting to appeal to the desire to favour the underdog. For example, Virgin Atlantic's challenge to British Airways.

Market follower – a business with a small market share that closely follows (and copies) the strategies of the market leaders.

Marketing mix – the combination of Product, Price, Promotion and Place used to implement marketing strategy.

Mass market – a market containing large numbers of consumers purchasing similar products.

Niche market – a small, clearly identifiable segment of a larger market.

Competetive advantage – refers to the ability to offer consumers something different from, or superior to, the market competition.

Summary questions

1 State **two** different marketing objectives that a business might have.
2 Suggest a suitable marketing objective for each of the following:
   • T-Mobile (formerly One-2-One)
   • a small local pet shop
   • Egg (online bank)
3 Distinguish between marketing objectives and marketing tactics.
4 Identify **two** factors that might influence marketing objectives.
5 Distinguish between niche and mass marketing.
6 Why might a business wish to focus on a niche market?
7 State and explain **two** disadvantages of a cost-leadership strategy.
8 Give **two** examples of mass-market products.
9 What is a 'me-too' strategy?
10 Suggest and explain **two** strategies a market leader might use to defend its position.
11 Draw a fully labelled copy of Ansoff's Matrix and include the following examples in the correct boxes:
   • Nescafé coffee, advertising to improve brand loyalty
   • Dyson, moving into the broader home appliances market (washing machines)
   • Oasis Clothing, opening branches in Europe
   • the launch of Cadbury's Snowflake.

Exam practice

The Sky's the limit

The Simpson's, *Buffy*, and *Friends* all have at least one thing in common – they were all shown first on Sky. Launched in 1989, Sky has transformed the way people in Britain watch and use their televisions.

Sky's achievements in its short life emphasise the importance of having a clear marketing strategy. Sky moved rapidly from a small niche market to becoming a truly mass-market product.

Sky's marketing strategy has been based around innovation and offering customers consistently better products and services. This is backed up by several important marketing aims:

● To create and acquire the best entertainment and information.
● To keep customers at the forefront of entertainment and IT.
● To give customers the best possible entertainment experience.
● To be inventive, creative, entertaining and challenging.

These marketing aims are then turned into specific marketing objectives that are clearly communicated throughout the business.

Sky's desire to be 'at the heart of 21st century living' has seen it expand into TV banking, TV shopping, TV games and information services. Constant innovations (such as Sky+), a focus on customer service and effective marketing strategies have enabled Sky to attain and retain market leadership, despite some very high-profile challenges from the likes of ITV Digital and cable TV.

Source: *The Times 100 Case Studies* (sixth edition)

1 Distinguish between marketing aims and marketing objectives. **[2]**
2 With reference to the case study, distinguish between niche and mass marketing. **[3]**
3 With reference to Ansoff's Matrix, suggest which marketing strategy is being used by Sky. Justify your answer. **[5]**
4 Discuss how the marketing strategies of market leaders, such as Sky, might differ from the strategies of market challengers. **[8]**
5 Critically evaluate the use of marketing models for businesses such as Sky in determining marketing strategy. **[12]**
Total 30 marks

9 Product

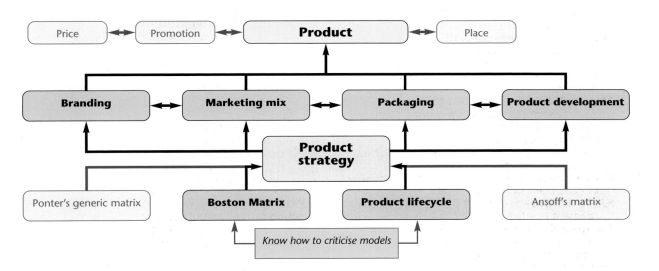

The product is a fundamental part of the marketing mix. It is, after all, the part of the mix that customers will use, eat or drink and so on.

 ## Product strategy

The decision as to the exact product or service to be sold is essentially a strategic one. As such, product strategy is determined in relation to corporate and marketing objectives. Use of strategic models (as discussed in Unit 8) will inform the way that product is used as part of the marketing mix. In addition, several product-specific models exist to help a business decide how best to use the marketing mix based on a market analysis of its current products.

1 Product portfolio analysis – the Boston Matrix

The Boston Matrix (see Figure 9.1) is a well-known marketing tool allowing businesses to conduct product portfolio analysis. It considers market share and the rate of market growth in the market:

- **Dogs** – are products with low market share in low-growth markets. They do not generate cash for the

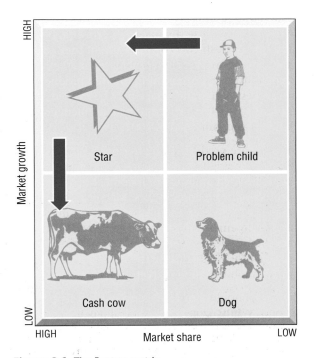

Figure 9.1 The Boston matrix

company; rather they tend to have a high **cash burn** rate. The most common strategy for 'dogs' is to divest – this involves selling off the product or ceasing production. An example of a low growth market is that for video recorders – overtaken in the technology and sales stakes by the DVD player.

- **Cash cows** – are products with a high share of a low-growth market. These are often mature markets with well-established products. Nescafé Original is an example of a cash cow. As the name suggests, cash cows generate more income for the business than is invested in them. This surplus cash can be 'milked' to support stars or problem children. Some cash must, however, be retained to help hold the product in its cash cow position. Cash cows may find their market positions frequently challenged by competitors – hence Nescafé continues to market and promote Nescafé Original.

Guru's views
'To control your cow, give it a bigger pasture.'
Suzuki Roshi, Zen Master

- **Problem children** – are products with a low share of a high-growth market. They consume marketing resources and generate little income. They may, because the market is growing, become the stars or cash cows of the future if they can gain greater market share. Increased marketing expenditure and attempting to build product awareness and brand image may be needed. Microsoft's X-Box proved to be a problem child when it was launched in 2001.

- **Stars** – are products in high-growth markets with a relatively high market share. Stars often generate high amounts of income, but may need protecting from competitors. Market leadership may not have been established in these markets, and companies will be fighting for market share and brand loyalty. The Nokia 3210 was a star product for Nokia during the rapid growth period in the mobile phone market.

A business should aim for balance within its product portfolio. Whilst 'dogs' should be avoided, 'stars' and 'problem children' are required to (hopefully) become future 'cash cows'. Cash cows are needed to generate income for product development and new product launches. Ideally, a business would have a product development cycle that follows the path indicated by

STOP & THINK

What has happened to the X-Box? Did Microsoft manage to turn it into a star or cash cow? Has it become a dog?

the arrows in Figure 9.3. Examining its product portfolio allows a business to consider whether it has got this balance right and adjust its strategy accordingly.

Criticisms of the Boston Matrix

There is an assumption that profit is directly related to high market share. This may not always be the case – when Boeing launches a new aeroplane, it may gain market share quickly but it still has to cover very high development costs.

The strategic responses suggested by the models will not suit all business situations. Many marketers argue that 'milking' a cow is likely to hand competitive advantage to other firms in the market.

The matrix oversimplifies a complex decision-making process – management experience and intuition remain important.

Conducting a product portfolio analysis is of little use if it does not lead to action.

Activity

Prepare a portfolio analysis for a mobile phone manufacturer.

1 Pick a mobile phone manufacturer (Nokia or Siemens, for example.). List all the mobile phones that they manufacture. Take a look at the manufacturer's website or, if you need to, go to www.carphonewarehouse.co.uk.

2 Think about the mobile phone market at the moment, is it growing or is it relatively static? This is important for the next section.

3 Draw a portfolio matrix and try to place each of the phones on the chart. Discuss with your classmates your selections, do they agree?

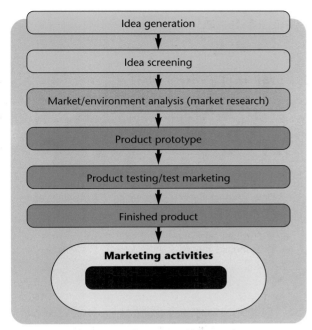

Figure 9.2 Product development and innovation

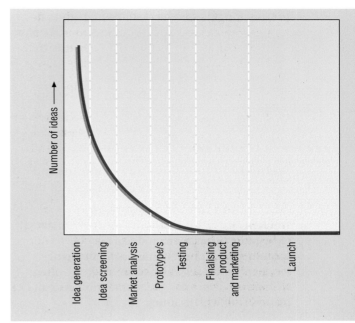

Figure 9.3 New product fall-out rate

2 Product development

There are many reasons why new products are important to businesses, some of these reasons include:

● To counter competitors actions.

● To smooth out seasonal fluctuations.

● To spread risk through diversification into new markets.

● To increase or maintain market share.

● To replace old, unpopular or discontinued products.

The stages necessary to bring a new product to market are shown in Figure 9.2.

Fewer than one in seven (or one in ten for food) product ideas ever make it successfully to market (see Figure 9.3). Some, despite all the testing and checking, fail once they reach the market. Mattell, the toy company, launched a toy doll that was designed to che plastic food, but it was also found to chew children's hair and fingers – the company had to buy back the 500,000 units it had sold!

> ### Guru's views
> 'Sometimes when you innovate, you make mistakes. It is best to admit them quickly and get on with improving your other innovations.'
> *Steve Jobs, Apple Computers*

3 The product lifecycle

After initial development, a product will be *introduced* to the market. Hopefully, its sales will *grow* and eventually the market will stabilise and become *mature*. Then, as new products are launched, sales for the original product will start to *decline*. This process is known as the product lifecycle and is shown in Figure 9.4.

Stages of the product life cycle

● **Introduction.** After research and development, which may inlcude **test marketing**, the product will be launched onto the market. Costs incurred

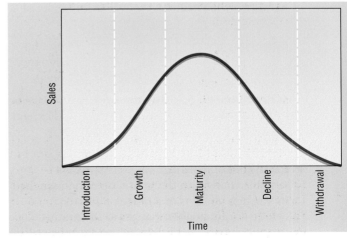

Figure 9.4 A typical product lifecycle

in launching the product will be high and sales may be low. The product is unlikely to make any profit at this stage. Tablet PCs are currently in their introduction stage.

- **Growth**. Sales begin to grow and competitors enter the market. Having covered its development costs the product may become profitable. Recordable DVD is an example of a product in its growth stage.

- **Maturity.** Sales grow at a decreasing rate and then stabilise. DVD players are currently in the maturity stage.

- **Decline.** Sales, for most products, eventually fall. New, more innovative products may be introduced or consumer tastes might change. Products that reach the decline stage are often withdrawn from sale. The market for personal CD players is slowly declining.

Knowledge of the product lifecycle concept allows managers, in theory, to adjust marketing strategy accordingly.

Different types of lifecycle

Not all products follow the classic lifecycle shown in Figure 9.5. Many products fail, some have very short lifecycles and others enjoy extremely long lives – Bisto gravy, for instance. Figure 9.6 (opposite) shows some of these different lifecycles.

Extension strategies

A variety of **extension strategies** (see Figure 9.6) can be used to prevent sales decline:

- **Encourage increased usage.** Doritos tortilla chips were marketed under the slogan '*friendchips*' in an effort to encourage people to buy more of the product.

- **Find new users.** Mobile phone companies have developed phones and airtime packages designed to appeal to younger children and pensioners.

- **Find new uses for the product.** Helly Hansen managed to increase brand awareness and extend the life of its sailing clothing by selling it as fashion items.

- **Change the product.** This may involve tangible changes to the product (Dyson launched its vacuum cleaners in a range of different colours) or intangible changes to the product's image (Pepperami was relaunched under the slogan 'a bit of an animal').

Activity

Draw product lifecycle sketches for the products and services listed below:
- Playstation One
- Big Brother (the TV programme)
- WAP mobile phones
- Kit Kat

For example …

A Mini success

The BMW Mini enjoyed a very successful launch and, as it creeps into maturity, has lost none of its appeal. When the Mini was launched in the UK, sales in the first three months of its life reached 27,691, boosting BMW's (the Mini's owners) overall car sales by 17.4 per cent. The story was very similar at the car's US launch, 787 cars were sold in just nine days. Sales in Japan totalled 900 in February 2002 – big numbers for a little car.

Source: *The Guardian* 9 April 2002

1 Identify **four** factors that might be important to a successful product launch. [4]
2 The Mini became a 'star' in BMW's product portfolio. Examine two implications this might have for the Mini? [4]
3 Evaluate the usefulness of product portfolio analysis to BMW. [8]
Total 16 marks

	Introduction	**Growth**	**Maturity**	**Decline**
Features of stage				
Sales	Low	Growing	Slow growth	Declining
Profits	Small	Highest	High but declining	Low
Cash Flow	Negative	Positive	Positive	Positive, but falling
Customers	Early adopters	Early majority	Mass market	Laggards
Competitors	Few	Growing	Many	Falling
Marketing strategy				
Marketing Expenditure	High	High (cost per sale falling)	Falling	Low
Price	Skimming or penetration strategy	Price cut/increase demanding on introduction strategy	Going-rate or competitor-based	High
Product	Basic	Improved	Differentiated	Basic
Promotion	Focus on awareness	Generate brand preference	Retain brand loyalty	Targeted promotions
Place (distribution)	Few outlets	Increasing	High number of outlets	Falling

Figure 9.5 The features and marketing implications of the product lifecycle

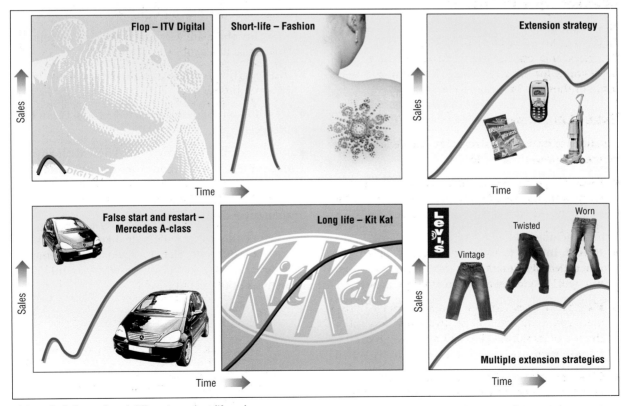

Figure 9.6 Examples of different product lifecycles

For example ...

Many of today's best-known 'manufacturers' no longer actually produce products and advertise them; but rather buy products and brand them. Companies such as Nike and Gap have divested themselves of all production capacity and focus solely on branding. The intention is to sell a lifestyle and an image. Nike defines itself as 'a sports company', not a sports clothing manufacturer. Money previously spent on production is now poured into promotion to support and develop the brand's identity.

Source: Naomi Klein, *No Logo*, Flamingo 2001

1 What is a brand?   [2]
2 Explain why promotion is important in supporting a brand's identity.   [6]
Total 8 Marks

Want to know more?

www.nike.com or www.nologo.org

2   Branding

Branding refers to the use of a name, symbol or design to identify a particular product. Popular brands include Nike, FCUK, Sony and Heinz.

Brand image is the 'personality' given to a product through marketing activities. This brand image will be deliberately created to appeal to a specific market segment; for example, Tango has been given a 'wacky' image to appeal to younger people. Branding is also used to:

- **Create and maintain brand loyalty.** When Kit Kat, at great expense, changed its packaging by removing the silver foil inner wrapper, loyal customers were outraged. The brand loyalty generated by the ritual of opening a Kit Kat was immense. Brands create familiarity and encourage long term repeat purchasing.

- **Expand product ranges.** Consumers are more likely to try a new product if they trust the brand. Boots was able to enter the beauty treatment market because customers trust the Boots brand.

- **Differentiate products.** A brand may be the only thing that makes one product different from another. This was, in fact, the original purpose of brands. The Cadbury's brand was borne out of the need to distinguish itself from other chocolates on the market.

- **To aid recognition.** The presence of a distinctive brand logo can help products to stand out on supermarket shelves. Coca-Cola bottles have a distinctive colour and shape, both aiding recognition.

- **To gain price flexibility.** The fact that the product is 'different' and has established brand loyalty or has a desirable brand image allows firms to charge higher prices.

Criticisms of the product lifecycle concept

When considering lifecycle analysis it is important to take into account the following factors:

- In reality there are very few products that follow the classic lifecycle.

- The length of each stage varies enormously between products.

- It is difficult to identify where a product is in its lifecycle.

- It is impossible for mangers to know with any degree of certainty when a product will enter the next stage of its life. Any changes to marketing strategy are therefore going to be reactive rather than proactive.

- Usage of the product lifecycle, like all business tools, needs to be balanced against management experience, personal intuition and a sound analysis of the market.

Product: summary

KEY TERMS

Brand image – the personality given to a product through marketing activities.

Branding – the use of a name, symbol or design to identify a particular product.

Cash burn – the rate at which a product or business uses up the cash available to it.

Extension strategy – marketing strategy to prevent sales from declining.

Test marketing – launching the product in a small area or testing the product with small groups of consumers.

Summary questions

1 List the main stages in a product's development.
2 Give an example of a recent, successful new product launch.
3 Identify the main stages of the product lifecycle.
4 Explain how the promotional support given to a product might differ in each stage of its lifecycle.
5 Sketch product lifecycles for the following:
   • a failed product
   • a successful extension strategy.
6 Explain **two** ways in which a firm might use product lifecycle analysis.
7 State and explain **three** product lifecycle extension strategies.
8 What is the Boston Matrix?
9 Explain, with reference to portfolio analysis, what is meant by a 'dog' product.
10 What strategies might a firm use with a product identified as a problem child?

Exam practice

Planning an extension

Coca-Cola, the US soft drinks company, worked secretly throughout 2002 on plans to launch Vanilla Coke.

Coke is the world's most valuable brand and the Coca-Cola Company has traditionally been extremely cautious about extending it to other drinks for fear of diluting the brand. Although a lemon-flavoured Diet Coke was introduced in 2001, the only flavoured version of standard Coke is Cherry Coke, launched in 1985.

However, cola drinks are losing market share to other soft drinks in the US, putting Coca-Cola executives under pressure to maintain and extend the brand's appeal.

Vanilla Coke already has a popular following in the US. People often make it by adding a shot of vanilla syrup to a glass of ordinary coke.

Source: *Financial Times* 1 April 2002

1 Explain what is meant by market share and examine **one** reason why Coca-Cola may be 'losing market share'. **[4]**
2 Why might Coca-Cola be fearful of diluting their brand? **[6]**
3 Explain, with reference to product lifecycle theory, Coca-Cola's rationale for launching the new variety. **[5]**
4 Evaluate the usefulness of product lifecycle analysis to companies such as Coca-Cola. **[15]**
Total 30 marks

10 Price

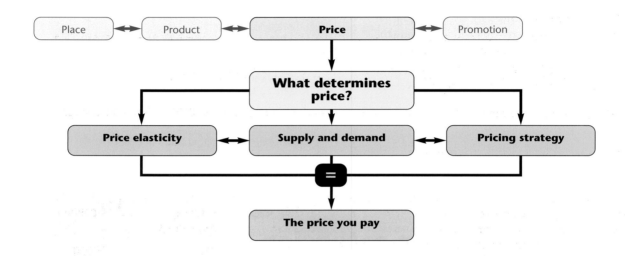

A variety of factors influence the price of a product, for example:

- the cost of production
- the target customers (market segment)
- marketplace competition
- the business's overall objectives, marketing objectives and marketing strategy
- where the product is in its life cycle (see unit 9).

1 Pricing theory

Figure 10.1 shows a basic supply and demand diagram. Supply and demand diagrams represent the conflicting interests of buyers and sellers. Buyers are willing to purchase more (demand) as the price falls and producers are willing to sell more (supply) at higher prices. The point where the demand and supply curves meet is known as the **equilibrium price**. Here, buyers and sellers are in agreement about price and quantity – producers are willing to sell the same amount demanded by customers at that price.

The equilibrium price is also known as the market

price. Knowledge of the influence of supply and demand is a useful tool in helping businesses to plan their pricing strategies. (See also Unit 40.)

Price elasticity of demand

Elasticity of demand measures the responsiveness of demand to a change in price or, in simple terms, 'a measure of to what extent sales of a product are affected by a change in its price'.

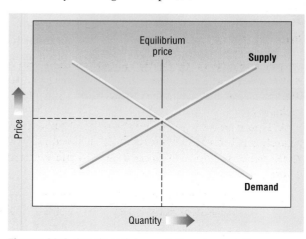

Figure 10.1 Supply and demand diagram

Percentages and percentage changes

There are many different ways of calculating percentage change. If you have been taught a different method, you may wish to stick with that.

Percentages

One way to remember how to work out percentages is to *'divide what you have by what you could have and multiple by 100'*. For example, in a test, you get 80 out of 125 marks:

$$\frac{80 \text{ (your score)}}{125 \text{ (what you could have scored)}} \times 100 = 64\%$$

Percentage changes

The same method is used but with one extra stage. You now have to calculate the difference between your answer and 100. So, using one of the price elasticity examples:

$$\left(\frac{£30 \text{ (what you have} - \textit{new price)}}{£25 \text{ (the price you could still be getting} - \textit{old price)}} \times 100 = 120\%\right) - 100 = \textbf{+20\%}$$

If the percentage is less than 100, then the percentage change is a minus value. So 80% − 100 = − 20 change.

Figure 10.2 Calculating percentage change

A product that is very price sensitive might see demand fall by, for example, 20 per cent if price rose by as little a 5 per cent. A product for which sales are not very price sensitive might see a fall in demand of only 5 per cent despite a 10 per cent price increase.

The basic concept of price elasticity is worked out by comparing the percentage change (see Figure 10.2) in quantity demanded with the percentage change in price, as shown in the following formula:

$$\text{Price elasticity (PED)} = \frac{\text{percentage change in quantity demanded}}{\text{percentage change in price}}$$

A business must know how responsive their products are to price changes so that they can analyse the potential impact of, say, special offers or a price increase.

Price inelastic demand

Despite heavy taxation by the government, smoking is still a popular habit. The purchase of cigarettes is, therefore, not very sensitive to price changes (price inelastic).

As Figure 10.3 shows, when the price of a packet of cigarettes is increased from £5 to £6 demand falls by 7,000 packets. Applying these figures to the formula gives:

$$\text{PED} = \frac{\text{percentage change in quantity demanded}}{\text{percentage change in price}} = \frac{-5\%}{20\%}$$

$$= -\textbf{0.25} = 0.25$$

Price per pack	Quantity demanded	Revenue
£4	150 000	£600 000
£5	140 000	£700 000
£6	133 000	£798 000

Figure 10.3 The price inelasticity of the demand for cigarettes

Minus signs are ignored when calculating price elasticity so −0.25 simply becomes 0.25.

The figure of 0.25 confirms that, in this example, demand for cigarettes is **price inelastic**. The figure is less than one, indicating that any percentage change in price results in a proportionally smaller percentage change in demand (hence all products with price elasticities less than one are considered to be price inelastic).

Due to the price inelastic nature of the product, revenue (total income received) has actually risen as a result of the price increase (from £700 000 to £798 000).

It is important to realise that there are also different degrees of price inelasticity. A figure closer to zero means the product is very price inelastic (demand is hardly affected by price at all) whereas a figure closer to one means the product is only slightly price inelastic.

Price	Quantity demanded	Revenue
£20	30 000	£600 000
£25	20 000	£500 000
£30	10 000	£300 000

Figure 10.4 The price elastic demand for perfume

Price elastic demand

While cigarettes have a price inelastic demand, Figure 10.4 shows that perfume has a price elastic demand.

In this example an increase in price from £25 to £30 (+20 per cent) results in a fall in quantity demanded from 20,000 to 10,000 units (−50%). Applying these figures to the formula (ignoring the signs):

$$PED = \frac{\text{percentage change in quantity demanded}}{\text{percentage change in price}} = \frac{50\%}{20\%}$$

$$= 2.5$$

As the resulting figure is greater than one demand for the product is said to be **price elastic**.

Revenue, in this example, falls by £200,000 (from £500,000 to £300,000).

Other considerations

Several factors affect how price elastic or inelastic a product is:

- **Availability of substitutes.** The more choice consumers have, the greater the price sensitivity. Breakfast cereal is likely to be price elastic as so many alternative brands are available.

Examples of other elasticities

- Cross elasticity of demand (XED)

$$XED = \frac{\text{percentage change in quantity of good A demanded}}{\text{percentage change in price of good B}}$$

- Income elasticity of demand (IED)

$$IED = \frac{\text{percentage change in quantity demanded}}{\text{percentage change in income}}$$

- Advertising elasticity of demand (AED)

$$AED = \frac{\text{percentage change in quantity demanded}}{\text{percentage change in advertising spend}}$$

- **Buyers knowledge.** The more aware buyers are that alternative products exist, the more price sensitive a product will be.

- **Switching costs.** If the cost of switching to a substitute product is high, demand may be relatively price inelastic. On the other hand, where customers can switch easily, the product may be price elastic.

Ideally, all businesses would like price inelastic products. That way they can increase prices without significantly affecting demand. The strategies a business might use to reduce a product's price elasticity are shown in Figure 10.5.

The effect on revenue and profit

Price changes, as highlighted, can have a significant impact on revenue. The extent of this impact will depend on price elasticity. It is important to also consider the impact on profit (revenue minus costs).

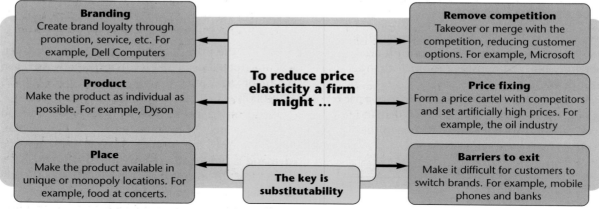

Figure 10.5 Strategies to reduce price elasticity

For example, cutting prices where only a small amount of profit is being made on each unit will require significant price elasticity to make the price change worthwhile in profit terms (that is, a large increase in demand will be required).

 Different pricing strategies

The most commonly used pricing method is **cost plus**, which forms the basis of all pricing decisions. The average cost of one item is calculated (total cost ÷ number of units) and then a mark-up is added to give the final selling price (see Example, part one).
　Other methods of pricing are:

- **Contribution**. The price is set at a level that covers the direct costs of making a good (variable costs) and adds (*contributes*) an amount to paying other costs (see Example, part two).

Example, part one

A business produces headphones for personal music players. The total production costs are £500,000, the business produces 100,000 units.

$$\text{Average cost } \frac{£500\,000}{100\,000} = £5 \text{ per unit}$$

If the business then decides its mark up will be 150 per cent, the selling price will be:

£5 + (£5 × 150%) = £12.50 selling price

Tip – *It is important to remember to add in the original cost when calculating mark-up.*

Example, part two

The total cost (£500,000) is made up of *fixed costs* plus *variable costs*. If the *variable cost* of making one set of headphones were £2, the *fixed cost* would be £300,000. (It follows that 100,000 units produced at £2 per unit cost £200,000; as the total cost of production was £500,000, the *fixed costs* must be £300,000.)

If the business charges £4 for the headphones, it would cover its variable costs of £2 per unit, and each unit sold would *contribute* £2 towards fixed costs – a total of £200,000.

In this case, if this were the business's only product, it would make a loss of £100,000. In practice, the business is likely to have a range of goods and the profits from other sales may offset this loss.

For example ...

DVD Demand

Price (000s)	Demand
£14	36 000
£16	28 000
£18	20 000
£20	6000

Figure 10.6 Demand for DVDs

1 Calculate the price elasticity for an increase in DVD price from:
- £14 to £16 **[3]**
- £16 to £18 **[3]**
- £18 to £20. **[3]**

Total 9 marks

- **Captive product pricing.** Companies are able to charge a premium price where the consumer is 'forced' to use complementary products. For example, a Gillette Sensor razor is relatively cheap; but the blades, by comparison, are expensive.

- **Destroyer (or predatory) pricing.** Prices are set deliberately low in an attempt to force other producers out of the market. Microsoft, for example, gave *Internet Explorer* for free in order to establish dominance over *Netscape Navigator* in the internet browser market.

- **Discriminatory pricing.** Different prices are charged to different groups of people at different times. For instance, cinemas charge different prices for daytime and evening showings.

- **Geographical pricing.** Prices vary according to the location of the store or outlet – petrol pricing is an example.

- **Going rate or market price.** The price charged is set at the same level as other products in the market, and at such a level that customers either expect or are willing to pay. The 'going-rate' for the average magazine, for example, is about £3.50

- **Loss leader.** Certain products are sold at below cost price in order to provide 'headline grabbing' prices that encourage customers to visit a particular store. Supermarkets often sell their 'own brand' basic foodstuffs, such as baked beans, as loss leaders. They hope that once customers are in the store the 'loss' will be made up as customers purchase other, higher-profit-margin items.

- **Penetration pricing.** When a product is launched into an established market, its price may be set low to attract customers. *Front* magazine was launched at just a £1, to encourage young males to trial it. The price is usually increased once market share has been gained.

- **Premium pricing.** This approach is used where a product has significant competitive advantage, or is clearly differentiated from the competition. It might also be used where a strong brand image has been developed. For example, flights on Concorde are premium priced.

- **Price skimming.** Where a product is first to market, a high price is often charged. New

technologies are often launched at a high price to recoup development costs as quickly as possible, and to benefit from the high profit margins available when a product is new and desirable. Plasma TV screens used a price skimming strategy.

- **Psychological pricing.** The price is set, for example, at £39.99 rather than at £40. This relates to perceived price barriers that customers may have – £40 may seem too expensive for the product in question. Most retailers use this strategy.

3   How important is price?

To most customers, price is very important. Yet few people actually buy the cheapest product available. A wide range of factors affect the price customers are willing to pay:

For example ...

Flying high?

Budget air carriers continue to enjoy success while traditional full-cost airlines struggle with the increasingly competitive market conditions. As the table shows, British Airways still carries more passengers in total than the low-cost airlines, but is losing passengers to these cheaper services. BA's, belated, response was to slash fares on some of its most popular European flights.

	Number of passengers	Percentage change
easyJet	0.8 m	+ 39%
Go	0.4 m	+ 81.5%
Ryanair	1.01 m	+ 48%
British Airways	2.17 m	− 4%

Source: *The Guardian* 9 April 2002

1 Identify the pricing strategy that the low-cost carriers might be employing. Justify your reasons. **[4]**
2 Suggest reasons why BA may have resisted cutting its prices. **[4]**
3 Identify what factors, other than price, might affect the popularity of airlines. **[6]**
Total 14 marks

Figure 10.7 Passenger numbers, March 2002

- degree of product differentiation or unique selling point (USP) – see price inelastic

- brand image or reputation

- product quality (perceived and actual)

- customer service

- speed of service and/or delivery

- availability.

An important distinction is made between **pricing strategies** and **pricing tactics**. Strategies will reflect the long-term objectives of the business, such as securing profit margins through premium pricing. Tactics will reflect short-term goals, such as securing market share via penetration pricing.

Price: summary

KEY TERMS

Equilibrium price – buyers and sellers are in agreement about price and quantity – producers are willing to supply the same amount demanded by customers.

Price elastic – demand for a product is responsive to changes in price (represented by a price elasticity greater than one).

Price inelastic – demand for a product is not very responsive to changes in price (represented by a price elasticity less than one).

Pricing strategy – the range of pricing tools used to achieve long-term objectives; for example, achieving above-average profit margins through premium pricing.

Pricing tactics – the use of pricing tools over the short term to achieve specific objectives; for example, the use of loss leaders.

Summary questions

1 Describe **three** factors that will affect a firm's pricing decision.
2 When might a firm use price skimming?
3 What is meant by the term 'loss leader'? When is this pricing strategy used?
4 What pricing strategy might a firm use when trying to gain a foothold in a competitive market?
5 What is price elasticity a measure of?
6 Comment on the following price elasticities:
  - 0.2
  - 6
  - 1.1
  - 0.89
7 What types of good might be price inelastic?
8 How might a firm attempt to reduce a product's price elasticity?
9 If a product's sales have risen by 30 per cent after a price cut from £5.99 to £5.49, what is its price elasticity? What type of product might it be?

Exam practice

Tough times for top brands?

In 2001 and 2002, the luxury goods business was hit in swift succession by a weakening global economy, an enduring slump in Japanese spending and the 11 September 2001 terrorist attacks on New York. The Japanese, who previously accounted for a third of all luxury goods purchases, cut foreign travel in half during the period and tightened their Louis Vuitton purse strings.

Luxury is an unusual business, though. The response of a small number of retailers to this downswing was to put prices up in an attempt to wrest back some of their exclusivity. The result? Demand fell certainly, but against a falling market the reduction in demand was favourable compared to competitors. Some luxury products, it would appear, display a degree of price inelasticity.

Source: *The Economist* 23 February 2002

A Louis Vuitton handbag

Exam practice continues ➤

Price: summary (continued)

The big easy

easyJet founder, Stelios Haji-Ioannou, plans to open a cinema in London that will sell tickets for as little as 20p. He believes that going to the cinema is price elastic. A ticket for a Tuesday morning showing, booked online one month in advance will cost just 20p. Ticket prices for the busy weekend showings will be comparable with other London cinemas. Stelios intends to significantly improve on the cinema industry's average seat occupancy of 20 per cent. He will also make money from the sale of popcorn and other refreshments that will, more than likely, be premium priced.

Source: *The Sunday Times* 7 April 2002

Stelios Haji-Ioannou believes the time is right for easy Cinema

1 Explain, with reference to cinema tickets, what is meant by the term 'price elastic'.   **[2]**
2 Define the term 'price inelasticity'.   **[2]**
3 Explain why cinemas can be said to be price discriminating.   **[2]**
4 Explain what is meant by premium priced?   **[2]**
5 Explain, using the theory of contribution, why Stelios can 'afford' to sell tickets at just 20p.   **[4]**
6 Examine why some luxury products might continue to enjoy healthy sales in economic slumps.   **[4]**
7 Calculate and comment on the price elasticity data in Figure 10.8?   **[6]**
8 Examine the likely response of other cinema chains and the impact that this might have on cinema pricing.   **[8]**
9 Luxury brands are often heavily reliant on promotion. To what extent might other elements of the marketing mix be more important than price in a product's success?   **[10]**
    Total 40 marks

Want to know more?

www.easyjet.co.uk

	Original	New (after price change)
Brand X	£100	£110
	1,000 units	950 units
Brand Y	£40	£44
	8,000 units	5,000 units

Figure 10.8 The price elasticity of Brand X and Brand Y

11 Promotion

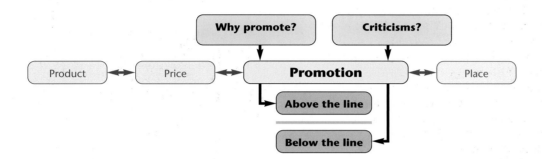

Promotion is the part of marketing that most people are familiar with. It cannot be emphasised enough that promotion is *just one part* of marketing. Keep this in the back of your mind as you work through this unit, try to put what you read into the wider context of *marketing as a whole*.

Equally, promotion is not just advertising. There are many other ways that a business can promote its products or services. Promotion might also include:

- personal selling
- sales promotion
- public relations (PR)
- direct marketing
- trade fairs and exhibitions
- sponsorship.

Promotion is about communicating with customers and potential customers. Through promotion a business communicates:

- who they are (developing a corporate image)
- what they sell (informative promotion)
- why consumers should buy their products (persuading)
- the brand image of a product (reminding and reinforcing)
- where customers can get the product (informative)
- how much the product costs (informative).

Why promote?

Consumers are faced with so much choice that it is often the business that 'shouts the loudest' about its products that gets noticed. Promotion is essential to:

- increase demand for products
- establish a price for products
- create, enhance or maintain a brand image
- raise awareness, emotion or concern for an issue or product
- maintain, protect or increase market share.

How important is promotion?

The extent to which promotion is important, relative to other aspects of marketing, depends on:

- the degree of competition in the market
- the extent to which promotion is the norm in a particular market
- the market segment (a niche product may need little promotion)
- the marketing emphasis (if the product is differentiated, whether this difference is tangible or intangible? Intangible differences may require heavy promotional support.
- stage in the product lifecycle (established products may need little promotion)

- the extent of supply (a product that is widely available may need little promotion).

3   Methods of promotion

A distinction is often made between 'above the line' and 'below the line' promotion. Choice of promotion method might depend on:

- the target market (what they read and watch)
- if the market is local or national
- the advertising budget
- where the product is in its lifecycle
- what type of product is being advertised (food needs to be advertised in colour)
- any legal constraints (for example, the Tobacco Advertising & Promotions Bill regulates tobacco advertising in the UK)
- whether the method chosen will complement other elements of the marketing mix.

Above the line methods

Above the line promotion involves the use of advertising media over which a firm does not have direct control, such as television or newspapers. The following are examples of some above the line methods of advertising.

- **Television** is the most familiar face of advertising. Because of its wide reach most mass-market consumer goods are advertised on television. Television is a relatively expensive

medium, but on a 'per viewing' basis is very cost effective. If, for example, a business paid £500,000 for one advertisement during the *Big Brother* finale of 2002, that advertisement would potentially have reached 10 million people. The cost of reaching each person is therefore only £0.05 (or £50 per thousand people), which, in advertising terms, is good value for money – despite the artificially high-cost example used.

> **Guru's views**
> 'The codfish lays ten thousand eggs;
> the homely hen lays one.
> The codfish never cackles
> to tell you what she's done.
> And so we scorn the codfish;
> while the humble hen we prize –
> which only goes to show you,
> that it pays to advertise.'
>
> *Anon*

- **Radio** has the advantage of low cost, and the ability to target specific regions. However, commercial radio accounts for only 45.5 per cent of total radio listening – the rest being made up by BBC stations (where advertising is not allowed). As digital radio becomes more popular, the number of commercial stations (and the promotional possibilities) should, however, increase (see Figure 11.1).

- **Newspapers** are the most popular medium for advertising. In 2002, 57 per cent of the £38.3 billion spent on advertising was spent on newspaper advertisements. As Figure 11.2 shows,

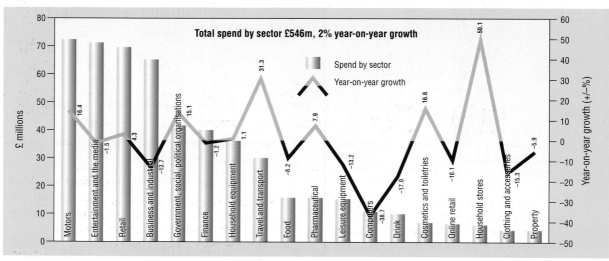

Figure 11.1 Radio spend on advertising by sector, June 2001 to June 2002

Source: ACNielsen MMS

despite a general fall in newspaper circulation, individual newspapers still reach wide audiences. In addition, newspaper publishers are able to clearly define their target audiences, making newspapers attractive to advertisers looking to reach specific market segments.

- **Magazine publishers**, like newspaper publishers, also have a clear idea of who their readers are (see the *Max Power* example in unit 7), and use this information to attract advertisers seeking to target specific market segments. Magazines are useful for building brand image – clothing seen in Vogue or FHM gains fashionable status almost by default!

- **Cinema** advertising depends, to some extent, on the success of the movie industry. Big blockbuster films, such as The Lord of the Rings, have helped to boost cinemas popularity over recent years – in the year to July 2002, expenditure had increased by 26 per cent. Cinema advertising is often used to reach young audiences who are difficult to communicate with via other mediums.

Title	Circulation	Year on Year
Daily Mail	2,416,895	–1.91%
Independent	226,641	1.56%
Times	682,672	–2.63%
Mirror	2,092,034	–5.86%
Sun	3,609,493	2.58%
News Of The World	3,862,029	–4.67%
Mail On Sunday	2,381,151	–1.09%
Sunday Mail	650,165	–7.32%
Sunday Times	1,340,996	1.88%

Source: Mediatel

Figure 11.2 ABC figures July 2002

- **Outdoor** advertising, includes advertisements at bus stops, on the sides of buses and taxis, billboards and posters.

- **Internet** advertising blossomed during the dotcom boom of the late 1990s. Expenditure on internet advertising was growing faster than for

For example ...

Want to know more?
www.brad.co.uk

The writing is on the wall

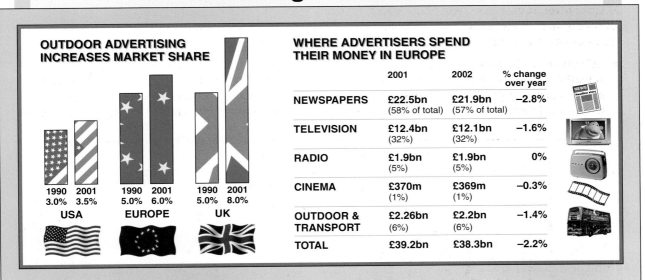

Source: *The Times* 4 April 2002

1 Suggest **two** reasons why outdoor advertising may be increasing its market share. [2]
2 Suggest **two** reasons why newspaper advertising accounts for over 50 per cent of advertising expenditure. [2]
3 Calculate the new total advertising spend for 2003 assuming a 3 per cent reduction from 2002. [3]
4 Examine the factors a firm will take into account when selecting advertising media. [8]

Total 15 marks

Guerrilla marketing

Modern marketing campaigns often include what is known as *guerrilla marketing*. This essentially

involves small-scale publicity stunts targeted directly at key market segments. Virgin Student, a marketing company, uses guerrilla marketing to reach university students throughout the UK.

For example, Brylcreem wanted to raise awareness of a new product among the student market. Virgin Student female representatives were transformed into 'Glo-Girl hit squads'. Their mission was to storm Student Unions around the country promoting Brylcreem's new UV glo-gel. They were dressed in branded T-shirts and demonstrated, in practice, the benefits of the new glo-gel by applying it under portable UV lights to male student's hair. By creating such a storm in Student Unions, and portraying the really fun nature of the product, the campaign was a true success!

Want to know more?

www.virginstudent.com

any other media type. When the dotcom bubble burst, so did the bubble surrounding internet advertising. Despite the fact that banner and 'pop-up' advertisements can be closely targeted to market segments, the advertisements often receive very few hits.

Activity

In small groups, prepare a presentation on the advantages and disadvantages of two media types. (Others groups could present different media types.) You may want to prepare a handout to support your presentation – these handouts can be distributed to the whole class to support your course notes.

Below the line promotion

Below the line promotion involves use of promotional media over which the firm has control, such as direct mail and trade fairs. Some examples are:

- **Personal selling**, which involves the use of a sales team who make regular visits to customers and potential customers.

- **Sales promotions**, including 'BOGOF' (buy one get one free), money-off coupons, competitions, free gifts (for example, a bonus CD when you buy an album), introductory offers (for example, buy Sky TV and get free installation), tasting sessions and demonstrations.

- **Public relations (PR)** involves a business communicating with its different stakeholders, often at little or no cost to the business. This might be through press releases or press conferences, for example. PR can be seen in action all the time – think of the media coverage generated when a pop star is launching a new album.

- **Direct marketing** includes all activities where, as a direct result of the promotion, consumers are able to immediately purchase the product. Direct mail, catalogue shopping, TV shopping, telemarketing and internet shopping are all examples of direct marketing. Figure 11.3 highlights some of the advantages and disadvantages of direct marketing.

- **Sponsorship** involves a business paying to be associated with a particular event, cause, individual star or even TV programme. Nike's sponsorship of Tiger Woods has helped Nike to become one of the leading suppliers of golf clothing.

4   Control of promotion

The Office of Communications takes principal responsibility for regulating advertising in the broadcast media. Within this, promotion is controlled and regulated by the BCAP (British Code of Advertising Practice). The code states that all promotions must be:

Advantages	Disadvantages
<ul><li>Accurate targeting of potential customers</li><li>Message can be personalised</li><li>Easy to measure customers responses</li><li>Competitors less aware of marketing activities</li></ul>	<ul><li>Direct mail often seen as intrusive and a nuisance ('junk mail')</li><li>High initial costs (market data is expensive)</li><li>Often low response rates to direct mail</li><li>Gives poor results if market data is out of date or incorrect</li></ul>

Figure 11.3 Advantages and disadvantages of direct marketing

- legal, decent, honest and truthful

- prepared with a sense of responsibility to consumers and society

- produced in line with the principals of fair competition.

These rules are enforced by:

- **The Advertising Standards Authority (ASA)** – Controls all advertisements except TV and radio.

- **The Independent Television Committee (ITC)** – Controls advertising on TV.

- **The Radio Authority** – Controls radio advertising.

These bodies are industry-funded and self-regulatory. Where an advertisement is deemed unacceptable the advertiser must withdraw or amend it.

 5   Criticisms of promotion

The increasing popularity of anti-capitalist and anti-globalisation pressure groups has seen a backlash against corporate promotion in recent years. Criticisms of advertising include:

- it raises costs without adding tangible product value

- it is used as a way of maintaining monopoly power

- it can be misleading

- it stimulates wants that cannot be met (creating a materialist society)

- the benefits of advertising (higher prices) are not passed on to product manufacturers (a Nike factory worker in Indonesia might earn $2 a day for producing $120 Nike trainers).

> **Guru's views**
> 'If advertisers spent the same amount of money on improving their products as they do on advertising then they wouldn't have to advertise them.'
>
> *Will Rogers*

The ASA investigated advertisements for the Austin Powers movie 'The Spy Who Shagged Me' after 310 complaints were received. The ASA found that the ads were unlikely to cause serious or widespread offence and allowed the advertisements to run.

Want to know more?

www.asa.org.uk

For example ...

French Connection UK

Fashion group French Connection has more than a passing acquaintance with the ASA. The group's founder and chairman Stephen Marks has turned his nudge-nudge FCUK logo into an international brand with straplines such as 'fcuk fashion' and 'fcukinkybugger'. Not without objection though, the ASA has received numerous complaints and a TV watchdog banned some adverts because of their 'unacceptable level of innuendo'.

Source: *The Guardian* 13 March 2002

1 What do the initials ASA stand for? [1]
2 Explain briefly the role of the ASA. What principles does it uphold? [3]
3 Despite the negative publicity, why do some businesses launch contentious advertising campaigns? [6]
4 Using French Connection as an example, suggest **two** other advertising constraints that a business might face. [4]

Total 14 marks

Promotion: summary

KEY TERMS

Above the line promotion – promotion through media such as TV, radio and cinema.

Below the line promotion – a range of promotional techniques, such as personal selling, direct marketing and PR, over which firms direct (some) control; usually led by the firm and not involving payment to independent agencies.

Summary questions

1 Distinguish between above-the-line and below-the-line promotion.
2 Give **three** examples of above-the-line promotion.
3 Give **three** examples of below-the-line promotion.
4 Examine the benefits offered by TV advertising.
5 Examine why internet advertising has declined over recent years.
6 Discuss the relationship between promotion and market segmentation.
7 Give **two** arguments against advertising.
8 What is personal selling?
9 What is public relations (PR)?
10 State **one** advantage and **one** disadvantage of personal selling.
11 What factors might influence the success of a promotional campaign?]
12 What is direct mailing?
13 Which independent body controls TV advertising?
14 What does the British Code of Advertising Practice state that all advertisements must be?

Exam practice

Direct to your door

Companies are starting to buy into direct mail in a big way. The once 'poor cousin' of trendier, below-the-line promotional techniques is gradually becoming more popular.

It is not hard to understand why. In theory at least, direct mail is accountable, flexible, targetable and profitable. Combined with other promotional techniques and a coherent marketing mix, direct mail can be a very potent marketing tool.

Not everyone agrees though, Mark Ritson, professor of marketing at the London Business School, observes 'there are two kinds of direct mail – the targeted, timely and relevant letter and the unfocused mass mailing. While the *vision* has always been the former, the reality is much closer to the latter.' So much mail, he claims, is unwanted that the entire direct mail medium has become tarnished. Good direct mail campaigns can produce excellent results, but poor campaigns can do serious damage to brands. A significant proportion of the population claim to dislike direct mail – it might be effective for the 2 per cent who respond to mailings, but for the 98 per cent who don't, it can be a considerable nuisance.

Source: *Financial Times* 23 April 2002

1 Explain what is meant by 'below-the-line' promotion.   **[2]**
2 Using relevant examples, describe **two** factors that might determine the success of a direct mail campaign.   **[6]**
3 Explain why poor direct mail campaigns 'can do serious damage to brands'.   **[4]**
4 Outline and examine the reasons why a business might choose a below-the-line marketing campaign over an above-the-line campaign.   **[8]**
5 Evaluate the importance of promotion in the marketing mix.   **[12]**
   Total 32 marks

12 Place

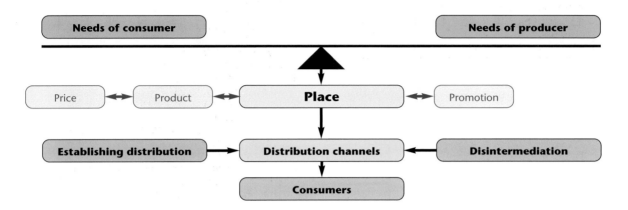

Place is *not* about a business's actual physical location. Place (or more properly distribution strategy) refers to the way in which a product is distributed – how it gets to the end consumer. The product must get to the end consumer at the right time, in the right quantities and in the right condition (that is, not broken or perished).

A **distribution channel** includes a number of **intermediaries** (stages in the distribution chain) through which a product passes before it reaches the end consumer. These intermediaries (sometimes called middlemen) might include wholesalers, retailers and import or export agents.

 What determines how a product is distributed?

A product's distribution channel will be determined by a number of factors:

- **Marketing aims.** A business aiming to increase sales volume will try to secure as wide a distribution as possible

- **Product characteristics.** The cost of the product, its shelf life and product type all affect how it is distributed. For example, a product with a short shelf life needs to get to customers quickly.

- **Market coverage.** The number of outlets where a product is sold affects the distribution method.

Getting Walker's crisps into newsagents, for example, requires many different stages in the distribution channel.

- **Cost considerations.** The longer the distribution channel, the more costly distribution will be. Short channels can increase stockholding costs (see unit 35) because the same amount of stock is shared among fewer intermediaries.

- **Special services.** Some intermediaries offer specialist purchasing advice (DIY stores) or specialist storage conditions (for example, industrial chemical distributors).

- **Degree of control required.** The longer the channel of distribution, the less control the original producer has.

- **Customer expectations and brand image.** Customer perceptions about retail outlets and a desire to create or maintain brand image may affect distribution. Levi's managed to stop Tesco selling its jeans at discounted prices.

- **Legal restrictions.** It is illegal to sell alcohol at petrol stations, for instance.

- **Product lifecycle.** Different channels can be used at different points in the product lifecycle, for example mobile phone 'top-up' cards were once available in just a few outlets, now they are available almost everywhere.

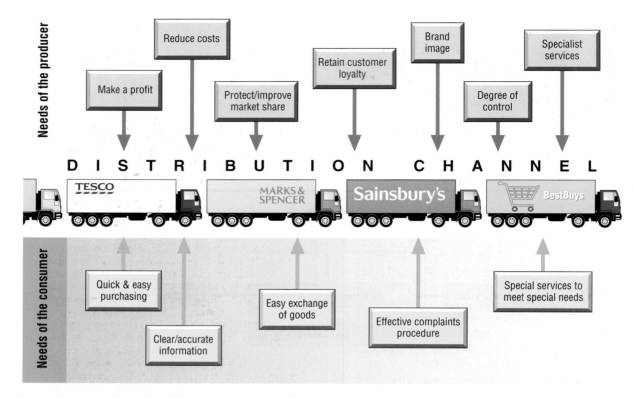

Figure 12.1 The distribution balance

The choice of distribution channel reflects a balance between these considerations. Essentially, this means that a business must balance its own needs (a desire for cost efficiency, for instance) against the needs of the consumer. This balance is shown in Figure 12.1.

2 Distributions channels

Figure 12.2 shows the main channels of distribution, which are:

- **Direct distribution.** The producer sells goods directly to the end consumer – no intermediaries are used (small local bakers and Mesh Computers plc are examples). The main

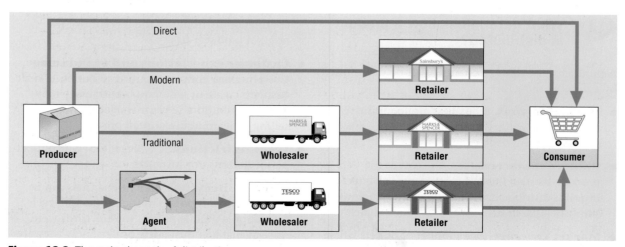

Figure 12.2 The main channels of distribution

Direct selling

Direct selling has become commoner in recent years due to the introduction of internet and TV shopping. Products traditionally sold through long distribution chains have undergone a process of **disintermediation** ('cutting out the middleman'). Producers can sell directly to large numbers of consumers at relatively little cost. Niche products can be sold to wider audiences. For example, specialist skateboard equipment can be easily purchased from the USA via the internet. Online businesses, such as Mesh and Dell, have become successful by exploiting the advantages of direct selling.

advantage of direct distribution is that, by cutting out the intermediaries (who add their own mark-ups), the product can be sold to the consumer at a competitive price. The producer is also able to develop a relationship with consumers and benefits from direct product feedback. Producers are able to react much faster to consumers' needs and changing market conditions.

- **Retailers.** Even though direct selling is becoming more popular, the majority of consumer products are still sold via retailers. Retailers allow producers to achieve wide distribution and can help to support or develop brand image (designer clothing is usually sold in small boutiques). Some retailers, such as Harrods, have strong brand images themselves, helping to boost the image of products sold there. Retailers can help to promote and merchandise products for example by point-of-sales displays or special offers. While retailers, such as Comet or Dixons, offer credit to customers for big purchases.

However, products sold via retailers usually have to fight with the competition for precious shelf-space. Comet, for instance, sells several different brands of televisions. It is this wide choice that attracts customers to retailers, but draws attention to other elements of a product's marketing mix (for example, the factors that differentiate Sony from JVC televisions).

- **Wholesalers.** In many markets, wholesalers act as a link between producers and consumers. Where a retailer does not have the purchasing power to buy directly from a manufacturer they will buy from a wholesaler. Wholesalers break down 'bulk' into smaller quantities for resale by a retailer. An

For example ...

The MP3 Revolution

The development of the online music business is one of the most important issues facing the global music industry. Direct selling facilitated by the internet presents a potential threat to traditional music retailers. Faster broadband internet connections and the increasing popularity of MP3 (and other digital formats) make this disintermediation all the more possible. Growth of online music has so far been constrained by slow download speeds – many consumers prefer to pay for a whole CD of tracks rather than wait (often an hour or more) for one track to download. However, as internet speeds increase, the threat of digital music becomes all the more real.

Source: *Financial Times* 11 March 1999

1 Explain what is meant by direct selling. [2]
2 Examine why the internet facilitates disintermediation. [4]
3 Discuss how traditional music retailers might respond to the 'digital threat'. [10]
Total 16 Marks

independent grocer may use this method. Wholesalers provide a means for small producers to get their products into retail outlets. A large supermarket chain may be unwilling to buy directly from the manufacturer until certain production volumes are reached or until sufficient demand has been established – wholesalers provide an alternative route to market.

When a business sells many products, it may use a wholesaler to bear the distribution costs of shipping those products to thousands of retailers. Wholesalers can provide storage facilities and can reduce producers' stockholding costs (see unit 35). Wine merchants (wholesalers) often buy 'young' wine relatively cheaply (taking the storage cost away from the wine producer), the wine is then stored until in reaches maturity and sold to retailers at a profit.

Some producers want to limit direct contact with customers (reducing the need for a large customer service department). Wholesalers can act as a buffer between producers, retailers and consumers. Faulty goods are returned in bulk via the wholesaler making the process more efficient. JBL (a speaker manufacturer) uses this strategy.

STOP & THINK

Look around you. Pick any three products you can see and attempt to draw a distribution chain for each of them. This could include anything – food, clothes, MP3 player, car or so forth.

- **Agents.** In contrast to wholesalers, agents never actually own a product. Agents usually connect buyers and sellers and manage the transfer of the good. Agents usually take a commission on sales, or charge a fee for their services. Estate agents are a good example.

Agents are often used by businesses trading overseas. Agents specialise in managing complex import and export procedures, and can provide a range of advice services. Differences in local product laws and customs procedures can, among many other things, make exporting goods very challenging. Businesses with little experience of foreign trading often find that agents offer a relatively safe way of entering new markets.

2 Establishing distribution

Establishing effective distribution can be one of the biggest challenges facing small businesses. A great, new product idea is unlikely to be successful if distribution cannot be secured. Retailers are often very reluctant to give valuable shelf space to new products. Convincing a major national supermarket chain to stop selling an established product in the hope that the new product will generate higher sales represents a significant barrier to success. Many new products are sold via smaller, specialist retailers, where a brand image and customer demand can be established before supermarkets are approached. Häagen-Dazs took this approach when it entered the competitive ice-cream market in 1989.

Guru's views
You can't sell what customers can't see.'
Anonymous

For example ...

Big Buddha

While on holiday in Thailand, Jenny thought she'd spotted a business opportunity. She'd noticed how cheap Buddha ornaments and trinkets were in Thailand and remembered the trend for 'ethnic' interior design back in the UK. She decided that importing and selling Buddha ornaments within the UK might be the business idea she'd been waiting for. If the business grew, she could also start importing items from other Asian countries.

1 Suggest, and justify, a suitable distribution strategy for Jenny's products.   **[6]**
2 Suggest and explain **three** problems that Jenny may face when importing the goods from Thailand.   **[6]**
Total 12 marks

Place: summary

Some important points to remember about place are:

- It is an essential (and often overlooked) element of the marketing mix. Effective distribution will be a major factor in a product's success. An excellent promotional campaign is useless unless supported by the distribution needed to meet demand.

- Place must complement all other elements of the marketing mix and marketing strategy. Increasing market share might require a significant increase in distribution, establishing a premium price suggests restricted distribution.

- More is not always better. Not all products require wide distribution: for example, designer brands closely control distribution to maintain brand image and exclusivity. Consumers do not expect Bose hi-fi equipment to be widely available and are willing to travel to buy it.

KEY TERMS

Intermediary – the different stages in the distribution channel are known as intermediaries. The stages a product must pass through in order to reach the end consumer (retailer, wholesaler, and so on)

Distribution channel – the method used by a business to get its product/s to consumers.

Disintermediation – a move towards direct distribution. Reducing the stages a product must pass through to reach the consumer by 'cutting out' intermediaries.

Summary questions

1 What is an intermediary?
2 State and explain **three** factors that influence the choice of distribution channel.
3 What is the role of a wholesaler?
4 What do distribution agents do?
5 State and explain **two** benefits of using direct distribution methods.
6 Examine the impact of the internet on distribution.
7 Explain the role of agents in distribution.
8 Examine the relationship between cost of distribution and product price.

9 Suggest, and justify, a suitable method of distribution for the following products:
- a breakfast cereal.
- books
- computers
- motorbikes

Exam practice

Within arm's reach of desire

Sales growth in the chocolate confectionery market has, over the last few years, remained relatively static. The trend for healthier eating has made the traditional confectionery market very competitive. The three main competitors (Cadbury's, Nestlé and Mars) have been attempting to maintain profits by finding new distribution outlets for their products. Cadbury's have introduced themed shops into Alton Towers, vending machines (including in pubs) and linked up with McDonald's to provide a range of chocolate-based 'McFlurry' ice creams. The aim is to ensure that Cadbury's chocolate is available wherever and whenever people might fancy a chocolate snack. Or, as Cadbury's puts it: 'within arm's reach of desire'.

1 Draw a diagram representing how confectionery is traditionally distributed. [2]
2 Suggest and explain why manufacturers often use wholesalers to distribute their products. [4]
3 Suggest and justify **two** other methods that Cadbury's might use to increase distribution of their products. [6]
4 Examine the issues that Cadbury's may face as a result of its increased distribution. [8]
5 Evaluate the importance of 'place' in the marketing mix. [10]
Total 30 marks

Getting the grade: Marketing

MARKETING is often the area of business studies that students find the easiest to grasp. Yet, very often, marketing questions are answered poorly in examinations.

The accessible nature of marketing means that students usually have many examples to throw at examiners, and can write at great length about the use of the marketing mix. This might be fine for short-answer questions, but does not often score highly on the more evaluative, long-answer questions. Several things must be borne in mind when answering marketing questions:

No business function stands alone

An evaluative marketing question will almost certainly require you to consider the impact of marketing on other aspects of the business.

- What is the financial impact?
- Do staff need training?
- Are new production facilities required?

These and many other factors may be relevant to the answer.

There are no magic solutions

The use of clever business models is never the sole answer to marketing success. Should a business really be basing its entire marketing strategy on knowledge of the product lifecycle? By all means, suggest their use, but balance this against the need for management experience and intuition. Remember, the models themselves can be criticised – they are certainly not perfect! If the question suggests it, don't be afraid of referring to this criticism.

Marketing is not the key to success

Marketing is just *one* of the many important keys to business success. More market research, more promotion or more distribution will not on its own secure success. Business history is littered with failed marketing campaigns. You must consider what other factors might affect the success of a marketing strategy.

- How will the competition react?
- How will the state of the economy affect any decision?
- What legal considerations are there?

All business are different

Businesses have different objectives, different strengths, and different markets. Any marketing strategy will, therefore, need to be focused on the specific circumstances a business faces. Your answer must be specific to the *context*, relate your textbook knowledge to the exam case study.

Not-for profit marketing

Marketing is not just relevant to profit-driven, private sector businesses. Whatever the goals of an organisation, marketing has a vital role to play. For every organisation, whether it is a school, a hospital or a local charity, has 'customers' whose needs it must serve. Marketing within these organisations seeks to identify these needs, and how best the organisation can meet them. The aim will still be to 'add value', but in terms of service rather than of profit.

Don't follow the trend

The business world is full of trends, fads and 'buzz' words. Marketing is perhaps more guilty than any other business function for creating such trends. You must be able to see the bigger picture. Does the trend represent a fundamental shift in business practice or will another trend replace it within the year – how significant is it? The marketing quip is also quite common (we have even used some in the guru's views quotes). Chucking a few of these into an answer will not, however, improve your score. If you do use them, they must be backed up by solid marketing knowledge and a strong focus on the case study, supported by your own analysis and evaluation.

The branded world

Marketing itself has come under heavy and increasing criticism in recent years. Global corporations such as Nike, McDonald's, Gap and Starbucks are coming under attack as a result of their marketing strategies. This pressure is slowly forcing companies to rethink their marketing strategies. It should also prompt you to consider the broader impact of marketing – it is this kind of thinking that can lead to developing 'A' grade exam skills.

An ability to consider and reflect on these bigger issues, to see the links within marketing and between marketing and other business functions is essential to exam success.

As, hopefully, you have seen marketing is all around you. If you carefully read and digest the material in these chapters, and keep your eyes and ears open, you should start to see the world of marketing open up before you. The more that you can reflect on what you see, and relate it back to textbook theory, the better chance you will have of fully understanding this exciting, but complex topic. Just do it!

Section 3
Accounting and finance

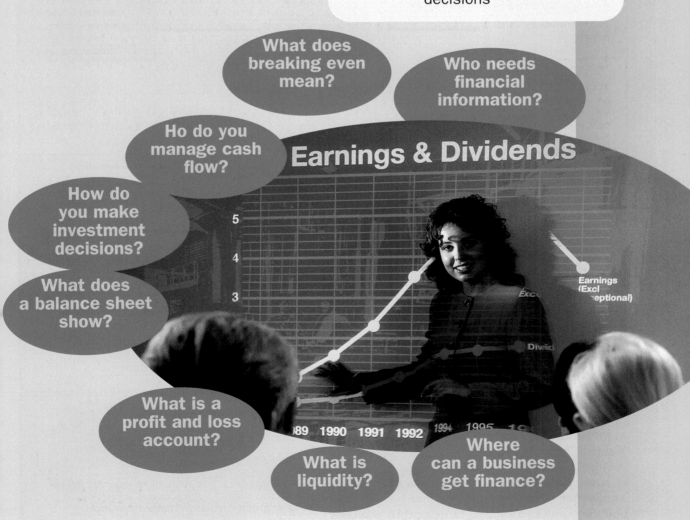

What does breaking even mean?

Who needs financial information?

Ho do you manage cash flow?

How do you make investment decisions?

What does a balance sheet show?

What is a profit and loss account?

What is liquidity?

Where can a business get finance?

13 Financial information

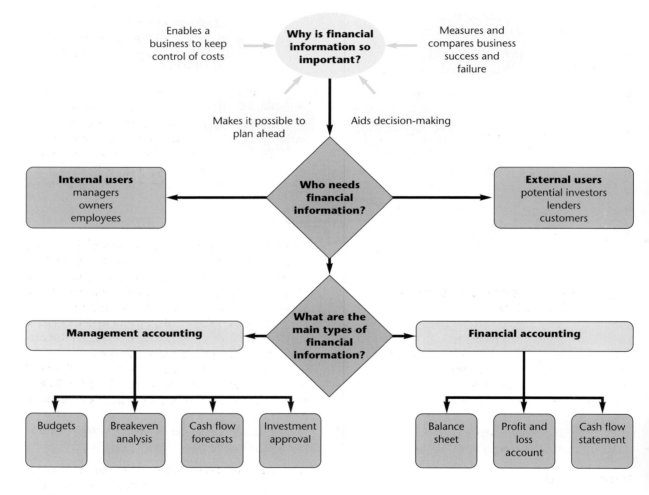

Enables a business to keep control of costs → **Why is financial information so important?** ← Measures and compares business success and failure

Makes it possible to plan ahead | Aids decision-making

Who needs financial information?

Internal users
managers
owners
employees

External users
potential investors
lenders
customers

What are the main types of financial information?

Management accounting

Financial accounting

| Budgets | Breakeven analysis | Cash flow forecasts | Investment approval |

| Balance sheet | Profit and loss account | Cash flow statement |

1 Why is financial information so important?

Why did Leeds United Football Club have to sell their best players in 2003? Why did the Stock Market falls of 2002 threaten the UK economy? Why did Morrison's bid to take over Safeway in 2003 spark a scramble between the UK's largest supermarket chains? The answers lie in an understanding of financial information. Finance is the language of business. Money is the unit that provides a means to compare and understand businesses, to judge their successes and their failures. Profit is the goal that inspires entrepreneurs and drives them to take risks.

Financial information can show:

- where money to set up a business has come from
- how this money has been used
- how much money is owed to others
- what a business is worth
- how much cash is available to pay off debts
- how much it costs to make a product

- how much profit (or loss) is being made.

However, the figures that provide answers to these questions do not give the whole picture of a business. Nor can they be taken as 'fact', because statistics are open to use and abuse, interpretation and misinterpretation. Nevertheless, using financial information is vital because it:

- allows business success or failure *to be measured*

- makes it easy *to compare performance* over time, and with the performance of other businesses

- helps business managers *to make decisions* about their prices, their production and their investment

- enables a business *to keep control* of its spending and use of other resources

- makes it possible *to plan ahead* so as to ensure cash is available when it is needed.

To understand further why financial information is so important, it is necessary to consider:

- who needs to use financial information

- the main types of financial information and the documents that can be used.

 ## Who needs to use financial information?

The 'stakeholders' in a business – all those who are affected by its success or failure – will be interested in financial information about the business. Different stakeholders will have different interests and so may want different information, or may look at information in different ways.

Stakeholders can be divided into **internal** and **external users** of financial information.

Internal users

- **Management.** Accurate and up-to-date financial information is essential to allow managers to run the business effectively. Information about costs and revenues, cash and profits will allow managers to:

  - keep records of what has happened and when, such as the value of sales over the past month
  - make informed business decisions, for example how much stock to purchase
  - monitor and evaluate the impact of their actions, such as whether a marketing campaign has been profitable

  - keep control of money flowing into and out of the business, so that cash is always available when it is needed.

- **Owners.** For small businesses such as sole traders and partnerships, owners can be classed as internal users. For limited companies, the owners are shareholders and could equally be classified as external users. In both cases, however, owners want to see if the money they have invested into the business is being used well and generating a healthy return. Comparisons could be made with other organisations or business opportunities to decide if the profit that the business is making is acceptable.

- **Employees.** The interest of the workforce is in the security of their jobs and in the pay and benefits they receive. Information about a business's costs, revenue and profits can help workers – or their trade union representatives – to make judgments about wage negotiations and whether the business could afford to pay more.

External users

Depending on the legal status of a business, varying amounts of financial information will be available to stakeholders outside of the business. Unlike sole traders and partnerships, limited companies are required by law to publish financial accounts. They are also required to have independent **auditors** check that the accounts are a true and accurate representation of the company's financial position.

All businesses will need to keep accurate financial records in order to meet the demands of the Inland Revenue, whose job it is to collect taxes on behalf of the government.

Other stakeholders interested in a business's financial information include:

- **Potential investors.** Individuals, businesses and investment companies will all be comparing the returns on different investment opportunities. Financial information can show them how secure the investment is likely to be, the business's current performance and its future potential.

- **Lenders.** Banks and other lenders will want to study financial information carefully before lending money to a business. They will want to be sure that their money is safe and will be returned on time and with interest!

- **Suppliers.** Firms that supply a business with large quantities of goods on credit will want to be sure that they will be paid. Financial information could show them whether the purchasing business is likely to have the cash to pay them on time.

- **Government.** The government and the Bank of England need to collect information about the economy and business performance in order make decisions about their policies on, for instance, interest rates or taxes.

- **Customers.** Often customers take no interest in a business's financial performance when they purchase a product, but this is not always true. Some will want to be sure about future aftersales service. When the customer is a business, it will be looking for a stable and reliable supplier, and financial information will be needed to help choose a business that meets these needs.

- **Competitors.** A business may seek to gain as much financial information as possible about its rival, as this could help give it a competitive advantage. It might, for example, identify the cost inefficiency of a competitor and exploit it by starting a price war.

3 Main types of financial information and documents

As shown in Figure 13.1, the two broad areas of financial information are **financial accounting** and **management accounting**.

1 **Financial accounting** is the recording and publishing of financial information to meet the necessary legal requirements. The accounts published by limited companies will allow a wide range of external users, together with internal users such as owners and employees, to assess the business's financial position. The accounts summarise the financial position of the whole business on a given date and show what happened in the period (normally a year) leading up to that date.

2 **Management accounting** is for the use of managers: to help them plan, make decisions and control the business effectively. Rather than taking the business as a whole, management accounting will share out the revenues and costs to individual units, divisions or departments. The goal is to provide valuable up-to-date information that will show managers what is going on within the business and allow them to monitor and review the impact of their decisions.

STOP & THINK

For two different internal users of financial information, explain which of the documents in Figure 13.1 they would be most likely to use and why. Do the same for two different external users.

Activity

Obtain a copy of the financial accounts of a well-known plc. You may be able to download them from the relevant website, or send for a copy. What do the accounts show you about the financial health of the business?

The Bank of England determines the base rate, from which all interest rates are derived

Financial accounting

Balance sheet

A summary of a firm's financial position at a specific point in time, showing:

- what it owns (its assets)
- what it owes (its liabilities)

(See Unit 18)

Profit and loss account

A record of the costs and revenues of a business over a period of time, showing:

- the final profit or loss it made
- how any profit was used

(See Unit 19)

Cash-flow statement

A summary of the cash that has come into and out of the business over a period of time, showing:

- where cash has come from
- how it has been used

(See Unit 15)

Cash-flow forecasts

A plan of the expected movements of cash into and out of the business in the year ahead, allowing managers to:

- ensure enough cash is available to meet outgoings
- plan how to finance any anticipated shortages of cash

(See Unit 15)

Management accounting

Budget

A financial plan for each unit or department within the business, showing either:

- expected costs, or
- expected revenues.

Actual performance can then be monitored against what is expected.

(See Unit 16)

Breakeven forecast

By calculating the different types of costs and the revenue to be gained from different levels of sales, managers can show:

- what level of production is needed to 'breakeven' (make neither a profit nor a loss)
- what level of profit or loss will be made at a given output

(See Unit 14)

Investment appraisal

A calculation of the expected costs and revenues arising from a new investment. This allows managers to decide:

- if a proposed investment would be profitable
- whether better returns could be gained from an alternative investment

(See Unit 21)

Figure 13.1 The documents used in finanacial and management accounting

Financial information: summary

KEY TERMS

Profit – the amount left over after subtracting costs from revenue.

Internal users – groups within a business that need financial information: for example, managers, owners and employees.

External users – groups outside the business that need financial information about the business: for example, lenders, suppliers and customers.

Auditors – independent verifiers of the accuracy and honesty of a business's financial information.

Financial accounting – the recording and publishing of financial information necessary to meet legal requirements.

Management accounting – financial Information for the use of managers to help plan, make decisions and control the business effectively.

Exam practice continues ➤

Financial information: summary (continued)

Summary questions

1 Why is financial information so important?
2 What use can managers make of financial information?
3 Why do external users of financial information know more about limited companies than sole traders or partnerships?
4 Name **three** different external users and explain what use each might make of financial information.

5 Explain the differences between financial and management accounting.
6 Give details of **three** types of financial document that are used in:
   a financial accounting
   b management accounting.

Exam practice

Marks & Spencer

	2002 £m	2001 £m	2000 £m	1999 £m	1998 £m
Turnover					
UK retail	6,575.2	6,293.0	6,482.7	6,601.1	6,695.8
Operating profit					
UK retail	505.2	334.8	420.1	478.9	871.5
Balance sheet					
Net assets	3,081.3	4,581.4	4,849.0	4,806.6	4,781.8
Capital expenditure	290.5	255.7	450.6	683.1	750.2
UK retail footage (000 sq ft)	12,229	12,440	12,265	11,960	10,977
Staffing (full-time equivalent)					
UK retail	40,854	41,573	41,699	40,814	38,349

1 Is the information shown in Figures 13.1 and 13.2 categorised as 'financial accounting' or 'management accounting'? Explain your answer. **[3]**
2 Explain how each of the following might use this information:
   a internal users **[6]**
   b external users **[6]**
3 To what extent has Marks & Spencer been successful during the period shown? **[10]**
   Total 25 Marks

Figure 13.1

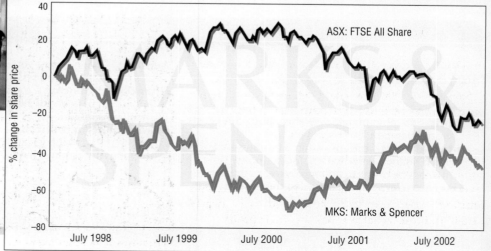

Figure 13.2

14 Costs, revenue and breakeven

Variable cost per unit	×	Number of units sold

=

Selling price per unit	×	Number of units sold

Fixed costs	+	Total variable costs

=

=

Total revenue − **Total cost**

=

**If negative: loss
If positive: profit
If zero: breakeven**

Know how to

Calculate breakeven numerically: $\dfrac{\text{Fixed costs}}{\text{contribution per unit}}$	Draw breakeven charts

Understand

Benefits of breakeven analysis	Limitations of breakeven analysis

 ## 1 Profit

In October 2002, the department stores operator Debenhams announced a profit for the year of £153.6 million. **Profit** is what is left from sales revenue once the costs of production have been subtracted:

Profit = Revenue − Costs

Debenhams sold products to their customers amounting to £1,690 million. This was their sales revenue. The costs of making these products and running the business amounted to nearly £1,540 million. What was left was their profit.

Debanhams, a successful high-street business

Revenue

Sales revenue (also known as turnover) is the value of goods and services sold to customers over a year. Revenue can be calculated using the formula:

Number of units sold × selling price per unit = Sales revenue

A sandwich bar that sells 100 sandwiches at £2 each will earn:

100 × £2 = £200 sales revenue

Where different products are sold at different prices, it is necessary to find an average selling price and multiply this by the volume of goods sold.

 Costs

Business costs consist of the value of resources used both in making the product and in running the enterprise. Some resources, such as raw materials, are directly used up in the production of the good or service. The costs of these resources are known as **direct costs**.

Other costs are not directly related to the production of a specific good or service but are the costs of running the business. These are called **indirect costs** or **overheads**. They include management salaries, administration expenses and marketing costs.

Another method of categorising costs is to divide them into *fixed* and *variable* costs.

Fixed costs

Costs that do not vary directly with the level of output in the short-term are called **fixed costs**. This does not mean that these costs cannot change from one month to the next, due to inflation for example. Rather it means that if the business increases or decreases its volume of production, the fixed costs will not be affected.

An example of a fixed cost is rent. A sandwich bar will have to pay the same rent for its premises whether it attracts 500 customers a day, 100 customers or none at all. In the short term at least, it faces a fixed cost. In the longer term, the business may want to expand and rent bigger premises, which would lead to an increase in its fixed costs.

Other fixed costs include the salaries of managers, insurance and depreciation (see Unit 19).

Variable costs

Costs of production that vary directly with changes in output are called **variable costs**. For example, if a business increases its production, costs of raw materials and wages will rise because of the need for more materials and more workers.

In the case of the sandwich bar, if it costs 40p to provide the ingredients for each sandwich and involves 10p worth of workers' time, the variable cost for each sandwich is 50p. So each extra sandwich brings an additional variable cost of 50p. This extra cost of producing one more unit of output is known as the **marginal cost**.

For example ...

Curbing costs

Europe's most powerful football clubs, including Manchester United and Real Madrid, have considered a series of ground-breaking measures aimed at curbing spiralling costs. The clubs hope to reduce the pressure to spend beyond their means, which some see as threatening football's stability.

One of the key measures would limit the size of the squad to 25. This would reduce the pressure on smaller clubs to buy large numbers of players. Cost control is a key issue facing small clubs as they struggle to balance player transfer fees, salaries and ground costs against fragile revenues.

Source: *The Financial Times*, 16 May 2002

1 Explain, with reference to football clubs, what is meant by the term revenues. **[4]**
2 Explain, with reference to football clubs, the difference between fixed costs and variable costs. **[6]**
Total 10 marks

The total variable cost for any level of output can be calculated as:

Variable cost per unit of output × number of units produced

If 100 sandwiches are made, the total variable cost will be:

50p × 100 sandwiches = £50.00

If production were doubled to 200 sandwiches, the total variable cost would also double:

50p × 200 sandwiches = £100.00

Semi-variable costs

Some costs, such as electricity, could be labelled as semi-variable because they combine aspects of both variable and fixed costs. An electricity or water bill, for example, may combine a fixed element – a standing charge that has to be paid whatever the usage – and a variable element, which increases with use. To keep things simple, semi-variable costs are included in either fixed or variable categories.

Total costs

The total cost of production for any given level of output can be found by adding the fixed and variable costs together:

Fixed costs + Total variable costs = Total costs

If the business produced 100 sandwiches per day, its total variable costs would be £50. Assuming its fixed costs average £300 per day, its total cost of production would be £350. Figure 14.1 shows how the total cost changes at different levels of production.

With no customers and no production, variable costs are zero but fixed costs still have to be paid. As output increases, the fixed costs become a smaller proportion of the **total costs**. This brings down the average cost of each unit and gives the business an incentive to expand its production.

 Profit, loss and breakeven

As explained earlier, the level of profit (or loss) can be calculated using the formula:

Total revenue – Total costs

Total revenue is calculated by multiplying the number sold by the selling price. The total costs are the sum of fixed and variable costs at that level of output.

Figure 14.2 shows the profit and loss made by the sandwich bar at each level of output.

- Where costs are greater than revenues, a *loss* is being made.

- Where revenues are greater than costs, a *profit* is made.

Output (number of sandwiches per day)	Fixed costs (£ per day)	Variable costs (£0.50 per sandwich)	Total costs (£ per day)
0	300	0	300
100	300	50	350
200	300	100	400
300	300	150	450
400	300	200	500

Figure 14.1 Ouput and costs per day for a sandwich bar

Output (number of sandwiches per day)	Total revenue (£ per day)	Total costs (£ per day)	Profit / Loss (£ per day)
0	0	300	−300
100	200	350	−150
200	400	400	0
300	600	450	+150
400	800	500	+300

Figure 14.2 Ouput and profit and loss per day for a sandwich bar

● Where costs and revenue are equal, neither a profit nor a loss is made. This is known as the *breakeven point*.

 5   Calculating the breakeven point

A business will find it useful to estimate the number of units it needs to sell to break even. This can be done numerically or by plotting a breakeven chart.

To calculate the breakeven point numerically, a business needs to know:

● the level of fixed costs

● the selling price per unit

● the variable cost per unit.

The selling price will normally be set higher than the variable cost. That way, each unit sold is covering its own cost of production as well as providing a surplus that can be used to pay off the fixed costs. This surplus on each unit sold is known as the *contribution per unit*. It is calculated as:

Selling price (per unit) – Variable cost (per unit) = Contribution per unit

It is known as **contribution** rather than profit because it is needed to pay off the fixed costs of running the business.

For the sandwich bar discussed earlier, the contribution per sandwich is:

£2.00 – £0.50 = £1.50

It is now only a short step to calculating the breakeven point. If fixed costs are £300 per day, how many sandwiches – generating £1.50 contribution each – must be sold to cover these fixed costs?

The answer can be calculated using the formula:

$$\frac{\text{Fixed costs (£ per day)}}{\text{Contribution per unit (£)}} = \text{Breakeven output (number of units per day)}$$

In this example, the answer is:

$$\frac{£300}{£1.50} = 200 \text{ sandwiches per day}$$

The 200th sandwich to be sold will generate the final £1.50 contribution needed to cover all the fixed costs. The 201st sandwich sold will generate a £1.50 contribution, and this time it will be profit.

 6   Breakeven chart

A breakeven chart (see Figure 14.3) is a visual representation of a business's revenues and costs at different levels of output. It enables the business to identify:

● how many units need to be sold to break even

● what level of profit or loss will be made at any output

● what effect a change in costs or selling price might have on the breakeven point and the level of profit or loss.

The horizontal axis shows the output scale (the number of units per period of time). The vertical axis displays the possible values of costs and revenues in pounds (£s). For the sandwich bar, the scales need to show an output of up to 400 sandwiches per day. If every sandwich were sold, revenue would be £800, and so this is the maximum value that needs to go on the vertical axis.

Constructing the chart

There are four stages to constructing a breakeven chart, as shown in Figure 14.3.

● **Stage 1: Plot total revenue line**
   If no sandwiches are produced or sold, there will be £0 revenue, and so the total revenue line begins at the origin. Each sandwich is sold for £2. Multiplying any level of output by £2 will give the appropriate level of revenue on the vertical axis. The easiest way to plot the total revenue line is to calculate revenue for the maximum level of output, plot this point and then draw the line from this point back to the origin.

● **Stage 2: Plot fixed cost line**
   Even if there is no output, fixed costs must be paid. As an increase in output has no effect on fixed costs, the fixed cost line will be horizontal. For the sandwich bar, the fixed cost is at £300 per day.

Stage 1

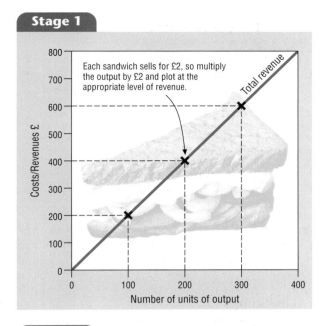

Each sandwich sells for £2, so multiply the output by £2 and plot at the appropriate level of revenue.

Stage 2

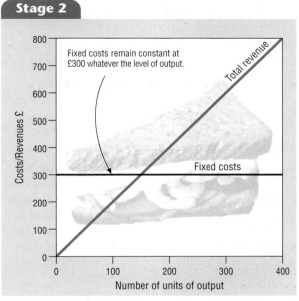

Fixed costs remain constant at £300 whatever the level of output.

Stage 3

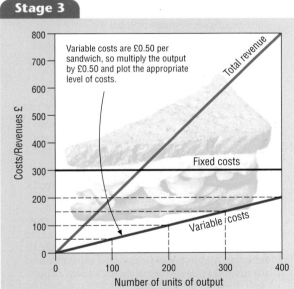

Variable costs are £0.50 per sandwich, so multiply the output by £0.50 and plot the appropriate level of costs.

Stage 4

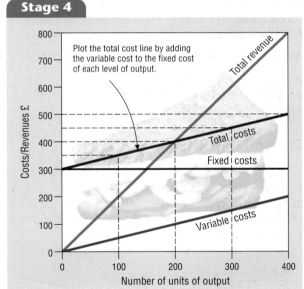

Plot the total cost line by adding the variable cost to the fixed cost of each level of output.

Figure 14.3 Constructing a breakeven chart

- **Stage 3: Plot variable cost line**
  If no sandwiches are produced, variable costs will be £0, and so this line begins at the origin. Each sandwich produced costs an additional £0.50. Multiplying any level of output by £0.50 will give the appropriate level of cost on the vertical axis. As with total revenue, the easiest way to plot the variable cost line is to calculate the variable costs for the maximum level of output and draw the line from this point back to the origin.

- **Stage 4: Plot total cost line**
  To plot the total cost line, add the variable cost at each level of output to the fixed cost line. The total cost line will begin at £300 for zero output, rising to £500 at an output of 400 units [£300 fixed cost + (£200 variable cost)].

7   Analysing a breakeven chart

Once the breakeven chart has been drawn, it can be interpreted to show the following (see Figure 14.4):

- **Breakeven level of output.** The point at which the total cost line crosses the total revenue line is the breakeven point. Reading down from this point, it can be seen that, to break even, 200 sandwiches must be sold each day.

- **Level of profit or loss at each level of output.** At levels of output below 200, total costs are greater than total revenue, so the business is making a loss. The level of loss is represented by the vertical distance between the two lines. The amount of loss can be read off the vertical scale. The level of profit can be found at levels of output above 200 sandwiches per day.

- **Margin of safety.** The number of units currently being produced above the breakeven level is called the **margin of safety**. For example, if the sandwich bar were to produce 300 sandwiches per day, the margin of safety would be:

300 units – 200 units = 100 units

(Current output) – (Breakeven output) = (Margin of safety)

The higher the margin of safety, the more profitable the business and the less likely that a fall in demand will lead to making a loss.

Breakeven analysis

Benefits

- Breakeven charts provide a clear, visual demonstration of some vital financial information. They show at a glance breakeven output and levels of profit or loss. This knowledge allows a business to predict its likely profit from a certain output and to plan how many units it needs to make and sell in order to reach a profit target.

- Breakeven analysis is not a complex, expensive or time-consuming process, and so could prove particularly useful to those starting up or running a small business.

- Breakeven charts can be used to show the likely financial impact of changes in costs or selling price. (See Figures 14.5 and 14.6.)

Limitations

- To keep breakeven analysis simple, a number of assumptions are made that are unrealistic. For example, it is assumed that:

  - all the output is also sold. Breakeven analysis cannot cope with items that are made but not sold.
  - the total revenue and variable cost lines are linear – that is, they increase at a constant rate. In reality, both selling price and the variable cost per unit will change as output increases. Economies of scales (see Unit 31), such as bulk-buying discounts, are likely to mean that variable costs per unit will fall at higher levels of output.

- The analysis is intended to help predict the effects of changes such as to selling price. It says nothing about the effect that such a change may have on customer demand and hence on actual level of profit or loss. This will depend on the price elasticity of demand (see Unit 10), which is not considered in the breakeven chart.

- The constantly changing nature of costs and prices in the real world means that a breakeven chart is unlikely to remain valid for very long.

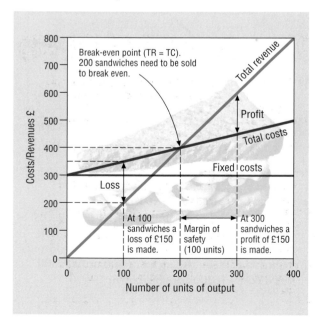

Figure 14.4 Analysing a breakeven chart

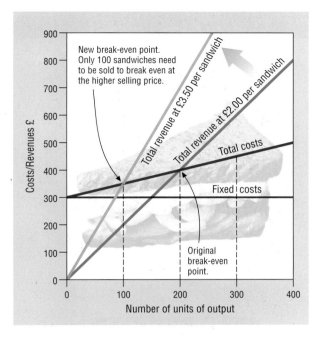

Figure 14.5 Impact of raising the price on breakeven ouput

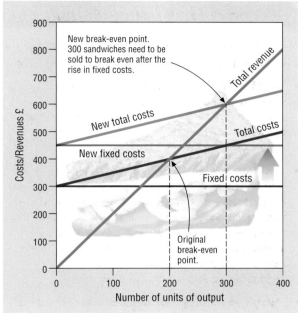

Figure 14.6 Impact of higher fixed costs on breakeven output

Figure 14.5 shows the impact of a higher price. The total revenue line becomes steeper as revenue rises at each level of output. An increase in the price per sandwich to £3.50 would cause the breakeven output to fall to just 100 sandwiches.

Figure 14.6 shows the impact on the business of higher fixed costs – such as an increase in rent. The fixed cost line shifts upwards from £300 to £450, and so the total cost line shifts upwards by the same amount. The impact is to raise the breakeven level of output from 200 to 300 sandwiches per day.

Costs, revenue and breakeven: summary

KEY TERMS

Profit – what is left from sales revenue once the costs of production have been subtracted (Profit = Revenue – Costs).

Total revenue – the value of goods and services sold to customers over a period (Sales revenue = Number of units sold × Selling price per unit).

Direct costs – the cost of resources, such as raw materials, that are directly used up in the production of a good or service.

Indirect costs – the overheads involved in running a business – costs, such as management salaries and administration expenses, that are not directly related to production.

Fixed costs – costs, such as rent, that do not vary directly with the level of output in the short term.

Variable costs – costs of production, such as raw materials and wages, that vary directly with changes in output.

Marginal cost – the additional cost of producing one more unit of output.

Total costs – Fixed costs + Total variable costs at any given level of production.

Breakeven – the point at which a business is making neither a profit nor a loss, where Total revenue = Total costs.

Contribution – the surplus on each unit sold, after the variable cost has been subtracted from the selling price, that contributes towards covering fixed costs and making a profit.

Margin of safety – the number of units that a business is currently producing above the breakeven level.

Exam practice continues ➤

Costs, revenue and breakeven: summary (continued)

Summary questions

1 What is profit?
2 Calculate total revenue when 2,500 units are sold at £6 each. Show the formula and your working.
3 Explain, using examples, the difference between direct and indirect costs.
4 Give **two** examples of fixed costs and **two** examples of variable costs for a hairdresser.
5 What are semi-variable costs?
6 Calculate total cost when:
   a fixed costs are £3000
   b variable cost per unit is £10
   c current output is 500 units.
   Show your working.
7 Calculate profit/loss when:
   a fixed costs are £10,000
   b variable costs per unit is £100

c selling price per unit is £200
d number produced and sold is 150.
Show your working.
8 What does breakeven mean?
9 Calculate the breakeven level of output when:
   a fixed costs are £500
   b variable costs are 50p
   c selling price is £2.50.
   Show your working.
10 What is a margin of safety?
11 Explain **two** benefits and **two** drawbacks of using breakeven analysis?

Exam practice

Summer Trade

M ARY AND JACK TWEDDLE own and run the Cotswold Hotel in Bourton-on-the-Water. They rely on the summer tourist trade to generate their profit. Their fixed costs are £12,000 per month. Their variable costs amount to £10 per customer per night. They currently charge £40 per customer per night. They can accommodate 20 customers at a time, totalling a maximum of 600 customers during a month.

From June through to August, the hotel is completely full. On average, the hotel is only half full for the rest of the year. Mary and Jack are keen to find ways to increase the profitability of their business and are considering a range of options:

- increasing their charge to £55 per customer per night
- seeking to reduce the variable cost per customer per night to £8
- building additional rooms to increase the hotel's capacity to 800 customers per month.

1 Define the terms:
   a fixed costs
   b variable costs.
   Give examples of those likely to be experienced in running a hotel.   **[6]**
2 Calculate numerically the breakeven number of customers per month for the Cotswold Hotel. Show your working.   **[4]**
3 Draw a breakeven chart for the Cotswold Hotel, marking on the chart:
   a the breakeven point
   b the margin of safety during the summer months
   c the monthly profit or loss during the rest of the year.   **[7]**
4 Show on the breakeven chart the impact of an increase in charges to £55 per customer per night.   **[4]**
5 How useful is breakeven analysis in helping Mary and Jack to decide which of the options would be most profitable?   **[9]**
   Total 30 marks

15 Managing cash flow

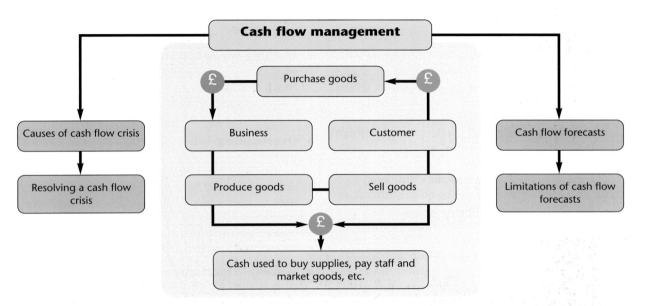

Cash flow management

- Causes of cash flow crisis
  - Resolving a cash flow crisis
- Purchase goods
  - £
  - £
  - Business
  - Customer
  - Produce goods
  - Sell goods
  - £
  - Cash used to buy supplies, pay staff and market goods, etc.
- Cash flow forecasts
  - Limitations of cash flow forecasts

 Difference between cash and profit

Cash is essential. Without cash, a business cannot buy stock, pay its workers or pay its bills. Without cash, a business would find it impossible to trade.

There is an important and fundamental difference between **cash** and **profit** (see 'Harriet's cash flow crisis'). It is quite possible for profitable businesses to fail due to a lack of cash. It is equally possible for a business to trade for many years without making a profit (as was the case with lastminute.com).

Harriet's cash flow crisis

Harriet sets up a specialist mountain bike business. She rents a shop for £1,000 a month – the first payment is due one month after taking up the lease. She buys 10 bikes on one month's credit. Each bike costs £1,000 and is sold for £1,300. She sells all the bikes within the first two weeks, generating income of £13,000 (and an initial profit of £3,000).

Cash = £13,000   Profit = £3,000   Stock = £0

Towards the end of the first month she uses the £3,000 profit to buy three more bikes, hoping to sell them quickly. Unfortunately, a competitor reduces its prices and Harriet finds that she cannot sell her bikes.

Cash = £10,000   Profit = £3,000   Stock = £3,000

At the end of the month, Harriet is faced with two bills. She pays her supplier £10,000, but no longer has the cash to pay her landlord.

Cash = £0   Profit = £3,000   Stock = £3,000

She has still (on paper) made £3,000 profit. This profit is tied up in stock (the bikes) that she cannot sell. Unless the landlord is generous or she can find the rental money from elsewhere, then despite being profitable, Harriet has a cash flow crisis on her hands.

Cash and working capital

Cash forms a large part of what is known as **working capital**. Working capital is the amount of money available to fund the day-to-day running of a business. It is calculated by comparing what a business owns with what it owes. However, money that a business has tied up in fixed **assets** (things that it owns – buildings, land, machinery and so on) is not immediately available. If a business needed cash, it could sell some fixed assets, but this might take time. Hence, fixed assets are ignored when considering working capital.

Current assets are those that are considered to be *liquid*. This means that they can be quickly turned into cash. Essentially it refers to the money a business can 'get its hands on' at short notice – money in a bank, money from selling stock, money from debtors (people who owe the business money) and cash 'at hand'. The business will owe money (current **liabilities**) for stock purchases, rental, utility bills, staff wages and so on.

Working capital can be calculated using the formula:

Working capital = Current assets − Current liabilities

A business needs to have more current assets than current liabilities to ensure that its short-term debts can be met. It is usually considered that having twice the value of current assets to current liabilities will leave a business with enough working capital to cover **liquidity** problems (see unit 20 for more detail). Even if all liabilities were payable in the short term the business would have enough cash to cover its debts and continue trading. In reality many businesses can run with much lower current asset to current liability ratios. The size of the business (and its strength with lenders) and the nature of the industry (some give much longer credit periods than others) all have an impact on 'safe' liquidity levels.

A lack of working capital causes the same problems as a lack of cash (remembering that cash is just one part of working capital). A business will be unable to meet its short-term debts (such as paying for stock, or paying staff) and will face a financial crisis.

 ## Reasons for cash flow and working capital problems

Working capital and cash flow problems (often called liquidity crisis) can have a variety of causes.

- **Investing too much in fixed assets.** Unnecessary spending, for example, on expensive machinery or vehicles, can tie up cash in non-liquid assets. It may be better to lease assets or to avoid overspending to ensure cash availability.

- **Holding too much stock.** Holding too much stock can reduce liquidity. It may not be possible to sell stock fast enough to generate the necessary cash (especially if the stock is still in raw material or work-in-progress form).

- **Overtrading.** When a business expands too fast for the funds available, this can result in overtrading. A business trying to increase production capacity rapidly may over-commit itself to staff wages or the purchase of machinery. If sales do not match forecasts, the business will face a liquidity crisis. Boo.com, the failed internet retailer, was, in part, a victim of overtrading.

- **Seasonal fluctuations.** Seasonal businesses, such as theme parks, may find cash flow management difficult. Income may be very variable seasonally while outgoings remain relatively constant. This will drain working capital during the out-of-season period.

- **Giving too much credit.** Many businesses offer their customers credit terms. Purchases made are usually charged for 30, 60 or 90 days after the actual goods are delivered. The longer the credit period, the longer the business has to

Petrol stations faced stock shortages but increased demands during the 2000 fuel crisis wait before it receives the cash from the sale. This can be a problem if, to attract sales, a business offers its customers a longer credit period than it is offered by its suppliers. The time between paying for its supplies and receiving payment from customers is when a business is most likely to suffer a cash flow crisis.

- **Using too much credit.** Lengthy credit periods from suppliers are, to some extent, an advantage. The longer the payment can be delayed, the greater the likelihood that the business will have the necessary cash. However, taking too much credit can lead to problems. A business may be overexposed to debt if demand for its products falls. If a business is unable to pay its **creditors**, they often refuse to deliver more goods, leading to problems if the business needs new stock to generate sales.

- **Unexpected events.** Changes in the economic climate, unexpected non-payment by customers and other unforeseen events can all seriously affect demand and cash flow. The fuel crisis of 2000 caused short-term cash flow problems for many businesses that relied on road haulage.

  Resolving a liquidity crisis

In general, cash flow problems can be avoided by careful management. Yet, unforeseen events do occur. Occasionally, even careful businesses may face a cash flow crisis. Resolving the crisis can include a number of possible measures.

- **Chase debtors.** Debtors can be encouraged to pay sooner (perhaps by offering early payment discounts), and slow payers can be pressured to pay on time.

- **Cut cash outflow.** By cutting down on expenses (such as the owner's personal withdrawals), enough cash may be generated to cover a short-term liquidity crisis.

- **Debt factoring.** Specialist debt collection agencies can be used to help smooth cash flows or to take over a business's debts. The business will receive part of the value of the debt immediately from the debt factor, who will then collect the full amount from the debtor.

- **Delay payments.** A business might try to negotiate longer credit periods or higher credit limits to delay creditor payments.

- **Increase cash inflow.** Selling stock at a discount may, at the expense of profit, generate positive cash inflows.

- **Overdraft.** An overdraft is essentially a short-term bank loan, allowing a business to draw more from the bank than the business has deposited. Overdrafts usually have high interest rates and should only be used for short periods. Although in practice they are often used for longer periods.

- **Bank loan.** A long-term loan may have a lower interest rate than an overdraft.

- **Sale and leaseback.** An asset is sold and then leased back from its new owner. Doing this generates an immediate inflow of cash, but at the price of long-term rental payments (see Unit 17).

- **Sell unused assets.** Any unused assets, such as unused buildings, can be sold off to generate cash inflows.

A cash flow crisis focuses a business's attention on survival rather than profit. However, businesses should be aware of the impact that resolving a liquidity crisis can have in the long term. Sale and lease back creates a long-term drain on finances. Selling unused assets may limit the potential for medium-term growth. It is important for a business to take such factors into consideration in deciding how best to resolve a liquidity crisis.

  Cash flow forecasts

Because cash is so important to business survival, businesses must carefully and constantly monitor their cash flow position. To do this, many businesses produce cash flow forecasts for the months, year or years ahead. A **cash flow forecast** lists:

- cash inflows (money coming in from sales and other sources)

- cash outflows (money being used to pay bills and other expenses)

- the effect on net cash flow (inflow minus outflow) on the business's cash balance.

An example of a cash flow forecast is given in Figure 15.1, on page 104. Each month, the closing balance becomes the opening balance for the next month. Net cash flow is then added or subtracted from the opening balance. Brackets are used in accounting to represent minus figures.

	Sept	Oct	Nov	Dec	Jan	Feb	Total
Cash inflows							
Sales reveue	1500	1600	1750	2000	1500	1100	9450
Total cash in	**1500**	**1600**	**1750**	**2000**	**1500**	**1100**	**9450**
Cash outflows							
Water	–	–	100	–	–	100	200
Electricity	–	–	100	–	–	100	200
Raw materials	750	800	875	1000	750	550	4725
Wages	100	100	100	200	100	100	700
Advertising	–	50	500	1000	–	–	1550
Maintenance	–	–	30	50	10	10	100
Office equipment	50	–	100	–	–	–	150
Premises rent	250	250	250	250	250	250	1500
Misc. expenses	10	10	100	200	10	10	340
Total cash out	**1160**	**1210**	**2155**	**2700**	**1120**	**1120**	**9465**
Net cash flow (+/–)	340	390	(405)	(700)	380	(20)	(15)
Opening balance	0	340	730	325	(375)	5	–
Closing balance	340	= 730	= 325	(375)	5	(15)	–

+ (bracket marking cash outflows)

Cash in – cash out = (annotation pointing to Net cash flow)

Figure 15.1 An example of a company's six-month cash flow forecast

Activity

Copy and then complete this cash flow forecast, by calculating the missing figures indicated by question marks.

	May	June	July
Cash inflows			
Start-up capital	5,000		
Sales revenue		1,000	?
Total receipts	**?**	**1,000**	**1,200**
Cash outflows			
Payments			
Insurance	100	100	100
Stock purchases	0	650	780
Miscellaneous	50	50	50
Rent	1,000	1,000	?
Electricity			100
Telephone			75
Marketing costs		20	24
Shop fittings	?		
Water			150
Total payments	**3,150**	**?**	**2,279**
Total receipts	5,000	1,000	1,200
Total payments	3,150	?	2,279
Net cash flow	**?**	**?**	**?**
Opening balance		1,850	1,030
Closing balance	**1,850**	?	?

Cash flow forecasts

Usefulness

- Cash flow forecasts enable businesses to identify cash shortages. If a business identifies a cash shortage, it can plan to avoid or manage the situation.

- Banks require cash flow forecasts to be prepared before they grant a business a loan. This ensures that the business will be able to pay back the loan and that it understands the importance of cash flow management.

- Using a cash flow forecast, a business can plan expenditure based on a future cash surplus, or delay expenditure to avoid a cash shortage.

- By completing a cash flow forecast, using a spreadsheet, the business can consider 'what ifs'. The spreadsheet will automatically work out the cash implications of, for instance, offering customers longer credit periods.

Limitations

- Cash flow forecasts are only estimates. Sales may be lower than forecast or costs may be higher. A wide range of factors will affect the accuracy of the forecast.

- It is impossible to forecast every item of expenditure.

- The cash flow statement may reveal a problem, but may give little indication of the underlying causes (although, at least, management will be aware of the problem).

- Management must use cash flow forecasts as a working tool. Once a cash flow forecast has been prepared, it should be monitored regularly and updated to take into account changing economic circumstances.

The cash flow forecast in Figure 15.1 shows that the business will have a cash shortage at the end of December, caused by the negative cash flow in November and December. The business will run into difficulties again in February. Drawing up a cash flow forecast enables the business to plan ahead to avoid such cash shortages.

A **cash flow statement** is different from a cash flow forecast. It details what has happened, rather than what might happen in the future. Limited companies are required to publish cash flow statements with their annual accounts.

> **Guru's views**
> 'Happiness is a positive cash flow.'
> *Fred Adler, venture capitalist*

STOP & THINK

What are the main causes of the cash flow problems experienced by the business in Figure 15.1? How might these problems be resolved?

Activity

Using the figures provided, complete a 12-month cash flow forecast for Wolf Clothing Stores. If possible, use a spreadsheet package to complete this exercise – you will find it much easier.
Note: The first month will be a non-trading month (no sales will be made, but all other relevant costs will still be incurred).

Capital introduced. £15,000 is invested in the business by the owners.
Sales. Sales are estimated at £1,000 in the first month, increasing by 35 per cent each month thereafter.
Insurance. £1,200 is paid in equal monthly instalments.
Stock. Cost of purchases is 65 per cent of sales. Loyalty discounts after 6 months will reduce this to 55 per cent (i.e. from the seventh *trading* month).

Miscellaneous. £25 per month.
Rent. £1,000 per month. The flat above the shop is rented out, bringing in £450 per month additional income.
Accountant's fees. £1,000 annual fee, paid in first month.
Electricity. £100 per quarter (July, October, January, April).
Telephone. £75 per quarter (July, October, January, April).
Vehicle costs. £200 in the first month, £75 per month thereafter.
Marketing costs. 2 per cent of sales for first six months, increasing to 6 per cent from the seventh trading month.
Water: £100 per quarter (July, October, January, April).
Salaries. Since Wolf are operating as a partnership, they do not intend to pay themselves for the first three months. After this time, salaries will equal 7 per cent of sales.
Shopfittings. £2,000 in the first month.

Managing cash flow: summary

KEY TERMS

Assets – items that a business owns, such as buildings, vehicles, and so on. Vehicles and stock also include intangible assets, such as brand names.

Cash – money held by a business in cash form (notes, coins, money in the bank).

Cash flow forecast – estimate of anticipated cash movements for a future period of time.

Cash flow statement – a record of actual cash movements over a period of time.

Creditor – person or organisation owed money by a business.

Debtors – person or organisation owing money to a business.

Liabilities – debts owed by a business to suppliers, banks and other people or organisations.

Liquidity – ease with which assets can be turned to cash; a measure of how easily a business can generate cash.

Profit – difference between total revenue and total expenditure.

Working capital – money available to fund day-to-day business activities.

Summary questions

1 What is meant by 'cash inflow'?
2 What items might a business include under the heading 'cash outflow'?
3 State and explain **two** reasons why it is important for businesses to draw up cash flow forecasts.
4 How might an overdraft be used to aid cash flow?
5 What is debt factoring?
6 How does debt factoring help business to manage cash flow?
7 State **two** limitations of cash flow forecasting.
8 Distinguish between cash and profit.
9 In what ways might a business use a cash flow forecast as a 'working document' when making business decisions?
10 Explain the significance of time lags in the cash flow management process.

Exam practice

Managing the money

Cash flow management is a staple component of business courses everywhere. It is taught at GCSE and A level, right through to degree level and beyond. Businesses employ accountants, at great expense, to prepare cash flow statements, and a cash flow forecast is one of the first things a well-prepared entrepreneur will draw up before setting up their business. For business start-ups in search of finance, cash flow forecasts are an absolute necessity.

Despite this, many businesses set up without the aid of a cash flow forecast. Even more businesses attempt to draw up an accurate cash flow, but struggle with the inherent limitations.

Because of the importance of cash flow, many specialist firms offer cash flow management solutions. Debt factoring companies provide a service whereby all bills are collected or paid through their offices. Businesses using this service pay an annual fee, but benefit from smooth cash flows. The debt factoring company will pay, on behalf of its client, all or part of the value of an invoice as soon as it is received, before recovering the full debt from the debtor.

Just as the cash in your pocket is important to you, so the cash in a business is essential to its survival.

1 What is the difference between a cash flow forecast and a cash flow statement?   **[2]**
2 Outline **three** ways in which a business might try to resolve a cash flow crisis.   **[6]**
3 Discuss the limitations of cash flow forecasting.   **[6]**
4 To what extent does cash flow forecasting guarantee the success of a business start-up? **[12]**
   Total 26 marks

16 Budgeting

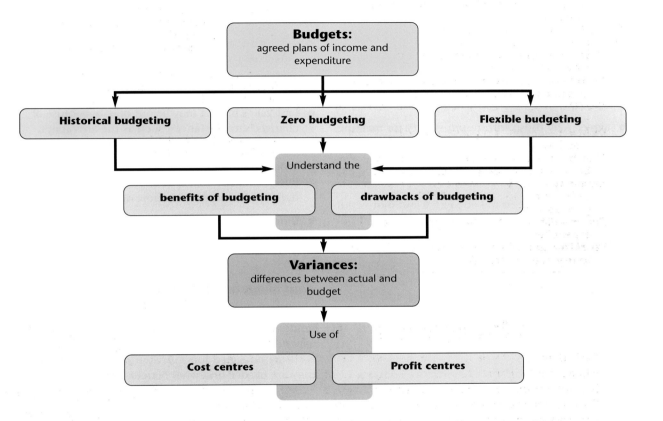

Figure 16.1 A simple budget

1 Budgets and planning

We can all recognise the concept of a **budget** – an agreed plan of income and expenditure. You may have your own budget, based on how much you earn from a part-time job and what this will allow you to buy. Budgeting in business is based on exactly the same principle – setting targets for revenues and costs over a period of time.

At its simplest, a budget could look like the one in Figure 16.1.

Budgets do not have to focus just on costs and revenue. A budget could be drawn up for output, profit, cash, investment or the sales and expenditure of a specific part of the business.

(£'000)	Jan	Feb	Mar	Apr	May	Jun
Revenue	50	50	60	80	120	160
Costs	60	60	65	75	95	115

What information would you need to obtain to draw up the budget in Figure 16.1? What does this budget tell you about the business in question?

2   Setting a budget

The process of setting the budget is vital to achieving its aim. The budget needs to be:

- realistic – to ensure that the targets set are achievable

- agreed – by those with responsibility for meeting the budget

- coordinated – with corporate objectives and other budgets within the business

- challenging – to ensure efficiency and motivation in seeking to meet the targets

- flexible – to take account of unforeseen changes during the budgetary period.

There are three main methods of setting a budget: historical budgeting, zero budgeting and flexible budgeting. Each method has its strengths and weaknesses.

Historical budgeting

The method most used for setting a budget is to base this year's targets for costs or revenue on last year's budget. Sales figures from the previous 12 months provide the baseline for this year's revenue budget, perhaps with a targeted small increase. Budgeted costs for this year would be based on last year's budgeted or actual expenditure, with an allowance made for any increases due to inflation.

This method, called **historical budgeting**, has the benefit of being realistic, as it is based on what has already been achieved. The process of setting the budget becomes a simple and swift exercise. However, using last year's budget can have drawbacks.

- Last year's budget may be out of date because of changed circumstances, such as the arrival of a major new competitor in the market.

- It does not focus on the specific priorities of the business in the year ahead, or take account of the need for resources to support new initiatives.

- It does little to encourage cost efficiency, as it is accepted that costs will be as high as – or even higher than – the previous year's.

Zero budgeting

The **zero budgeting** approach requires each budget-holder within the business to justify every £1 of expenditure. The budget is initially set at zero, and costs are budgeted for only after demonstrating why they are needed and what benefits they will bring.

A marketing manager, for example, would be

Zero budgeting

Advantages

- Cost efficiency can be improved. As all expenditure has to be justified, resources are less likely to be wasted.

- Allocation of funds can be better targeted. Where resources are not needed this year, they can be reduced and switched to other parts of the business where they may be more effective.

- Coordination can be enhanced. Funds can be allocated to those areas essential to meeting the business's overall objectives for the year.

- Motivation can be increased. Managers have been involved in the budget-setting process, weighing up the costs and benefits of alternative proposals. They are therefore more committed to the success of their plans and to meeting the set budget.

Disadvantages

- Budgeting becomes more complex. The required consultation and evaluation are time-consuming procedures that put an additional burden on managers.

- The process could become more political and divisive. Zero-budgeting forces managers to justify their need for expenditure and, by doing so, increases competition between managers for funds. This could result in disagreement and even conflict within an organisation.

required to bid for funds to finance specific marketing campaigns. This bid would need to show which marketing methods would be used, how they fit into the corporate plan for the year ahead and how they will benefit the business.

Flexible budgeting

Flexible budgets allow targeted figures for revenues or expenditures to change as circumstances change. An unexpected recession that caused sales to fall would lead to the budgeted sales figure being revised downwards. The lower than expected sales target may in turn cause the expected expenditure on production to fall, as less output is needed.

The **flexible budgeting** approach has the benefit of remaining realistic and up to date in the face of changing conditions. What is lost, however, is the concept of a budget as a set and agreed target that needs to be met. Poor performance, excused by changing conditions, could lead to targets being reduced to make them achievable.

Activity

Find out how budgets are set in your school or college. What are the benefits and problems of how this system works in practice?

3   Budgetary control

Setting the budget is only the first stage of the process of **budgetary control**. This process involves monitoring the performance of the business and comparing it to the targets that have been set. It can be done on a monthly, weekly or even daily basis, to allow managers to respond swiftly to poor performance.

Variance

When comparing actual performance with the budgeted figures, managers are looking for areas of variance – differences between actual and budgeted figures.

A **favourable variance** occurs when the actual performance produces more profit than had been budgeted for, either because:

- actual sales have been *higher* than budgeted for
- actual costs have been *lower* than budgeted for.

An **adverse variance** occurs when the actual performance is less profitable than had been budgeted, either because:

- actual sales have been *lower* than budgeted for
- actual costs have been *higher* than budgeted for.

Budgetary control

Advantages

The effective use of budgetary control enables a business to:

- plan ahead – identifying what financial resources will be needed to achieve its objectives
- improve coordination – ensuring that all parts of the business are working towards the same objectives and that overall business objectives will be met
- set targets – providing measurable objectives to aim for, against which performance can be judged
- improve efficiency – ensuring expenditure stays within the budgeted level and identifying areas where there is overspending
- delegate responsibility – allowing junior managers to take charge of a budget, while senior management maintains ultimate control through the setting of the budget
- motivate – providing a target for everyone to aim for, and helping to establish a sense of achievement when it is met.

Disadvantages

Budgetary control may cause problems when budgets are:

- too rigid and inflexible – where circumstances have significantly changed, budgets may be left out-of-date, unachievable and irrelevant
- a source of conflict – individual managers may see the budget as an opportunity to increase their spending power and their status within the organisation, perhaps leading to conflict between departments or individuals
- unfairly or inaccurately prepared – where managers and staff feel that budgets have been set unrealistically or without consultation, they may become demotivated or refuse to cooperate with the budgetary process
- viewed by the business as the only important targets – a focus on meeting sales or cost targets may cause the business to ignore the interests of other stakeholders, such as employees or the local community. In the long-term, this could seriously undermine the organisation's success.

For example ...

A juicy business

Nature's Bounty Ltd manufactures a range of organic fruit juices for sale in supermarkets and health food stores. It has set sales and cost budgets for each of the different fruit juices it makes. Information for the last year of trading has been collated in the table below to show the budgeted and actual performance of each type of fruit juice.

Fruit juice	Sales variances (£'000)			Cost variances (£'000)		
	Budget	Actual	Variance	Budget	Actual	Variance
Sunshine Orange	450	400	50 adverse	200	180	
Orchard Apple	350	380		180		30 adverse
Tangy Tropical	400	480			240	40 adverse
Morning Grapefruit		120	30 adverse	100	120	

1 Complete the missing information in the table. **[7]**

2 Of what value is the information in the table to Nature's Bounty Ltd? **[5]**

Total 12 marks

Having identified variances, the business needs to seek explanations for why they have occurred. The reasons could lie within the business – the consequences of its own actions – or in the wider business environment, where trading conditions may be different from those anticipated. It is also important to know whether the variance was a one-off or whether it is likely to be repeated in the future.

This process of monitoring, identifying and explaining variances is of great value in finding solutions that will help to improve performance. Future budgets can be set more accurately once it is understood why actual performance differed from what was budgeted for in the previous year.

 ## 4 Cost and profit centres

A **cost centre** is a part of a business for which it is possible to identify the costs that it incurs. Each part can be set its own cost budget against which its performance can be measured. Where it is also possible to establish the revenues, and hence the profit, of this part of the business, it can be identified as a **profit centre**.

The cost or profit centre may be:

- a functional department – such as marketing or IT. A school or college will make its subject departments the cost centres, setting them a budget for their expenditure.

- a geographical area – such as a sales region or factory location. BMW operates the Cowley car plant, in Oxford, which manufactures Mini Coopers, as a separate cost centre.

- a brand or product type – a large company, like Unilever, will want to distinguish between the

Businesses can establish individual products or brands as profit centres

Cost and profit centres

Benefits

- Accounting. The use of cost and profit centres enables firms to identify specific areas of the business that are inefficient or making a loss. British Airways, for example, identified its London–Belfast route as a loss-maker, once it had made each of its routes a separate profit centre. By cutting this route, BA increased its profitability.

- Organisational. Creating cost and profit centres enables budgetary control to be exercised at a lower level and for smaller units. As explained earlier, doing this can provide measurable objectives, clear lines of responsibility and improved coordination.

- Motivational. Allowing managers and workers to take responsibility for meeting costs and revenue targets within their own profit centre could act as a valuable motivator. It provides opportunities for achievement in meeting targets to be recognised and for involvement in the budget-setting process.

Drawbacks

- Accounting. Allocating costs to an individual cost or profit centre is not always straightforward. Whereas direct costs, such as raw materials, can easily be attributed to a cost centre, indirect costs – overheads, such as marketing – are much more difficult to allocate to individual cost or profit centres. Different methods of allocating overheads to an individual cost centre may create very different impressions about its efficiency.

- Organisational. Establishing separate cost and profit centres may lead to conflict rather than co-ordination. Each centre may be pursuing its own interests, rather than those of the whole business, and competing for funds, financial rewards or even for customers! Furthermore, decisions to close loss-making profit centres may have a negative impact on the business as a whole. Marks & Spencer's decision to close loss-making European stores had a disastrous public relations effect on the company in the UK.

- Motivational. Additional responsibility to achieve budget targets for sales or costs may prove demotivating. Managers may feel excessive stress, while feelings of job insecurity may undermine the morale of workers who fear the closure of a loss-making profit centre.

costs of each of its main product types, such as Bird's Eye Frozen Foods and Wall's Ice Cream.

- a type of equipment or individual machine – a business may wish to study the cost of running a machine, such as a photocopier, to see if it can be use more efficiently.

- an individual – such as a salesperson or manager, whose costs and revenues can be identified to evaluate their benefit to the business.

A product or brand can be made a profit centre if both the costs incurred by the product and the revenues it brings into the business can be identified. A separate profit and loss account can be drawn up for each product, allowing the business to make decisions on the basis of what are its most profitable, or loss-making, products. Some parts of a business cannot be made full profit centres, because identifying the revenues that they bring in is not possible. The administration element of a business is an example. In this instance, it can, at most, be made a cost centre.

Budgeting: summary

KEY TERMS

Budget – an agreed plan that sets targets for revenues and costs over a period of time.

Historical budgeting – setting this year's budget on the basis of last year's budgeted or actual cost and revenue figures.

Zero budgeting – a method that initially sets the budget at zero, with costs being budgeted for after it has been shown why they are needed and what benefit they will bring.

Flexible budgeting – an approach to budgeting that allows targeted figures for revenues or expenditures to change as circumstances change.

Budgetary control – monitoring the performance of a business, by comparing performance to the targets that have been set, and seeking to understand why differences occur.

Adverse variance – when the performance of a business is financially worse (that is the business is less profitable) than indicated in the budget.

Favourable variance – when the performance of a business leaves it financially better off (that is more profitable) than had been indicated in the budget.

Cost centre – part of a business for which the costs that it incurs can be identified.

Profit centre – part of a business for which it is possible to identify the costs, revenues and, therefore, profits that it generates.

Exam practice continues ➤

Budgeting: summary (continued)

Summary questions

1 What is a budget?
2 What criteria should a successful budget meet?
3 Explain the difference between historical and zero budgeting.
4 Identify **two** benefits and **two** drawbacks of zero budgeting.
5 What is a flexible budget?
6 Explain what the process of budgetary control involves.

7 What is a variance?
8 Explain **two** benefits and **two** potential drawbacks of budgetary control.
9 What is the difference between a cost centre and a profit centre?
10 Weigh up the positive and negative effects of cost and profit centres.

Exam practice

Between the sheets

Coulthers is a well established manufacturer of quality bed linen, supplying many major department stores. In the late 1990s, Coulthers experienced a slump in sales and, for the first-time in its history, made a loss. A new finance director, James Melwood, was brought in to identify ways in which the financial health of the company could be improved.

Melwood focused initially on the company's budgeting process. Expenditure seemed to have grown each year, with few attempts to improve cost efficiency. The budgeted expenditure had been based on that of the previous year, with a percentage increase added for inflation. Even when sales and output had fallen, expenditure had continued to grow. Managers within the firm were defensive, each claiming that their own area needed the financial resources it was being given. There was also considerable confusion as to where the problems lay within the

business. No one seemed to know which of the company's products were profitable and which were not.

Melwood's proposals were for a complete reform of the budgeting process. Each product type – duvet covers, sheets and pillowcases – would be made into a separate profit centre. Each would have its own revenue and expenditure budgets set, using a process of zero budgeting. Variances from budgeted figures would be carefully scrutinised to identify and solve potential problems.

The new system produced some startling results. Costs were cut by 20 per cent in the first year, as managers were forced to justify every £1 of expenditure. Analysis of each profit centre revealed that pillowcases were a major loss-maker for Coulthers. Melwood took this information to a meeting of the board of directors to discuss the case for stopping the production of pillowcases.

1 Define the terms:
  a profit centre   [2]
  b variance.   [2]
2 How would a move to zero budgeting change the process of setting budgets at Coulthers? [4]
3 Explain, using examples from the case study, the benefits and drawbacks of using budgets.   [8]
4 Discuss the case for stopping the production of pillowcases on the basis of the information gathered.   [9]
  Total 25 marks

Product type	Revenues (£'000)		Direct Costs (£'000)		Share of overheads (£'000)		Profit/Loss (£'000)	
	Budget	Actual	Budget	Actual	Budget	Actual	Budget	Actual
Duvet covers	850	700	450	400	200	200	200	100
Sheets	500	450	200	200	200	200	100	50
Pillowcases	300	200	150	200	200	200	(50)	(200)

17 Sources of finance

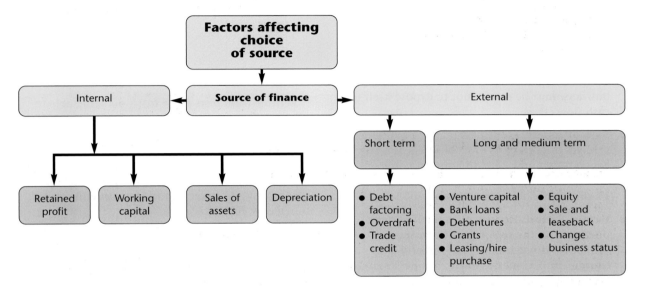

```
                    ┌─────────────────────┐
                    │  Factors affecting  │
                    │       choice        │
                    │     of source       │
                    └──────────┬──────────┘
                               ▼
┌──────────────┐    ┌─────────────────────┐    ┌──────────────────────────────────────┐
│   Internal   │◄───│   Source of finance │───►│                External                │
└──────┬───────┘    └─────────────────────┘    └──────────────────────────────────────┘
```

Internal				Short term	Long and medium term	
Retained profit	Working capital	Sales of assets	Depreciation	● Debt factoring ● Overdraft ● Trade credit	● Venture capital ● Bank loans ● Debentures ● Grants ● Leasing/hire purchase	● Equity ● Sale and leaseback ● Change business status

1 Raising and using money

It cost Manchester United £30 million to buy the footballer Rio Ferdinand in 2002. Yates's, the pub chain, invested over £6 million in refurbishing 40 of its premises during 2001–2. Finding large sums of money, even for big businesses such as these, is not always easy. This chapter looks at the **sources of finance** available to help businesses, large or small, raise the money necessary to fund operations.

How a business uses money can be broadly split into two categories:

- **capital expenditure** – money spent on purchasing fixed assets such as buildings, machinery and vehicles. Capital expenditure adds to the value of the company.

- **revenue expenditure** – money used to help generate sales such as stock purchases, wages and so on. Revenue expenditure does not add fixed value to the company.

Football clubs rely on private investment and sponsorships to provide the capital to purchase top-rate players

2   Internal finance

There are several ways to raise money for a business from internal sources:

- **Retained profit.** Once a business starts to make a profit, it can use this profit as a source of finance. Ploughing profit back into a business is inexpensive and very popular.

- **Working capital.** Reducing stockholding, delaying payment to creditors and encouraging debtors to pay on time can help to generate cash from working capital (see Unit 15). This 'spare' cash can be used as a source of finance, but the business must be careful not to expose itself to a cash flow crisis.

- **Sale of assets.** A business may sell buildings, vehicles or even parts of its business as a way of generating funds. Richard Branson raised an estimated £1.3 billion from the sale of parts of his Virgin empire between 1999 and 2002.

- **Depreciation.** Depreciation is a long-term provision for the replacement of assets. As vehicles and machinery wear out and IT equipment becomes obsolete, businesses make a deduction for depreciation in calculating their profit. In effect, this is an allowance for saving towards the cost of replacing these assets. However, in practice, the cash is available to the business.

Internal sources of finance have the advantage of being inexpensive and relatively convenient. Most businesses, however, have limited internal funds and need to seek external sources of finance.

3   External finance

External sources of finance are often grouped according to the time frame over which money is borrowed, as shown in Figure 17.1.

Paying the piper

Venture capitalists often insist on being able to have a say in the running of the business. In 1999, Apax Partners, a venture capital firm, invested £12 million into QXL, the online auction site. As part of the deal, Apax insisted on bringing in new management. The company's founder had to step aside in favour of a new chief executive.

Short-term finance

There are several possibilities for raising finance for the short term.

- **Debt factoring.** A debt-factoring company will pay to its client all or part of the value of an outstanding invoice and then recover the debt from the creditor.

- **Overdraft.** An overdraft is effectively a short-term bank loan. A bank will allow a business to withdraw from its account more money than it has deposited. Overdrafts are often used to cover cash shortages, so a business may be overdrawn only for a matter of days. Interest is paid only when the account is overdrawn. An overdraft is a flexible way for businesses to borrow small sums of money as and when required.

	Time frame	Possible usage
Short term	Under 1 year	Working capital
Medium term	1–5 years	Capital expenditure (vehicles, refurbishment, etc.)
Long term	Over 5 years	Major capital expenditure (buildings, land, etc.)

Figure 17.1 Borrowing money: time frames and possible uses

Inflating the bubble

During the dotcom boom of the late 1990s and early 2000s, Clickmango.com, the ill-fated health product website fronted by the actor Joanna Lumley, managed to raise £3 million in just a few days. Venture capitalists were clambering over themselves to acquire stakes in internet businesses. At the time, owning equity in a dotcom was viewed like owning a winning lottery ticket. Boo.com, another star-crossed e-retailer, managed to raise over £40 million in venture capital during 1999. Both businesses rapidly burned through this cash and disappeared as quickly as they had appeared.

Source: *dot.bomb* Rory Cellan-Jones (2001) Aurum Press, London

1   What is venture capital? Why is it sometimes known as risk capital? **[4]**
2   What is meant by the term 'equity'? **[2]**
3   Evaluate the arguments for and against a start-up business financing itself through venture capital. **[6]**
    Total 12 marks

Want to know more?

www.boo.com (click on the boo.com link)

Trade credit. Most business-to-business transactions are completed on a credit basis. Goods purchased are not paid for immediately. Using trade credit, a business can get stock even if it does not have the cash to pay for it at the time. It is intended that, by the time payment is due, the stock will have been sold and the necessary cash generated to pay the bill.

Medium- and long-term finance

Finance for the medium or long term can be provided in a number of ways.

- **Venture capital.** Venture capitalists are specialist finance providers. If a business is unable to raise sufficient funds, venture capital is often used. Venture capitalists usually invest in smaller, risky ventures and do not ask for security. Rather, they will loan a business money in return for a share of business ownership or of any eventual profits. Venture capital is often used in a **management buy-out** – where the management of a firm raise sufficient finance to purchase all or part of a company from its original owners. Often this is done because the mangers want to stop the business from closing down.

Guru's views
'A bank is a place that will lend you money if you can prove that you don't need it.'
Bob Hope, American comedian

- **Bank loans.** A bank loan is usually repaid on a monthly basis over a number of years. It can be medium or long term and incurs interest charges. Bank loans are a relatively safe source of finance. With a fixed interest rate, repayment amounts are known and can be planned for. However, banks usually require some form of security on the loan (a building or, in the case of a sole trader, a personal asset such as a house). If the business is unable to repay the loan, the bank will seize this asset.

Activity

Investigate the activities of several venture capital companies. Using the internet, research the following:
- what services are offered
- what recent loans have been made
- what criteria have to be met for a loan to be made.

Want to know more?

www.bvca.co.uk *or* www.3i.com

- **Debentures.** A **debenture** is a form of long-term loan to a business. It carries a fixed interest rate and is repayable over a specified period (often 15–25 years).

- **Grants.** A variety of UK government and EU grants are available to businesses. The amounts on offer range from less than £100 to many thousands of pounds. Grants are available for businesses setting up in certain locations, producing certain products or creating employment opportunities.

- **Leasing.** By leasing an asset instead of purchasing it, a business can reduce the amount of finance it needs to raise. A business pays a set fee to lease the asset for a set time. After this, the asset is returned to the leasing company. The business might then renew the leasing contract and receive a new asset. Leasing is useful for equipment such as computers, which quickly become outdated. Leasing companies will also maintain an asset and replace it if it breaks.

- **Hire purchase.** Using hire purchase is similar to leasing, except that the company owns the asset once all the monthly payments have been made.

- **Share capital/equity.** Limited companies may raise funds through the sale of shares. Share issues can be used to raise capital – called share capital or **equity** – for start-up or for additional capital at any time. Raising share capital can be expensive, but it can generate large amounts of permanent capital.

- **Changing business status.** A change in business status can be used to generate funds. A sole trader might take on a partner who would bring in additional funding, or a partnership might convert to a limited company to benefit from being able to sell shares.

- **Sale and leaseback.** An asset is sold and then leased back from its new owner. This generates an immediate inflow of cash, but at the expense of long-term rental payments. Sale and leaseback

Sale and leaseback provides many benefits for companies requiring ready cash

For example ...

The B&B Sale

Bradford & Bingley, the building society, sold property worth £30 million during 2002. The bank copied the deal under which larger rival Abbey National sold and leased back £457 million worth of property. B&B's objective was not to release capital – the bank already had almost £150 million of surplus cash. Christopher Rodrigues, B&B's chief executive, was thought to be looking for suitable acquisitions to help drive business growth. B&B was also hoping to reduce its exposure to the property market, an area that was making banks increasingly nervous.

Source: *Financial Times*, 21 May 2002

1 What is meant by the phrase 'sale and leaseback'?   **[2]**
2 Why do businesses usually use sale and leaseback?   **[2]**

3 Evaluate the use of sale and leaseback in the case of Bradford & Bingley.   **[8]**
Total 12 marks

can be used to resolve short-term cash flow problems, or to help fund long-term growth. By releasing cash tied up in assets, a business can generate the funds needed to pursue growth. The additional income generated by growth would, hopefully, more than cover the rental payments.

Businesses often reduce the amount of finance they need to raise by engaging in **joint ventures.** A joint venture is where two or more businesses join forces to finance a new business venture or product. Virgin Mobile is a joint venture with T-Mobile. Both businesses put £50 million into the venture.

 4   Factors affecting choice of finance source

The source of finance chosen must be appropriate to its usage. Short-term finance, such as an overdraft, should not be used to fund long-term asset purchases. Equally, long-term finance should not be used to fund revenue expenditure.

When choosing sources of finance, a business needs to consider a range of factors.

- **Availability of internal funds.** If a business has internal funds available, it must consider whether using these funds would be appropriate. What would be the impact on working capital? How might shareholders react to lower dividends?

- **Time.** The time frame of repayments or exposure to debt must relate to the purchase being made. A fixed asset may pay for itself over many years and could be funded with long-term finance.

- **Type of business.** A sole trader may have only a limited range of financial options. A public limited company usually has a wide range of sources of finance available. Because of the size of loans undertaken and the security offered, plcs are also often able to negotiate lower interest rates on bank loans.

- **Current financing.** The current financial make-up of a company can determine the sources of finance available to it. Thus, a business that already has several bank loans may find it difficult to secure another (this is related to the concept of **gearing**, see page 124). In any case, a business that is already highly geared (having a high proportion of loans compared to equity) may put itself at risk if it takes on additional loans. Any increase in interest rates will have a significant effect on the firm's debt burden.

- **Control.** The degree of control that the owners of a business wish to maintain affects whether venture capital or conversion to limited status can be considered as potential sources of finance.

- **Cost.** A business will take into account the cost of raising finance. The cost will be closely related to the time frame of any debt that is undertaken. Share issues are expensive, but can raise large sums. Trade credit is usually interest free, but is only available for short periods.

- **Security.** Small businesses, in particular, may have little to offer as security against borrowing and may find it difficult to get a bank loan. Larger, more established businesses will have proven track records, and assets that can be used as security, making it more likely that banks will lend them money.

Whatever source of finance is chosen, it must be appropriate to the business situation and the motive for needing finance. Business growth requires both adequate short-term cash flow and long-term finance for expansion. The two requirements may well be met by very different sources of finance.

> **Guru's views**
> 'Out of debt, out of danger.'
>
> *Proverb*

Sources of finance: summary

KEY TERMS

Capital expenditure – money spent on purchasing fixed assets (buildings, machinery, etc.).

Debenture – a form of long-term loan to a business.

Equity – money generated through the sale of shares; another term for share capital.

Gearing – the proportion of funds raised from loans relative to equity.

Joint venture – two or more businesses joining forces to finance a new business venture or new product.

Management buy-out – purchase of all or part of a company by its managers.

Revenue expenditure – money used to help generate sales (stock purchases, wages, etc.).

Sale and leaseback – selling an asset and then leasing it back from its new owner.

Summary questions

1   List **two** internal sources of finance and **two** external sources of finance.
2   State **three** factors a business may take into account when deciding on sources of finance.
3   Why might a business prefer a bank overdraft to a bank loan?
4   What is debt factoring?
5   What is venture capital?
6   What is the difference between leasing and hire purchase?
7   What is trade credit?
8   What is a debenture?
9   Distinguish between equity and debt.
10 How do the sources of finance available to plcs and Ltds differ?

Exam practice

By the skin of their teeth

Lister-Petter is a maker of diesel engines. The firm has a history of nearly 150 years and combines two of the best-known names in the diesel industry. Since Victorian times, Lister and Petter engines have been exported around the globe.

In 1996, the business was the subject of a management buyout backed by Schroder Venture Capital. Under its previous ownership, Lister-Petter had been so starved of investment that parts of the manufacturing plant were unchanged since the 1970s. After the buyout, and with a downturn in engineering, the firm could not find the £15–20 million that it would cost to improve the plant.

To make matters worse, the board, typically for a venture capital backed operation, was drawn from all of the financial backers, and there were inevitable conflicts of interest. After putting the business up for sale, the board, lacking potential buyers, started to prepare the company for receivership.

The company was saved at the eleventh-hour by the South West Regional Development Agency. They agreed to pay £15 million for the company's land, with Lister-Petter continuing to occupy a small part of it. This funding formed the basis for the management to secure additional sources of finance. The management team raised £13.5 million from two banks and relied on the goodwill of local tax and VAT offices and suppliers to overcome their 'awesomely tight' working capital problems. The day that the funding was approved was the day the banks were due to take their decision about receivership. Lister-Petter were saved by the skin of their teeth!

Source: *The Times*, 14 May 2002

▶▼ **LISTER PETTER**

1   What is a management buyout? **[2]**
2   What is working capital? **[2]**
3   Suggest and explain **one** alternative method Lister-Petter could have used to raise all or part of the funding required. **[4]**
4   Examine the drawbacks of financing through venture capital. **[6]**
5   'Internal sources of finance are always preferable to external ones'. To what extent do you agree with this statement? **[11]**

Total 25 marks

18 Balance sheet

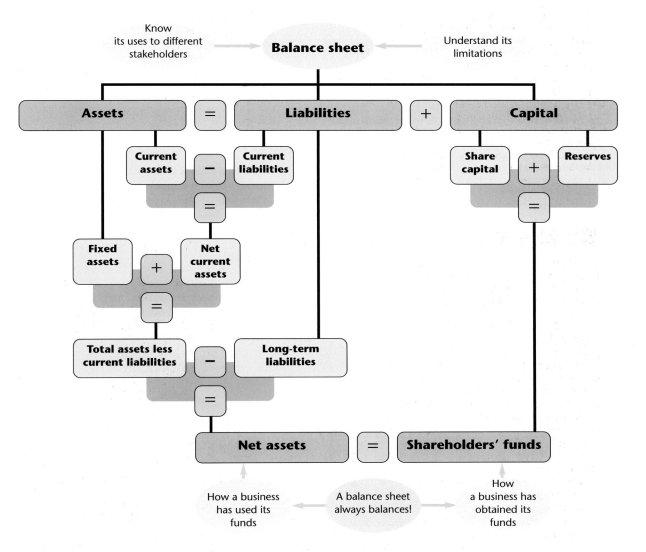

1 What is a balance sheet?

A **balance sheet** shows what a business owns – its assets, and what it owes – its liabilities. It is a snapshot of what a business is worth at a particular time, showing how it came to be worth that much. The balance sheet is one of the three key financial accounting statements. It is used by a variety of external users – such as shareholders and lenders – to judge the financial position of the business.

A balance sheet is so-called because it shows how what a business owns – its assets – is balanced by the sources of finance that have funded these assets. Funds must either have come from:

- **liabilities** – money the business has borrowed and needs to repay

115

- **capital** – money invested by the owners, or profits that they retained within the business.

The ways that funds have been used (assets) will always balance the value of where those funds have come from (capital and liabilities).

2 Assets

An **asset** is a resource of some value that is either:

- owned by the business – such as buildings or equipment
- owed to the business by someone else – such as money owed by a customer who has bought on credit (that is, a debtor).

A balance sheet first lists the value of these assets under two main headings, fixed assets and current assets.

Fixed assets

Resources that a business will use and reuse over a period of more than a year are called **fixed assets**. These may be:

- **tangible assets** – physical resources owned by the business, including:
    - land and buildings: such as a factory premises
    - equipment: such as machinery or vehicles
    - fixtures and fittings: such as furniture

- **intangible assets** – a resource of value but not a physical item that can be touched, including:
    - brands: the name and identity of products, which may be of great value in ensuring future sales
    - goodwill: the reputation of the business, which may create customer loyalty, making the business as a whole more valuable than just the sum of its individual assets
    - patents, copyright or trademarks: legal rights guaranteeing that the business will be the only business to sell a specific type of product or use a certain name. This will help to boost future sales, and so has a real and measurable value to the business.

- **financial assets** – investments held by the business, such as shares in other companies.

STOP & THINK

How can the value of intangible assets be measured? How reliable is this measurement? What are the arguments for omitting intangible assets, such as brands, from a balance sheet?

Current assets

Resources that a business expects to sell or turn into cash within one year are called **current assets**. The most common types of current asset are:

Activity

Look at the photographs a–d. Explain the type of asset shown in each picture and say which category it belongs to.

a

b

c

d

- **stocks** – which will include:
  - raw materials: components waiting to be used in production
  - work-in-progress: semi-finished items going through the production process
  - finished goods: items waiting to be sold

- **debtors** – the value of money owed to the business by customers who purchased goods or services on credit

- **cash** – cash deposits held in bank accounts together with any petty cas' held on the premises.

 Liabilities

A business's debts are called liabilities. They show from where finance was obtained and to whom it is owed. A balance sheet shows two types of liabilities, current and long-term.

Current liabilities

Debts that must be paid back within 12 months are **current liabilities**. On a plc's balance sheet, these are labelled as 'Creditors due within one year'. They will include:

- **trade creditors** – other firms that have allowed the business to purchase goods and services, such as raw materials, on credit (in effect, a form of a short-term loan)

- **bank overdraft** – borrowing from a bank, using an overdraft facility or a short-term loan

- **taxation and dividends** – tax that the business owes to the Inland Revenue, or dividends that are due to be paid to shareholders.

Long-term liabilities

Debts that are not due for repayment within 12 months are long-term liabilities. These will include:

- **bank loans** – longer-term borrowing that may, for example, have been used to purchase vehicles or equipment

- **mortgage** – borrowing to purchase land or buildings, where the property is offered as security on the loan.

 Capital

If finance has not been obtained through borrowing, it will have come from the investment of capital. Capital refers to the funds provided by the owners of the business. The owners may be a sole trader, business partners or shareholders, depending on the type of business ownership.

There are two main types of capital for a limited company:

1 **share capital** – funds provided by shareholders when they purchased shares. These funds show the total value of shares when they were first sold, not the current share price.

2 **retained profit** – profits that have been earned and not distributed as dividends, so the value of the company will have increased. Profits will have been reinvested in equipment or premises. The accumulation of retained profit is often labelled 'reserves'. This does not mean there is a sum of money in reserve, waiting to be used. It reflects how the value of the company has grown, but the use to which the money has been put will be shown in the assets section.

Share capital and retained profit together are known as shareholders' funds. These are treated as a liability for the business. This is because a company has its own legal status, separate from that of its owners. Capital belongs to the shareholders and is ultimately owed back to them.

Activity

Use the internet to find the published accounts of any well-known company. From the balance sheet, find the value of:
- fixed assets
- current assets
- current liabilities
- long-term liabilities
- capital and reserves.
Look for examples of items that this company has under each category. What has happened to the value of each category since the previous year? Why do you think this has happened?

 Vertical balance sheet

The most common way to construct a balance sheet is in the vertical format similar to that shown in

Figure 18.1. This is the format that all public limited companies are legally required to use.

The heading shows the name of the company and the date on which the balance sheet was drawn up. The two-column format helps to improve the presentation. Individual items are listed in the left-hand column, while the right-hand column shows the key totals and how they are calculated.

Referring to Figure 18.1:

- figures for the fixed assets (1) are added together

- as are the figures for current assets (2) and for current liabilities (3)

- current liabilities are subtracted from current assets to calculate **net current assets** (4) – also known as 'working capital'.

This shows whether the company will be able to pay its immediate debts out of its available assets. If the net current assets figure is positive, the business should have enough money to cover its day-to-day outgoings. Negative working capital could mean debts are not paid on time and creditors such as banks or suppliers could ultimately take legal action to get their money back. However, many large businesses, such as supermarkets, routinely operate with negative working capital (see Unit 20).

- Fixed assets (1) and net current assets (4) are added together to produce 'total assets less current liabilities'(5).

- Long-term liabilities, labelled as 'creditors due after one year' (6), are listed and added together.

- They are then subtracted from 'total assets less current liabilities' (5)

- to calculate 'net assets' (7).

The value of **net assets** shows what the business is worth. The money that the business owes has been subtracted from the value of what it owns, and what is left belongs to the shareholders. For this reason, it is this figure of net assets that must always balance with the bottom line of the balance sheet – the shareholders' funds.

- Share capital and reserves (8) are added together to produce 'shareholders' funds', equal to net assets (7).

ABC Construction Ltd

Balance sheet as at 31 December

		£'000	£'000
(1)	**Fixed assets**		
	Premises	450	
	Equipment	300	
	Vehicles	350	
			1,100
(2)	**Current assets**		
	Stocks	250	
	Debtors	200	
	Cash in hand	300	
		750	
(3)	**Current liabilities**		
	Trade creditors	200	
	Bank overdraft	150	
	Taxation	100	
		450	
(4)	**Net current assets**		
	(Working capital)		300
(5)	**Total assets less current liabilities**		1,400
(6)	**Creditors due after 1 year**		
	Bank loan	200	
	Mortgage	400	
			600
(7)	**Net assets**		800
(8)	**Capital and reserves**		
	Share capital	550	
	Retained profit	250	
(9)	**Shareholders' funds**		800

Activity

Using the balance sheet in Figure 18.1, explain the effect that each of the transactions described might have on it (*Hint*: each transaction has two effects on the balance sheet that keep it in balance).
- £10,000 of raw materials are obtained, but the supplier has given 30 days' credit before payment needs to be made.
- A bank loan of £50,000 (repayable over 10 years) is used to purchase additional equipment.
- Cash is used to pay the company's tax bill.
- Profit of £100,000 is reinvested in an expansion to the premises.
- All the customers who owed the company money pay in cash.

Figure 18.1 Balance sheet for ABC Construction Ltd

Balance sheet

Usefulness

- Shareholders will be able to gain a valuable insight into the performance and financial strength of the business. The balance sheet will show how their share capital has been used, whether the worth of the company is increasing and whether it is in a position to pay dividends.

- Potential Investors can judge the company's financial stability and potential for future expansion. The bigger the proportion of finance that has been borrowed, rather than invested as capital, the riskier the business situation. The balance sheet will also indicate the value of the company to any individual or organisation considering taking over the business.

- Employees can judge their job security and pay prospects, as the balance sheet shows the financial resources that the business has available.

- Creditors (banks and suppliers) will use the 'working capital' figure to show whether the business is in a position to meet its repayment of short-term debts. The 'asset structure' of the business – the relative proportions of fixed versus current assets – is crucial in ensuring a business has sufficient working capital.

Limitations

- A balance sheet is no more than a 'snapshot' of the value of a business on a given day. It can quickly become out of date. To be meaningful, it needs to be compared with previous years' balance sheets to identify key changes.

- Many of the values included on a balance sheet are estimated. Goodwill, brand names, even the current value of fixed assets such as equipment, are all difficult to evaluate. The value of the business may, as a result, be overestimated or underestimated.

- Recent accounting scandals, such as the one at Enron, the American energy giant, have shown that documents such as balance sheets can be used to hide and mislead stakeholders. Even where there is no illegal activity, creative accounting – also known as 'window dressing' – can be used to make the company's financial position look better than it really is.

- The balance sheet cannot be considered in isolation. The situation in the economy, trends in the company's own market and the performance of its competitors all need to be weighed up alongside the balance sheet to gain a full picture of the business's prospects.

6 Differences between balance sheets

The exact layout and items included in a balance sheet will vary, depending on whether the business is a sole trader, a private limited company or a public limited company.

- The 'capital account' of a sole trader's balance sheet will show the 'owner's capital' that has been put into the business and the 'drawings' of money that the owner has taken out of the business for personal use. Capital minus drawings will produce a balance that shows what is owed back to the owner, and will be equal to the value of net assets.

- The balance sheets for limited companies show shareholders' funds and whether these are made up of share capital or retained profit. There are differences between private and public limited companies. A plc, for example, will list:

  - called up share capital: meaning the value of different types of shares issued, including ordinary and preference shares

  - revaluation reserve: which reflects any increase in the value of fixed assets such as land. If a piece of land increases in value after it is purchased, the value of fixed assets will increase. The 'capital and reserves' section needs to be increased by the same amount to keep the balance sheet in balance.

- Under the Companies Act of 1985, limited companies must meet certain standards of content and presentation in their balance sheets. The previous year's figures must be set alongside the current year's to allow comparisons to be made. Notes to the accounts will include details and explanations of the figures in the balance sheet.

Do not to be put off by differences you may encounter between different types of balance sheet. They all show the same kinds of information and have been constructed using the same basic concepts and methods.

Different stakeholders can use the balance sheet to identify what the listed assets of the business are worth, how it obtained its finance and how it has used that finance. To make best use of a balance sheet, you can do a series of calculations known as 'ratio analysis'. This is explained in Unit 20.

Balance sheet: summary

KEY TERMS

Balance sheet – a 'snapshot' of what a business is worth at a particular point in time; showing what a business owns – its assets, and what it owes – its liabilities.

Liabilities – money that the business has borrowed as a source of funds.

Capital – money invested by the owners, or profits that they have retained within the business.

Asset – a resource of some value that is owned by the business.

Fixed assets – resources that a business will use and reuse over a period of more than one year.

Current assets – resources that a business expects to sell or turn into cash within one year.

Debtors – the value of money owed to the business by customers, having purchased goods or services on credit.

Current liabilities – debts that must be paid back within one year.

Net current assets – the value of the 'working capital' available to a business to pay its day-to-day debts; calculated as current assets minus current liabilities.

Net assets – what the listed assets of the business are worth, calculated as 'total assets less current liabilities' minus long-term liabilities.

Summary questions

1 What is a balance sheet?
2 Why must a balance sheet always balance?
3 What is a fixed asset?
4 Give an example for a high street retailer of:
   a a tangible asset
   b an intangible asset
   c a financial asset.
5 Explain, using examples, how current assets differ from fixed assets.
6 What is a liability?
7 Explain, using examples, how current liabilities differ from long-term liabilities.
8 What are the two main types of capital for a limited company?
9 Why is negative working capital a potential problem for a business?
10 Why will net assets equal shareholders' funds on a balance sheet?
11 How does the balance sheet of a plc differ from that of a sole trader?
12 Explain how **three** different business stakeholders might valuably use a balance sheet.
13 Explain **three** limitations to the usefulness of a balance sheet.

Exam practice

Figure 18.1
Balance Sheet for lastminute.com as at 31 March 2002

lastminute.com plc provides last minute travel, leisure and gift solutions to its customers via the internet.

	At March 2002 £000s	At March 2001 £000s
Fixed assets		
Intangible assets	36,661	51,306
Tangible assets	11,048	15,216
Investments	638	350
Total fixed assets	**48,347**	**66,872**
Current assets		
Stock	107	133
Debtors	9,893	14,279
Cash at bank and in hand	34,747	61,801
	?	?
Creditors:		
amounts falling due within one year	(24,172)	(29,372)
Net current assets	**20, 575**	**46,841**
Total assets less current liabilities	68,922	113,713
Creditors:		
amounts falling due after more than one year	(116)	(149)
Provisions for liabilities and charges	(554)	(1,079)
Total net assets	?	?
Capital and reserves		
Called up share capital	1,743	1,711
Share premium account[2]	112,950	112,936
Profit and loss account	(113,845)	(70,023)
Other reserves[3]	67,404	67,861
Shareholders' funds	?	?

Notes: 1   All figures in brackets are to be subtracted
         2   The value of shares issued at a premium to the nominal value
         3   Includes merger reserve

Source: lastminute.com Annual Report and Accounts 2002

1 Explain the following terms in relation to lastminute.com:
   a intangible assets
   b tangible assets
   c debtors.   **[6]**
2 Calculate for 2001 and 2002 lastminute.com's:
   a current assets
   b total net assets
   c capital and reserves. **[6]**
3 Why do you think the value of lastminute.com's intangible assets is three times greater than its tangible assets?   **[4]**
4 How might the decline in total net assets in 2002 be explained?   **[4]**
5 How useful is this balance sheet to lastminute.com's different stakeholders?
                               [10]
                       Total: 30 marks

19 Profit and loss account

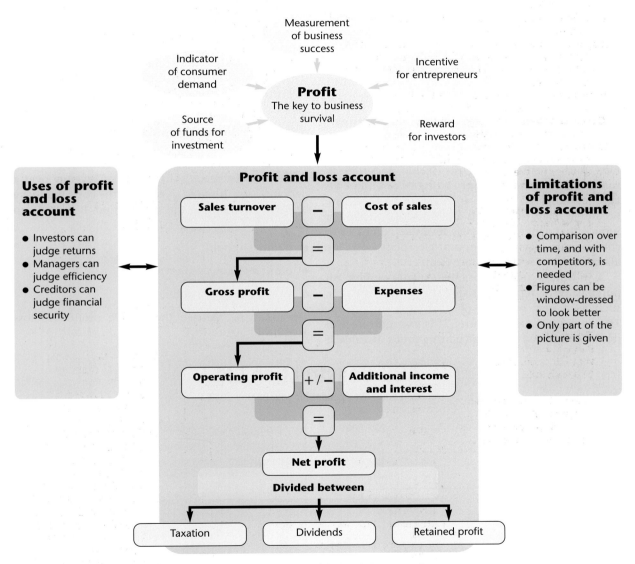

Measurement of business success

Indicator of consumer demand

Incentive for entrepreneurs

Profit
The key to business survival

Source of funds for investment

Reward for investors

Uses of profit and loss account

- Investors can judge returns
- Managers can judge efficiency
- Creditors can judge financial security

Profit and loss account

| Sales turnover | − | Cost of sales |
| = |
| Gross profit | − | Expenses |
| = |
| Operating profit | + / − | Additional income and interest |
| = |
| Net profit |

Divided between

| Taxation | Dividends | Retained profit |

Limitations of profit and loss account

- Comparison over time, and with competitors, is needed
- Figures can be window-dressed to look better
- Only part of the picture is given

 1 **Profit**

Profit is the amount of money left over from sales revenue once all costs have been deducted (see Unit 14). It plays a crucial role in business because it:

- provides an incentive for entrepreneurs to take risks in setting up businesses

- acts as a reward for investors who are willing to provide finance for a business opportunity

- enables businesses to reinvest profits in new equipment or in expansion

- makes it clear that consumer demand is sufficient for businesses to succeed in that market

- acts as a measurement of business success and efficiency.

While, in the short term, a business may be able to make a loss and yet still survive, loss-making businesses will, in the longer term, be forced to close. The resources they use (such as land and labour) will be shifted to other areas of business that can return a profit.

> **Guru's views**
> **'In the state of nature, profit is the measure of right.'**
>
> *Thomas Hobbes, 1651*

2   Capital and revenue expenditure

When calculating profit over a period of time, a business must identify the costs it has incurred in running the business and generating its revenue. This type of costs is known as **revenue expenditure** because it refers to the costs of producing the good or service that generates its sales revenue. Purchases of components, paying wages and electricity costs are all examples of revenue expenditure.

A business may also have spent money on purchasing or replacing fixed assets (see Unit 18), such as a new building or computer equipment. This is **capital expenditure**. This expenditure will not be subtracted when calculating profit, because it

> **Activity**
>
> State whether each of the following is an example of capital or revenue expenditure:
> - salespersons' salaries
> - purchase of a delivery van
> - addition of a refrigerator unit to delivery van
> - purchase of a piece of land for development
> - advertising expenditure
> - purchase of a new office computer.

represents a long-term investment rather than a short-term cost. Instead, a business will include an allowance, called **depreciation**, for the use and deterioration of fixed assets over the period. Depreciation is explained on the page opposite.

3   Profit and loss account

The profit and loss account is the formal accounting statement that records a firm's sales revenue over a period of time (usually a year) and the costs that have been incurred during the same period. It is made up of three sections:

- trading account
- profit and loss account
- appropriation account.

These can be seen in the sample profit and loss account in Figure 19.1.

ABC Construction Ltd

Profit and Loss Account for year ending 2003
£

		£
	Turnover	232,000
(less)	Cost of sales	112,000
=	**Gross profit**	120,000
(less)	Expenses	78,000
=	**Operating profit**	42,000
(plus)	Non-operating income	2,800
(less)	Interest	1,300
=	**Profit on ordinary activities before tax**	
	(net profit)	43,500
(less)	Corporation tax	2,500
=	**Profit on ordinary activities after tax**	41,000
(less)	Dividends	22,000
=	**Retained profit for the period**	19,000

The trading account
Shows revenue from selling products and the costs of making them. What is left is 'gross profit'.

The profit and loss account
Expenses are subtracted from gross profit to produce operating profit. Adjustments for other income and interest lead to net profit.

The appropriation account
Shows how the net profit earned by the business is distributed.

Figure 19.1 The profit and loss account for ABC Construction, year ending 2003

Depreciation

Capital expenditure on fixed assets, such as buildings or equipment, is not considered in a profit and loss account. This is because the expenditure would provide assets that could be used in production over many years and could not all be attributed to the trading of that year.

However, a proportion of the cost of capital expenditure *should* be included in a profit and loss account to represent the cost of using fixed assets during the year. This is known as depreciation.

Depreciation is an estimate of how much of the original value of fixed assets has been used up during the year. It is not an actual expense that the business will have to pay out to anyone during the year. But depreciation must be included in a profit and loss account if the full costs of trading are to be taken into the reckoning. It is also important to reduce the values of assets in the balance sheet to ensure they remain accurate.

Equipment or buildings may fall in value as they are used because:

● they wear out or become damaged

● they may be poorly maintained

● they become out-of-date as technology improves.

There are two main methods of estimating a value for depreciation.

1 **Straight-line method.** This method assumes that each fixed asset loses an equal amount of its value each year. To calculate this, the business needs to know:

– its original value
– its useful life span (in years)
– whether it will have any residual (scrap) value at the end of this life span.

The yearly depreciation expense will then be:

$$\frac{\text{Original value} - \text{Residual value}}{\text{Useful life span (years)}}$$

If a machine originally costs £50,000 and is expected to last four years, with a final scrap value of £2,000, the annual allowance for depreciation will be:

$$\frac{£50,000 - £2000}{4 \text{ years}} = \frac{£48,000}{4} = £12,000 \text{ per year}$$

This is the simplest and most commonly used method in the UK of calculating depreciation. However, it depends on estimates of useful lifespan that may be no more than guesses. In addition, the method is not realistic for some assets (such as vehicles) whose value declines dramatically when they are first used and then much more gradually after that.

2 **Reducing balance method.** This method assumes that assets lose most of their value in the first years of their life and less later on. Depreciation is calculated by reducing the value of an asset by a set percentage each year.

If a £50,000 asset lost 50 per cent of its value in the first year, this would represent depreciation of £25,000. In the second year, with the asset now only worth £25,000 a further 50 per cent fall would equal depreciation of £12,500. Each year, a 50 per cent fall is assumed, but the value that this represents declines.

The percentage chosen to depreciate the asset each year must reduce the value of the asset to its residual value over the expected lifetime. You are not likely to be asked to work out the percentage, but rather to work out the annual depreciation from a given percentage and original value.

As Figure 19.2 illustrates, the reducing balance method will produce higher depreciation values in the early years of an asset's life and lower values in the later years. This is one of the virtues of the method, as it tends to mirror the real decline in the value of assets. On the other hand, it will mean that any new investment incurs a hefty depreciation charge in the profit and loss account in its first year. Because of this, some businesses may think twice about whether to invest at all.

Figure 19.2 Straight line versus reducing balance methods of calculating depreciation

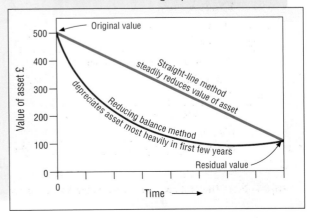

Trading account

The trading account section shows the total value of sales revenue (also known as 'turnover') during the trading period and the direct costs of producing that output. These costs are known as the **cost of sales** (or sometimes 'cost of goods sold').

The sales revenue figure excludes the value of any indirect taxes, such as VAT or duties, because these are handed directly to government rather than being retained as revenue by the business.

The cost of sales figure will include any costs arising directly from the production of those goods that have been sold, such as raw materials, wages or electricity. Costs of producing finished goods that have not yet been sold are *not* included.

To calculate 'cost of sales', it is necessary to identify the value of stock that has been used in production. The value of stock at the start of the year (opening stock) is added to the value of stock that has been purchased during the year. The value of any stock left over at the end of the year (closing stock) is subtracted. What is left is the value of what has actually been used up and sold.

Cost of sales = (Opening stock + Purchases) − Closing stock

For example, if a business begins the year with £5,000 of stock and then purchases a further £10,000 of stock during the year, the combined value of this stock is £15,000. If £3,000 of stock remains at the end of the year, then £12,000 of stock must have been used and sold during the year.

Cost of sales = (£5,000 + £10,000) − £3,000 = £12,000

The cost of sales figure is subtracted from sales revenue to calculate **gross profit**. Gross profit is not yet a good indicator of how much profit the business has made, because only the direct costs of production

---

For example ...

Computers to order

Computertronics is a small company, based in Reading, that builds computers to individual customer specifications. Its profit and loss account for 2002 is shown on the right.

1 Calculate the value of the missing figures.   **[4]**
2 Give **two** possible examples of the types of costs that would be included in Computertronics accounts under the headings of:
  a cost of sales
  b administrative expenses.   **[4]**
3 Why might Computertronics have decided to:
  a pay dividends
  b retain some of its profits?   **[6]**
                           Total 14 marks

Computertronics Ltd – Profit and Loss Account for year ending 31 December 2002

	(£'000)
Sales turnover	1,284
Cost of sales	?
Gross profit	**786**
Expenses:	
Salaries	84
Rent	120
Administrative	24
Depreciation	35
Other	88
Operating profit	**?**
Income from non-trading activities	32
Interest	?
Profit on ordinary activities before tax (Net profit)	**419**
Corporation Tax	88
Profit on ordinary activities after tax	**?**
Dividends	18
Retained profit	**313**

have been subtracted from turnover. But it does show the mark-up the business is achieving on making and selling its product.

Profit and loss account

Confusingly, the second section of the profit and loss account is given the same name as the whole document. The profit and loss account section subtracts expenses from the gross profit figure to produce **operating profit**.

The expenses to be subtracted are all the overheads of running the business. These are the indirect costs that were *not* subtracted under 'cost of sales'. They can include:

- management salaries

- rent

- administration costs

- heating and lighting

- marketing costs

- depreciation.

Depreciation was explained in detail in a separate feature on page 115.

Any additional income from non-trading activities is now added. This may include returns on financial investments (such as dividends or interest) or rent on property that the business owns and lets out to others.

Any interest that the business has had to pay is shown separately and subtracted.

The final figure is called 'profit on ordinary activities before tax' – also known as **net profit**. This profit figure is of crucial interest to a business and its stakeholders. It shows how much profit has been made once all costs have been subtracted.

Appropriation account

The final section of the overall profit and loss account is known as the appropriation account. It shows how the net profit earned by the business is distributed. This may be:

- to the Inland Revenue as taxation. Corporation tax must be paid by all companies making a profit over a certain level.

- to shareholders as dividends. A company is not required to pay out dividends, but may choose to do so to reward shareholders and encourage investors.

- retained within the business for future use, such as capital expenditure or expansion. In a plc's accounts this may be called **transfer to reserves**.

4   Legal requirements

The Companies Act requires all limited companies to produce a profit and loss account each year. Together with the Financial Reporting Standards issued by the Accounting Standards Board, the Act sets out the formats that may be used, what must be included and the supporting information that is required.

Notes to the accounts should include details of:

- depreciation amounts

- directors' earnings

- employee earnings and pension schemes

- auditors' fees.

Companies must provide details of any large 'one-off' expenditures or revenues, known as exceptional items. These costs or incomes that arose from trading and are not expected to recur, such as the failure of a major customer to pay the business – a so-called 'bad debt'

Plcs must publish their accounts, making them available to shareholders and other stakeholders. They will usually display at least the previous year's figures for comparison. Where a large company owns a group of smaller companies, it must produce a consolidated account to show the combined profit and loss of the whole group.

Activity

Using the internet, obtain a profit and loss account for a plc. Identify the company's:
- Turnover
- Gross profit
- Operating profit
- Profit before tax
- Profit after tax
- Retained profit
What does this information tell you about the financial success of the company?

Profit and loss acount

Usefulness

- Shareholders and potential investors will be able to judge the success of the business on the basis of its profitability. They will see how this profit is being used and the returns being provided on their investment.

- Managers will be able to see how well the business is controlling its costs – both the cost of sales and the overheads. They can also see how much profit is being retained, and therefore be able to plan for future growth or new investment.

- Creditors will be able to judge whether the business is in a sound financial state and able to repay its debts.

To interpret a profit and loss account and gain maximum benefit from it requires the use of financial ratios. These are explained in Unit 20.

Limitations

- On its own, a profit and loss account will be of limited value, as the figures it shows need to be compared with previous years' figures and those of other companies. Only then can success or failure be properly judged.

- There is scope, even within accounting guidelines, to 'window dress' the figures in a profit and loss account – that is, to disguise problems and manipulate statistics to create the most favourable impression.

- Financial figures alone do not tell the whole story of a business's performance. Its effect on its stakeholders, the conditions of the market, the future opportunities for the business and threats to it are just as important in making judgments about a business.

Profit and loss account: summary

KEY TERMS

Revenue expenditure – day-to-day costs of consumable items involved in running a business, such as stock, wages or electricity.

Capital expenditure – money spent on fixed assets, such as a new building or computer equipment, that will be used on a long-term basis.

Cost of sales – the value of the direct costs incurred in making the products that are sold.

Gross profit – sales revenue (turnover) minus cost of sales.

Net profit –- equals gross profit plus other income less expenses. Also known as 'profit on ordinary activities before taxation'.

Depreciation – an estimate of the reduction in value of fixed assets over a period of time.

Operating profit – gross profit minus expenses.

Summary questions

1 Why is profit so important?
2 Explain the difference between capital and revenue expenditure.
3 What are the three sections of a profit and loss account?
4 How is gross profit calculated?
5 Calculate the cost of sales if:
   a opening stock = £75,000
   b purchases of stock = £120,000
   c closing stock = £50,000.
6 Explain how net profit is calculated.
7 Why do fixed assets depreciate in value?
8 Explain the difference between the straight line and reducing balance methods of calculating depreciation.
9 What does the appropriation account show?
10 What requirements does the law place on the profit and loss accounts of plcs?
11 In what ways are profit and loss accounts:
   a valuable
   b limited
   in their usefulness to stakeholders?

Exam practice continues ➤

Profit and loss account: summary (continued)

Ryanair profits increase by 44 per cent

Ryanair claimed yesterday that it was Europe's only 'low fares' airline, as it announced a 44 per cent increase in net profits in spite of an 8 per cent fall in average fares.

The results were achieved in the most difficult year the aviation industry has faced in the past decade. It weathered the effects of the sharp global fall in demand for air travel following the September 11 terrorist attacks.

Michael O' Leary, chief executive, said Ryanair was the Wal-Mart among airlines, with the formula of 'piling them high and selling them cheap'. The formula is based on the strictest control of costs. Ryanair does not worry about the revenue side of the balance. It simply lowers the fares to the level needed to fill its aircraft and tries to make sure that as fares fall, costs fall faster. Using low-cost, secondary airports such as Frankfurt Hahn, is crucial to this cost-cutting.

On the back of this success, Mr O'Leary is planning to add more planes, routes and operational bases in the coming years.

Source: *Financial Times*, 11 June 2002

Ryanair Consolidated Profit & Loss Account for the year ended March 31 2002

	2002 €'000	2001 €'000
Total operating revenues	624,050	487,405
minus		
Operating expenses		
Staff costs	(78,240)	(61,222)
Depreciation	(59,010)	(59,175)
Other expenses	(323,867)	(252,997)
Total operating expenses	(461,117)	(373,394)
Operating profit	162,933	114,011
plus		
Other income/(expenses)	9,441	9,377
Profit on ordinary activities before tax (Net profit)	172,374	123,388
minus		
Tax	(21,999)	(18,905)
Profit for the financial year	150,375	104,483

1 Define the terms:
   a consolidated profit and loss account **[2]**
   b net profit. **[2]**
2 How might Ryanair's net profit be used? **[6]**
3 How might Ryanair have calculated its depreciation expense? **[4]**
4 Explain why depreciation is likely to be a major expense on the profit and loss account for an organisation like Ryanair. **[4]**
5 How have Ryanair managed to increase net profits by 44 per cent in a year that was so difficult for the air travel industry? **[7]**
6 How useful is the profit and loss account to Ryanair's stakeholders? **[10]**

Total 35 marks

20 Analysing accounts

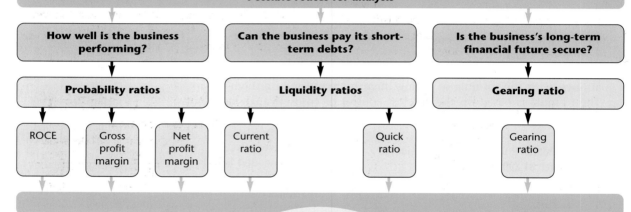

Analysing accounts
What is the question?
Pick out the figures
Calculate
Interpret
Compare

Possible routes for analysis

How well is the business performing?	Can the business pay its short-term debts?	Is the business's long-term financial future secure?
Probability ratios	Liquidity ratios	Gearing ratio
ROCE / Gross profit margin / Net profit margin	Current ratio / Quick ratio	Gearing ratio

Limitations of ratio analysis
Relies on accuracy of accounts
Needs comparisons with other firms
and previous years
Does not consider wider issues

1   Measuring performance

In February 2003 Lloyds TSB declared profits of £2.6 billion, while those for easyJet were £71.6 million. Which company had performed better? MyTravel, the tour operator, reported losses of £73 million in 2002 while Abbey National's losses were around £1.5 billion. What had caused the losses and which company was best placed to reverse its fortunes?

The financial figures in the balance sheet and the profit and loss account seem to pose more questions than they answer. If a stakeholder is to understand what the accounts show about a business, a careful analysis of the figures is required.

In 2002, easyJet's profits were £71.6 million

What stakeholders want to know

How stakeholders analyse the accounts will depend on what they want to find out.

- **How well is the business performing?**
  Managers, shareholders and potential investors will all look to profitability as a measure of business performance. Judgments will need to be made as to whether the level of profit reflects a good performance when compared to previous years and to competitors.

- **Can the business pay its short-term debts?**
  Creditors will be particularly concerned about whether the business has the **liquidity** to repay current liabilities out of its current assets.

- **Is the financial future of the business secure?**
  Employees, investors and creditors will all want to judge whether the funding of the business – its **gearing** – is safe, or whether it is at risk because of an overdependence on borrowed funds.

Guru's views

'The ability to sign a cheque is the least reliable guide to a company's fitness.'

David Plowright

Once the focus for analysis has been chosen, relevant figures must be selected from the accounts. Calculations can then be made that allow the figures to be interpreted and compared. This process is known as 'ratio analysis'.

The most useful way to see how this is done is to use a set of accounts, make the relevant calculations and interpret what these mean. A profit and loss account and a balance sheet for Mulberry's Wine Bars Ltd are shown in Figure 20.1.

STOP & THINK

What are the problems with using just the raw figures shown in Figure 20.1 to judge Mulberry's financial position?

Mulberry's Wine Bars Ltd

Balance sheet

	31 December 2002 (£'000)	31 December 2001 (£'000)
Fixed assets	2,000	1,800
Current assets		
Stocks	900	600
Debtors	150	250
Cash in bank	300	375
	1,250	1,225
Current liabilities		
Trade creditors	450	500
Tax payable	150	125
	600	625
Net current assets (Working capital)	750	600
Total assets less current liabilities	2,750	2,400
Creditors: amounts falling due after 1 year	1,825	1,625
Net assets	**925**	**725**
Capital and reserves		
Ordinary share capital	625	625
Retained profit	300	100
	925	**725**

Mulberry's Wine Bars Ltd

Profit and loss account

Year ending	31 December 2002 (£'000)	31 December 2001 (£'000)
Turnover	1,600	1,290
Cost of sales	400	430
Gross profit	1,200	860
Expenses	800	640
Operating profit	400	220
Non operating income	150	100
Profit on ordinary activities before tax and interest (Net profit)	550	320
Interest	50	50
Tax	150	70
Net profit after tax	350	200
Dividends	150	100
Retained profit	200	100

Figure 20.1 Accounts for Mulberry's Wine Bars Ltd

3 ## Profitability ratios

Ratios that indicate the degree of profitability fall into two categories: return on capital employed and gross and net profit margins.

Return on capital employed

The most useful indicator of how well a business has performed is the return on capital employed (**ROCE**). This ratio compares the profit made in a year to the size of the business, as shown by the value of the funds invested in it. In this way, it highlights the return of invested funds and the significance of the level of profit relative to the size of the business.

ROCE is calculated as:

$$\frac{\text{Operating profit}}{\text{Capital employed}} \times 100 = \% \text{ ROCE}$$

The figure for operating profit is taken from the profit and loss account. For Mulberry's in 2002 this was £400,000, as shown in Figure 20.1.

Capital employed is the value of shareholders' funds together with any long-term liabilities. This is shown in the balance sheet as 'Total assets less current liabilities' and represents all the long-term funds that the business has used to make its profit. For Mulberry's in 2002 this figure is £2,750,000.

ROCE for Mulberry's in 2002 is therefore:

$$\frac{£400,000}{£2,750,000} \times 100 = 15\%$$

A figure of 15 per cent means that for every £1 of funds used by Mulberry's, 15p profit has been earned. Some of this will have to be paid in tax, some may be paid in dividends and some may be retained. Nevertheless it indicates a return on funds borrowed or invested, so the higher the ROCE the better.

To know whether 15 per cent indicates a good performance, the business must:

● compare it to the previous year's ROCE to see if it has increased

● compare it to its competitors' performance to see if it is higher than their ROCE

● compare it to rates of interest that funds could have earned in bank or building society accounts. Unless it is higher than these, funds could have been more profitably invested elsewhere.

Gross and net profit margins

To help a business understand how and why it earned the profit it did, it can examine its profit and loss account more closely. This will show managers and investors what type of costs the business has had to pay and how much gross and net profit left were from the sales turnover. A profit margin expresses the level of profit *as a proportion of* the original sales turnover.

Gross profit margin is calculated as:

$$\frac{\text{Gross profit}}{\text{Sales turnover}} \times 100 = \% \text{ Gross profit margin}$$

For Mulberry's in 2002 this was:

$$\frac{£1,200,000}{£1,600,000} \times 100 = 75\% \text{ Gross profit margin}$$

Net profit margin is calculated as:

$$\frac{\text{Net profit}}{\text{Sales turnover}} \times 100 = \% \text{ Net profit margin}$$

For Mulberry's in 2002 this was:

$$\frac{£550,000}{£1,600,000} \times 100 = 34\% \text{ Net profit margin}$$

The higher a profit margin the better, because this would show that a bigger proportion of sales turnover is being made as profit and less is being paid out as costs.

The **gross profit margin** shows what proportion of turnover is left after the direct costs of production have been paid. A figure of 75 per cent shows that only 25 per cent of the turnover has had to be spent on the cost of sales – the selling price is four times greater than the direct cost of making the product.

Although higher is better, the main determinant of a gross profit margin will be the type of industry that the business operates in. In some industries, such as food retailing, the costs of buying stocks are high, so gross profit margins are typically low. In other industries, such as air travel, the cost of taking each passenger on each flight is only a very small proportion of the ticket price. Gross profit margins will therefore be high. To judge how impressive the figure of 75 per cent is, Mulberry's will have to compare it with figures for:

● competitor businesses

● its own business in previous years.

The **net profit margin** shows what proportion of turnover is left after all costs, including overheads, have been deducted. A figure of 31 per cent shows that out of every £1 sales revenue, 31p is left as net profit. Once again, this figure needs to be compared with competitors and with previous years. A higher net profit margin would be preferable.

Given that 75p in every £1 was left as gross profit, to produce a 31 per cent net profit margin a further 44p in every £1 must have been spent on overheads. Overheads therefore make up a bigger proportion of the business's costs than the cost of sales. This might reflect the nature of the industry, or it might indicate that the business has a problem in controlling its overheads. Comparisons of each type of expense over time will help to determine whether it is a growing problem for the business.

 4   Liquidity ratios

Liquidity is how much possible cash a business can raise. It can be measured by the 'current ratio' and the 'quick' ratio. (See unit 15.)

Current ratio

The **current ratio** shows whether a business has sufficient current assets to cover all of its current liabilities. This is known as the liquidity of the business, as it indicates whether the business has sufficient assets in cash (the most liquid of all assets) and in stock or debtors that could soon be turned into cash. A business that cannot pay its current liabilities may be forced to close.

The information needed by a business to calculate liquidity ratios is found on its balance sheet.

$$\frac{\text{Current assets}}{\text{Current liabilities}} = \text{Current ratio (expressed as } x:1)$$

For Mulberry's in 2002, the current ratio is:

$$\frac{£1,350,000}{£600,000} = 2.25:1 \text{ Current ratio}$$

A current ratio of 2.25 : 1 means that for every £1 of current liabilities, the business has £2.25 of current assets. Mulberry's has a significant, positive working capital that would allow it to pay off its current liabilities two-and-a-quarter times over.

A guideline for the ideal current ratio is between 1.5 : 1 and 2 : 1. If the current ratio were less than 1 : 1, a firm could not pay all its current liabilities should it need to do so. Given that some of the current assets – in the form of stock and debtors – might not be easily turned into cash, and current liabilities may turn out to be higher than expected, a current ratio of less than 1.5 : 1 is potentially risky. Despite this, many large companies get away with low current ratios – many less than 1 : 1 – because they can use their size

and influence to avoid having to pay all their current liabilities at any one time.

On the other hand, a ratio above 2 : 1 suggests that too many of the business's assets are in the form of cash, stock or debtors. These are unlikely to gain much interest and so represent an unproductive use of the business's resources. Mulberry's current ratio of 2.25 : 1 means that some of its current assets could be switched into fixed assets to make a more profitable use of them, reducing the current ratio to below 2 : 1.

Quick (acid test) ratio

The **quick ratio**, or acid test ratio as it is often known, is a further, tougher test of liquidity. Given that stock is not easily converted into cash and so may not prove a very liquid current asset, it is excluded from the quick ratio. The quick ratio shows whether current liabilities can be paid from the most liquid of current assets: cash and debtors. It is calculated as follows:

$$\frac{(\text{Current assets} - \text{Stock})}{\text{Current Liabilities}} = \text{Quick (acid test) ratio } (x:1)$$

For Mulberry's in 2002 the quick ratio is:

$$\frac{(£1,350 - 900)}{£600} = \frac{450}{600} = 0.75:1$$

Once again, the result is examined to judge whether the business is able to pay off its current debts out of its liquid assets. A ratio of 1 : 1 is considered the ideal for the quick ratio, because it allows the business to pay its creditors solely from cash and debtors, without relying on converting stocks into cash.

Mulberry's 0.75 : 1 is potentially risky, with only 75p of liquid assets to cover every £1 of current liabilities. This is in contrast to its current ratio, which suggested Mulberry's had too many current assets. How has this happened? The problem lies with its stocks – worth £900,000. These very high stock levels are tying up financial resources that could be more productively used elsewhere. But they have also left the organisation unable to pay its current debts from its most liquid assets – cash and debtors. The business should seek to convert some of this stock into higher cash holdings and some into fixed assets. As with the current ratio, however, many larger businesses survive on ratios much lower than this 'ideal'.

> **Guru's views**
> 'Revenue is vanity...margin is sanity...cash is king.'
>
> *Unknown*

5   Gearing

Gearing shows the proportion of a business's funds that have come from long-term borrowing rather than from share capital and reserves. This then indicates how risky investment in this business will be, and the higher the level of debt the greater the risk. A business that has borrowed a high proportion of its funds is more at risk from higher interest rates, as it will be more affected by higher interest payments. Moreover, if sales are falling – due to a recession or increased competition – a firm will find it very difficult to make a profit given that interest payments must be maintained. So the risk of insolvency is much greater where gearing is high.

It is the balance sheet that contains the vital information to calculate gearing.

$$\frac{\text{Long-term liabilities}}{\text{Capital employed}} \times 100 = \% \text{ Gearing}$$

Long-term liabilities are those described as 'Creditors falling due after 1 year' in Mulberry's balance sheet in Figure 20.1. Capital employed is the value of all long-term funds used by the business, shown as 'Total assets less current liabilities'.

For Mulberry's in 2002 the Gearing ratio is:

$$\frac{£1,825,000}{£2,750,000} \times 100 = 66\% \text{ Gearing}$$

A business with a gearing ratio of more than 50 per cent is said to be 'highly geared', one with less than 50 per cent 'low geared'. Highly geared means that a high proportion of the organisation's funds have been borrowed, and as a result the risk level is higher. At 66 per cent, Mulberry's gearing is considered high and it may find it difficult to raise further funds through borrowing.

On the other hand, it may have used borrowing to raise money, rather than dilute the ownership of the business by bringing more share capital into the business. Borrowing could also have been used to improve profitability through expansion. These can be seen as strengths of high gearing. Low gearing is certainly safer, but could be the result of an unambitious growth strategy. High gearing can swell earnings for shareholders very effectively.

Activity

Using Mulberry's accounts for 2001 in Figure 20.1, recalculate each of the ratios and compare them to the results for 2002. Explain how these have changed and comment on what this shows about the performance and financial position of the business over the two-year period.

Limitations to ratio analysis

Although the different types of ratio analysis described can provide valuable information about a business, the methods have their limitations.

The accuracy and relevance of the ratios will depend on how reliable and up to date are the figures being used. It was recognised in Units 18 and 19 that the balance sheet and the profit and loss account can be 'window dressed' to look more favourable. If so, the analysis using ratios will suffer as well.

The results calculated often mean very little on their own. They need to be compared with previous years and with other similar firms to understand what they show about the performance and financial position of the business.

Even after comparisons have been made, the figures fail to show the context in which they have been achieved. Other factors, such as the state of the economy, trends in consumer spending and the level of competition, all need to be taken into account. Information from other sources, such as the chairman's report, also need to be considered.

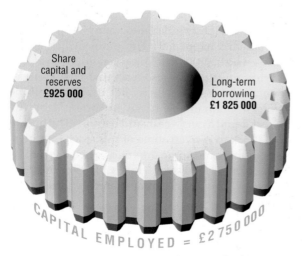

Gearing = 66%

Figure 20.2 Gearing for Mulberry's Wine Bars Ltd

Analysing accounts: summary

Summary questions

1 What **three** key questions does ratio analysis help to answer?
2 What **two** financial documents are needed to carry out ratio analysis?
3 Why is ROCE the most useful indicator of how well a business has performed?
4 How should a business interpret an ROCE of 5 per cent?
5 What is a profit margin?
6 Why will businesses in some industries achieve lower gross profit margins than others?
7 What could cause a net profit margin to be low even though the gross profit margin was high?
8 Why is a current ratio of 1.5 : 1 considered ideal?
9 How does the quick ratio differ from the current ratio?
10 What does it mean for a business to be 'highly geared'?
11 Why is low gearing not necessarily preferable to high gearing?
12 In what ways is the usefulness of ratio analysis limited?

Exam practice

Margin of success for clothing retailers

A dramatic increase in gross profit margins at Burberry, the luxury brand famous for its check-lined raincoats, highlights a trend among fashion retailers. Burberry revealed that it had increased its gross profit margin to 55.7 per cent in the first half of this year, from 47.8 per cent the year before.

Other clothing retailers have achieved similar improvements through a variety of strategies. Marks & Spencer's decision to move production away from the UK two years ago enabled it to add between six and seven percentage points in terms of gross margin. Retailers have also driven down their purchasing prices by using fewer, more flexible suppliers who can design, make and supply products far more swiftly in response to customer demand. This helps margins by reducing the need for retailers to discount their products in an attempt to sell unwanted stocks. Finally, quality, image and branding have all helped to justify higher price premiums on the clothes they sell.

This is a world away from the 'pile 'em high. sell 'em cheap' techniques of Britain's big super-market chains, whose profit margins fall each year. Their gross profit margins hover around the 25 per cent mark, while their operating (net profit) margins are far lower – Tesco's, the market leader, is around only 6.1 per cent. And yet the supermarkets do not appear to be overly

Operating margins
Operating profit as a proportion of sales

Burberry	17.1%
French Connection	11.2%
Austin Reed	7.9%
Arcadia	7.4%
Tesco	6.1%
Safeway	4.6%
J Sainsbury	3.5%

Gross margins
Gross profit as a proportion of sales

Arcadia	51.5%
Burberry (*interim*)	55.7%
Austin Reed	55.0%
French Connection	52.0%

concerned with chasing higher margins. For them, the main goal is higher sales and greater market share, and their strategy to achieve it often involves aggressive pricing policies. Supermarkets achieve their 'return on capital' through higher turnover rather than higher margins.

Source: *The Times*, 20 November 2002

1 Define the terms:
   a gross profit margin
   b return on capital.   [4]
3 Why is Burberry's operating margin so much lower than its gross profit margin?   [4]
4 Explain why clothing retailers are able to achieve higher gross profit margins than supermarkets?   [6]
5 Explain the meaning of the sentence 'Supermarkets achieve their return on capital through higher turnover rather than higher margins.'   [6]
6 How useful are profitability ratios in assessing the financial position of a business?   [10]

Total 30 marks

21 Making investment decisions

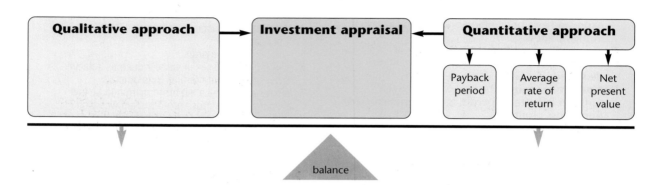

1 Investment and risk

Businesses make capital investments all the time. But, because finance is limited, they often have to choose between different investments. For instance, a business may have to choose:

- between two alternative production locations
- to launch one product rather than another
- to purchase one machine rather than another.

Capital investment is, by its very nature, risky. It is usually expensive, meaning that potential losses are high. It is often long term, making forecasting difficult, and it is usually at least semi-permanent. Take, for example, building new production facilities. This will almost certainly be expensive, it may take a year or more to complete and, by the time it is complete, market conditions may have changed – hence it is risky. Once complete, the builing may not be easy for the business to sell if the facility is no longer required. Therefore the decision is, to some extent, permanent.

Because of the risk and expense involved in capital investment, a range of techniques, which we collectively referred to as 'investment appraisal', has been developed to help businesses evaluate investment decisions.

2 Payback method

The simplest form of investment appraisal is the payback method. This measures how long an investment takes to pay back its original investment. A business comparing investments would choose the project with the shortest payback period.

Example 1

Investment	Launching a new product
Cost	£1,000,000
Expected returns	Year 1– £250,000
	Year 2 – £250,000
	Year 3 – £250,000
	Year 4 – £250,000

£250,000 + £250,000 + £250,000 + £250,000 = **£1,000,000**

The project has a **payback period of 4 years**.

Things will not, however, always be that simple! Payback will usually occur at some point *during* a year. It is then necessary to calculate both the year and month of payback.

Example 2

Investment	New production facility
Cost	£300,000
Expected returns	Year 1– £100,000
	Year 2 – £100,000
	Year 3 – £150,000
	Year 4 – £240,000

£100,000 + £100,000 + £150,000 = **£350,000**

The investment clearly pays back its original investment in the third year, but by the end of the third year £50,000 more has been generated than is needed.

To work out the month of payback, the following formula is used:

$$\text{Month of payback} = \frac{\text{Income required}}{\text{Contribution per month}}$$

Income required at the end of year 2 is £100,000 (the difference between the amount already paid back at the end of Year 2, £200,000, and the amount required, £300,000).

Contribution per month is calculated by dividing the income during the year by 12:

$$\frac{£150,000}{12} = £12,500 \text{ per month}$$

Therefore

$$\text{Month of payback} = \frac{\text{Income required}}{\text{Contribution per month}}$$

$$= \frac{£100,000}{£12,500}$$

$$= \textbf{8 months}$$

The investment has a **payback period of 2 years 8 months**.

It is important to note that what happens after an investment has repaid its original outlay is ignored. Based solely on the payback method, a profitable investment would be rejected in favour of one with a shorter payback period, even if total received were less. For instance, in Example 3, Project 24 would be favoured. For this reason, the payback method is often used alongside other methods of investment appraisal.

Example 3

	Payback	Total income generated
Project 24	2 years	£1,000,000
Project 7	3 years 3 months	£2,000,000

Payback method

Advantages

- easy to calculate
- takes into account cost of investment
- focuses on short-term cash flow (a business might want to know how quickly new IT equipment will pay for itself, as it is likely to have a very short useful life).

Disadvantages

- ignores the overall return on a project
- ignores the time value of money
- encourages a short-term approach (an investment with a longer payback period may actually be more profitable for the business).

Activity

Use the following information to calculate the payback period for this investment:

Investment	Extension to factory
Cost	£500,000
Expected returns	Year 1 – £100,000
	Year 2 – £100,000
	Year 3 – £150,000
	Year 4 – £240,000

Average rate of return (ARR)

The **average rate of return (ARR)** method measures the average annual income of a project as a percentage of the total investment cost. This allows businesses to compare the average income from different projects and to see which gives the best percentage return on its initial outlay (the cost of the project).

The formula used is:

$$\text{ARR} = \frac{\text{Average annual return}}{\text{Initial outlay}} \times 100$$

Example

Investment	Extension to factory
Initial outlay (cost)	£200,000
Expected returns	Year 1 – £100,000
	Year 2 – £100,000
	Year 3 – £100,000
	Year 4 – £100,000

Average annual return is calculated by dividing the total profit from an investment by the number of years over which that profit is earned:

£100,000 + £100,000 + £100,000 + £100,000 = **£400,000**

Net profit = Total income – Initial outlay = £400,000 – £200,000 = **£200,000**

£400,000 – £200,000 (Initial outlay) = **net profit**

$$\text{Average annual profit} = \frac{£200,000}{4 \text{ years}} = \textbf{£50,000}$$

$$\text{ARR} = \frac{\text{Average annual profit}}{\text{Initial outlay}} \times 100 = \frac{£50,000}{£200,000} = \textbf{25\%}$$

Once calculated, the percentage return of one investment can be compared with the percentage return of other investments. Investment with higher ARRs will

For example ...

Food for thought

A food company is considering launching a new product, and has to choose between two possibilities. For secrecy's sake, the products have been given codenames.

	Product Egg	Product Chicken
Initial outlay	(£100,000)	(£125,000)
Projected income		
Year 1	£50,000	£20,000
Year 2	£50,000	£30,000
Year 3	£40,000	£50,000
Year 4	£30,000	£60,000

1 Carry out an investment appraisal on the two potential investments, using payback period and ARR, and decide which product should be launched. Justify your answer.   **14 marks**

be preferred. However, where the ARR is very low the investment might be rejected in favour of an alternative investment, such as a high-interest bank account. ARR can therefore be used to compare investments and to set a lower limit on expected returns below which a business would reject all investments.

ARR focuses on the overall profitability of an investment, but ignores the timing of cash flows. The quicker a project pays back its initial outlay, the lower the risk. ARR ignores this fact. A project with a high ARR but a long payback period would be favoured over a quick payback period and a lower ARR.

As the example at the top of page 141 shows, based solely on the ARR method, project 7 would be chosen.

Average rate of return (ARR) method

Advantages

- measures profitability
- easy to compare percentage returns against other investments
- considers total revenue.

Disadvantages

- ignores the timing of cash flows
- ignores the time value of money
- ignores the risk factor of having a long payback period.

Example

	Payback	ARR
Project 24	2 years	19%
Project 7	3 years 3 months	25%

 Discounted cash flow

The payback period and ARR methods of investment appraisal do not consider the impact of time and its effect on the value of money. The length of time over which investment returns are made affects the true value of those returns.

For a start, inflation (see unit 40) erodes the value of money. A pound (£1) today is worth more than it will be in five, ten or fifteen year's time. What you can buy today with a pound may well cost two pounds in five years time. From an investment point of view £100,000 received today is worth more than £100,000 received in five years time.

Added to this is the opportunity cost of investing. If interest rates are 5 per cent then £50,000 left in a bank would increase to £63,814 over five years. As shown with ARR, any investment must better the potential return from merely investing money in the bank. It can also be seen that £50,000 kept 'under a mattress' will effectively decrease in value over that

Example

The projected future revenue is multiplied by the relevant discount factor (in this case 6 per cent).

Discount factor
Year 1 – 0 .94
Year 2 – 0.89
Year 3 – 0.84
Year 4 – 0.79

Option	Relaunch	Discount factor	Discounted cash flow
Initial Cost	(£250,000)		
Projected revenues			
Year 1	£100,000	× 0.94	£94,000
Year 2	£100,000	× 0.89	£89,000
Year 3	£125,000	× 0.84	£105,000
Year 4	£150,000	× 0.79	£118,500
Total income	**£475,000**		**£406,500**

The discounted income (i.e. expressed in its relative value today) is £406,500.

period. No interest will be earned over that period and inflation will erode its purchasing power – its relative value has therefore fallen.

For a business this means that the money it receives from an investment in future years will not have the same value as it does today.

Receiving £1m from an investment in five years might sound good, but how much will £1m *really* be worth in five year's time, relative to its value today? A business must consider whether to risk investing the money now or whether it will be better just to put the money into a bank account.

At a simple level, to determine the true value of investment returns over their life, interest rates are used to calculate a **discounting** factor. Future returns from an investment are discounted (reduced) according to predicted interest rates for the years ahead. In practice, firms often use discounting factors over and above the rate of interest. This is done to take account of the level of risk involved and the potential returns of other, perhaps safer, investments.

Once discounted income is known a business can calculate the **net present value (NPV)** of an investment. This compares the discounted income against the cost of the project:

Total income	£406,500
Initial cost	(£250,000)
Net present value	£156,500

At today's values, the project returns £156,500. When comparing investments the project with the highest NPV will be chosen. Where the money being spent today is greater than the net present value of the money being returned the project would be rejected. In this case, £250,000 has to be spent to generate just £156,500 (in today's terms) the investment would therefore be rejected.

 Other investment considerations

When conducting investment appraisal, a business will take into account **qualitative** data as well as **quantitative** data. Profitable investments may be rejected in favour of less profitable ones for a variety of qualitative reasons:

● **Corporate objectives.** Which investment most closely suits corporate objectives? Are profit objectives long-term or short-term? A firm with long-term profit horizons may consider investments with long payback periods, whereas a business facing a cash flow crisis may prefer shorter payback periods.

Discounting: NPV method

Advantages

- Considers the effect of inflation
- Considers all cash inflows

Disadvantages

- Complex to calculate
- Cannot compare projects with different initial costs

For example ...

Magazine Makeover

A publisher is considering whether to relaunch its most popular magazine. The magazine is aimed at teenage girls and has enjoyed great success. It has a loyal subscriber base and has been popular for a number of years. Recently though, competition in the market has increased and sales have started to decline. The company is considering two options.

Option 1: A complete relaunch, with the magazine renamed, redesigned and rebranded. The content remains similar, but upgraded to appeal to a wider age range.

Option 2: The magazine undergoes a makeover. It would keep its current title and content would remain virtually unchanged. The style of the magazine would be changed to reflect a more modern design.

The following investment information has been drawn up.

Discount rate – 10%

Discount factor
Year 1 – 0.91
Year 2 – 0.83
Year 3 – 0.75
Year 4 – 0.68

Option	Relaunch	Makeover
Initial cost	(£150,000)	(£50,000)
Projected Revenues		
Year 1	£45,500	£27,300
Year 2	£41,500	£20,750
Year 3	£37,500	£12,750
Year 4	£34,000	£8,840

(If you have ICT equipment available to you, see if you can attempt this activity using a spreadsheet package. It will make the maths much easier and will allow you to consider 'what if' scenarios. For example, try changing the discount factor.)

1 Calculate the net present value of each option. [12]
2 Suggest which option you think the publisher should choose. Justify your answer. [8]

Total 20 marks

- **Corporate image.** A business will consider how an investment project will affect its overall image and brand (for example, it would be unwise for Ferrari to invest in speed camera manufacture!).

- **Human factors.** A business may reject an investment simply because it is not favoured by management. The opinions of staff, the need for staff training and the effect on workplace culture may all be taken into account.

- **Risk.** The degree of risk a business is willing to take might affect investment decisions. Virgin is willing to take risks, whereas, Marks & Spencer has traditionally avoided risk.

- **Operations.** Which investment most suits current production capacity? What effect will the investment have on current production? Will quality standards be maintained? A business may have close links with its currents suppliers and be reluctant to trade with new suppliers.

- **State of the economy** – The current state of the economy and economic forecasts will have a big effect on investments. If economic conditions are difficult (such as those faced in early 2003) a business is unlikely to invest heavily.

Making investment decisions: summary

KEY TERMS

Average rate of return (AAR) – a measure of the net return of an investment per annum as a percentage of the original outlay.

Discounting – the process of reducing future cash inflows to account for the time value of money. The discount factor is used to reduce the value of the cash inflow such that it is expressed relative to its actual value in current terms.

Interest rate – the cost of borrowing money or the return on money deposited in a bank.

Net present value (NPV) – the total return of an investment expressed in current terms (total discounted cash inflow less initial investment).

Qualitative – based on subjective data (opinions, feelings, qualities, hunches).

Quantitative – investment considerations based on the opinions, feelings, hunches attitudes and opinions of an individual, or as a result of broader qualitative research.

Summary questions

1 What is meant by 'investment appraisal'?
2 Distinguish between quantitative and qualitative investment appraisal information. Provide examples.
3 How is payback period calculated?
4 Outline the drawbacks of using payback period for investment appraisal.
5 How is average rate of return (ARR) calculated?
6 When might ARR be used as the prime method of investment appraisal?
7 State **two** drawbacks of using ARR.
8 What does the phrase 'time value of money' mean?
9 How are the discount factors used in net present value (NPV) arrived at?
10 How is NPV calculated?
11 Consider the following data:

Investment	Machine One	Machine Two
Payback	2 years	2.5 years
NPV	+£15,000	+£16,000

On purely **quantitative** grounds, which investment would you choose? Justify your answer.

12 Outline **three** qualitative factors a firm might consider when choosing to relocate its factory to one of two new locations.

Exam practice

Tricky decision

Trick-Audio Ltd is a manufacturer of high end home audio products. The speakers are made in the UK and are sold mainly in Europe and Asia. They sell at premium prices.

To compete with Asian suppliers, Trick-Audio is considering purchasing new machinery that will lower production costs. The machine will also increase Trick-Audio's total capacity, enabling it to sell more products. Some staff training will be required, and installation will cause disruption to current production.

Staff at Trick-Audio tend to be highly skilled, and most have been with the company since it was started in 1990. They are reasonably well paid by industry standards, but some have been attracted away by higher salaries in a local engineering business.

Management see the new machine as a way of helping the company to move out of its current niche market.

Investment in new machinery by Trick-Audio Ltd

Year	Cost of buying machinery (£)	Cash inflows (£)
0	50,000	0
1	0	25,000
2	0	20,000
3	0	15,000
4	0	10,000
5	0	10,000

Discount factors:

Year 0	1.00
Year 1	0.96
Year 2	0.91
Year 3	0.86
Year 4	0.81
Year 5	0.76

1 Calculate the payback period for the new machine. Show your workings. **[3]**
2 Examine why Trick-Audio may not wish to base its investment decision solely on the payback period. **[5]**
3 Calculate the net present value of the investment decision. Show your workings. **[7]**
4 Considering both quantitative and qualitative information, analyse whether Trick-Audio should purchase the machinery. **[12]**

Total 27 marks

Getting the grade: Accounting and finance

THE finance component of most AS syllabuses is relatively short. You should not make the mistake, though, of thinking that this makes it is any less important.

Finance is many students favourite topic because a correct answer gets full marks – something that is often difficult to achieve with written responses. Though many students would prefer to give a written answer rather than 'dust off' their calculators!

When examining financial issues and revising finance consider the following:

Don't be scared

Love it or loathe it, the financial content of AS Business Studies is not that difficult. If you do find it difficult you must, however, give it more of your time. If you can do basic sums you can 'do' finance. If you approach it logically, slowly and don't give up then you ought to be able to get it. Get plenty of practice and if you do find it difficult don't avoid the issue – ask for help.

Have a go

Above all you must be willing to have a go at finance questions. Even if you get the answer wrong you may well pick up valuable marks for your method. Remember that examiners apply the 'own figure' rule – you can still get good marks even if your financial answer is wrong, but your analysis is right according to *your* answer. Missing these questions out entirely will not get you a top grade.

For what audience

If you are presented with a set of figures in the exam, consider for whom they have been prepared.

● Are they internal figures?

● Are they taken from published accounts?

● Might they have been 'window dressed' (altered to suit company aims)?

Other data

Always consider what other data may be required to make an accurate decision.

● Is it possible to compare performance over time or against other businesses?

● Would having this information help your analysis?

As with all topics remember to consider finance within context – considering other data (or making reference to the lack of it) will allow you to build up a better picture of this context.

And so what ...

Ultimately most financial data is not the answer in itself – it is the prompt for other questions. You need to consider:

● What the figures show?

● What they don't show?

● What might be the cause

● What might the solutions be?

The big picture

Treat all the topics within finance as an integrated whole. How will one financial decision impact on other elements of finance? Remember that profitable businesses can still face cash flow problems.

● Is the cash flow position strong enough to support expansion?

● How high is gearing?

● Consider the long-term impact of financial decisions.

● Sale and leaseback may seem to be the best short-term decision, but what about the long-term?

The key is to think about the big picture, don't treat figures in isolation.

The bigger picture

Financial decisions must be taken in the light of other business issues and the qualitative side of a financial decision may be more important than overall profitability. Lowering the breakeven point by cutting staff may make financial sense, but what about the impact on motivation and morale? A particular investment may seem ideal from a boardroom perspective, but do staff have the required training to implement the decision?

A good mark on financial questions can make a real difference. Remember that financial information and other numerical data may be present in all your exam papers. Most business decisions will be taken with at least one eye on finance, make sure that your answers pay the same respect to this important topic.

Section 4

People in organisations

What is the difference between managing and leading?

Why do motivation theories have their limitations?

How does motivation work in the real world?

How do you make sure you appoint the right people and keep them?

Why is corporate culture important?

What makes for effective communication?

What is organisational structure?

How do you plan your workforce to meet your future needs?

22 Organisational design

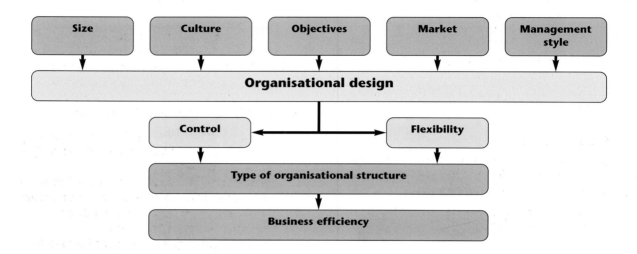

1 Organisation charts

Next plc, the high-street retailer, employs over 24,000 people. Such a large and complex organisation requires good organisational design. 'Organisational design' refers to the formal and logical way that an organisation is managed. The foundation for efficient business operations is good organisational design.

To represent organisation design, many businesses produce **organisational charts**. An organisation chart shows, in pictorial form, the structure of a business. An example is shown in Figure 22.1.

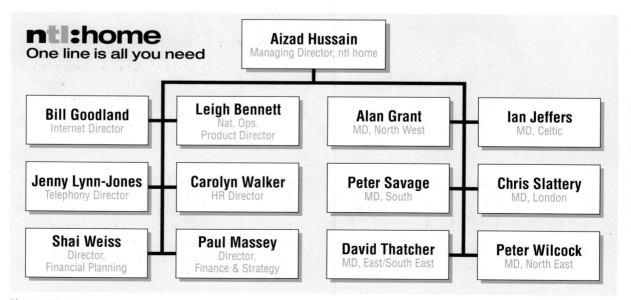

Figure 22.1 An organisation chart

Organisational charts

Advantages

- The preparation of an organisation chart requires detailed consideration of organisation design.
- Formal relationships between different employees and departments can be highlighted.
- They are a useful source of information for new recruits, highlighting position, responsibilities and lines of authority.
- They provide a useful starting point for changing organisation design.
- They can highlight potential communications problems.

Disadvantages

- They present a static picture (the organisational structure is likely to change regularly).
- They do not show 'informal' relationships.
- Large and complex organisations can be difficult to represent.

As with many business tools, simply producing an organisational chart is not enough. Organisation charts must be seen as working business documents used to support analysis of business efficiency.

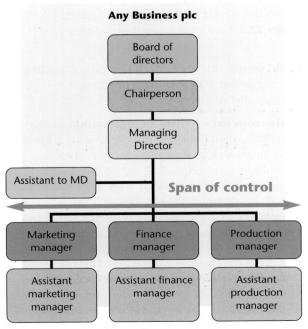

Figure 22.2 Span of control

2 Principles of organisational structure

Organisational charts allow managers to consider a number of important issues.

- **Hierarchy.** A general term used to refer to the number of levels within an organisation. A 'hierarchical' organisation will have many levels of management.

- **Authority and responsibility.** An organisation chart will show areas of responsibility (for example, marketing manager) and lines of authority (a marketing assistant will be accountable to the marketing manager). Several different types of authority exist:

  - *Line authority*. This is straightforward authority as illustrated above. A subordinate will report directly to his or her line manager.
  - *Staff authority*. A manager has the authority to advise members of other departments. Personnel managers usually have the authority to advise staff and managers in all other departments.
  - *Functional authority*. Business specialists have the authority to make departmental managers accept their decisions. For instance, finance managers might be able to veto (prevent) a sales manager making a stock purchase.

- **Span of control.** The number of subordinates reporting to a manager is known as the **span of control**. According to business theorists, the ideal span of control ranges from five to eight (see Figure 22.2).

STOP & THINK

What is your Business Studies teacher's span of control in relation to your class? What would be the benefits if it were smaller? What problems might arise if this span of control were doubled?

- **Chain of command.** The hierarchy – number of levels in an organisation – represents the chain of command (see Figure 22.4). An instruction will be passed up or down the chain of command through the hierarchy. Shorter chains of command result in faster and more efficient internal communications.

Wide span of control	Narrow span of control
Manager may lose personal contact with subordinates	'Tall' organisations with many levels of hierarchy may suffer high administration costs
Manager may lose control over group	Long chain of command means a lengthy communication process
Subgroups (with unofficial leaders) may emerge	Tight supervision may be required in low-skilled, part-time work or where strict quality standards must be met
Too much supervision might be resented by staff	
Managers may find it difficult to monitor the quality of individuals' work	
Increased possibility for delegation may be motivating for subordinates	
Training and supervision may suffer, leading to low motivation among staff	

Figure 22.3 The problem of wide or narrow spans of control

As shown in Figure 22.5, a tall organisation structure has a long chain of command and narrow span of control. A flat structure has a broader span of control and shorter chain of command. The advantages and disadvantages of each structure are listed in Figure 22.3. The 'correct' structure for a business will depend on the size, type and culture of the business.

- **Delegation.** A manager may **delegate** (pass down) the *authority* to complete a task, but *responsibility* for the completion of the task remains with the manager. A finance director might delegate budgetary control to a finance manager, but the director would be ultimately

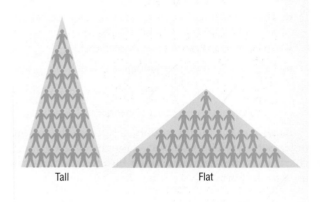

Figure 22.5 Tall and flat organisation structures

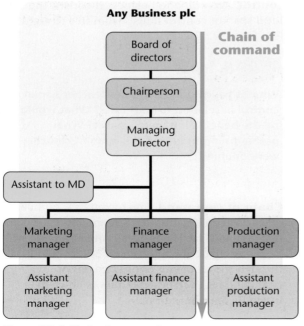

Figure 22.4 Chain of command

responsible for the budget. Delegation can help to empower staff and may contribute to improved motivation.

- **Bureaucracy.** Where an organisation closely follows rules, policies and systems, this is known as 'bureaucracy'. Bureaucracy often involves multiple form-filling and tight control over authority – a decision may have to be given the 'OK' by several managers, before it can be implemented. Bureaucracy is usually found in large organisations with tall hierarchies. It often results from senior managers wanting to retain control over large organisations. Decision-making tends to be slow and the corporate culture quite formal. Marks & Spencer underwent a major reorganisation during the late 1990s and early 2000s to eliminate excessive bureaucracy.

- **De-layering**. The removal of one or more levels of hierarchy from the structure of an organisation is called de-layering. This may mean simply the reorganisation of the business, or it may involve **downsizing** – that is, making some jobs redundant. Fewer levels of hierarchy can help to improve communication (see Unit 23), remove bureaucracy and reduce overhead costs. De-layering can, however, lead to the problems associated with wide spans of control discussed earlier.

> **Guru's views**
> 'There are two types of business – the quick and the dead.'
>
> *Unknown*

Activity

Task 1
Draw an organisational chart to represent the business described here.
The business has four levels of hierarchy. The managing director has a span of control of four. Each of the four functional directors controls a supervisory team of two per function. Functional supervisors are jointly responsible for ten staff per function.

Task 2
Draw an organisation chart to represent all or part of an organisation with which you are familiar. Consider the following issues:
- How wide are the spans of control of managers/supervisors?
- Are there any communication problems in the business? Does the organisation chart highlight why these problems occur?
- Is the organisation 'tall' or 'flat'? What impact does this have on business performance?

3   Types of organisational structure

An organisational structure can usually be categorised as entrepreneurial, functional/hierarchical or matrix. Other structures are also possible.

Entrepreneurial

Often found in small businesses, the entrepreneurial structure is relatively informal. Larger businesses frequently mimic the entrepreneurial structure so as to benefit from the quick decision-making that it allows. Key decision-makers are very important, as is the central manager or business owner. Wide spans of control are common, and the organisation will be relatively flat (see Figure 22.6). Amazon.com has an

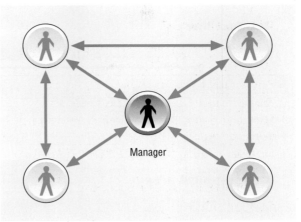

Figure 22.6 Entrepreneurial structure

entrepreneurial structure, with the founder, Jeff Bezos, at its centre.

Functional/hierarchical

The traditional structure for most businesses is functional/hierarchical (see Figure 22.7). Departments and employees specialise in individual tasks, and roles are clearly defined. Speed of decision-making depends on the size of the business, but there is a potential for poor communications because of bureaucracy. However, specialisation might enable the business to benefit from economies of scale.

Matrix

Matrix structures involve a team-based approach to organisational design. Departmental specialities still

Matrix structure

Advantages
- allows fast decision-making
- allows for creativity and flexibility
- more efficient than departments working on projects in isolation
- can motivate employees through greater empowerment and job variety.

Disadvantages
- may be resented by senior managers, as power is concentrated down the hierarchy
- allows few people to have a complete overview of business activities
- may make control difficult.

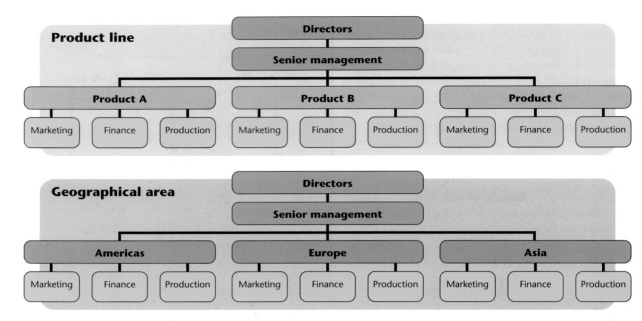

Figure 22.7 Other formal structures

exist, but staff from different departments work together on projects. A project team might include representatives from finance, marketing, production, personnel and operations. An individual might report to both the team leader and the department head. Cisco Systems, a provider of internet hardware and equipment, use matrix management both internally and together with its many business partners, including Microsoft and Hewlett Packard.

Proctor & Gamble, for instance, have product managers with global responsibility for different brands.

Others

A business may also be structured according to geographic regions or according to product lines (see Figure 22.7).

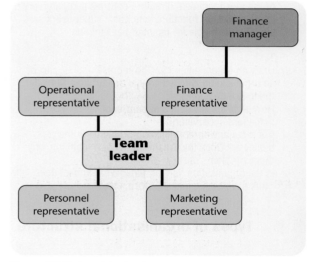

Figure 22.8 A matrix structure

4   Centralisation and decentralisation

When every business decision is made by senior management, this is called **centralisation**. All authority is retained at the top of the hierarchy. As shown in Figure 22.9, in a traditional high-street retail chain this might mean that all decisions are made at head office. All stocking, staffing and operational decisions will be taken centrally. Local managers would merely implement head office instructions. McDonald's uses a very centralised strategy to control more than 25,000 restaurants.

Decentralisation involves delegating decision-making power down the hierarchy. An individual shop, for instance, might be given the authority to decide what goods it stocks and whom it employs.

In practice, where a business is geographically spread, authority is likely to rest with both local branches and head office. Local branches are often free to adapt head office decisions to suit local conditions.

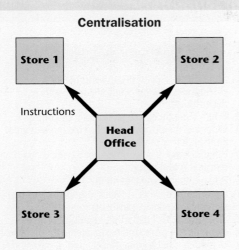

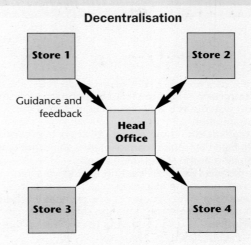

Centralisation

Advantages

- Senior management have tight control over an organisation.
- The marketing message, appearance and quality will be almost identical at every outlet.
- The organisation can gain from economies of scale.

Disadvantages

- Local conditions and differences are ignored.
- Local management's experience and expertise are not taken into account.
- Local staff can become demotivated.
- Change will occur slowly.

Decentralisation

Advantages

- Staff are empowered and may be more motivated.
- Local conditions and differences are taken into account.
- Local management's experience and expertise are acknowledged.
- Communications problems and bureaucracy are reduced, which might also reduce costs.

Disadvantages

- Scope for economies of scale are limited.
- Corporate image may not be consistent across outlets or branches.

Figure 22.9 The advantages and disadvantages of centralisation and decentralisation.

 5 **Factors that influence organisation design**

A variety of factors can influence organisation design.

- **Management style.** Some managers will prefer to retain direct control over an organisation whereas others may be more willing to delegate. Sir Richard Greenbury's autocratic management style was part of the reason for the hierarchal and bureaucratic organisation at Marks & Spencer.

- **Business size.** The larger a business is, the more likely that it will need formal control systems and formal, systematic lines of communication. Small businesses are more suited to entrepreneurial structures.

- **Market.** A business that operates in a market where change is frequent, such as technology, or in a highly competitive market, will need a structure that promotes quick decision-making and allows flexibility.

- **Culture.** Organisation structure and culture are very closely linked (see Unit 29). The structure of an organisation will affect its culture. Equally, culture will affect the structure – staff used to an informal culture may resent attempts at formalisation.

Organisation design: summary

KEY TERMS

Bureaucracy – the close following of rules, policies and systems as a way of running of an organisation.

Centralisation – business set-up where decisions are taken by senior management and authority is retained at the top of the hierarchy.

Decentralisation – delegating decision-making power down the hierarchy.

De-layering – the removal of one or more levels of hierarchy from an organisation structure.

Delegation – passing authority to complete a task to a subordinate, but responsibility for completion of the task remains with the manager.

Downsizing – reducing the total headcount within an organisation by means of redundancy.

Organisational chart – a pictorial representation of the structure of a business and its lines of communication.

Span of control – the number of subordinates reporting to one manager.

Summary questions

1 State **three** uses of organisation charts.
2 Distinguish between centralisation and decentralisation.
3 What is meant by the term 'span of control'?
4 What are the disadvantages of having a span of control that is too wide?
5 What are the disadvantages of having a chain of command that is too long?
6 What is matrix management?
7 Describe **two** ways in which organisational design can affect business performance.
8 What is the purpose of de-layering?
9 Examine the problems associated with de-layering.
10 Distinguish between authority and responsibility.
11 What is 'staff authority'?
12 What is delegation?
13 Explain **two** factors that determine organisation design.
14 Briefly explain the link between organisation structure and culture.

Exam practice

Cannon's people can

Cannon, which produces automotive, aerospace and cinematography products, is renowned for giving its engineering teams as much autonomy (independence) as possible. 'Someone once said that in a bureaucracy the boss is your only customer', says Harry Gilfillan, the business development manager. 'Management teams and long chains of command often stifle creativity because they put people in boxes. We don't operate in a hierarchy and there are no management teams.'

This approach leaves staff free to apply their skills and creativity, streamlines product development and keeps lead times short. Purchasing is delegated to shop-floor personnel, who have budgetary responsibility and deal directly with salespeople. Matrix style teams are set up to work on particular projects. The structure of the company is based on the customer, not on a formal hierarchy.

Source: *The Times*, May 26 2002

1 What is meant by the term 'chain of command'?   **[2]**
2 What is meant by the term 'on a formal hierarchical basis'?   **[2]**
3 Examine the disadvantages of matrix management.   **[6]**
4 Discuss the circumstances in which a matrix management structure might not be suitable.   **[6]**
5 Evaluate how Cannon's shop-floor workforce might respond to the autonomy that they are given.   **[12]**
Total 28 marks

23 Communication

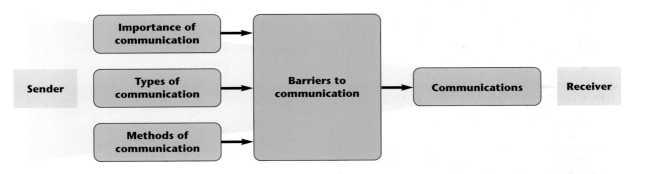

1 Effective communication

Good teams rely on good communication. For the crew of a yacht, good communication can mean the difference between life and death; for a hockey team it might be the difference between winning and losing. The same is true in the business world.

Effective communication is essential to business success. Without it, a business would not be able to function. It might receive the wrong supplies at the wrong times and customers may not even know what the company does.

A business may communicate with:

- staff
- customers and potential customers
- shareholders
- suppliers
- media
- pressure groups
- trade unions
- government.

2 Types of communication

Communication within an organisation can take many forms, as shown in Figure 23.1.

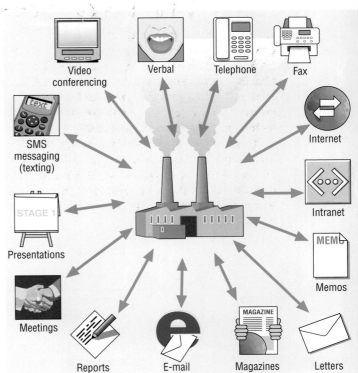

Figure 23.1 Methods of communication

Investigate the advantages and disadvantages of different types of communication. Using IT, produce a handout/presentation on one or more methods of communication. Take into account the following:
- speed of communication
- ease of communication
- whether a permanent record is generated
- whether several people can communicate at once
- whether it is possible to communicate overseas
- whether the message is likely to get distorted
- whether the method is two-way (is feedback possible?).

Communication is often described as being internal, external, horizontal, formal, informal or vertical. In most cases, communication will be a combination of these methods. A letter sent to a supplier (external, formal) might generate a verbal response over a lunch meeting (external, informal). The different categories of communication are considered in Figure 23.2.

Figure 23.2 Communication types, examples and comments

Type of communication	Explanation	Examples	Comments
Internal	Communication within an organisation	Memos, notice boards, meetings, intranet	Communicating corporate goals, motivating staff etc
External	Communication between an organisation and external stakeholders	Telephone, e-mail, brochures, internet	Often (and ideally) two-way (between business and suppliers)
Formal	Recognised, approved and directed by an organisation	Memorandums, notice boards, meetings, letters	Message controlled, but often slow
Informal	Communication through unofficial channels	The 'grapevine'	High potential for message distortion and rumour. Sometimes used by management to test ideas
Vertical	Communication up/down the chain of command	Requests to complete a task, feedback to management (telephone, memo, letters)	
	Top-down	Communication from management to subordinates	Traditionally used by management to instruct subordinates
	Bottom-up	Communication from the 'shop- floor' to management	Now often used as a two-way process
Horizontal	Communication between people at the same level within an organisation (i.e. supervisor to supervisor)	Discussion of projects, marketing, informing production of problems (team briefings, reports, e-mail)	Often communication slowed by rivalry between departments

Activity

List **four** ways in which your school/college, head teacher/senior management communicates with students. Draw and complete a table like the one below.

Method	Internal or external?	Formal or informal?	Use of ICT?	Two-way?	Barriers to effective communication?	Advantages of method	Disadvantages of method
Notice board	Internal	Formal	No	No	Notices not read. Removed by students. Defaced	Easy, cheap. Reach wide audience	No written record. Often ignored

The choice of communication method might be determined by answering certain questions.

- How important is the message? Does it need to get there quickly? Is it personal? Should it be delivered face to face?

- How many people are receiving the message?

- Is feedback required?

- Where is the message going – internal or external, national or international?

- Who is the message going to? What communications equipment do they have?

3 Communications and IT

Businesses are increasingly using information technology (IT) in communications. Not only can **information communications technology (ICT)** greatly speed up communications, but it helps to provide permanent communications records and allows the transfer of pictures, drawings and diagrams as well as words or speech. ICT is often relatively cheap to use (compare the cost of an international telephone call with the cost of an e-mail) and has encouraged more regular communication between organisations and their stakeholders.

Many retailers use ICT to help managers make important decisions. Up-to-the-minute sales figures are available, using **management information systems (MIS)**, and stock ordering can be done electronically, with computer systems communicating with suppliers and head office automatically. In theory, this method reduces the amount of paperwork involved and vastly speeds up the communication process.

However, communications technology has also raised a number of issues. Training staff to use ICT can be expensive, as is buying IT hardware and frequently having to replace it. Moreover, the amount of information now available with ICT has created 'information overload', with managers sometimes finding that they have too much information to deal with. It is estimated that the average middle manager gets over 200 messages every day. Also, ICT has become a major cause of 'lost time' in the workplace. The availability of e-mail and internet systems for personal use has made it much easier for workers to 'time waste'.

4 Communications failure

There are a number of barriers that can prevent effective communication from taking place (see Figure 23.3):

- **Problems with the message.** A message can become distorted as it moves through a

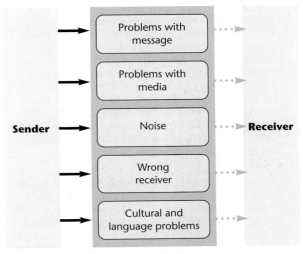

Figure 23.3 Barriers to communication

communications channel (just like in the game 'Chinese whispers'). A message may not have been expressed in terms that the receiver can understand, or the message may simply have been wrong in the first place. Both the sender and the receiver need the skills to complete the communications process effectively (a secretary may not understand the technical language in a letter and might send a message containing errors).

- **Problems with the media.** If the medium breaks down, or the recipient does not have the necessary equipment, a message may fail to be delivered.

- **Noise.** 'Noise' might refer to the effects of actual noise (a shouted instruction on a factory floor being misunderstood), the distortion of the message in transit (a blurred fax) or information overload (so many messages are received that some are missed amid the 'noise').

- **Wrong receiver.** A message may be sent to the wrong person. Costly delays, lost sales or disgruntled employees might be the result.

For example ...

The Italian Job

Haseeb's business partners in Italy were getting edgy. A big order was at stake and they had not yet received the final proposal document, sent by courier from the London office. The client was due at the Italian office that evening.

Haseeb had e-mailed a copy of the document to Italy, but some issue with computer incompatibility was causing printing problems, and the proposal had to look professional. Haseeb contacted the courier, but was unable to speak to anyone who could answer his query. He tried to pacify his Italian partners, but they did not share his optimism and he found himself on the receiving end of some fiery tempers.

Haseeb breathed a sigh of relief when a blurred fax, which had been sent to the wrong department in London, was rushed to him by a concerned secretary, confirming arrival of the proposal in Italy.

1 What is a communication barrier?   **[2]**
2 Identify at least **three** communication barriers in the case described.   **[3]**
3 Propose and justify a solution to **one** communication problem identified in the story.   **[5]**
                                        Total 10 marks

- **Cultural and language problems.** A message may well be altered in translation from one language to another. The slight differences in word meanings might have a significant effect on the overall meaning of the message.

> **Guru's views**
> 'Many attempts to communicate are nullified by saying too much.'
> *Robert Greenleaf, ATT*

5 Communications and business size

Small businesses with few employees may have very direct lines of communication. Thus, the decision-makers can quickly be informed of important issues and the business can react quickly to market changes. Any changes needed to be made to the business can then be communicated throughout the organisation and promptly put into effect.

As a business grows, so does the difficulty in ensuring effective communication. The more employees a business has, the more difficult communication becomes. And the more levels of hierarchy a message has to pass through, the more likely that a barrier to communication will arise.

To combat this problem, large organisations often have extensive formal communications processes (numerous meetings, reports, publications and so on). Although these may help to keep staff informed, they can also contribute to information overload and create bureaucracy. Decision-making is slowed, because managers are not free to make quick decisions. Also, before any decision can be acted upon, it has to be communicated through the various channels.

As discussed in Unit 22, large businesses often attempt to minimise the negative effects of size on communication, by mimicking the organisational structure of smaller firms (matrix structure) and by de-layering.

6 Problems of ineffective communication

Good communications is essential to business success. A business must be able to react to changing internal and external pressures. Poor communications can lead to a number of serious problems:

- **Lack of strategic direction.** Corporate

strategy must be clearly communicated and understood throughout a business. An organisation will be most effective when all departments are working together towards a common goal.

- **Poorly motivated staff.** Recognition of both staff and individual sense of worth are essential to motivation – they cannot be achieved without communication.

- **Missed opportunities.** Selling opportunities or changes in consumer needs may be missed if marketing and sales do not communicate with customers.

- **Resistance to change.** Communication between staff and key decision-makers is essential when managing change. People do not like change, but are much more responsive if there is a two-way discussion before the change is made.

- **Stakeholder pressure.** Keeping different stakeholder groups informed and being aware of their needs can help businesses to avoid negative publicity and criticism from pressure groups.

Communication: summary

KEY TERMS

Communications channel – route through which a message is passed before it reaches the receiver.
Information communications technology (ICT) – the use of electronic means (e-mail, internet, fax) to transfer information.
Message and media – the information being transferred and the method of transfer.
Management information systems (MIS) – electronic systems that provide management with up-to-date sales and stock figures on which they can base decisions.

Summary questions

1 Identify **three** methods of internal communication.
2 Identify **two** methods of external communication.
3 Outline **two** advantages of face-to-face communication.
4 Identify **one** barrier to communication. Suggest how a firm might attempt to remove this barrier.
5 Explain the significance of IT in communications.
6 Why are some firms now encouraging workers to use more traditional methods of communication, rather than solely relying on IT?
7 Suggest and explain **two** reasons why poor communication might lead to poor motivation.
8 Discuss how communications problems might differ in large and small organisations.

Exam practice

Getting the message

When Peter Murtagh agreed to appear on the BBC's 'Back To The Floor' series he could not have realised how bad his firm's internal communications would be made to look. Murtagh, who runs a Hoover production factory, did a stint on the shop-floor to see how the business might be improved.

It was an eye-opener for him. When he was asked about internal communications, he explained that there was a notice board and a monthly meeting. But it was clear that any communication that did exist was strictly 'top-down'. Shop-floor workers had become fed up with trying to draw management's attention to defects and being ignored.

Women on the assembly line, who appeared as savvy as any of the management, were being made redundant, despite offering their support and ideas to help the company win a lucrative new contract.

The Hoover management had made no serious attempt to communicate with their obviously willing but frustrated staff. The company was an almost textbook example of how not to communicate. After his journey 'back to the floor', Peter Murtagh quickly set about improving things.

Source: *Sunday Times*, 28 April 2002

1 Explain what is meant by 'top-down' communication?   **[2]**
2 Suggest and examine **one** disadvantage of 'strictly top-down' communication in relation to Hoover.   **[5]**
3 Examine the relationship between communication and motivation within Hoover.   **[8]**
4 To what extent do internal communications determine the success or failure of a business?   **[10]**
Total 25 marks

24 Motivation theory

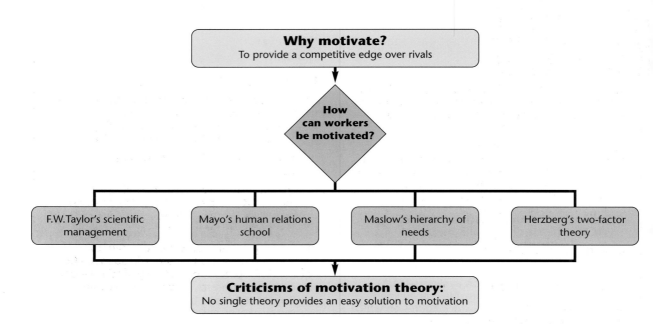

Why motivate?
To provide a competitive edge over rivals

How can workers be motivated?

| F.W.Taylor's scientific management | Mayo's human relations school | Maslow's hierarchy of needs | Herzberg's two-factor theory |

Criticisms of motivation theory:
No single theory provides an easy solution to motivation

1   What is motivation?

Motivation is *wanting* to do something or wanting to achieve a certain result. What motivates you to complete your Business Studies work, or to work hard in your part-time job? What are the factors that make you *want* to get the work done well and on time? What makes you want to get out of bed in the first place and go to work?

Your answers to these questions are the key to what motivates you personally. The answers are likely to be similar to those given by others around you, but no two people are motivated in identical ways. The challenge facing business is to find ways to motivate each and every one of its workers.

A motivated workforce is important because it can help a business to boost its profitability, through both increased revenues and reduced costs.

● Increased effort results in higher productivity.

● Pride in the work leads to improved quality.

● Loyalty to the business reduces labour turnover.

● Commitment to the business reduces absenteeism and the likelihood of industrial conflict.

● Personal development can allow the business to get the very best from its workers' skills.

Different theories of motivation have been put forward to explain which factors are important in encouraging people to give their best. If a business can identify what it is, in theory, that motivates most of its workforce, the business can find ways to achieve this in practice. The end result could be a real competitive edge over its rivals. That is why motivation theory matters so much.

A wide range of theories have been proposed by business thinkers, managers and psychologists. Four of the most important theories are:

● scientific management, developed by F W Taylor

● school of human relations, founded by Elton Mayo

● hierarchy of needs, Abraham Maslow's theory

● two-factor theory, devised by Fredrick Herzberg.

F.W. Taylor

the father of 'scientific management'

Guru's views

'When a naturally energetic man works for a few days beside a lazy one, the logic of the situation is unanswerable: "Why should I work hard when that lazy fellow gets the same pay that I do and does only half as much work?"'

F.W. Taylor

The work of Frederick Winslow Taylor (1856–1917) shaped the views of managers on motivation for most of the twentieth century and remains influential today.

Taylor studied the movements and working practices of workers in the USA at the turn of the twentieth century – most famously, those involved in pig-iron production at the Bethlehem Steel Works in Bethlehem, Pennsylvania. These 'time and motion studies' found that workers took their own decisions about the methods and speed required to do a job, and that many of their ways of working were inefficient.

Theory of scientific management

Taylor's ideas to improve efficiency became known as **scientific management**. He believed managers could find the 'best way' to complete a job through a scientific procedure of observation, experiment and calculations. Based on these ideas, he set out a number of recommendations.

- Managers should study the tasks being carried out by workers and identify the quickest way of doing each one. Any unnecessary movement or tasks should be eliminated.

- The skills of each employee should be matched to the tasks that need to be carried out, and each given specific instructions on what to do and how to do it.

- All workers should be supervised and controlled, and those who do not work efficiently should be punished – the 'stick'.

- Workers should be rewarded financially for being efficient, and pay schemes designed to pay more to those who produce more – the 'carrot'.

Taylor believed that money motivates – 'a fair day's pay for a fair day's work'. Workers seek to maximise their pay, he said, and want managers to design a system that will allow them to do this.

Theory into practice

Taylor's ideas formed the basis for the mass-production assembly lines that dominated manufacturing in the twentieth century. To put 'scientific management' into practice involves:

- eliminating wasted time and resources in production

- closely supervising workers, controlling their methods and speed of work, possibly through the use of a conveyor-belt system, which dictates the speed they must work at

- introducing either a **piece rate** system of payment – where workers are paid so much for each unit ('piece') of output they produce – or a financial incentive system based on meeting output targets.

Problems

A number of objections have been raised to Taylor's theory.

- The theory assumes there is a scientific 'best way' to organise production, but this ignores differences between workers, which may affect the success of any one method.

- The approach treats workers as machines to be used and controlled, creating an atmosphere of conflict between workers and managers.

- Money is not the only motivator, nor is it the most important one for some people. Taylor's ideas ignore the personal and social needs of individuals at work.

A typical mass-production line

Elton Mayo

believer in teamwork and rest breaks

Elton Mayo lectured on psychology in Australia in the early twentieth century, and from 1922 in the USA. Following F W Taylor's work-study research, Mayo studied the impact of rest breaks on workers' productivity. Just as Taylor had found that the right type of work methods and payment systems could improve productivity, Mayo was investigating whether there was a similarly ideal length or frequency of rest break. Initial experiments suggested regular breaks boosted productivity, and led Mayo to call for the more humane treatment of employees at work.

Mayo's most famous studies took his ideas a stage further. Experiments between 1927 and 1932 at the Hawthorne Plant of the Western Electric Company in Chicago became the foundation for the 'human relations school' of management theory. The Hawthorne studies involved varying working conditions, such as lighting, heating and hours of work, and measuring the impact on the productivity of small groups of workers. A change in conditions was made every 12 weeks, but beforehand researchers would discuss the change fully with the workers. The results surprised everyone.

Every change that was introduced brought *higher* productivity. Productivity went up even when no changes were made. The final change was to go back to the original working conditions – with the effect of achieving the highest productivity of all.

Theory of human relations

Mayo drew two, different, but equally important conclusions from the surprising results of his workplace experiments.

1 **The importance of teamwork.** The experiments had led to groups of individuals becoming a team, whose members worked closely in cooperation with each other. A sense of team spirit, and doing what the group expected, motivated employees to work harder.

2 **The need for managers to take an interest in their workers.** Workers responded well to being observed and to the feeling of importance that this produced. The morale-boosting effect of

the experiments suggested that managers who communicated closely with workers and showed an interest in them would be rewarded with an increase in productivity – the so-called **Hawthorne effect**.

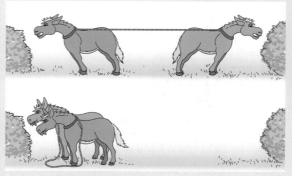

The benefits of working together

Theory into practice

Mayo's findings led to a number of practical conclusions for motivating workers.

- Getting the physical conditions of work and the financial rewards right is less important than getting right the social conditions – teamwork and good communication are essential.

- Giving workers the opportunity to be involved in making decisions and to be creative is more likely to motivate them than Taylor's assembly-line approach.

- Personnel departments that focus on the well-being of workers are central to business success.

Guru's views
'**British management doesn't seem to understand the importance of the human factor.**'

Prince Charles

Problems

Mayo's theory has been criticised on at least two grounds.

- The experiments themselves were far from scientific – only small groups of workers were observed, and subsequent experiments have failed to confirm the findings.

- Workers will not always share the goals of managers, despite their best efforts. Trade unions may see these efforts as management attempts to fool workers into boosting productivity when there is little gain for workers in doing so.

Abraham Maslow

put forward the theory of the hierarchy of needs

In 1954 the American psychologist Abraham Maslow put forward his theory of what motivates human beings. His ideas did not apply solely to the workplace but nevertheless had an important message for business.

Theory of the hierarchy of needs

Maslow suggested that all human beings have the same types of needs and that these could be organised as a **hierarchy of needs**. The five levels of needs he referred to are shown in Figure 24.1.

At the base of the hierarchy lie 'physiological needs' – the essentials for human survival, such as food and rest. Maslow placed this type of need at the bottom of the hierarchy because such needs are the most fundamental set of needs for any human being. They will always be the first type of need that must be satisfied.

Once this level of needs is met, it no longer remains a focus or a motivation. Instead, it is the next level of needs in the hierarchy that an individual seeks to satisfy. So, once their physiological needs have been met, people seek the 'safety' needs of security and freedom from anxiety. Motivation stems from each individual's desire to have their next level of needs met. The final level of needs, 'self-actualisation', refers to the need to fulfil one's potential. Once all other levels of need are met, it is this need that can continue to motivate.

Guru's views

'It is quite true that humans live by bread alone – when there is no bread. But what happens to their desires when there is bread?'

Abraham Maslow

Theory into practice

Maslow's theory has important practical implications for business.

- To motivate a workforce requires an approach that will identify the level of need of each individual.

- Each worker will first need sufficient pay to provide for his or her basic physiological needs, then will seek job security and a safe working environment. Figure 24.1 shows how businesses might seek to meet each level of needs in the hierarchy.

- Financial rewards alone will not motivate. Boosting workers' esteem and developing their talents will be crucial. But, without decent pay and job security, these are worthless.

Problems

Opponents of Maslow have found his theory unconvincing on several grounds.

- Any generalisation about 'levels' of human needs is bound to have exceptions – businesses may find they have workers who place little value on gaining praise or developing their potential. Some workers – such as artists or musicians – may even seek creativity needs before financial reward.

- Even if Maslow's theory holds good, workers may not seek all levels of need within the workplace. They may be satisfied with pay alone from their job, meeting other needs through their leisure time.

- Matching rewards to needs for each and every worker is a well-nigh impossible task in practice.

What people need

What businesses can offer

What people need	Level	What businesses can offer
Achieving your full potential	Self-actualisation	Training, challenges and opportunities to develop each individual's skills
Gaining the respect of others; feeling valued; having confidence and self respect	Esteem needs	Reward for achievement; promotion and status
Being part of a group; giving and receiving affection and friendship	Love and belonging needs	Opportunities for teamwork; social facilities and positive working relationships
Security; absence of danger and freedom from anxiety	Safety needs	High standards of health and safety; job security; absence of bullying
Food, water, air, rest, activity	Physiological needs	Decent pay to enable needs to be met; acceptable working hours and conditions

Figure 24.1 Maslow's hierarchy of needs

Frederick Herzberg

proposed the 'two-factor theory'

Frederick Herzberg, an American psychologist, conducted research in the 1950s that directly addressed the question of motivation. He asked 200 engineers and accountants which factors in their work created job satisfaction and which caused dissatisfaction. His results are presented in a simplified form in Figure 24.2.

The results showed that six factors, including achievement and recognition, were frequently mentioned as causing satisfaction at work. On the other hand, ten factors, such as company policy and working conditions, were often mentioned as causes of dissatisfaction, but rarely as a source of pleasure!

'Two-factor theory'

Herzberg used this research to develop his 'two-factor theory' of motivation. This states that there are two sets of factors – **motivators and hygiene factors** – that are both important in motivating workers, but for very different reasons.

1 **Motivators.** The factors that have the potential to motivate workers by providing job satisfaction include:

   – a sense of achievement
   – recognition of effort
   – interesting work
   – responsibility
   – opportunities for promotion
   – opportunities for self-improvement.

These factors help to meet the human need to grow psychologically. If a job can provide these motivators, workers will want to work and will enjoy their work. If the motivators are absent from the job, this does not by itself create dissatisfaction – only a lack of motivation.

2 **Hygiene factors.** Just as poor hygiene can cause illness, the factors that can cause dissatisfaction in the workplace are all related to the working environment. They include:

   – company policy
   – relationships with supervisors or colleagues

   – working conditions
   – pay and status
   – security.

Herzberg believed that our 'animal' nature leads us to seek the avoidance of pain. If a job can avoid problems in all of the areas listed, it will stop us feeling that work is a painful experience. It will prevent dissatisfaction. However, no matter how good these factors are in a job, they will not, by themselves, motivate someone – that is down to the motivators. Good hygiene can stop you getting ill, but it cannot make you happy.

Theory into practice

Several practical conclusions can be drawn from the two-factory theory.

   – To motivate a workforce, a business must first make sure that all of the hygiene factors are being met – a decent salary, fair rules and policies and pleasant working conditions.
   – The motivators must be there – ensuring that the job itself is meaningful and interesting, that workers are trained to do their jobs well and that they have the opportunity to develop their skills.

Specifically, Herzberg advocated 'job enrichment' – building a variety of tasks, skills and responsibilities into each job (see Unit 25).

Guru's views
'How do I motivate someone to play the piano? First, I teach them how to play it.'
Frederick Herzberg

Problems

Herzberg's theory has encountered major criticisms.

   – Subsequent research around the world has failed to confirm that Herzberg's theory can generally be applied to workers in every business.
   – Some jobs, especially low-skilled ones, cannot be easily 'enriched', and many workers may not seek responsibility or advancement.

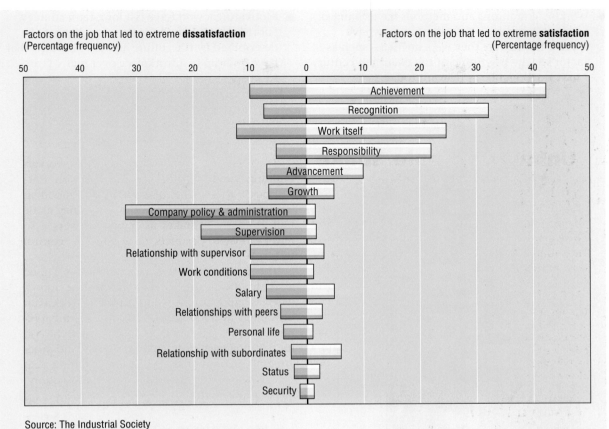

Factors on the job that led to extreme **dissatisfaction** (Percentage frequency)

Factors on the job that led to extreme **satisfaction** (Percentage frequency)

Source: The Industrial Society

Figure 24.2 Factors leading to job satisfaction and dissatisfaction

2 Criticisms of motivation theories

One of the problems with motivation theories is already obvious. Four different views have been presented, each with a different prescription for how business can motivate its workers. But they cannot all be right. A manager makes assumptions about human nature in adapting a theory about motivating people at work. Only then can the manager put motivational policies into practice.

Even then, the motivation theory chosen will not easily solve the problem of motivating a workforce, for a number or reasons.

- Each worker will have his or her own needs and priorities. No general theory of motivation can accurately capture the needs of each individual.

- Even what motivates any one individual is likely to change over time. Money may well be a priority while pay negotiations are going on, but at other times others issues may dominate.

- Working conditions and methods have changed over the decades, so theories that may have applied to the time they were devised – such as Taylor's at the beginning of the twentieth century – may no longer be as relevant today.

- Motivating a workforce is a long-term strategy. Short-term motivation is therefore likely to be determined by the culture and relationships that have built up in a workplace over many years.

For example ...

Unhappy people 'make the best workers'

Psychologists from the University of Alberta have found that miserable people make better workers than happy ones. Cheerful people waste too much time trying to maintain their happy mood, while their miserable co-workers simply get on with the task in hand. The findings fly in the face of previous research on the subject, which suggested that happy workers were more productive, and put a question mark over the millions spent each year on ensuring a happy working environment.

The researchers studied four groups of workers building circuit boards on a production line. Although those who described their mood as 'sad' did not produce any more work, they made half as many mistakes as happy workers – so fewer of their products failed quality control tests.

The study found that miserable people used work to distract themselves from their mood, whereas happy people tended to regard work as an unwanted distraction and a source of unhappiness. If these ideas catch on, it could spell the end for bonding weekends, company songs and other attempts at corporate jollity – something that could put a smile on the face of the most stony-faced employee.

Source:
http://news.bbc.co.uk/1/hi/business/1386484.stm,
13 June 2000

Grumpy rarely whistled while he worked

1 According to the new research, why will attempts to produce happy workers not help a business? **[4]**

2 How would different motivation theorists explain these findings? **[7]**

3 Should a business make any attempt to motivate its workers? **[7]**

Total 18 marks

Motivation theory: summary

KEY TERMS

Motivation – wanting to do something or to achieve a certain result.

Scientific management – Taylor's theory that there is a 'best', most efficient way to complete a task, which managers should identify, implement and enforce.

Piece rate – a payment method that rewards the worker for each unit of output produced.

Hawthorne effect – the idea that the interest of management in their workers can itself prove motivating.

Hierarchy of needs – Maslow's idea that human needs can be grouped into five types, shown as building up from the most basic needs of survival to the ultimate need for self-development.

Motivators – those factors, such as responsibility, that can create job satisfaction.

Hygiene factors – issues that can cause job dissatisfaction, such as poor pay or unfair rules.

Summary questions

1 What is meant by 'motivation'?
2 Why is worker motivation important to a business?
3 Explain the concept of 'scientific management'.
4 How would Taylor recommend that a business should motivate its workers?
5 Briefly summarise Mayo's main findings from the Hawthorne studies.
6 Explain why Maslow shows the five levels of human needs as a 'hierarchy'.
7 Explain **two** ways in which a business might use knowledge of Maslow's theory to motivate its staff.
8 Explain, using examples, the difference between 'motivators' and 'hygiene factors'.
9 Why is it important that a business considers both sets of factors?
10 What criticisms can be made of motivation theories?

Exam practice

Two views of Wal-Mart

t to know more?

w.walmart.com

al-Mart's statement of motivation

s a Wal-Mart "Associate", you are art of a continuously growing, obal family. We are a group of edicated, hard-working, ordinary eople who have teamed up together o accomplish extraordinary things. We believe that every individual deserves to be treated with respect and dignity. We are committed to equal opportunities and to sexual harassment prevention.

'Every Associate is encouraged to bring any suggestions to their supervisor. Wal-Mart is committed to providing state-of-the-art training resources and development time to help achieve career objectives. Our Associates have boundless limits on career advancement, without ever leaving the company.

'Bonuses are paid to Associates based on individual and company performance. Whilst a paycheck will buy one kind of loyalty, nothing can substitute for sincere words of praise. They're absolutely free – and yet worth a fortune.'

Source: www.walmart.com

Wal-Mart's critics: 'It was like a cult'

Wal-Mart, the world's biggest retailer, with 1.2 million employees and 3,250 stores throughout the USA, is being sued by thousands of current and former employees in 28 states. They claim the company demanded a slave-like commitment, expecting them to work overtime with no pay, and bullying workers into long hours. Many employees have complained that they often went without breaks, missing the opportunity to eat or go to the toilet. Hourly rates are so low that most workers cannot afford basic living expenses.

One employee, Liberty Serna – a 25-year-old restaurant manager in a Wal-Mart store – claims that store managers refused to hire more staff, leaving her to do basic jobs like cleaning and waitressing. Paid overtime would be refused, but she would be expected to work an extra three or fours hours per day unpaid to get the work done. 'I knew that if I didn't, I would lose my job,' she says. Another employee added, 'I think about the Wal-Mart cheers and the chants and I think it was like a cult. I am angry at a company that has no feelings for the people that have made it what it is.'

Source: *The Times*, 16 July 2002

Exam practice

1 What is meant by the term 'motivation'? **[2]**
2 Why does a company such as Wal-Mart seek a motivated workforce? **[5]**
3 In what ways have Wal-Mart used money as a motivator? **[6]**
4 Using Maslow's hierarchy of needs, explain how, in theory, Wal-Mart seeks to motivate its workers. **[10]**
5 Using Herzberg's two-factor theory, evaluate why many Wal-Mart employees have become demotivated. **[12]**
Total 35 marks

Want to know more?

www.walmartwatch.org

25 Motivation in practice

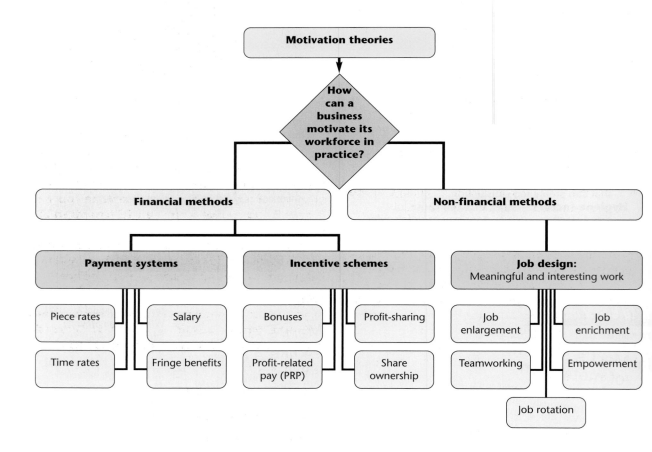

1 Theory and practice

Even with the aid of motivating theory, creating a motivated and productive workforce in practice is not straightforward. Numerous financial and non-financial rewards are available to an organisation. The 'package' of rewards must achieve certain objectives:

- a motivated and productive workforce

- a workforce that is flexible in meeting the organisation's needs

- the recruitment and retention of the best workers

- value for money in ensuring the reward is cost-effective in what it achieves.

2 Financial rewards

No theory of motivation ignores the relevance of money. Some theorists, such as Taylor, see it as a factor of primary importance; others, such as Herzberg, see money as important in preventing dissatisfaction but not in itself as a motivator.

Financial rewards can be divided into two types, which nevertheless overlap. They are:

1 payment systems – methods of calculating and providing the basic pay for a job

2 incentive schemes – rewards to recruit, retain and motivate workers.

Payment systems

Businesses pay their employees in a variety of ways, all of which have their benefits and their drawbacks.

Piece rates

A piece-rate system pays workers for each unit of output that they produce. There is no guaranteed level of basic pay, and no sickness or holiday pay. **Piece rates** ae most commonly used in manufacturing industries, such as clothing. According to Taylor, piece rates motivate because they directly reward those who work harder.

Piece rates, however, have been criticised for:

- producing low pay and insecurity, even for those who work hard (undermining the lower order needs of Maslow's hierarchy)

- encouraging workers to sacrifice quality in the search for a greater quantity of output

- making the workforce resistant to change, for fear that it will harm their rate of earnings.

Time rates

With **time rates**, employees are paid for the length of time that they work. This may be an hourly rate, common in the retail sector, or a weekly wage for completing a set number of hours. Overtime, possibly at a higher rate, may be paid for working longer than the agreed number of hours. Time rates encourage workers to produce a higher quality of work than do piece rates, as there is no focus on the quantity produced.

However, their power to motivate is questionable, in that:

- there is no reward for those who work the hardest or achieve the most within the time

- there is still little security of income, leaving pay a potential source of anxiety and dissatisfaction

- workers on a weekly wage have no encouragement to be flexible in how or when they work, leaving businesses overstaffed at times and understaffed at others.

Salary

Employees on a salary system are paid an agreed sum for a year's work. There is much greater flexibility in terms of when and how long an employee may work in a day, week or month. Secondary school teachers are paid a salary for working 1,265 hours per year at school, and for additional time spent marking and preparing lessons.

It is not just money that can satisfy people's needs for status

Herzberg believed that salaries are the best type of payment scheme because they provide the opportunity to meet workers' financial 'hygiene' needs and then to focus on other motivators. A salary encourages workers to be flexible and open to change, knowing that their financial rewards will be unaffected.

Taylor would criticise a salary system for providing no incentive to work hard, knowing that the financial reward will be the same regardless of effort.

Fringe benefits

In addition to money payments, many organisations offer other forms of reward as part of a worker's basic pay. These are called **fringe benefits**, and include:

- company cars

- private medical insurance

- discounts on company products

- leisure and social facilities.

Fringe benefits have become increasingly important as part of the total payment package given to employees – particularly for management and executive positions. They offer status that can help to provide the 'esteem needs' identified in Maslow's hierarchy, but can swiftly become an expected 'right', which could equally be a cause of status envy and dissatisfaction.

Incentive schemes

Business use a number of ways to improve the pay package and so motivate employees to work harder.

Bonuses

A bonus is the general term for an additional financial reward given to a worker in recognition of the contribution that he or she has made. Examples include:

● piece-rate bonus – an additional payment to workers for each unit of output that they produce above a stated target

● commission – a percentage of the sales price of a product that is paid to the salesperson as a reward for making the sale

● one-off payment – a lump sum paid to an individual, team or whole workforce as a reward for their efforts. It may be a seasonal bonus, such as a Christmas bonus, or a reward for attendance, quality or service.

Door-to-door sales personnel often work on a commission basis

Bonuses, such as **commission**, can act an incentive because they offer the prospect of additional reward for additional commitment or for achieving a certain target. On the other hand, bonuses may come to be expected as part of the overall payment package, breaking the link between effort and reward. In addition, bonuses can cause conflict due to jealousy between workers.

Performance-related pay (PRP)

Another type of bonus scheme is **performance-related pay (PRP)**. This provides a financial reward to an employee for meeting agreed, individual targets. PRP is closely linked to the annual appraisal process, in which a member of staff will agree, and later review, performance targets with a line manager. Performance is measured against the targets set, and the size of the reward payment reflects the degree of achievement.

PRP is now commonly used for executives in both the private and the public sectors. It represents a management equivalent to piece rate, in the sense that it provides a financial reward for the 'output' of managers. However, some companies have become sceptical of its benefits, because of:

● the potential for conflict between employees and their line managers over the achievement of targets and the level of reward they should receive

● the failure of PRP to promote teamwork and a spirit of unity, by focusing exclusively on individual performance

● the need to keep financial rewards to an affordable level, leaving PRP payments too small to make any great motivational impact

● the insignificance of financial reward – according to theorists like Herzberg – compared to other motivational factors.

Profit sharing

Employees are offered a share in the annual profits of the organisation. **Profit sharing** encourages them to work collectively to the benefit of the whole organisation, in contrast to the individual approach of PRP. The level of the incentive will depend on the proportion of the organisation's profit to be shared out, and whether worker commitment is sufficient to make that organisation successful.

Share ownership

Incentive schemes that provide company shares as the reward produce similar benefits to profit-sharing schemes. As shareowners, employees will benefit financially from the success of the business, the issuing of dividends and growth in the share price.

At the heart of most share ownership schemes is the concept of a **share option**. A share option is the right to buy a share at an agreed price at a given future date. The agreed price is likely to be the share's market price at the beginning of the scheme, or even a discounted rate below this. If the share price rises over the period of the scheme, the employee will gain significantly. On the agreed date, the employee will be able to 'exercise' the option and then sell the shares at a much higher price.

Share ownership schemes are, typically, of two types:

● savings-related schemes, which allow staff to save a set amount each month over a period of time and then exchange these savings for share options

For example ...

Big bucks

Many company executives earn salaries that most people can only dream of. Often however, this salary is made up of complex PRP arrangements and share options with extended lock-ins. Basic salaries may be only a small proportion of potential earnings if performance targets are met.

Jonathon Bloomer (pictured), chief executive of Prudential, stood to gain a bonus of £900,000, with the potential of reaching £4.6 million, on top of a £660,000 salary, before shareholders stepped in and vetoed the deal. Jim Nicol, chief executive of Tomkins, has a potential bonus of 100 per cent of his £750,000 salary and share options worth four times his salary.

Directors Pay

	Lead executives	Finance directors
Basic salary (Avge £ per yr)	673,321	340,984
Total cash (Avge £ per yr)	1,167,277	600,236
Total earnings	2,073,606	1,355,908

Source: *Financial Times*, 6 March 2002 and 9 May 2002

1   Distinguish between share options, PRP and bonuses. **[6]**

2   Explain why such a large proportion of executive pay is linked to performance. **[4]**

3   Explain **two** reasons why shareholders might have vetoed Mr Bloomer's pay package. **[4]**

4   Evaluate the benefits of paying executives in share options as opposed to cash benefits. **[8]**

Total 22 marks

- incentives for executives, which often link the number of share options offered to status or performance.

Executive share option schemes have been much criticised for unfairly boosting 'fat cat' salaries. However, a period of instability in the stock market in the early 2000s has made this a much less attractive type of incentive.

3   Non-financial rewards

According to Mayo, Maslow and Herzberg, financial rewards by themselves are not enough to motivate workers. Other needs must be met – such as Maslow's 'higher-order' needs of esteem and self-actualisation. These focus not on the monetary reward for work, but on the personal rewards of doing the job.

The 'design' of the job is therefore crucial to motivation. Above all, a job must be meaningful and interesting, according to Herzberg. To achieve this end, each worker's job role should provide:

- variety – possibly through the use of 'job rotation'

- closure – the opportunity to see a job or product through to completion, using 'job enlargement'

- challenge – work that develops skills and offers advancement, achieved through 'job enrichment'

- control – over key decisions related to the job role, a process known as 'empowerment'

- cooperation – the opportunity to work and interact with others, achieved by promoting 'teamworking'.

Job rotation

The process of switching an employee between tasks or job roles over a period of time is called **job rotation**. For example, an employee at a fast food outlet might be switched between cooking, serving and cleaning duties on different shifts. The variety of tasks should help to prevent boredom, while the **multiskilling** of the employee adds to the flexibility of the organisation.

On the other hand, a worker may become less practised and so less productive in any one task. Moreover, switching between a variety of boring tasks does not necessarily make a job more motivating than performing just one boring task.

Job enlargement

Allowing a worker to perform more tasks in a production process may enable him or her to see the complete product. This is known as **job enlargement**, because it involves giving workers more tasks to do of the same type and in the same process. The theory is, they will gain greater job satisfaction by performing more tasks and seeing the end result of their efforts.

Job enlargement is not, however, a solution on its own. Giving workers more work to do can cause resentment if they feel they are being asked to work harder without financial reward. As with job rotation, increasing the 'horizontal loading' of a job – doing more of the same – may not in itself make a job more interesting.

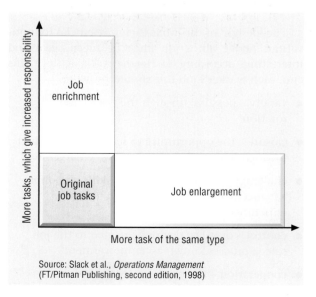

Source: Slack et al., *Operations Management* (FT/Pitman Publishing, second edition, 1998)

Figure 25.1 Job enlargement versus job enrichment

Job enrichment

Different ways have been tried to make a job more challenging or rewarding, called **job enrichment**. They include:

- providing a range of roles and activities within the job

- allowing workers to use and develop different skills

- offering opportunities to demonstrate an individual's capabilities

- enabling workers to take responsibility for their actions and working environment

- training workers to enable them to advance their own skills.

It is these factors that comprise Herzberg's motivators and contribute towards the achievement of Maslow's 'higher-order' needs. Workers will be motivated because they enjoy their work and feel that it is allowing them to grow as an individual.

Job enrichment, however, is not easy to achieve for all job roles. Unskilled, manual labour rarely lends itself to the right opportunities for enrichment, and some workers may not want more responsibility. The changes required in the way a business is organised to enable job enrichment could also prove expensive and disruptive.

Empowerment

Giving employees the power to take the decisions that affect their working lives is known as **empowerment**. This could include the right to make decisions over how and when work is done, and taking responsibility for those decisions.

To empower workers is to go a stage further than to delegate. **Delegation** involves being given the authority by a manager to take decisions in a specific area – such as quality control. Empowered workers, however, would be given a far more wide-ranging power to implement their own ideas in any aspect of their jobs – such as changing the layout of the factory floor and the flow of work.

One way of putting this into practice is through the use of 'quality circles'. These are small groups of employees who meet regularly to identify potential improvements in their work area and oversee their implementation. (See Unit 35.)

Empowerment is at the heart of Herzberg's theory of motivation – giving responsibility, providing opportunities for advancement and making work itself more interesting. Not only can empowerment motivate, but it can get the best out of the workforce by making use of their talents and ideas. If decisions are taken by those who know most about the issues involved, they might be better decisions.

In practice, empowerment may cause a number of problems.

- The reality may fall far short of the theory, with little power really being given by managers who do not trust the workforce.

- Empowerment may be used as an excuse to cut costs by removing levels of middle management and increasing the workload of the remaining employees.

- Genuine empowerment poses the danger that effective control and coordination may be lost, leading to expensive mistakes or a lack of strategic direction.

Teamworking

Mayo's 'Hawthorne studies' emphasised the importance of teamwork in motivation. Teamwork helps to meet workers' social needs for interaction and friendship in the workplace. Teamworking involves:

- organising employees into small groups (teams)

- setting objectives for the team to achieve

- giving the team responsibility and rewards for achieving targets, such as improved quality

- training workers to be able to carry out any role within the team.

Many organisations, such as General Motors, Levi Strauss and Jaguar, have reported benefits from teamworking. These include:

- increased job satisfaction

- higher productivity

- improved product quality

- reduced labour turnover and absenteeism

- enhanced flexibility.

Where teamworking fails it is often because:

- teams were not given clear objectives or the authority to achieve them

- individuals refuse to cooperate with the team approach

- teams are cut-off from management or from the rest of the organisation

- it is seen as a universal solution when an individual approach may be better in some situations.

Guru's views

'Individual commitment to a group effort – that is what makes a team work, a company work, a society work, a civilisation work.'

Vince Lombard

Activity

Working in groups, compare and contrast your own experiences of how firms attempt to motivate their workers. If you have a part-time job, what motivational policies are used at your workplace? How are your parents, friends or relatives motivated at work?

- Do the motivational strategies work?
- Do they work for all employees or just some?
- Do they cause any resentment among staff?
- Could they be improved?
- What other strategies might be better?

Motivation in practice: summary

KEY TERMS

Piece rates – payments for each unit of output that workers produce.

Time rates – payment at an agreed rate for the length of time that employees work.

Fringe benefits – payments to workers in ways other than money, such as a company car.

Commission – payment to a sales person of a percentage of the value of what he or she has sold.

Performance-related pay (PRP) – an incentive scheme that links bonus payments to the achievement of agreed targets.

Profit sharing – a scheme that offers employees a share in any profit made by the organisation.

Share option – the right to buy a share at an agreed price at a given future date.

Job rotation – the process of switching an employee between tasks or job roles over a period of time.

Multiskilling – training employees to perform a range of tasks or job roles.

Job enlargement – giving workers more tasks to do of the same type and in the same process.

Job enrichment – extending the role of the worker to include more responsibility and a wider range of activities.

Empowerment – giving employees the power to take decisions that affect their working lives.

Delegation – passing down to a subordinate the authority to carry out a set task.

Summary questions

1 What objectives might a business have for its rewards package?
2 Explain the difference between a piece rate and a time rate.
3 What are the drawbacks of using a time-rate payment system?
4 Why does Herzberg believe a salary is the best type of payment scheme?
5 What is a fringe benefit? Use examples to support your answer.
6 What are the problems of using bonuses to motivate workers?
7 Explain the benefits and problems of PRP.
8 What is profit-sharing.
9 List the **five** characteristics of a meaningful and interesting job.
10 What are the potential benefits and problems of job rotation?
11 Distinguish between job enlargement and job enrichment.
12 Why does job enrichment not always succeed in motivating a workforce?
13 Explain the difference between empowerment and delegation.
14 What are the potential benefits of teamworking? Why might they not be achieved?

Exam practice

Happy workers keep profits growing

General Dynamics, a company in the defence industry, has been through a difficult period. In 1997 it had to sack a third of its workforce. The remaining employees were apprehensive and very hostile towards management. Productivity inevitably suffered.

Today a campaign to win back the hearts and minds of staff and 'engage' them in the company's success has contributed to the doubling of profit margins and to healthy company earnings.

An 'engaged' worker is someone who will take an extra step, contributing that bit more to the organisation's success, rather than just going through the motions from nine to five. In short, engaged workers are motivated.

General Dynamics discovered that alongside financial rewards for excellent performance, equally, if not more, important in motivating staff were strong leadership and a genuine willingness to listen to employees.

Creating a positive work environment, based around fringe benefits and a friendly culture, also helped to boost motivation and productivity. Job empowerment and job enlargement further contribute to the engagement process.

Studies show that the benefits to profits of having a motivated workforce are so strong that organisations not practising effective people management will be left behind by the competition.

Source: *The Times*, 10 March 2002

1 Distinguish between job empowerment and job enlargement. **[4]**
2 Outline **three** benefits of having an engaged workforce. **[6]**
3 Identify and explain **two** reasons why improved motivation might *not* automatically lead to increased productivity. **[4]**
4 To what extent do you believe that financial rewards are the only way to motivate staff? Support your answer with relevant examples and with reference to at least one motivational theorist. **[16]**
Total 30 marks

26 Leadership and management styles

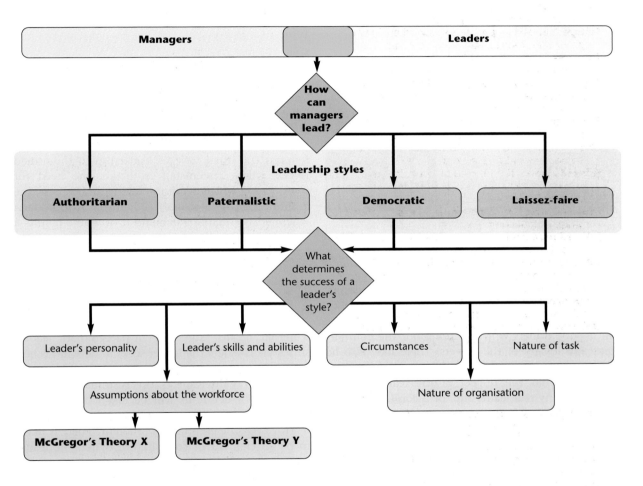

1   Managers and leaders

Think of a manager. Is that person also a leader? Think of a leader. Is he or she also a manager? Managers and leaders are not the same thing, but there will often be overlap between the two groups. Management is a position of authority created within an organisation whereas leadership is a personal skill that can be possessed by anyone.

Managers perform certain functions, including:

- setting objectives
- organising how work is to be done

- commanding, coordinating and communicating with others who do the work

- developing and motivating, to bring out the best in others

- measuring and evaluating the achievement of objectives.

Leaders possess certain qualities. They have:

- a vision of the direction in which the organisation should move

- innovative ideas as to how this objective might be achieved

- the commitment and dedication to follow their ideas through

- the ability, self-belief and personal qualities to gain the support of others.

> ### Guru's views
> 'Managers do right things. Leaders do things right.'
>
> *Warren Bennis, American management writer*

Source: *Sunday Times*, 30 September 1990

The world of sport has plenty of examples of leaders. A football team manager's position carries the authority to organise and command others. The best managers will also be leaders who can bring out the commitment and loyalty of the players. There may also be other leaders, such as the team captain or another player who has the respect of the team. But the absence of any real leadership, or a conflict between two or more leaders within the team, can cause problems that undermine morale and organisation.

> **STOP & THINK**
>
> Within the world of sport, identify:
> - a manager who shows true leadership skills
> - a player who shows true leadership skills
> - a manager who lacks the ability to be a leader
> - a conflict between two or more 'leaders' within a team.

2   Styles of leadership and management

Managers can adopt very different styles and methods in the way they seek to lead others. They range from authoritarian (the strictest) to laissez-faire (the least strict).

Authoritarian

With an **authoritarian** (also known as 'autocratic') style of leadership, the leader takes all the decisions him- or herself. Others are told what to do and are closely controlled in the way they do it. Autocratic leaders do not seek the opinions of others; they know what direction they want to go in.

The term 'authoritarian' is associated with political dictators, such as Hitler, Stalin or Napoleon. It remains the usual style of leadership in the armed forces, where circumstances dictate the need for swift, strong-willed decision-making. In business, the authoritarian style of management tends to be seen where crisis situations demand it or where it suits a leader's dominant personality. But it can cause problems when the dominance of the leader overshadows the abilities or ideas of others, leaving workers feeling ignored, resentful and demotivated.

Paternalistic

'Paternal' means 'father-like'. A **paternalistic** leadership style is where the leader seeks to do what is best for his or her workers, just as a father would for his children. In many respects, this is similar to an autocratic style – decisions will be taken by the leader alone and then enforced.

However, the emphasis is different. There is likely to be an element of consultation, when the leader listens to the views of others before reaching a decision. The decision is then made, taking into account the needs and views of the workforce. Finally, rather than just commanding others to implement the decision, the paternalistic leader will seek to persuade the workforce that the decision is in their best interests.

The paternalistic style is common among UK prime ministers, who seek to persuade the nation that decisions have been taken in their best interests. It is also the traditional style of UK business management: managers see to manage as being their role, and to work as being the workers' role. Decisions are taken on behalf of workers and 'sold' to them as being in their best interests.

The danger of this approach is that a '**them and us**' attitude persists. Managers and workers remain

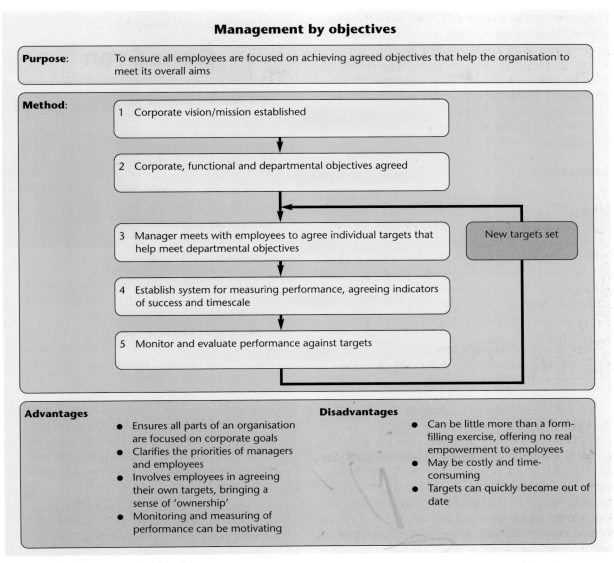

Figure 26.1 Management by objectives

divided and suspicious of each other – rather like an interfering parent and a rebellious teenager!

Democratic

The word 'democratic' means that decisions are taken by the people and for the people. A **democratic** management style is characterised by allowing workers to play a full part in decision-making. This may be achieved through:

- participation – worker involvement in suggestion schemes, in quality circles or even as 'worker directors', with members of the workforce invited to sit on the board of directors

- management by objectives – agreement between the leader and the workers on what their goals should be, and delegation of responsibility to them for achieving these goals (see Figure 26.1).

- autonomous teamworking – empowering groups of workers to take wide-ranging decisions about their own working environment. Managers seek to 'coach' teams to be successful, rather than to dominate. This is often part of a broader strategy to motivate a workforce, as described in Unit 25.

The aim of democratic management is to remove the 'them and us' distinction between managers and workers and to replace it with a **single status** culture in which all employees are treated the same.

Participation, **management by objectives** and **autonomous teamworking** are designed to help achieve this aim. Organisations such as the John Lewis Partnership, Honda and Unipart describe their employees as 'partners' or 'associates'. Practical changes to working conditions may be made to reinforce the 'single status' message, such as having the same uniform, canteen or car park for all managers and employees.

Laissez-faire

'Laissez-faire' literally means 'let it be'. The **laissez-faire** style of management is one in which managers leave employees to get on with their work with little or no interference. Broad aims and guidelines may be established, but the day-to-day role of the manager will be limited. Workers may enjoy the freedom, and respond by taking responsibility and showing creativity. However, others may feel aimless or take the opportunity to slack.

> **Guru's views**
> 'The real leader has no need to lead – he is content to point the way.'
>
> *Henry Miller*

3   Factors affecting leadership styles

There is no single 'best' style of leadership. Every one of those examined has proved successful in business – but equally, there are examples of each one having been disastrous. So what determines the style of leadership that is adopted and whether it proves successful?

- **Leader's personality.** Few leaders take a conscious decision to adopt a particular style of leadership; it reflects the leader's own personality. A dominant personality, for example, will tend to an autocratic style. The studies of F. Fiedler (1976) suggested that it was almost impossible for a leader to change his or her natural style of leadership; if a new style of leadership is needed, the business should change its leader.

- **Leader's skills and abilities.** Whether a leader's style proves successful will in part depend on whether that person has the necessary expertise and personal charisma. An autocrat will need to win the respect and loyalty of the workforce; a democrat will need to create a consensus out of very different opinions.

> *For example ...*

Guru Sven

Sven Göran-Eriksson's skills are as much in demand in the boardroom as they are in the dressing room. The manager of the England football team is already remarkable for transforming the status of an unpopular job (dependent on England's performances on the pitch), but he is also being hailed as a leadership and management guru. His leadership style has even prompted a book detailing his successful traits.

He is described as a mature, level-headed leader with a long-term viewpoint who learns from failure, encourages responsibility and 'keeps it simple'. His style is less hierarchical than that of a traditional British manager and he employs far more consensus-building when taking decisions. The Swedish business style is being taken up more often in the UK, notably in the businesses that show consideration for their wider stakeholders.

Source: 'The Business', *FT Weekend Magazine*, 6 April 2002

1 List **three** 'wider stakeholders' that a business may consider.   [3]
2 Using management theory, how would you define Sven Göran-Eriksson's management style? Justify your answer.   [4]
3 Explain **two** possible reasons why this management style can be so successful.   [4]

Total 11 marks

- **Circumstances.** A crisis, such as a potential business failure, requires swift and decisive leadership. The workforce is more likely to accept autocratic leadership if workers believe it can save their jobs!

- **Organisation culture.** The existing culture of an organisation is likely to prove crucial in determining the success of a leader's style. For example, a workforce that has become used to consultation and involvement will resist an autocrat's attempts to dominate decision-making.

- **Kind of task.** Where a task is technically complex or highly demanding, a skilled and knowledgeable leader is likely to dominate. Where the task is easily mastered, a laissez-faire approach can be successful.

- **Kind of workforce.** If a workforce is lazy, unskilled and unwilling to take responsibility, a more autocratic style could be the only way to get results. On the other hand, a highly trained, motivated and ambitious workforce would feel restricted and undervalued by the same autocrat.

For example ...

Bad times – good leaders

If bad times make good leaders, recessions must produce a host of them. During recession, some managers are frozen with indecision while others act with unnecessary haste. Across large organisations, the effects of such poor leadership can be disastrous. Those managers that survive the inevitable cull are likely to exit the recession as much better leaders, their skills honed under difficult market conditions where mistakes are difficult to hide. The best managers will utilise the skills learnt during a recession throughout the trade cycle. Creating an atmosphere in which waste and excess are unacceptable, whatever the market conditions, can significantly aid company performance.

Source: *The Economist*, 9 March 2002

1 Which management style might be the most appropriate in a recession? Why?   **[4]**
2 Identify **two** reasons why recessions might produce good leaders.   **[4]**
3 What might companies do to recruit and retain the best managers?   **[6]**
      Total 14 marks

Activity

Research the management styles of the following people:
- Bill Gates (head of Microsoft)
- Tony Blair (Prime Minister)

- Gordon Ramsay (restaurateur)

- Richard Branson (Virgin Group)
- Your headteacher/principal

Describe their style and explain why it is or is not effective.

 McGregor's Theory X and Theory Y

Douglas McGregor's research into business managers in the USA of the 1950s led him to conclude that the style of leadership they adopted was determined largely by the assumptions that they made about the nature of the workforce.

McGregor characterised two opposing views of workers that managers may hold. He labelled them as 'Theory X' and 'Theory Y'. The key aspects of each set of beliefs are shown in Figure 26.2. These views then shape the leadership style adopted by the manager.

- Managers that believe the workforce is **Theory X** in nature will use a more autocratic leadership style. This is because they believe workers need to be told what to do and be closely controlled, or they will not get the work done. There is little point involving workers in decision-making because they do not want such responsibility and are motivated only by money.

Theory X workers:	Theory Y workers:
• dislike work and are naturally lazy • are motivated by money • want to be controlled and directed • lack ambition and seek to avoid responsibility	• enjoy work • are motivated by a range of needs, including esteem and self-actualisation • prefer the independence of taking their own decisions • are ambitious to advance, develop their own abilities and take on responsibility

Figure 26.2 McGregor's X and Y theories

• Managers that believe the workforce is **Theory Y** in nature will use a more democratic leadership style. If workers are seen as creative, seek responsibility and are motivated by being empowered, a leadership style which allows them to fulfil all these needs will be adopted.

Whether the adopted leadership style is successful, depends on whether the manager has made the right assumptions about the workforce. A manager's attitiude has the power to become a self-fulfilling prophacy (that is, it becomes true).

• If it is assumed a workforce conforms to Theory X and it does, the autocratic style will be appropriate and necessary. If, however, the workforce conform to Theory Y, the autocratic style could prove disastrous. The demotivation that it would cause could even create a workforce that conformed to the Theory X label slapped on them – disinterested and uncooperative.

• If it is assumed that a workforce conforms to Theory Y and it does, choosing a democratic style will get the best out of workers' potential and will prove immensely successful. However, if the workers in reality conform to Theory X, the democratic style is doomed to fail. Workers will abuse the freedom from control and will contribute little to decision-making.

Once again, to get the best from their workforce, managers are left to make difficult decisions about human psychology. There is little doubt that managements in UK businesses have traditionally held a Theory X view of the workforce and this has reinforced a 'them and us' attitude. Even though democratic management styles, based on a Theory Y view of workers, have become more common in the UK in recent years, the traditional assumptions of managers seem slow to change.

Leadership and management styles: summary

KEY TERMS

Authoritarian (autocratic) – management style where the leader takes all the decisions and workers are told what to do and are closely controlled.

Paternalistic – management style where the leader seeks to do what is best for his workers, in a father-like way, perhaps involving consultation but with the leader making all the key decisions.

Democratic – management style where the leader allows workers to play a full part in decision-making.

Laissez-faire – management style where the leader leaves employees to get on with their work with little or no interference.

Management by objectives – the process whereby managers agree targets with workers and delegate the responsibility to them for achieving the targets.

Autonomous teamworking – empowering groups of workers to take wide-ranging decisions about their working environment.

Single status – a culture in which all employees are treated the same way.

'Them and us' attitude – a culture in which barriers exist between managers and workers.

Theory X – a set of assumptions about workers that characterise them as lazy, disliking work and wanting to avoid responsibility.

Theory Y – a set of assumptions about workers that characterise them as creative, wanting to work and keen to take on responsibility.

Summary questions

1 How does a leader differ from a manager?
2 Explain the characteristics of an authoritarian leadership style.
3 How does a paternalistic style of management differ from an authoritarian style?
4 What is a democratic leadership style?
5 What is management by objectives (MBO)?
6 How can managers use teamworking to achieve a democratic leadership style?
7 Explain how a single status culture can break down barriers between managers and workers.
8 What is a laissez-faire management style?
9 Why may it be difficult for a leaders to change their style of leadership?
10 What factors determine the success of a leadership style?
11 Contrast how a Theory Y manager would view workers compared to a Theory X manager.

Exam practice

Player managing

The 'golden age of management' in which the manager becomes the pillar of the workplace is, according to Philip Augar and Joy Palmer, coming to an end. The pair have identified what they describe as 'the rise of the player manager', in a book of the same name.

Leaner management structures, enforced by a concentration on shareholder value and the rise of 'knowledge workers', whose expertise is valued more than management skills, have all begun to displace the need for the management generalist. Technical experts today are expected increasingly to incorporate management into their daily work. These 'player managers', who are often among the best in their field, struggle to cope with the competing demands of production and management responsibilities. They often display consultative management styles, but find that stress and time pressure frequently result in them being autocratic.

Player managing is currently practised as a step down the road to self-managed teams – groups of 'knowledge workers' without predefined managers responsible for their own workloads. As ever, managers are finding that they have got to develop new skills to survive in these environments.

Source: *Financial Times*, 4 April 2002

1 Define what is meant by a 'consultative management style'. **[2]**
2 Outline **two** drawbacks of a consultative management style. **[4]**
3 Examine the reasons why 'player managers' might be more likely to display a consultative management style. **[6]**
4 Contrast consultative management styles with autocratic styles. **[6]**
5 Evaluate the pros and cons of an organisation implementing more self-managed teams. **[12]**
Total 30 marks

27 Workforce planning

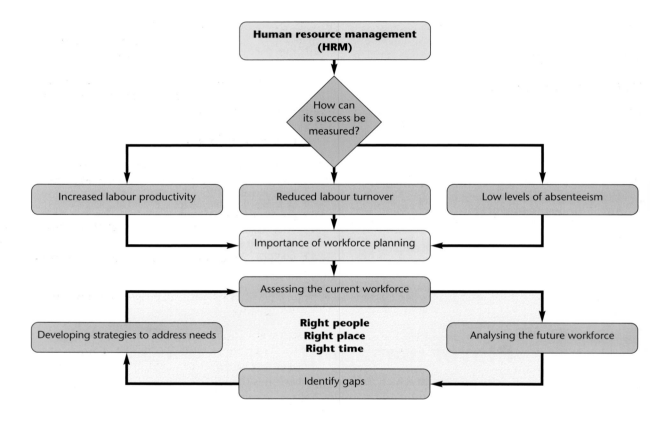

1 The importance of human resource management

Recognition of the fact that people are an organisation's most valuable asset has led to the emergence of **human resource management (HRM)** as a key function in business. HRM is an approach to managing people that emphasises the importance of planning and developing the workforce to achieve the overall aims of the business.

HRM aims to:

- match the skills and energies of the workforce to the strategic direction of the business

- build a competitive advantage over the business's rivals by maximising the quality and motivation of employees

- maximise the efficiency of the business through its management of the workforce.

2 Measuring the success of human resource management

The success of an organisation's approach to HRM may be measured in relation to a range of specific targets: increased labour productivity; reduced labour turnover; reduced absenteeism.

Increased labour productivity

Labour productivity is a measure of the average output per worker over a period of time (see Unit 30). Higher productivity means that each worker is producing more units of output, on average, in the same period of time. This helps to cut production costs and to make the business more cost-competitive. Increased labour productivity is a measure of the success of HRM policies because it is likely to reflect the skills, attitudes and motivation of the workforce – aspects that it would otherwise be difficult to measure.

Reduced labour turnover

Labour turnover is a measure of the rate of change of personnel within a company's workforce. It is calculated as:

$$\frac{\text{No. of staff leaving per period of time}}{\text{Average no. of staff per period of time}} \times 100 = \% \text{ Labour turnover}$$

So if, during one year, five members of staff left out of a workforce of 50 people, the rate of labour turnover would be:

$$\frac{5}{50} \times 100 = 10\% \text{ Labour turnover}$$

Reducing labour turnover is a target for HRM policies, because high labour turnover brings with it a number of costs:

- disruption and lost output or sales when an employee leaves

- costs of recruiting, selecting and training a replacement employee

- unsettling impact on remaining employees, which could harm morale.

Tackling high labour turnover will depend on its causes. Possible causes can include:

- uncompetitive wage rates

- poor morale among the workforce

- low job satisfaction

- poor working conditions

- failure of recruitment and selection processes to find the appropriate person for a job

- failure to develop skills and talents of the workforce.

The HRM function will need to identify the specific causes and plan how to redress them effectively.

However, a successful HRM policy will not necessarily mean a zero per cent labour turnover, which represents no changeover of staff over a period of time. This is because:

- there will always be some staff wanting to leave for personal reasons (retirement age etc)

- new staff can add fresh ideas and enthusiasm to a business

- a business may need new skills in its workforce that are best gained through new recruitment rather than retraining existing staff.

Effective HRM will seek to balance the benefits against the costs of labour turnover to achieve a low, but healthy rate of turnover.

Reduced absenteeism

Absenteeism refers to the number of staff that miss work compared to the overall size of the workforce. It is measured as:

$$\frac{\text{No. of staff absent per period of time}}{\text{Total no. of staff per period of time}} \times 100 = \% \text{ rate of absenteeism}$$

HRM seeks to reduce absenteeism, because high rates of absenteeism:

- reduce productivity – since output is lost when staff miss work

- increase employment costs – because additional workers need to be employed to cover absences, or overtime needs to be paid to existing workers

- harm the morale and motivation of the whole workforce.

Once again, the solutions to a problem of absenteeism lie in the causes specific to each case. Potential causes and solutions are shown in Figure 27.1

3 Workforce planning

To maximise the quality and efficiency of the workforce, so that future business needs can be met, requires effective forward planning. **Workforce planning** is the process of forecasting and providing for the future needs of the business, in terms of both the number of employees required and the skills that they will need. For a business to achieve its objectives, it must employ the right number of people, in the right places and with the right skills.

Workforce planning must be carried out on a short-term and long-term basis. Short-term planning

Possible causes of absenteeism	Appropriate solutions
Failure to ensure health and safety in the workplace, causing accidents or illness to members of staff	Improve working conditions to remove hazards and create a more pleasant working environment
Stress caused by poor relationships with managers or colleagues, e.g. by bullying	Strong action against bullying or harrassment, as well as efforts to encourage teamwork and create a positive social atmosphere
Boring, stressful and unrewarding job	Job redesign to include enrichment and opportunities for staff development
Lack of financial incentive, e.g. no loss of pay through absence	Financial incentives to link pay to productivity attendance, e.g. piece rates/PRP or attendance bonuses

Figure 27.1 Possible causes and solutions of absenteeism

will involve meeting staffing needs over the following weeks and months – for example, to ensure there is sufficient cover scheduled for staff on holiday. Longer-term planning will be based on the strategic plans of the whole business, to make sure that the workforce achieves the goals set out. The stages involved in long-term workforce planning are summarised in Figure 27.2.

> ### Guru's views
> **'The person who figures out how to harness the collective genius of his or her organisation is going to blow the competition away.'**
>
> *Walter Wriston*

Assessing the current workforce

The starting-point for workforce planning will be to ask, 'Where are we now?' – an assessment of the size and skills of the existing workforce. **A workforce audit** of current employees will examine all of the business's personnel records to identify:

- the number of employees working in each part of the business

- the job roles that they are carrying out

- the characteristics of employees in terms of their age, length of service etc.

- the skills and experience within the workforce.

This information will prove vital in allowing the business to estimate the likely size and skills of the workforce in the future.

Analysing the future workforce

Carrying out an analysis of the future workforce involves forecasting and estimating.

- **Forecasting.** A forecast of the likely supply of workers and skills from within the business in the future is needed. Using the current workforce audit, the business can begin to assess the likely future supply of workers and skills. It will also need to estimate future labour turnover to predict how many of the existing staff will leave through retirement or for other reasons.

- **Estimating.** The business must estimate the likely future demand for workers and skills. It will need to decide:

  – how many staff will be needed and when

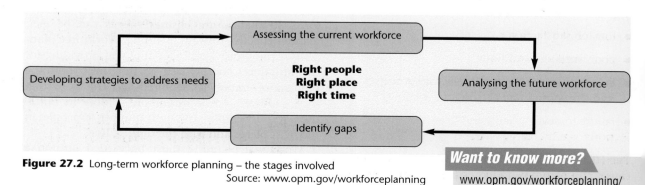

Figure 27.2 Long-term workforce planning – the stages involved
Source: www.opm.gov/workforceplanning

Want to know more?
www.opm.gov/workforceplanning/

– what skills and training they will require

– in what parts of its organisation they will be required.

These future needs will depend on several key factors.

- **Business goals.** The workforce will need to be able to carry out the business strategy and achieve the business's goals. Business growth will require an expanded workforce, while a move into new foreign markets may require additional language skills.

- **Future demand for the product.** Expected growth or decline in the level of demand for the final product will affect the size of the future workforce. Growth in demand will need to be *anticipated* so that the workforce is recruited and trained, ready to meet the higher demand.

- **Changing productivity levels.** It may be possible to meet higher demand through the increased productivity of the existing workforce or through greater use of technology. The potential economies or diseconomies of scale (see Unit 31) caused by a growth in business size will need to be taken into account.

- **Changing business environment.** An increase in competition, the development of new technology or new employment laws could all influence the number or type of workers needed.

STOP & THINK

How will workforce planning be affected by a changing business environment?

4 Strategies to address needs

Once a business has forecast its future *demand* for employees and compared this with the estimated *supply* of workers available from within the business, it will be able to identify the gaps between the two. These may indicate a need to:

- expand the workforce
- contract the workforce
- develop new skills or attitudes within the workforce.

Expanding the workforce

Recruitment of additional workers from outside the organisation needs to be carefully planned (see Unit 28). The firm's ability to recruit both locally and nationally will be affected by:

- level of unemployment, and so overall labour supply

- availability of the specific type of labour and skills required

- level of competition and the reward package offered to employees

- availability of affordable housing, allowing new workers to move into the area

- demographic trends, such as more women entering the labour market

- government assistance and constraints, such as training schemes

- employment laws.

Contracting the workforce

A reduction in staff could be achieved through:

- 'natural wastage' – not replacing workers when they choose to leave the business (encouraged by offering 'early retirement' incentives to those still under the official age of retirement).

- redundancy – shedding workers whose jobs are no longer needed.

- de-layering – removing management levels from the company hierarchy to produce a 'flatter' organisational structure (see Unit 22).

- flexible working – encouraging job-sharing, or part-time or short-term employment while keeping a smaller 'core' of full-time employees.

Activity

Study the following information about a business:
- absenteeism – 5% (2% higher than previous year)
- labour turnover – 15% (down 2.7% on previous year)
- average length of service (shopfloor staff) – 4 years
- average length of service (management) – 8 years
- 15% of the workforce, 30% of managers and 3% of senior management under 35 years of age
- 5% of the workforce eligible to retire within three years
- males – 68% of all staff
- females – 4% of management and 46% of shop-floor workers.

In light of the information provided, write a report explaining why workforce planning is important to this business.

Workforce planning: summary

KEY TERMS

Human resource management (HRM) – an approach to managing people that emphasises the importance of planning and developing the workforce to achieve the overall aims of the business.

Labour turnover – a measure of the rate of change of personnel, including leavers and joiners, within a company's workforce.

Absenteeism – the number of staff who miss work compared to the overall size of the workforce.

Workforce planning – the process of forecasting and meeting the future needs of the business, in terms of the number of employees required and the skills that they will need.

Workforce audit – a check on the size and skills of a current workforce.

Summary questions

1 What are the aims of human resource management (HRM)?
2 Why is labour productivity an important measure of the success of HRM policies?
3 How is labour turnover calculated?
4 How might high labour turnover be reduced?
5 Why might a labour turnover of zero per cent be undesirable?
6 What is meant by 'absenteeism'?
7 Explain two problems associated with high absenteeism.
8 Briefly explain why workforce planning is necessary.
9 What are the critical stages in workforce planning?
10 What will a business need to consider when forecasting:
   a the future internal supply of workers
   b the likely future demand for workers?
11 What strategies could a business use to address the gaps between its future demand for workers and the available internal supply?

Exam practice

Older and idler?

Modern pensions are often no longer enough to support people through what can be lengthy retirements. As Figure 27.3 shows, between 1992 and 2002 there was a steady increase in the number of older workers (defined as 'over 50') in the workplace. Older people are now finding that they need to rejoin the workforce to bolster their pensions.

Sheer common sense, you might think. But in practice there are hurdles. Physical strength declines with age, as does memory, and companies are often reluctant to employ older people. However, the benefits to be gained by employing older workers can more than offset the supposed disadvantages. A Nottingham University survey found that older workers show less absenteeism, lower labour turnover, fewer accidents, higher job satisfaction and a more positive work ethic than younger workers. They also bring a range of valuable skills and experiences.

Older workers will be getting help from the EU in 2006, when a directive will make age discrimination illegal. In fact, some companies such as B&Q already actively seek to recruit older workers in order to benefit from some of the factors mentioned.

Source: *The Economist*, 23 March 2002

1 Define the term 'labour turnover'. [2]
2 What is meant by 'less absenteeism'? [2]
3 Outline two benefits of employing skilled and experienced workers. [6]
4 Analyse the benefits a firm may gain from low labour turnover and low absenteeism. [8]
5 Evaluate the implications for workforce planning of B&Q's policy actively to recruit older workers. [12]

Total 30 marks

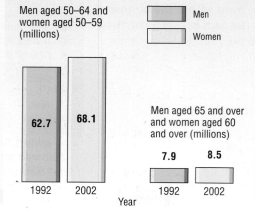

Figure 27.3 Average number of women and men over 50 in employment in 1992 and 2002

28 Recruitment, selection, training

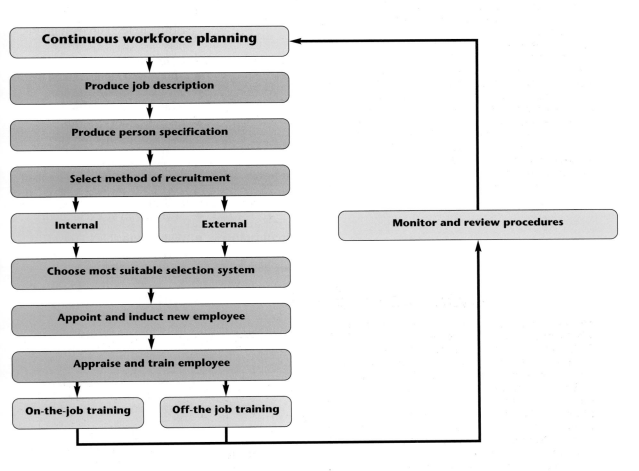

1 Three vital processes

Unit 27 emphasised the importance of people in enabling the strategic aims of a business to be met. Maximising the quality of the workforce involves a business in three vital processes:

- recruitment – attracting the best-quality people into the workforce
- selection – ensuring the most suitable candidates are chosen from a pool of applicants
- training – developing the skills of the workforce to make the most out of the abilities they possess.

2 Recruitment

Many of Britain's top companies spend more than £1 million a year on recruiting new workers. They know that attracting the very best applicants will help to give them a competitive edge over their rivals. To ensure that only the most suitable individuals apply for positions, the business must make careful decisions about:

- what the job involves – expressed in a **job description**, which provides a 'word picture' of the tasks and working conditions. The job description (see example in Figure 28.1) shows prospective applicants what they would be expected to do if appointed.

Job title:	**TV football commentator**
Department:	Sports broadcasts
Main job role:	To provide knowledgeable commentary on top football matches for weekly TV broadcasts
Responsible for:	Guest summarisers
Responsible to:	Head of Sports Broadcasting
Duties:	<ul><li>To prepare thoroughly in advance of each match, including looking up relevant statistics</li><li>To sit in the commentary box for the duration of each match and to commentate on the play lucidly but with enthusiasm</li><li>To interview players and managers in a relaxed, non-confrontational manner.</li></ul>

Figure 28.1 Job description for a TV football commentator

Job title:	**TV football commentator**
Attainments:	<ul><li>Background in radio or TV journalism</li><li>In-depth knowledge of football</li><li>Preferably some experience of playing the game or coaching</li></ul>
Skills:	<ul><li>Ability to speak quickly and clearly to keep up with up the play</li><li>Good eyesight</li><li>Ability to conduct interviews</li><li>Excellent knowledge of football in all its aspects</li><li>An outwardly cheerful disposition whatever the weather</li></ul>
Interests:	<ul><li>Everything to do with football</li></ul>
Disposition:	<ul><li>Enthusiastic</li><li>Able to convey excitement</li></ul>
Circumstances:	<ul><li>Willing and able to travel</li></ul>

Figure 28.2 Person specification for a TV football commentator

- the qualities of the ideal candidate – set out in a **person specification**. This identifies the skills and abilities needed to do the job successfully (see Figure 28.2 for an example). The person specification provides an ideal checklist against which to judge the desirability of each potential candidate.

- the most appropriate methods of recruitment to be used – chosen from a range of **internal recruitment** and **external recruitment** methods. These are described in Figure 28.3.

In managing the recruitment process, a business has to balance the need to attract the best applicants against the expense of the process. This can be gauged by monitoring how much the recruitment of a new employee costs on average and how long that person stays with the business – an indicator of the success of the appointment.

STOP & THINK

What are the benefits and the drawbacks of each of the methods of external recruitment shown in Figure 28.3?

Activity

Using the internet, investigate the recruitment processes of the following businesses:
Virgin Ltd (www.virgin.com)
Egg plc (www.egg.com)
Cisco Systems (www.cisco.co.uk)
Demon Tweeks (www.demon-tweeks.co.uk)
Topshop (www.topshop.co.uk)

- What is each of these businesses looking for in potential recruits?
- How much information about vacant positions does each of them provide?
- Can you apply online?
- Are job descriptions and person specifications available online? What do they include?
- What recruitment process does each business use?

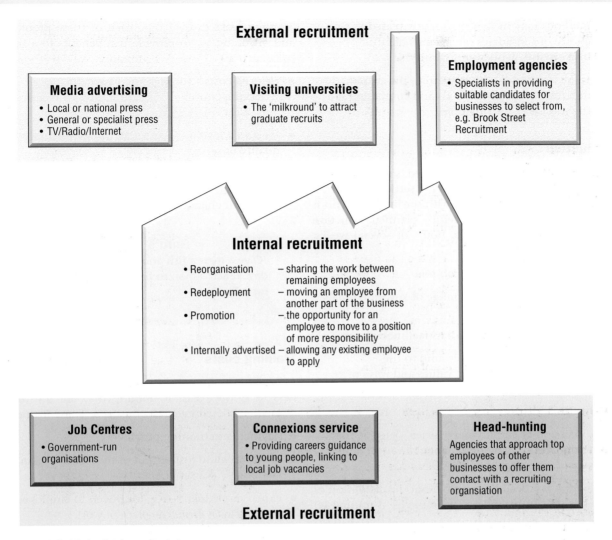

Figure 28.3 Methods of recruitment

 ## 3   Selection

The selection process is about choosing the right candidate for the job. The costs of selection procedures in time and money can be considerable, but the costs of a wrong decision will be even greater in terms of:

- low productivity

- poor quality or customer service

- demotivation

- high labour turnover

- further costs in recruiting a replacement once someone has left.

Because selection is recognised as being so important, developing effective selection systems has become a priority for businesses in recent years.

Figure 28.4 lists the selection methods in widespread use and identifies their respective benefits and drawbacks.

In most European countries, the most widely used selection tools are the application form, interview and references. However, there are some differences in the techniques used between countries. For example, in France the majority of firms use handwriting analysis to judge personality traits – a method little used elsewhere.

In seeking the right combination of methods, a business will need continually to review the outcomes of its selection procedures. It can study:

- the predictive success of selection methods – by examining the performance and retention of previously successful candidates

- fairness – by analysing whether selection

methods may have been unfairly biased in the choice of candidates on grounds of ethnic background, gender or disability

- value for money – by measuring the cost of different selection methods and comparing it to the success of the outcome.

Induction

When a new employee is appointed, specific training will be required to help him or her settle into the new job and become acquainted with the business. This is known as **induction**. A carefully planned induction programme can last several hours or several weeks, but is likely to include:

- specific training for the job role

- opportunities to meet a range of key individuals within the business

- a tour of the business and its facilities

- explanation of the background to the organisation – its vision, values and ways of working

- health and safety instruction

- discussion of employment issues – such as the terms of employment, payment arrangements etc.

Induction is crucial in ensuring that the disruption to the business of having a new employee is minimised and that the employee feels secure and positive in his or her new environment.

 4   Training

Training is the process of teaching employees new skills or developing the skills and qualities they already possess. Without the ongoing training of its workforce, a business could experience a number of problems:

- low labour productivity

- poor product quality or poor customer service

- demotivation of staff

- high rates of labour turnover or absenteeism

- inability to cope with change – such as new technology or new working practices

- poor health and safety record, producing high accident or illness rates among staff.

Training seeks to overcome each of these problems and, in doing so, to provide real benefits to a business, such as:

- reduced costs – through increased efficiency, reduced recruitment costs or improved health and safety

- increased revenues – through improved image, quality or service

- innovation and flexibility – through a workforce that is highly skilled, generating ideas and able to cope with change.

Guru's views
'Give a man a fish and you feed him for a day. Teach a man to fish and you feed him for a lifetime.'

Proverb

Training costs

Although training brings a range of benefits to a business, it is the costs of training that are the most immediately obvious to the business. These include:

- payments to training providers

- disruption and lost output of those undertaking training

- expenses payments (e.g. for travel) to employees training away from the place of work

- administrative/management time and effort needed to organise, implement and review training.

Such costs can be considerable. To train one employee to NVQ Level 2 standard in Food Retailing costs over £1,000, while in Construction this figure rises to nearly £9,000.

During a recession, when businesses need to cut costs to remain profitable, it is often expenditure on training that is cut. Short-term cost-savings prevail over the long-term benefits that training would bring. This is one example of a type of **market failure** – where the 'ideal' level of training is not provided because the true, long-term benefits are not given sufficient weight against the short-term costs.

Another reason why businesses may not spend the optimum (ideal) amount on training is that they do not always get to see the full benefits of the training that they provide. Trained employees may move to another firm, which then gets the skills and training

Selection method	Description	Benefits	Drawbacks
Application forms/Curriculum vitae (CV)	<ul><li>how 97% of UK businesses collect information about candidates – through use of their own application form or a **curriculum vitae (CV)** prepared by the candidate.</li><li>summary of a candidate's qualifications, skills and experience.</li></ul>	<ul><li>enable key data to be compared with the person specification, so that unsuitable candidates sifted out; provide a good basis for interview questions for the rest.</li><li>advantage of a standard format offered by application forms – easier to sort – and the opportunity to ask carefully chosen questions.</li></ul>	<ul><li>leave important questions unanswered – cannot alone provide for effective selection</li><li>the information desired by the business perhaps not provided by CV.</li></ul>
Interviews	<ul><li>face-to-face meetings to question short-listed candidates and find out more about their suitability for the job.</li><li>should be conducted in a structured and objective way that allows candidates to be compared fairly.</li></ul>	<ul><li>provide an opportunity to discuss the written details submitted by the candidate as well as wider issues about the job and the candidate's qualities and ambitions.</li><li>enable the business to evaluate whether the candidate would fit in, and relate well to colleagues.</li><li>allow the business to sell itself to candidates and thereby encourage the best one to accept a job offer.</li></ul>	<ul><li>impressions formed on the basis of candidate's appearance or interview technique, due to subjective nature of interviews.</li><li>interviews unreliable indicators of a candidate's ability to succeed in a job, according to research findings.</li></ul>
References	<ul><li>contact details, provided by candidates, of previous employers or other individuals that will confirm a candidate's qualities or experience.</li></ul>	<ul><li>provide important evidence that the skills and experiences claimed by a candidate are genuine.</li></ul>	<ul><li>far from objective and not necessarily reliable – candidates choose referees that are likely to commend them for the job.</li></ul>
Testing	<ul><li>ability tests – testing a specific skill relevant to the job, e.g. numeracy.</li><li>personality tests – also known as **psychometric testing** – seeking to measure aspects of the candidate's attitudes and characteristics, e.g. risk-taking or risk-avoiding; increasingly common in the UK for executive recruitment.</li></ul>	<ul><li>a cost-effective and easy-to-use method, providing further evidence of a candidate's suitability.</li><li>can directly simulate the challenges and requirements of the job to see whether a candidate, if appointed, could cope.</li></ul>	<ul><li>not necessarily objective or fair – may be biased in choice or wording of questions.</li><li>some candidates becoming skilled in giving the 'right' answers in personality tests.</li><li>notion of 'ideal' personality type perhaps leading to an organisation full of personality 'clones'.</li></ul>
Assessment centres	<ul><li>short-listed candidates invited to an **assessment centre** to undergo a range of assessment techniques – interviews, testing, group exercises, simulations – that reflect the demands of the job.</li><li>performances of each individual observed and rated by trained assessors.</li></ul>	<ul><li>a reliable and valid selection technique using a wide range of methods relevant to the job role.</li><li>objectivity to the selection process brought by qualified assessors, while line managers involved in observation and decision-making.</li></ul>	<ul><li>a time-consuming and expensive method of selection which is therefore only appropriate for large firms and executive positions.</li></ul>

Figure 28.4 Benefits and drawbacks of different selection methods

of the new employee for free. This is a particular problem in the health service, where government expenditure on training for doctors and nurses is wasted if they move out of the NHS to work in private healthcare.

For all these reasons, the level of training provided by businesses will often be lower than the ideal. To encourage businesses to invest in their workforce, government can provide subsidies or tax incentives to businesses to help reduce the costs of training.

Types of training

Training can be divided into two types according to when and where the training takes place: **on-the-job training** and **off-the job training**.

- **On-the-job training.** This refers to training that takes place while the employee is working. It can be done through:

  - coaching – where a supervisor or coach guides a trainee through the stages involved in a job or teaches the trainee how to improve the quality of his or her work
  - mentoring – where a more experienced colleague offers advice to another on how best to carry out a job or solve problems
  - job rotation – moving employees from one task, or part of the company, to another to broaden their range of skills and experience.

- **Off-the-job training.** This includes a form of training that requires an employee to stop working to be trained. The training may still take place within the business, or the employee could go elsewhere to be trained. Off-the-job training methods include:

  - in-house courses – where a business arranges its own training programmes, often using the expertise of its employees to act as trainers. Larger businesses, such as HSBC, have training centres, where they run residential courses for employees from other parts of the country.
  - college/university courses – where employees go from the workplace to a local college or university to study for qualifications relevant to their job. The Chartered Institute of Marketing and the Institute of Personnel Management are professional bodies that offer vocational qualifications for employees working in their respective fields. Employees may also study for qualifications at home through distance learning programmes. Businesses can support them by giving them time-off to study or by meeting the costs of courses and qualifications.

For example …

Of course!

Training has become the Holy Grail to some organisations – evidence of how much management truly cares about the workforce. No wonder so many employers see it as an asset. Ideally, not only do staff acquire skills that will help them to work more efficiently, they also get a morale boost – it's gratifying to think you are perceived as worthwhile to invest in.

Unfortunately, it doesn't always work out that way. Even with carefully identified training needs and full management support, the most effective training is not always the result. Many off-the-job business courses are too long or try to cram too much into one day. It is often more efficient (though more hassle) to spread courses over several half-days. And, since – apparently – we forget 70 per cent of everything we have learned on a course within three days, some managers think twice before sending employees on expensive training programmes.

Source: *The Times*, 16 May 2002

1 What is meant by off-the-job training?   [2]
2 State **two** advantages to an organisation of having well-trained employees.   [2]
3 State and explain **two** problems that might be associated with having a poorly trained workforce.   [4]
4 Consider whether 'ineffective' training might be better than no training at all.   [6]
    Total 14 marks

Want to know more?

www.monster.co.uk

Recruitment, selection, training: summary

KEY TERMS

Job description – a summary of what the job involves, such as the main duties and working conditions.

Person specification – an outline of the skills and experience required in the ideal candidate for a job.

Internal recruitment – seeking to fill a vacant post from among current employees.

External recruitment – seeking to attract applicants from outside the business to fill a vacant post.

Curriculum vitae (CV) – a personal summary of an applicant's qualifications, skills and experience.

Psychometric testing – assessment of a candidate's personality traits and personal qualities relevant to a specific job role

Assessment centre – a venue for hosting a variety of selection exercises, including testing, interviews and simulations.

Induction – initial training to introduce a new employee to the business and to his or her job role.

Market failure – when the ideal level of provision of a good or service is not achieved through the forces of supply and demand, such as when training is under-provided by businesses because they do not realise its true long-term benefits.

Summary questions

1 Distinguish between a job description and a person specification.
2 Draw up a brief job description for a teacher or lecturer.
3 Explain the importance of job descriptions and person specifications in the recruitment process.
4 Explain how and why a business might use internal recruitment.
5 What are the advantages of external recruitment?
6 Suggest **two** reasons why a firm might prefer to use application forms rather than CVs when recruiting staff.
7 What types of testing can a business use in its selection process?
8 What is the value of using an assessment centre?
9 State **three** things that might be included in induction training.
10 Explain **two** reasons why training is important to business.
11 Distinguish, using examples, between on-the-job and off-the-job training.

On-the-job training – methods of training that take place while the employee is still working.
Off-the-job training – methods of training that involve the employee stopping work to be trained

Exam practice

Are you a high flyer?

The Caudwell Group (owners of Phones 4U) is a highly successful mobile phone business based in Crewe, Cheshire. The Caudwell Graduate High Flyer scheme was launched to attract and retain some of the world's very best university graduates. Candidates must be prickly, focused, intolerant of failure and shrewd achievers. The company seeks to recruit exceptionally talented graduates with between one and three years' commercial experience and a proven track record of excellence. Caudwell looks for over-achievers who feel that their current position does not offer the opportunities for development that they demand.

The application process is very rigorous. Candidates undergo numerous interviews and are eventually interviewed by John Caudwell himself, the entrepreneurial chief executive. Induction training is short and tough. The successful candidate is expected to hit the ground running and to make an immediate impact. Those appointed are often expected to improve the performance of some of the company's weakest phone stores within a matter of weeks.

The rewards are, however, excellent. Salaries start at £40,000–£60,000 a year, with healthy bonuses. A company car is provided, and earnings of £500,000 before reaching the age of thirty are perfectly possible. The group has, to date, created over twenty millionaires. If they get through the tough application process, candidates really could be flying high!

1 What is induction training? [2]
2 Explain why induction training is so important. [6]
3 Outline a suitable recruitment and selection process for Caudwell's High Flyer scheme. [10]
4 Prepare a suitable person specification for a Caudwell Graduate High Flyer. [7]
5 Lengthy recruitment and selection campaigns often cost businesses many thousands of pounds. Given that successful recruitment is never certain, evaluate why businesses invest so much money in it. [10]
Total 35 marks

29 Corporate culture and managing change

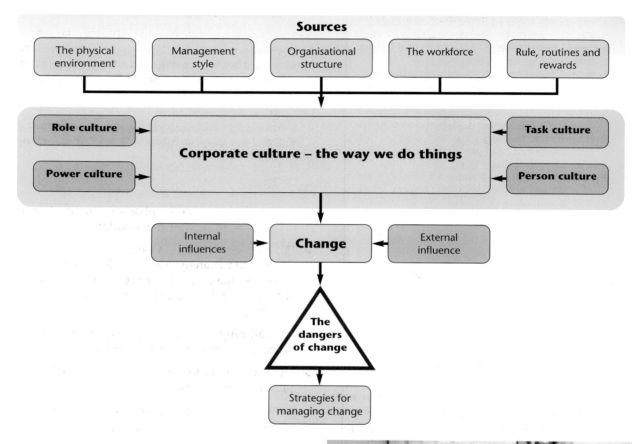

Sources

| The physical environment | Management style | Organisational structure | The workforce | Rule, routines and rewards |

Role culture → **Corporate culture – the way we do things** ← **Task culture**

Power culture → ← **Person culture**

Internal influences → **Change** ← External influence

The dangers of change

Strategies for managing change

1   What is corporate culture?

Richard Branson, chair of the Virgin Group, calls it 'the way we do things'. Sumantra Ghoshal of London Business School describes it as 'the smell of the place'. If you have ever watched *The Office* on TV you will be able to describe it. What is it?

'It' is **corporate culture** – the attitudes and values that are evident within an organisation. Culture includes the atmosphere, the rules, the habits and the image of the organisation. It is not something written down, though the written policies and statements of the business may shape the culture. It is something that may not even be visible to the casual observer. But someone who works within the organisation will

What kind of culture does David Brent create in *The Office*?

be able to describe it – culture is what it is like to be there.

When describing corporate culture, we mean:

- the atmosphere within the organisation – is it stressful or relaxed, bullying or supportive?

- the feelings created by the physical environment – do the facilities make staff feel valued or resentful?

- the attitudes of staff and management towards work – is it positive and hardworking, or negative and work-avoiding?

- what is valued most – is it initiative and risk-taking, conforming to the rules or even breaking the rules?

- how authority is used and shared out – is it used constructively or unfairly; is it centralised or are employees empowered to take their own decisions?

- the image people have of the organisation – is it perceived as successful or under-achieving?

Activity

Choose an organisation and research its culture. This may be a business where you work or your school or college.
Describe the culture of your chosen organisatoin, using the aspects listed under What is corporate culture? as a guide.

2   Types of business culture

Writers on business management have used a variety of labels to describe different types of business culture. Charles Handy, London School of Business founder and author, and Roger Harrison, a business consultant and author, suggest that organisational cultures can be classified under four headings: **power culture**, **role culture**, **task culture** and **person culture**.

Power culture

An organisation that has a power culture is like a web with a ruling spider. All those in the web depend on the central power source – a strong and dominant leader.

- The leader dominates the organisation, using personal charisma, an authoritarian leadership style or key middle-managers who ensure everyone's loyalty.

- What is valued is pleasing the boss. Rules do not dominate or constrain what individuals do – indeed those that exist may be broken if it suits the leader or those seeking to please.

- Work and achieving results are what matters – with the leader setting the goals.

- Success and promotion within the organisation are closely linked to the personal relationship between the employee and the centre.

A power culture can be effective, dynamic and swift to respond to change. On the other hand, many employees may feel unfairly treated and resentful at the power of the leader. Efforts may become focused on pleasing the boss, rather than on business success or meeting the needs of other stakeholders. Much will depend on the skills of the leader in motivating and managing staff – particularly in a growing organisation.

Role culture

With role cultures, the emphasis is on the formal rules and structures of the organisation.

- The business is likely to be organised as a 'functional hierarchy' (see Unit 22), in which employees have clearly defined job roles as part of a specialist department, such as finance or marketing.

- The authority of each employee is determined by his or her place within a 'pyramid' structure.

- Communication follows the formal lines of authority from top to bottom.

- Following rules and procedures is more important than showing initiative or taking risks.

One of the strengths of role culture is that both the organisational structure and what is expected of an individual are clear. This type of culture can achieve stability and consistency, presenting an unthreatening working environment. However, the bureaucratic nature of the culture may make it slow to respond to change. It will not encourage innovation from staff, nor make the best of their talents. This could prove frustrating and demotivating.

Task culture

An organisation with a task culture is one in which power and responsibility are distributed across a 'net' of small teams.

- These teams focus on results and getting things

done. They may have been set up to tackle specific projects or contracts – such as in a 'matrix' organisational structure.

- Job roles do not bring authority; rather it is the expertise and achievements of each individual that are recognised and rewarded.

- Individuals are empowered to make decisions and take risks to achieve results.

The emphasis on teamworking and results can make this type of culture flexible, motivating and responsive to change. However, it can lack some of the benefits of a role culture – namely, clarity of organisation and communication. And conflict between individuals and teams may harm the overall interests of the organisation.

Person culture

In a person culture, the individual worker is the central point.

- There may be little or no overall structure to the organisation and, where there is, it only exists to support the individuals who work there.

- This may be typical of a professional partnership such as barristers' chambers or an architects' practice, where office support is shared, but otherwise individuals work alone.

Person culture is likely to be the only one that individuals in these types of organisations will accept. Each individual may have very different values and beliefs about how things should be done. Problems can arise if one employee tries to impose his or her culture on others. Employees with a person culture may also be found working in other cultures, but 'doing their own thing'. 'Mavericks' like this can be very difficult for a different culture to manage.

3 Sources of business culture

Business cultures develop over a long time. They are largely based on tradition and what has come to be expected. Because of this, the culture that exists cannot be traced back to a single cause. Consequently, changing a corporate culture is often a difficult and

---

For example ...

Tough bosses reap what they sow

The founder of WorldCom, Bernie Ebbers, had so much praise heaped on him in the 1990s that, even now, many just cannot believe that his company perpetrated the biggest fraud in history. Mr Ebbers successfully cultivated the image of a 'popular hero' who brought jobs and wealth to the poorest state in America.

Yet, according to Lynne Jeter of the *Mississippi Business Journal*, the seeds of the disaster at WorldCom were sown from the start by the aggressive autocratic management style of Mr Ebbers. 'Bernie Ebbers was very arrogant and pompous. He was very dismissive of everyone,' she says.

Bernie Ebbers: aggressive and autocratic style

Ms Jeter points to rumours, now emerging, that senior managers had been fired simply for selling some of their WorldCom shares.

Such an atmosphere of fear – where employees lack the confidence to challenge their boss – is bound to lead to mistakes in the end. The fact that so many employees had not just their job tied up in WorldCom, but also most of their savings, also meant they were less likely to 'rock the boat' a little bit, for fear of what the consequences might be.

The willingness to tolerate an arrogant and bullying business culture therefore appears to have played a key role in the shocking financial scandals that have emerged in the past year.

Source: http://news.bbc.co.uk/ 1/hi/business/2097553.stm

---

1 What type of business culture developed at WorldCom? Explain your answer. **[5]**

2 What might the effects of this culture be? **[5]**

3 What factors may have created this culture? **[5]**

Total 15 marks

lengthy process. An organisation's culture may have been shaped by a number of factors.

- **Management style.** An autocratic leader is likely to create a power culture around him or her, whereas a democratic management style will shape a task culture or even a person culture.

- **Organisational structure.** A formal hierarchical structure requires a role culture if it is to operate effectively, whereas a matrix structure will help to build a task culture.

- **Nature of the workforce.** A workforce that conforms to Theory X (see Unit 26) will need a role culture, as they will show little personal initiative; a workforce that conforms to Theory Y will be best motivated by the empowerment offered by a task culture.

- **Rules and routines.** The existing procedures, the way that they are enforced and the habits and routines of employees will combine to shape an organisation.

- **Rewards.** What is rewarded – conformity or risk-taking, for example – and how it is rewarded, financially or through other means, will all help to shape what is valued and how people behave.

- **Physical environment.** The culture of the business will be reflected and reinforced by the physical environment, shaping attitudes towards work and towards the business.

4   Managing change

To be successful, an organisation must adapt to changing circumstances. It may need to change its:

- business culture
- organisational structure
- business size
- product portfolio
- target markets
- methods of production
- management style.

The need for change could arise from internal or external factors. Internal factors leading to change may be due to problems or successes. Problems might include:

- demotivated workforce

- negative business culture
- poor labour productivity
- lack of product quality or innovation.

Successes might include:

- increasing sales
- new product ideas
- investment in new technology or new premises
- growth through acquisition of other businesses.

Change is often forced on an organisation by changes in the external business environment, such as:

- market change – for example, increasing competition (as in the emergence of low-cost airlines) or a change in consumer tastes

- political/legislative change – such as new laws that give employees rights to flexible working hours

- economic change – recession or entry into the single currency, for instance

- social change – such as demographic change that leads to a growing elderly population

- technological change – that may open up new opportunities in the production process or affect competition.

Problems of change

Sudden or rapid change can cause a number of problems for an organisation, unless the process of change is carefully managed.

- **Loss of strategic focus.** A business could lose sight of its main strengths during the process of change. Business growth through diversification and acquisition, for example, could leave an organisation uncertain as to where its core business lies. ICI suffered such problems, leading it to 'demerge' and a return to its original product focus.

- **Disorganisation or distraction.** The process of change could itself become the focus of attention for managers and employees, rather than efficiency or customer service. New procedures or a new office location might serve to distract workers from their key tasks. New ideas or ways of working may need new structures or styles of leadership – without which change may be very difficult to achieve.

- **Financial dangers.** A business might be left short of cash, for example, if it seeks to expand too swiftly – the problem of overtrading. Mobile phone companies were left with huge debts, having purchased new-generation licences in an attempt to keep pace with technological and market change.

- **Resistance to change.** The motivation theory of Abraham Maslow (see Unit 24) identified a basic human need for security. Change will undermine this security, with threats to:
  - familiar routines and ways of working
  - job security or personal status
  - pay and existing working conditions
  - social ties within the business.

Employees may become demotivated and obstruct change. They may act collectively through trade unions to resist change, causing industrial relations problems.

> **Guru's views**
> ' "Progress" is a nice word, but change is its motivator ... and change has its enemies.'
> *John F. Kennedy*

Managing change effectively

If problems are to be avoided and change is to be successful, the management of change must be effective. Change must not just be allowed to happen, or occur without planning for the consequences. Managing change requires planning, implementation and review. For it to succeed, a number of key principles must be observed.

- **Careful strategic planning.** To identify the benefits of change, its consequences, any problems that may arise and how these will be addressed requires careful, strategic planning.

- **Limiting change.** Only some changes within an organisation are possible and desirable – and any ideas for change must fall within these constraints.

- **Understanding the effects.** Change can have an impact at many different levels – on the individual, on teams or groups, on the whole organisation and even on communities and the economy. To make change acceptable, the respective needs at each level should be considered and an effort made to meet them.

- **Involving those affected.** All the different groups of stakeholders that will be affected by change should be consulted, and ways found for them to be involved. Employees could participate in the change process, helping to make key decisions and to implement changes. This will give them 'ownership' of the change process and invite greater commitment to its success. Ensuring that customers, suppliers and the local community are kept informed of changes will help to build trust and reduce fears about the impact of change.

- **Meeting security needs.** If change is being resisted out of a sense of insecurity, it is essential to allay these fears. Guaranteeing job security, offering a pay rise and keeping employees informed would all contribute towards this end.

- **Positive, dynamic leadership.** Setting out a clear vision of what is expected from change and communicating this effectively will help to provide direction and motivation. The ability of a leader to win over the support of employees is vital to the success of change.

- **Training and support.** If employees are to adapt successfully to change, they may need to adopt new skills or attitudes. Training and support within the organisation will be crucial in achieving this end.

- **Developing a culture of change.** If resistance to change is an ingrained part of the business culture, this will be difficult to overcome. In time, businesses need to build a culture that accepts change and can adapt swiftly to changing circumstances.

STOP & THINK

Think of a major change you have experienced – in your own life or in an organisation you have been part of. Was the change successfully managed? Which of the principles of change management were apparent and which were not?

Corporate culture and managing change: summary

KEY TERMS

Corporate culture – the attitudes and values that are evident within an organisation.

Power culture – an organisation in which employees seek to please a strong and dominant leader.

Role culture – an organisation in which conforming to the formal rules and structures is what matters.

Task culture – an organisation in which power and responsibility are distributed across a 'net' of small teams and achieving results is what is valued.

Person culture – an organisation in which the individual worker is the central point, and there is little or no overall business structure.

Summary questions

1   Explain what features of an organisation make up its 'corporate culture'.
2   What is a power culture?
3   What is valued in a role culture?
4   How does a task culture differ from a role culture?
5   Why do some organisations have a person culture?
6   What factors shape an organisation's culture?
7   What (a) internal (b) external factors might force a business to change?
8   What problems can change cause?
9   Explain **three** key principles of effective change management.

Exam practice

1   Define the terms:
   a   business culture   [2]
   b   mission statement.   [2]
2   What type of business culture seems to have existed at Cummins before the VISION programme? Explain your answer.   [6]
3   Explain the meaning of the phrase 'employees were empowered'.   [5]
4   How did Cummins seek to ensure that change was successfully managed?   [8]
5   Evaluate the likely impact of changing the corporate culture on a business such as Cummins.   [12]
   Total 35 marks

Powering forward through culture change

Cummins Inc. is one of the world's leading manufacturers of diesel engines and power generation systems. Having grown steadily over more than 50 years, Cummins was facing rapid change in a global market. It had moved into new geographical markets across the world and into new product markets, using new technologies. This pace of change and the increasingly intense competition it faced exposed the need for Cummins to develop a business culture that was more adaptable, flexible and swifter to respond to change. If it was to succeed, Cummins would need to reenergise the company, creating a more dynamic culture that would make full use of the creativity and ideas of its employees.

In planning for change, Cummins recognised the importance of creating a new, clear vision that would help to shape a more consistent set of values and goals across its global organisation. The new vision statement came out of a series of focus workshops that gathered the views of a wide range of employees across the company's different locations worldwide. The vision – 'Making people's lives better by unleashing the Power of Cummins'– was supported by a mission statement that referred to 'motivating people to act like owners working together'. This was intended to communicate a shift to a culture in which employees were empowered to generate new ideas and to reduce costs.

To kick-start the change in culture, the VISION programme was rolled out – a series of special events that came as a real surprise to employees. These were motivational events, which were based on fun, informality, high energy and audience participation. Their purpose was to involve everyone in the new way of working – one in which their ideas would be listened to.

These events were followed by a series of practical changes in the way employees at Cummins worked.

●   Team-working was encouraged, and responsibility delegated within a 'cell structure'.
●   The performance of managers and employees was measured against the company's new values.
●   An internal web-site magazine offered guidance and the chance to see the results of change.

Cummins now believes its strategy has successfully reenergised the company and laid the foundation for a more innovative, efficient and profitable future.

Source: www.thetimes100.co.uk

Want to know more?

www.cummins.com

Getting the grade: People

PEOPLE management is at the heart of successful business. Poor people management can be the root cause of a wide range of business problems. Equally, effective people management can provide a springboard for above-average business performance.

For many businesses, staffing costs represent a significant proportion of total costs – for many school's it is over 80 per cent. Making best use of this expensive asset is clearly important.

While this is true, remember that people management is only one aspect of business management. Without successful financial management it may be difficult to pay sufficient salaries to attract the right people. Without a clear strategy even highly trained and well-motivated staff may be ineffective.

Understand the terms

The people topic is full of different business terms and business theories. The first stage in getting a good grade is to develop a solid understanding of the key terms and key theorists. Consider, though, that the examination will not be a test of how much you can remember. For instance, you must be able to *use* Maslow's theory of the hierarchy of needs, and apply it to business situation – it is not enough just to memorise the diagram.

More is not always better

Many students find motivation theory (and other people topics) quite easy to grasp and many exam answers often focus on using as many theories as possible. Unless the question states otherwise, it will usually be enough to focus your analysis on one or two theories, but to consider these theories in more depth.

It is also easy to assume that more motivation automatically equals more productivity, and that more motivation can easily be achieved through more empowerment, enlargement, promotion or so forth. Motivation must not be treated in isolation of other issues. Increased motivation *may* contribute to higher productivity, but it may be operational factors and not motivation that is constraining productivity. Empowerment will only work if staff are willing to be empowered. Not all motivational tools will be relevant to all situations (or individuals). Consider the situation you are presented with and analyse the relevance of the different tools within that *particular* context.

Links with operations

People management has many close links with operations management.

The number of staff and their skills may determine production capacity.

Choice of production method will influence the number of staff required and how skilful they need to be.

Questions often ask you to highlight and discuss these relationships. Consider why and where these relationships occur. What impact does each have on the other? Why?

Long-term issues

Workforce planning is an increasingly important business tool. Many industries (teaching for instance) are facing major skills shortages. Demographic and regional changes (and other external influences) may also affect a business's ability to recruit or retain suitable staff.

- What impact will this have on people management?
- What impact will this have on operations?
- Will the business be able to meet its long-term strategic goals?

Consideration of such issues is central to successful workforce planning and may well be important in shaping your answers.

The power of culture

Culture is a very difficult thing for managers to change. Suggesting a change of culture in an answer should be supported with an acknowledgement of how difficult this really is. Cultural change takes time and is often resented, improvements will not occur overnight. Culture can also have a significant impact on success. Getting all staff to 'buy into' corporate strategy requires a culture where staff see themselves as an integral part of the organisation – this is not as easy as it sounds.

If you have a part-time job then you are ideally placed to witness people management in action. You will be able to see the impact of culture

- Are all staff driven to give good customer service?
- Why?
- Why not?
- What motivational tools are used?
- Do they work?

If you can link people management theory to practice then you will have a much better chance of being able to analyse the people management issues presented to you in the exam.

Section 5

Operations management

How can the business maximise efficiency?

Why do some businesses grow while others stay small?

What is the importance of labour productivity?

Will a business gain from economies of scale?

Should a business vary its capacity to match changes in demand?

What is total quality management?

How does lean production improve efficiency?

How much stock should a business hold?

What factors will affect the choice of production method?

30 Efficiency and productivity

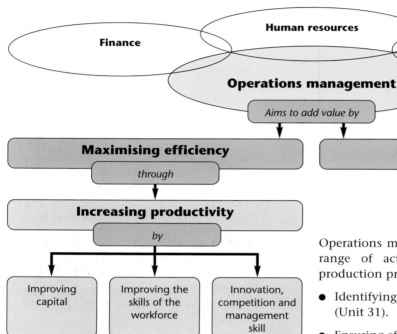

Operations management is responsible for a broad range of activities involved in managing the production process. These include:

- Identifying the most efficient scale for operations (Unit 31).

- Ensuring effective utilisation (use) of its production facilities (Unit 32).

- Planning and controlling the most appropriate methods of production (Unit 33).

- Managing stock control (Unit 34).

- Maximising the quality of the final product (Unit 35).

- Seeking ways to improve both efficiency and qualities – including the use of lean production techniques (Unit 36).

1 What is operations management?

Operations management is the organisation of resources to produce goods and services. Every product you buy and every service you use is the outcome of a *production process* – the transforming (changing) of inputs into outputs (as shown in Figure 30.1).

The twin objectives of operations management are:

- **To maximise efficiency** – by achieving the maximum output from a given set of inputs. This can be measured using the concept of *productivity* (see page 198).

- **To maximise quality** – by producing a good or service that satisfies the needs of consumers.

2 Adding value

Added value is created by producing an output that is worth more than the combined costs of the inputs (see pages 8-9). Using resources efficiently to produce goods and services allows the business to charge a price that is profitable:

- **Goods.** A production process is used to create a new product. For example, Benetton produces

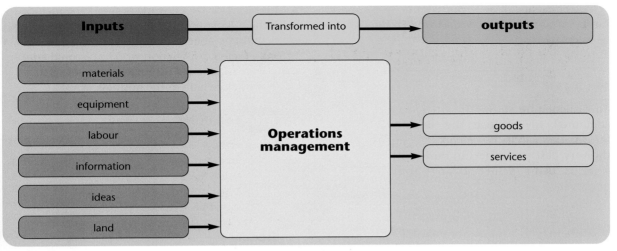

Figure 30.1 Transforming inputs and outputs

and sells clothing using a variety of inputs, such as raw materials, production machinery and labour, retail outlets and staff. The value of sales exceeds the costs of the inputs allowing Benetton to make a profit.

- **Services.** No physical production process occurs to provide a service, but there is still a transformation, which must be managed. An airline combines aircraft, pilots and aircrew with ground staff and computer booking facilities to provide flights for passengers. The challenge is to organise the process in such a way that the price of the flight exceeds the costs of providing it.

 Other business functions

In producing goods and services that determine the success or failure of the business, operations management overlaps with other aspects of the business.

- **Marketing.** In Unit 5 we saw how a market-orientated approach involved key product decisions being based on customers wants. This requires a very close relationship between marketing and operations management. Operations managers need market research and sales information to help them build customer needs into every aspect of their work, ensuring that the quality of the final product meets the needs. Marketing and operations work together to build the image and reputation that allows the business to add value.

- **Human resources.** To achieve the twin objectives of efficiency and quality, an organisation needs a flexible and motivated workforce. The operations and human resources departments work together to ensure that the:

  - workforce *size* matches the sale of production
  - workforce *skills* meet the operation needs
  - *flexibility* of attitudes and working practices allow change to occur
  - workers' *motivation* helps to maximise productivity and quality
  - workers' *health and safety* is ensured.

- **Finance.** Controlling production costs enables the business to keep prices down, and to make a profit. The business finance and accounting function needs the operations department to cost each aspect of its work in order to determine prices, wages, and profit or loss.

To successfully manage business operations there needs to be effective coordination between these different functions. Any conflict between individuals, or rivalries between departments or poor communication will undermine this relationship.

4 Measuring efficiency

Efficiency is about making the most of the resources you have either by maximising the output or minimising the inputs. To maximise output, the business must produce as much as possible from a given set of inputs such as labour, equipment and raw materials. To minimise inputs, it must ensure that no resources are wasted in the production process.

197

The efficiency of an organisation – or a country – can be measured by its *productivity*. Productivity can be calculated as:

$$\frac{\text{output (quantity or value of production)}}{\text{inputs (labour + capital + raw materials, etc.)}}$$

This calculation shows the efficiency of the inputs combined to produce the final product. This information can be *benchmarked* (compared) against the very best performers in business to understand what is being achieved, and how it could be improved.

> ### Guru's views
> There is no less fear from outside competition than from internal inefficiency …
> *Unknown*

Individual measures of productivity can be used to find out which inputs work efficiently, and where there may be problems. The commonest of these is **labour productivity**, which measures the average output of each worker over a period of time. This is calculated as:

$$\frac{\text{output (per period of time)}}{\text{number of workers}} = \frac{\text{number of units produced per worker}}{\text{(per period of time)}}$$

So, if a car factory with 200 workers produces 10,000 cars in a year, its labour productivity is:

$$\frac{\text{10,000 cars (per year)}}{\text{200 workers}} = 50 \text{ cars per worker (per year)}$$

To become more productive they must produce more cars (output) from the same number of workers – or the same output with fewer workers!

There are problems, however, with measuring labour productivity in this way:

- In many organisations it is difficult to measure the output of a worker. In service industries for example, such as banking, there may be no physical output to be measured. The number of customers dealt with may not be a relevant measure of a worker's output.

- It may be the quality, rather than the quantity, of the employee's work that matters. In schools, for example, it would be pointless to measure the productivity of a teacher in terms of the number of pupils taught when what matters is the quality and outcome of the teaching.

- It is not clear which workers should be included in the calculation. If it is the entire workforce, including management and administrative staff, a very efficient production workforce could appear to be unproductive because of high levels of staffing elsewhere in the business.

> ### STOP & THINK
> Consider how productive you are either in any part-time job you might have or in your studies. What determines your productivity? What constrains it? How could your productivity be improved?

5   The importance of labour productivity

Labour productivity is crucial for many organisations because it determines their ability to compete with their rivals. Where labour costs make up a major proportion of the overall costs of the business it is vital to keep these costs to a minimum by making the most efficient use of labour. If the business can keep labour costs down it can afford to keep prices low whilst still making a profit.

The **unit labour cost** is an important indicator of this ability to compete on price. It shows the cost of the labour needed to produce one unit of output:

$$\frac{\text{wage rate (per period of time)}}{\text{labour productivity (per period of time)}} = \text{unit labour cost}$$

A car manufacturer that pays its workers £20,000 per year to produce an average of 50 cars each will have a unit labour cost of:

$$\frac{\text{£20,000}}{50} = \text{£400}$$

Each car took an average of £400 of labour to produce. If labour productivity could be increased to 100 cars, the unit labour cost would be halved to £200 per car (assuming wage rates stayed the same).

Clearly, improving labour productivity is not the only major objective for operations managers. Where

Tough targets

The future of car production at Vauxhall's Ellesmere Port plant could be at risk if the group does not meet stringent productivity targets. Failure to meet the targets puts seriously at risk the factory's chances of securing production of the next generation Astra models, due to begin production in 2004.

Employees have been told that unless the tough productivity targets are met, 850 jobs may have to go. Some 450 jobs would be lost from assembly lines as part of general efficiency improvements and the remainder from outsourcing various services.

Morale amongst staff remained positive despite the announcement and management believe that suitable human resource systems are in place to ensure that the targets can be met. Trade unions were considering their response.

Source: *Financial Times*
23 February 2002

1 What factors, other than productivity, might determine Vauxhall's competitiveness? [6]
2 State, and explain, **two** important links between productivity and people management. [6]
3 Consider how the trade unions might react to these announcements.
[6]
Total 18 marks

labour costs are a small proportion of total costs, it may have little impact on overall competitiveness (the business may be capital rather than labour intensive). Quality is also crucial. The business must be careful that in trying to produce more efficiently it does not reduce the quality of the finished product.

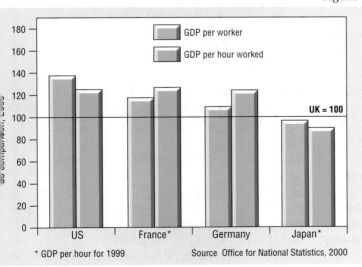

* GDP per hour for 1999   Source Office for National Statistics, 2000

Figure 30.2 Gross domestic product (GDP) per worker, per hour worked

6 Improving productivity in UK business

In recent decades a *productivity gap* has emerged between British business and its international rivals. Figure 30.2 indicates that labour productivity in Britain is significantly below that of businesses in the USA, France and Germany.

This makes it very difficult for British businesses to compete with their international rivals, who can produce more rapidly, more cheaply and respond to customer orders more swiftly. The Government has realised that improving productivity is central to the success of British businesses in the future and has committed to closing the productivity gap.

Finding ways to improve productivity depends on first identifying the causes of the poor productivity. Research by the National Institute of Economic and Social Research (NIESR)

in 1999 considered three sets of possible causes:

- **The amount and quality of capital available to each worker** – this sees poor productivity as the effect of inadequate, out-of-date equipment and technology.

- **The skills of the workforce** – this identifies the workers' low and inappropriate skill levels as causing poor productivity.

- **Other factors** – including innovation, the level of competition businesses face and the management techniques used.

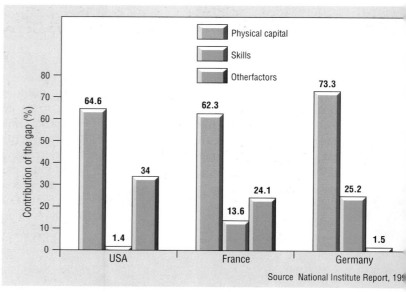

Source National Institute Report, 199

Figure 30.3 Accounting for the gap in labour productivity

Figure 30.3 shows NIESR's estimates of what caused the productivity gap between the UK and the US, France and Germany:

- The impact of poor capital and inadequate equipment is clear, accounting for between 62 per cent and 73 per cent of the productivity gap. This has been caused by a lack of investment by both business and government over several decades.

- In comparison with Germany, the poorer education and training of the workforce is also seen to have a major effect.

- Finally, compared to the United States, other factors such as the burden of government red tape and insufficient competition account for more than one-third of the productivity gap.

Figure 30.4 identifies the potential solutions to poor productivity, based on each of the competing explanations. Many of these ideas are developed in later units.

Causes	Potential solutions
Inadequate equipment	More investment by businesses in modern equipment, extending automation Government increase investment in infrastructure, technology, research and development
Low skill levels	Businesses train workers to higher skills levels, and be more flexible Government invest in education and training, raise standards of numeracy and literacy, and encourage lifelong learning
Burden of government red tape	Government seek ways of reducing the administrative burden on business, particularly on small firms
Insufficient competition	Tougher competition policy, Office of Fair Trading take more action against *anti-competitive* practices (such as *cartels*) Government measures to *liberalise* some markets (open them up to competition), such as that for the delivery of letters
Poor management techniques	UK businesses focus on motivating employees and working in partnership with them, not in conflict Use of lean production techniques, including a continual striving to improve productivity and quality (*kaizen* – see unit 36)

Figure 30.4 Solutions to poor productivity

Efficiency and productivity: summary

KEY TERMS

Efficiency – making the most of resources by maximising the output from a given level of inputs.

Labour productivity – the average output of each worker over a period of time.

Unit labour cost – the cost of labour needed to produce one unit of output.

Summary questions

1 What is productivity?
2 What are the main determinants of labour productivity?
3 How might a business attempt to improve labour productivity?
4 Explain the relationship between productivity and unit costs.
5 What is meant by the term 'labour intensive'
6 Why is it important to strike a balance between productivity and quality? Why might this be difficult to achieve?
7 Calculate labour productivity in the following examples and comment on the figures.

	output	number of workers
Factory Alpha	10,000	15
Factory Beta	70,000	100
Factory Charlie	100,000	125

Exam practice

Beaten by the Germans again

For some time, the Government has been worried that Britain is uncompetitive. We are less productive than both the French and the Germans and we lag behind the productivity of the Americans, even when taking into account the differences in hours worked.

Despite the capital investments of the past decade, relative output per worker is about a fifth higher in France and Germany, and more than a third higher in America. Even when measuring productivity per hour, as opposed to productivity per year, the gap is staggering and Britain appears to be struggling to improve its position.

Why is the UK so inefficient? Surveys suggest that a great part of the gap in manufacturing is because of investment levels. The rate of capital intensity per hour worked in French factories is almost double that of the UK. Modern management practices and greater emphasis on people skills for production managers might also account for some of the difference.

Even in financial services, where Britain leads the world, inefficiencies exist. The French and Germans might lag behind in terms of raw service volumes, but they are considerably more productive.

Source: *The Times*
May 1 2002

1 What is meant by the term 'capital intensity'? **[2]**
2 Define the term 'labour productivity'. **[2]**
3 State and explain **two** possible reasons why productivity may be higher in France and Germany than in the UK. **[6]**
4 Examine the relationship between productivity and international competitiveness. **[9]**
5 Examine the issues a firm might face when attempting to improve productivity. **[9]**
Total 28 marks

Want to know more?

www.dti.gov.uk

31 The scale of operations

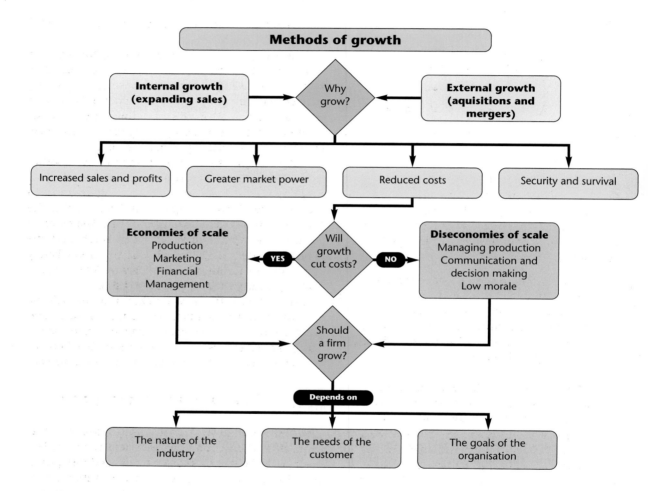

1 Growing the business

Growth is one of the key objectives of any business. It is the route to increasing profits and a reflection of a successful business. There are almost daily media reports about mergers of large companies to become huge and powerful organisations; yet there is no sign that small business is disappearing. So why do some businesses grow while others stay small? Is there an ideal scale (size) for the operations of a business?

2 Measuring business size

The size of a business can be measured in different ways. Because there is no single ideal measure of business size, it is important to look at a variety of indicators.

- The number of employees. The Department of Trade and Industry labels businesses as:

    - *micro*, fewer than 10 employees
    - *small*, between 10 and 100 employees
    - *medium*, between 100 and 500 employees
    - *large*, more than 500 employees.

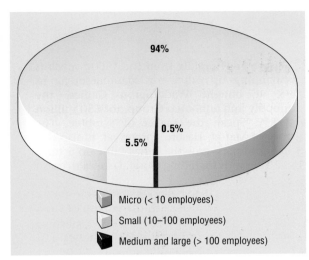

Figure 31.1 Numbers of workers employed by size of business

As Figure 31.1 shows, the vast majority of businesses in the UK are micro – they have fewer than ten employees. Just 0.5 per cent of businesses employ more than 100 people; but this small number of businesses employs 49 per cent of the total workforce!

This measure of business size is important, but not ideal. Some businesses need many workers to make or deliver their product – they are labour intensive – while others rely mainly on machinery and are said to be capital intensive. The true size of these businesses may be disguised.

● **Sales turnover.** The value of the products a business sells is its sales turnover. The larger the value of the product, the bigger the business size. The Companies Act 1985 states that a business is small when its turnover is less than £2.8m. In the UK, 80 per cent of businesses have a turnover of less than £100,000 – way below the £2.8m limit!

● **Profit.** Comparing the annual profits of businesses can indicate the scale of a business. The problem with this measure is that large companies may make a loss when times are bad and small businesses may make low, but consistent profits!

● **Company value.** Measuring the net worth of a business by looking at its balance sheet can be an important indicator of its size. If the value of the capital employed in the business is less than £1.4m, the Companies Act classes it as small.

 STOP & THINK

Which of these ways of measuring business size do you think is the most useful? Why?

3   How do organisations grow?

An organisation can expand through either internal or external growth.

Internal growth means expanding the scale of production to meet increased sales demand. Sales may be increasing because the business is gaining market share, moving into new markets or launching new products. McDonald's has grown into a global multinational by expanding its operations into new countries and increasing its market share.

External growth happens through buying other businesses, known as **acquisition** or **takeover**, or **merging** as an equal with another organisation to create a new, bigger company. In August 2002, the low-cost airline easyJet completed the takeover of its rival, Go. easyJet bought Go's 22 aircraft and the rights to fly to 38 destinations, immediately expanding its number of customers by 50 per cent – making it Europe's largest budget airline.

External growth is a quicker way to achieve growth than the gradual expansion of sales and production. The evidence suggests that many mergers or takeovers do not bring the desired benefits and some cause problems that can prove disastrous.

4   Why do organisations grow?

Organisations grow when they believe that expanding their operations will help them achieve their goals. These goals might be to maximise profits for shareholders, to serve other stakeholders or merely just to survive. Growth brings a number of benefits that can help achieve these goals:

● **Increased sales and profits.** Through producing and selling more, a business can raise its sales revenue and therefore its profitability.

● **Greater market power.** Expansion allows a business to boost its market share, providing greater power to influence price and to raise profit margins. It may also boost the status and image of the business in a way that meets the personal goals of managers and employees.

For example ...

Big boys dominate in the business of toys

Bob the Builder and Action Man, made by toy manufacturing giant Hasbro, may have been the victims of price-fixing says the Office of Fair Trading. The toy industry once had hundreds of small manufacturers, but as a result of soaring manufacturing and distribution costs, these days it is dominated by just two: Hasbro and Mattel.

Hasbro grew rapidly from the 1960s onwards by snapping up other toy manufacturers. In 1995, it bought Waddington Games, the Monopoly and Subbuteo Group, for £50 million and J.W. Spear, the maker of Scrabble. The history of Mattel, Hasbro's archrival, is also one of extraordinary growth. It has built up a huge stable of brands including Corgi, Fisher Price and Aviva Sports.

The traditional toy market has come under pressure in recent years with the growth of alternative products for children – such as electronic games, sportswear and even mobile phones. The result has been a stagnating market with very little if any growth in sales. Now the Office of Fair Trading is to examine whether manufacturers or big toy retailers such as Argos, Toys'R'Us and Woolworths are using their market power to fix prices and exploit the consumer.

Source: *The Times* 2 May 2002

1 What method of growth has Hasbro and Mattel used in recent decades? **[2]**
2 Why do you think these companies chose to grow in this way rather than the alternative? **[3]**
3 What benefits might Hasbro and Mattel have gained from this expansion? **[5]**

4 Discuss whether consumers gain from the growth of big manufacturers and retailers in the toy industry. **[7]**
Total 17 marks

Want to know more?

www.hasbro.com

- **Security and survival.** Faced with large and powerful rivals, growth may be the only route to survival. The accounting firms Coopers and Price Waterhouse claimed their merger was the only way they could survive in a global accounting industry dominated by American giants.

- **Reduced costs.** There are ways that larger firms can improve efficiency and cut costs through large-scale production; known as *economies of scale* (explained later in this unit). By helping to improve cost efficiency, growth can help to improve profitability.

Economies of scale

Economies of scale are the benefits of size – the cost savings that large organisations can make compared to smaller businesses. Big businesses can often find ways to keep their average costs – the cost per unit of output – below those of smaller rivals. These lower average costs are known as economies of scale and are illustrated in Figure 31.2.

Economies of scale are often quoted as one of the

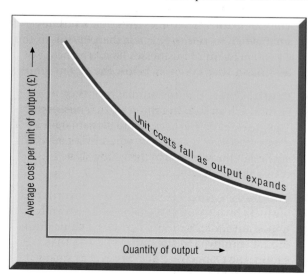

Figure 31.2 Economies of scale

main reasons behind a merger or takeover. Fiat, the Italian car manufacturer, believed that its alliance with General Motors in 2000 would lead to cost savings of up to €2bn within five years. Large organisations dominate industries such as oil, pharmaceuticals, and telecommunications. It is in these industries that the scope for cost savings by big companies is particularly great. Economies of scale can be categorised into four types:

1 Production

● When bought in bulk, raw materials and components may often be purchased from suppliers at a discount. It is the power that a big business, such as McDonald's, has over its smaller suppliers that allows it to reduce the costs of purchasing supplies.

● Larger firms have more opportunities for the *division of labour*, allowing workers to specialise in areas of expertise.

● Operating on a large scale allows a business to use *mass production* techniques (see Unit 33). The overheads are spread across a huge output, making the fixed costs proportionally lower than for small-scale production. Larger and more efficient machinery can also be used.

2 Marketing

● Marketing costs, such as research, advertising and employing a salesforce, are largely fixed costs. That is, the business pays much the same for them whether they sell 5,000 or 10,000 units of a product. So, by doubling output, very little is added to marketing costs, but the cost per unit of output can be almost halved. Following merger, AOL and Time Warner expected to increase profits by 30 per cent, mainly through combining marketing campaigns to cut costs.

● Additionally, larger firms can afford methods of advertising, such as television, out of the reach of smaller companies, as they require a big financial outlay. These methods are very cost-effective in terms of the number of customers reached.

3 Finance

● Larger firms find it easier to attract finance from lenders and investors because they have a successful track record, and have more financial security to offer the lender.

● As a consequence, lenders often charge lower rates of interest to large companies. This reflects the reduced risk, the increased security offered and the lenders' desire to attract the business of large organisations.

● Other sources of finance, such as shareholders' capital or retained profits, may be cheaper than borrowing. Yet these alternatives are often closed to small businesses as a way of expanding.

● Better access to the stock market and the accumulation of retained profit is another way in which large businesses can make costs savings when seeking finance for expansion.

4 Management

● A sole trader must try to be a 'jack-of-all-trades' in managing every aspect of their business. Lack of time and expertise may lead sole traders to make expensive mistakes or miss opportunities. Larger business can afford specialist managers with expertise in their own areas, such as marketing, personnel and production. This usually leads to better decision-making and cost savings.

● Larger firms can use more efficient, coordinated administrative systems, including computerisation, to improve communication and speed up manual procedures.

5 The problems of growth

Evidence suggests that a business cannot continue to grow and expect cost savings no matter how large it gets. Sooner or later, average costs begin to rise again – see Figure 31.3.

Why does this happen? One of the reasons is that eventually opportunities for further cost savings are exhausted. Beyond a certain point there will be few opportunities for:

● greater division of labour and specialisation

● further bulk-buying discounts

● even lower rates of interest!

Importantly, though, as businesses grow problems can arise that push average costs up. These are known as **diseconomies of scale** and include:

● **Problems in managing production.** Mass production can become increasingly difficult to organise on a very large-scale, leading to inefficiency. Bulk-buying of stock, for example,

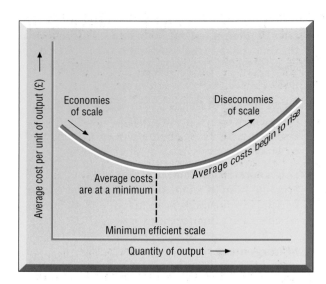

Figure 31.3 The economies and diseconomies of scale

6 Factors affecting choice of scale

A number of factors will combine to determine the scale of operations the business chooses.

- **The nature of the industry.** Industries such as oil and car manufacture have significant economies of scale and so tend to be dominated by large firms. These industries require huge investments in research and development (R&D) that can only be recouped through mass sales. It is estimated that one million cars need to be sold before a car manufacturer even recoups its R&D costs.

Finding the ideal scale of operations for a business is very much a matter of trial and error. If the business grows and finds its costs have fallen, it may seek further expansion. But if growth causes problems and rising costs, the organisation may decide it needs to shrink or to split. What the business is searching for is the so-called **minimum efficient scale**, shown in Figure 31.3, where its average costs are at their lowest.

- **The needs of the customer.** There is an opportunity for a business to expand to meet high demand or unfulfilled needs. Also, where customers seek low prices, economies of scale can provide a crucial marketing advantage. However, many small businesses survive and flourish because they meet different customer needs, such as quality or service.

- **The goals of the organisation.** Where an organisation seeks to maximise profitability, the benefits that growth can bring are likely to push it into expansion. However, many business owners do not seek to expand because their personal goals are being met by the business staying small.

may produce discounts from suppliers but also raises costs of storage, leaving valuable cash tied-up in stock.

- **Problems with communication and decision-making.** As the number of employees and the levels of management grow in an organisation, so it becomes more difficult to manage effectively. Decision-making may become more complex, making the organisation inflexible and slow to react to change.

- **Poor morale.** Individuals can feel unimportant and unvalued in a large organisation. Their views may not be listened to and their needs may go unmet, resulting in demotivation, poor productivity and high labour turnover.

Growth through merger or takeover brings further problems of its own. Merging two different business systems, cultures and management styles can cause chaos and resentment within the new business rganisation. The AOL–Time Warner merger, prompted by a desire for economies of scale, ran into just these kinds of problems. Time Warner managers were critical and distrustful of their counterparts from AOL. In recent years, demergers, for example Woolworths from the Kingfisher group, have highlighted the problems of growing too large.

The scale of operations: summary

KEY TERMS

Internal growth – the expansion of a business through increased production and sales.

External growth – expansion achieved through buying or merging with other businesses.

Acquisition or takeover – taking control of another business through buying at least half of its share capital.

Merger – the joining together of two businesses, usually as equals, to create a new organisation.

Economies of scale – the reductions in average cost (per unit of production) achieved by growing in size.

Diseconomies of scale – the increases in average costs that occur when a business grows beyond its ideal size.

Minimum efficient scale – the ideal level of output that achieves the lowest level of average cost.

Summary questions

1 Explain the difference between internal and external growth.
2 Why might a business choose to expand using external growth?
3 Explain **four** main benefits that growth brings to a firm.
4 What are 'economies of scale'?
5 Explain how economies of scale arise in the areas of:
   a production **b** marketing **c** finance **d** management.

6 What is the meaning of the term 'diseconomies of scale'?
7 Explain **three** main reasons why diseconomies of scale occur?
8 Using a diagram, explain the concept of 'minimum efficient scale'.
9 What factors might determine the scale of operations a business chooses?

Exam practice

Growing the business: Rolls-Royce and the marine market

The name Rolls-Royce has always been associated with high quality products. Most people link the company with high-quality aero-engines and cars. Rolls-Royce still makes aero-engines, but no longer manufactures cars. Instead, the company's goal has been to expand into new markets in which it can build on its expertise and its reputation for quality, to establish a leading position.

Through extensive market research, the marine market was identified as the ideal choice. It involved the provision of engines, propellers and other machinery for all types of shipping from cruise liners to aircraft carriers. It was a growing market in which shipping businesses were looking to buy more powerful engines that also met new and demanding regulations on emissions. Rolls-Royce believed it could become a market leader through developing a competitive advantage in supplying powerful, efficient and environmentally friendly products.

It was acquisition and takeover that was to be the main route to growth. In 1999, Rolls-Royce acquired Vickers Plc.

Vickers was already a key player in the marine market, providing leading-edge marine equipment.

The impact was dramatic. The acquisition of Vickers broadened Rolls-Royce's customer base and established the company as the market leader. Economies of scale were also gained, allowing the combined business to cut its costs. Size brought other benefits. Customers in the marine market want to deal with a supplier who operates on a scale that is sufficiently large as to be able to service and meet a range of complex needs. Rolls-Royce was particularly well placed to provide products and services at every stage in the development of marine vessels.

Today, more than 20,000 commercial and naval vessels use Rolls-Royce equipment. Marine activity accounts for about 15 per cent of the Rolls-Royce group's turnover and has the potential to move to about 30 per cent of the group's turnover over the next 10 years.

Source: *The Times* 100 case studies

Want to know more?

www.rollsroyce.co.uk

1 Define the terms:
   a takeover [2]
   b competitive advantage. [2]
2 What types of growth did Rolls-Royce use to expand its business in the marine industry? [4]
3 What benefits might Rolls-Royce have sought to achieve through its expansion? [6]
4 Explain the nature of the economies of scale that Rolls-Royce may have experienced following its takeover of Vickers. [7]
4 Discuss the problems Rolls-Royce may experience in doubling the size of its marine business over the next 10 years. [9]

Total 30 marks

32 Capacity management

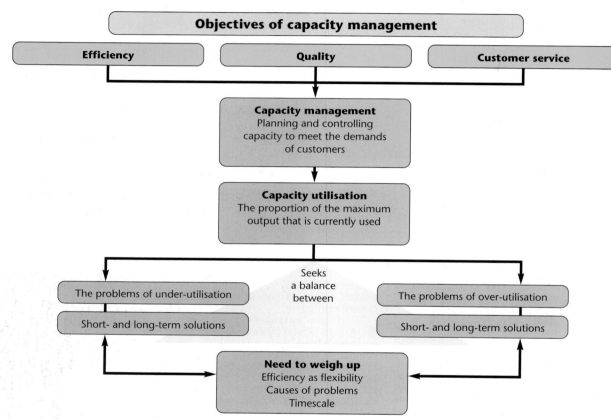

Objectives of capacity management

Efficiency	Quality	Customer service

Capacity management
Planning and controlling capacity to meet the demands of customers

Capacity utilisation
The proportion of the maximum output that is currently used

The problems of under-utilisation		The problems of over-utilisation
Short- and long-term solutions	Seeks a balance between	Short- and long-term solutions

Need to weigh up
Efficiency as flexibility
Causes of problems
Timescale

Airports must manage their capacity to cope with uncertain customer demand.

1 What is capacity management?

A police force must decide how many officers should be on duty without knowing in advance what the level of crime or disturbance will be at any given time. Manufacturers of suntan cream must plan how much to produce without knowing whether a hot summer is in store. An airline must decide how many flights and seats to offer without knowing how many passengers wish to fly.

Take any organisation that faces uncertain demand and try to decide how many resources it should employ and what its maximum possible output should be. This is **capacity management**.

Capacity refers to the maximum possible output from an organisation over a given period of time. The level at which this maximum is set will be determined by the resources available such as buildings, equipment and people. This physical capacity determines the largest output that could be achieved each day, month or year if resources are used to their maximum. For example, the capacity of a cinema is limited to 1000 seats, because there are five screens – each with 200 seats available. However, if each screen is able to run five performances a day, the capacity of the cinema is 5000 customers per day.

The key decisions in capacity management are:

● What maximum capacity level should the business settle on over the long-term?

● What proportion of this maximum capacity should the business be using at any one time (its capacity utilisation) – 100 per cent? 90 per cent? Or less?

● Should the business ignore short-term changes in demand and keep capacity constant? Should it attempt to vary its capacity to match fluctuations in demand? Or should it attempt to change demand to fit the capacity available?

2   The objectives of capacity management

In making capacity management decisions, an organisation must seek to balance three key objectives:

● **Efficiency.** The costs need to be kept down and waste avoided. If the maximum capacity is not being fully utilised (used) there is an element of waste that will raise unit costs. On the other hand, over-producing when there is a lack of demand will lead to a build-up of stock causing wasted space, time and money.

● **Quality.** The business must ensure that quality is maximised, and not suffering because capacity is being overstretched.

● **Customer service.** The flexibility to respond to unexpected changes in demand is vital.

3   Capacity utilisation

The term **capacity utilisation** refers to the proportion of the maximum capacity that is actually used during a period of time. It is measured as:

$$\frac{\text{Actual output (per period of time)}}{\text{Maximum possible output (per period of time)}} \times 100 = \text{\% capacity utilisation}$$

For example, if a cinema could cope with up to 5,000 customers per day and actually gets 3,000 on a particular day:

$$\frac{3,000}{5,000} \times 100 = \textbf{60\%} \text{ capacity utilisation}$$

Capacity utilisation is called different things in different industries. In a factory environment it may be called *uptime*. The proportion of seats occupied on an aircraft is called its *load factor*. Hotels measure their capacity utilisation by looking at *room occupancy levels*.

To be utilising its capacity fully, a business must make

STOP & THINK

What measures of capacity utilisation could be used by the following organisations:
● **a hospital**
● **a supermarket**
● **a university?**

Supermarkets may need more than one measure of capacity utilisation

use of all its available productive resources. Operating at, or near, full capacity is often taken as a sign of a successful business. It suggests that demand is high and that no potential output is being lost. The result should be that the business is maximising its sales. However, full capacity is not always ideal for reasons that will be explored later.

Under-utilisation

When actual production is well below the maximum capacity, it is known as **under-utilisation**. This can occur for a number of reasons:

- **Demand has fallen** due to changing consumer tastes, recession or seasonal fluctuations. A new competitor may be stealing market share and reducing the business's sales.

- **Capacity has been increased to too high a level**, with the expansion of assets or the workforce to a level well above that which is needed to meet demand.

- **Inefficiency in the production process**, caused by 'bottlenecks' in the system, poor working practices or shortages of raw materials.

Under-utilisation cannot always be put down to problems or inefficiencies on the 'shop floor' – the cause could lie elsewhere in the business or outside in its market. Under-utilisation brings a number of problems.

- **Costs will rise.** Businesses pay their overheads, known as fixed costs, for resources such as premises or equipment. When capacity is fully utilised overheads are spread across the maximum possible number of units of output. The fixed cost per unit is therefore at a minimum. However, when less output is produced, fixed costs do not fall and each unit of output must bear a higher share of the fixed costs. For example:

  - A factory spends £10,000 a week on paying its fixed costs.
  - At full capacity, it can produce 5,000 units per week.
  - As well as variable costs (cost of producing each unit), each unit must bear £2 of the fixed costs (£10,000 for 5,000 units).
  - If the factory only produces 2,500 units in a particular week, its capacity utilisation is 50 per cent.
  - Each of the 2,500 units must now cover £4 of the fixed costs. Fixed costs per unit have doubled.

- **Profits will fall.** As explained, the profit margin on each unit falls if unit costs have risen. In addition, potential output has not been produced and this translates to a loss of potential sales revenue. It may be that a lack of demand is the cause of under-utilisation, in which case the sales opportunities were never there. Nevertheless, the profitability of the business will suffer.

- **Prices may have to rise.** To cover the higher fixed costs per unit and to boost revenue, prices may be increased. Depending on the price elasticity of demand (see unit 10), this may or may not achieve higher sales revenues. Customers will suffer and demand may be further cut back.

- **Employees may feel insecure.** When a business utilises only a proportion of its capacity, employees may fear for their own prospects. The workforce may be cut in order to reduce capacity and costs. Part-time and temporary staff, who may have previously been brought in to raise capacity, may be the first to go; but all employees may fear for the prospects of the business.

For example ...

Boiling hot

Boil is a high-quality kettle manufacturer providing kettles to five-star hotels for guest rooms. Due to favourable economic conditions they anticipated increased demand and set about increasing capacity.

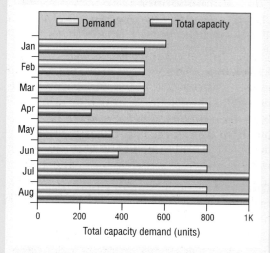

Figure 32.1 Capacity and demand analysis for Boil

1 What might have caused the reduction in capacity in April? What might have been happening in May and June? **[4]**
2 What might have been the effect on Boil of total capacity falling short of demand from April to June? **[4]**

Total 8 marks

Responses to under-utilisation

If a business experiences under-utilisation, it can respond in several different ways.

- **Reduce capacity.** Cutting capacity increases utilisation. On the first anniversary of September 11, British Airways cut half its flights to the USA. It anticipated passenger numbers would be low. So, rather than operate all its flights half-full, it halved the number of flights and ran near to full capacity. The effect of cutting capacity is to cut costs while still meeting customer demand. The result is greater efficiency and profitability.

There are a number of different ways in which capacity can be reduced:

- Cutting overtime or the length of the working week
- Switching staff to other operations
- Reducing the size of the workforce; for example, through redundancy
- Employing temporary or part-time workers instead of permanent or full-time
- Selling off or leasing out productive assets, such as premises or equipment.

This process of cutting back capacity when faced with excess capacity is known as **rationalisation**. Rationalisation means finding ways to reorganise production in order to reduce costs and become more efficient.

The wisdom of cutting capacity depends on what has caused the under-utilisation and how long this is expected to last. If caused by a long-term fall in demand or over-supply in an industry, a business would be foolish to maintain current capacity as costs would remain high and profits low. In recent years, industries such as steel and car manufacture have both had to face up to problems of over-supply, and both have seen companies cutting back their capacity.

On the other hand, if the cause of under-utilisation is either production inefficiencies or short-term dips in demand, cutting capacity would be a mistake. Rationalisation is not without costs of its own. Reducing the size of the workforce, for example, brings:

- redundancy payments ,
- insecurity and reduced morale
- a loss of skills and experience.

If demand rises again, the business may find itself unable to meet the new level of customer demand. Additional costs of recruitment and training will then be experienced.

- **Boost demand.** If under-utilisation is due to lack of demand, then finding ways to boost demand is an attractive alternative to cutting capacity.

Seasonal demand plays havoc with capacity management – pushing capacity to its limits at the height of demand and leading to substantial under-utilisation out of season. Finding ways to increase demand during these low points is one solution. New products may be introduced that will prove popular at different times of the year, or all-year round. For example, hotels that are half-empty during the winter could advertise themselves as conference or wedding venues.

Other strategies may involve *price-cutting* or *promotional campaigns*. Cutting the price of holidays during off-peak times is one way of ensuring better occupancy rates, for example.

The business may consider undertaking work for other firms – **subcontracting**. This is common practice in some industries, such as maintenance or building work, where small companies can only meet the needs of a large job through the use of subcontractors. The solution is not ideal for either business. The company with a lack of capacity may not be able to guarantee the quality of subcontractors' work. Equally, the subcontractors are not building their own direct customer links.

- **Do nothing.** If a business believes the low level of utilisation is short-term, and it can cope with the problems this causes, it may choose to do nothing and keep capacity constant. This allows it to plan with greater certainty and provide its workforce greater stability. It may even be producing below capacity intentionally (see below).

Over-utilisation

Seeking to run at 100 per cent of capacity all the time, or facing demand that is above capacity brings problems of over-utilisation.

- **Customer service may suffer.** The speed with which customers' needs are met is likely to be reduced if the business is running at full capacity. Queuing and delays could result when a business is struggling to meet demand. For example, running at full capacity in a fast food restaurant increases waiting times and reduces customer satisfaction. Product quality might also suffer if workers are encouraged to manufacture goods as quickly as possible.

- **Lost sales and profits.** When a business runs at full capacity there is no slack to meet an unexpected increase in demand. As a result, custom could be permanently lost to rivals. Toy manufacturers find crazes particularly problematic. They may be unable to meet demand for Teletubbies or Thunderbirds toys in time for Christmas and by the time they can, demand may have fallen away again. Spare capacity at least provides flexibility.

- **A strain on resources.** Working at full capacity places a strain on all the business's resources – workers and managers may become demotivated by the constant pressures on them. Flat-out usage of premises and equipment makes essential maintenance difficult, if not impossible. The result could be a sudden breakdown of resources with all the problems that this brings.

A business running at full capacity finds it difficult to respond in the short-term to increased demand. Its short-term and long-term options are shown in Figure 32.2.

STOP & THINK

What factors will a business need to weigh up in deciding between these options?

Short-term	Long-term
Increasing the hours of existing workforce	Investing in new premises or equipment
Moving workers to bottlenecks in production, or busy areas	Expanding the workforce through new recruitment
Leasing or renting new capacity	Seeking to increase productivity
Subcontracting work to another organisation	

Figure 32.2 Short- and long-term options for responding to increases in demand

---

For example ...

Motoring along

Mr Jean Martin Folz, chief executive of Peugeot-Citroën, was clear about the strategy needed to take the car group from takeover target to industry leader. Separate managers were running the Peugeot group, with little co-operation between Peugeot and Citroën. With the slogan 'one company, two marques', Mr Folz fused many of the two companies' activities to gain economies of scale.

Nowadays, beneath their metal skin, Peugeot and Citroën cars share the same engines, gearboxes and brakes. Peugeot's factories, one-third idle when he arrived now run flat out, with a third eight-hour shift allowing them to operate at 115 per cent of installed capacity. Output has increased by more than 50 per cent to over three million cars a year, with a target of four million by 2004. The increased capacity has been achieved without heavy investment, and Peugeot now boasts the best total shareholder returns of any European car company.

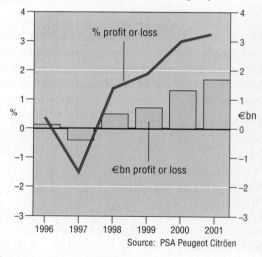

Figure 32.3 Increasing output at PSA Peugeot Citroën
Source: *The Economist*, 6 April 2002

1 What is meant by capacity utilisation? [2]
2 What proportion of capacity was being utilised when one-third of Peugeot's factories were idle. [2]
3 Explain **two** methods, other than the extra third shift, that Peugeot might have used to increase total capacity without heavy investment. [4]
4 Discuss the impact that operating at '115 per cent capacity utilisation' might have on the company? [7]
Total 15 marks

Want to know more?

www.peugeot.co.uk

Operational management: summary

KEY TERMS

Capacity – the maximum possible output that can be produced over a period of time.

Capacity management – the process of planning and controlling the capacity of an organisation to meet the demands of its customers.

Capacity utilisation – the proportion of capacity that is actually used over a period of time.

Under-utilisation – the use of well below 100 per cent of an organisation's maximum potential output.

Rationalisation – the process of reorganising a business to reduce capacity and increase efficiency.

Subcontracting – using the resources of another organisation to help fulfil customer demand.

Summary questions

1 What does the statement 'the firm is operating at 30 per cent of capacity' mean?
2 State, and explain, **three** implications for a business of operating at 100 per cent of capacity.
3 Why do businesses want to operate at the highest capacity utilisation possible?
4 What is meant by rationalisation? What does it often involve?
5 Outline **three** methods a firm can use to increase its total capacity.
6 Calculate the capacity utilisation if a firm is producing 1,500 units per day against a total capacity of 4,500.
7 Define the term 'excess capacity'.
8 Consider the issues facing a business attempting to rationalise its production process.

Exam practice

Even more motoring

Britain's motor industry is booming. Thanks to soaring domestic demand and decent export orders, in 2002 Britain reached a record number of cars produced (1.7m). Industry leaders believe that by 2005 the number of cars produced will exceed two million.

Odd then, that during 2002 both Ford and Vauxhall closed down production plants (Dagenham and Luton respectively). Both Ford and Vauxhall claimed global over-capacity as the reason for the closures.

In sharp contrast, both the Cowley Mini plant and the Ryton Peugeot plant increased capacity during 2002. Ten years ago, Ryton made about 80,000 cars a year. During 2002 it made approximately 200,000 and in 2003, with the addition of a fourth shift, intends to produce 230,000 cars. At Cowley, where teams of robots put the trendy Mini together, BMW also increased production targets and capacity during 2002. Some extra capacity was gained through the manufacturer's flexibility agreement; staff build hours in personal accounts to give managers extra flexibility in the use of the plant. The shift system also means that the plant now works nearly every day of the year.

Vauxhall claimed that, at a time when they needed less capacity to stem losses of £480m, the Luton plant required significant capital investment to make cost-efficient the capacity it already had. Ford ceased mainstream car production at Dagenham, but used the plant's infrastructure to increase its diesel engine manufacturing capacity.

Source: *The Guardian*, 21 March 2002 and *The Times*, 8 & 12 May 2002

1 What is meant by the phrase 'global over-capacity'? **[3]**
2 Outline **two** implications of the plant closures for either Ford or Vauxhall. **[6]**
3 How else might capacity has been increased at BMW's Cowley plant? **[6]**
4 Evaluate the issues facing car manufacturers attempting to match capacity with demand. **[10]**
Total 25 marks

33 Methods of production

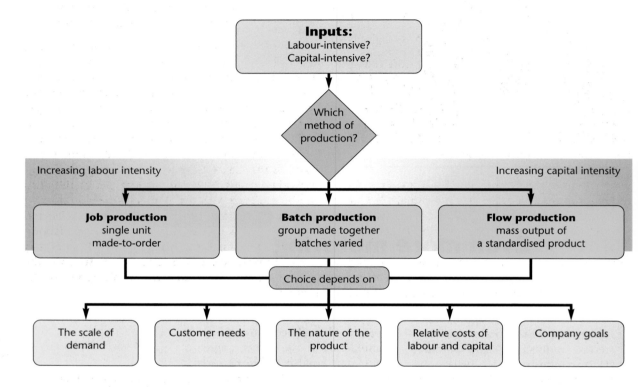

Inputs:
Labour-intensive?
Capital-intensive?

Which method of production?

Increasing labour intensity

Increasing capital intensity

Job production
single unit
made-to-order

Batch production
group made together
batches varied

Flow production
mass output of
a standardised product

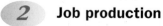

Choice depends on

The scale of demand

Customer needs

The nature of the product

Relative costs of labour and capital

Company goals

1 Organising the production process

Whether it is the manufacture of a good or the provision of a service, every organisation must make choices about how best to combine inputs – resources such as land, labour, and capital. A business that chooses to use a high proportion of labour (people) compared to capital (machinery) in its production process is said to be **labour-intensive**. Examples of labour-intensive methods include delivery services such as those for newspapers, milk or letters.

The alternative is a **capital-intensive** method of production. This is one that uses a greater proportion of machinery than labour in the production process. The replacement of labour with machinery in production is known as mechanisation and is to be found in manufacturing on a mass scale, such as in food production.

This decision over the mix of capital and labour to use in production is closely linked to the choice of production method facing a business. The three main alternative types of production method are known as:

- job production
- batch production
- flow production.

2 Job production

Think of a wedding you have been to. The bride's dress may have been handmade. The menu at the wedding reception will have been especially chosen for the event. The photographs, flowers and transport were planned to meet the preferences of the happy couple. All are examples of job production.

Job production involves creating a single good or

Making Jewellery – creating a unique product

unique goods and services can be produced to individual customer requirements. Typically, job production is used in:

- craft industries, such as pottery or jewellery-making

- personal services, such as hairdressing, dentistry and accountancy

- major, one-off construction projects, such as a bridge or the re-building of Wembley Stadium.

Job production is almost always labour-intensive, depending on the skill of an individual worker. Even where machinery is used, it is the way a worker chooses to use these machines that creates the uniqueness of the product. A carpenter, for example, may use a variety of tools but the emphasis remains on the craftsmanship in the way the tools are used.

Job production is, therefore, ideally suited to a business that bases its appeal on meeting customers' individual needs. If demand is low, profitability can still be achieved with a high-quality product offering high profit margins. The dilemma comes as demand rises. Job production is time-consuming and labour-intensive. Keeping the uniqueness of each order may mean turning customers away. But to lose the uniqueness may be to lose the whole appeal of the product.

service to meet the specific needs of a customer. Each order is a one-off – unique and individual. The order is seen through all the stages of production, from start to finish, by an individual or a group of workers. As each job is completed and before moving on to the next, a single unit is produced – rather than a batch or mass of identical products. Job production is the most flexible of all production methods in that

Job production

Advantages

- High added value – the uniqueness of the finished product means that a high price can usually be charged. This makes job production potentially very profitable, despite its low quantity of production.

- Customer satisfaction – the ability to make-to-order means that the business can meet customer needs and achieve a high standard of quality. The resulting customer satisfaction helps build reputation and loyalty.

- Employee motivation – the craftsmanship and variety of tasks involved, together with the opportunity to see production through from start to finish means workers have a high degree of job satisfaction. If this is translated into motivation, then the result is likely to be higher productivity and pride in the work done.

Disadvantages

- High production costs – as production is labour-intensive, often time-consuming and highly skilled, the costs of producing each item are likely to be high. The fixed costs can be spread across only a low level of output, making fixed costs per unit high. There are few-opportunities for economies of scale (see unit 31).

- Inefficient use of machinery – a variety of different types of equipment may be needed during job production, but each tool or machine may only be used occasionally. This could mean a high initial capital cost, followed by low and inefficient use of the machinery.

- Slow to meet customer orders – the nature of job production in making an item to customer order may mean there is a substantial delay before it can be produced and delivered. A lengthy *lead time* may deter some customers and sales may be lost. For example, a restaurant offering freshly cooked meals to order may seem slow compared to one where food is pre-cooked and heated only when required.

Batch production

Batch production is an alternative approach that

STOP & THINK

Why do you think Aston Martin use job production techniques to make cars when most car manufacturers use mass production techniques?

enables a business to expand the scale of its production, but with the loss of uniqueness that job production provided. It involves the production of a group of identical items at a time. The group (batch) are moved from one stage of production to the next until all processes are completed. Typical examples of batch production are the manufacture of food products, such as bread, or of clothing, where different sizes, styles and colours will be produced. The batch size could be anything from 10 to 10,000 units according to the scale of demand. Batch production is more capital-intensive than job production, making greater use of machinery and relying less on the skill of the employees.

Figure 33.1 shows how batch production is used in the manufacture of bicycles.

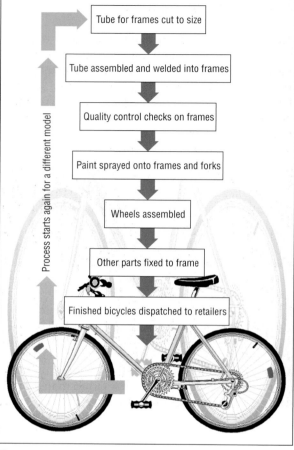

Figure 33.1 Batch production of bicycles

Batch production

Advantages

- Increased output – batch production enables a business to increase output volume compared to job production. By meeting high demand it can increase sales revenue and potentially its profits.

- Reduced costs of production – by working on a group of products at a time and making greater use of machinery in the production process, the unit production costs can be reduced. The process is less labour intensive, and the fact that workers no longer need to be as highly skilled means that labour costs will be cheaper. Greater output means that fixed costs can be spread across more output units, reducing the fixed costs per unit.

- Some flexibility is retained – batch production still allows a business to produce different types of a product to meet different customer needs.

Disadvantages

- Loss of uniqueness – if the one-off nature of the product attracted customers, a move to batch production could lead to damaged reputation and exclusivity.

- Demotivation of workforce – batch production is likely to involve more repetitive and less highly skilled work. The resulting boredom could be demotivating and reduce productivity.

- High stock levels and work-in-progress – at any one time, there will be raw materials waiting for use, work-in-progress at different stages of production and finished stock waiting to be sold. These high stock levels tie up space and cash, both of which could be used more productively.

- Complex organisation – production time can be lost in switching from one batch to another, with machinery having to be re-tooled. Careful scheduling is required to ensure the right quantities of each batch are produced to meet demand.

4   Flow production

Flow production is the continuous movement of items through each stage of production. Also known as **mass production**, this technique enables large quantities of an identical product to be produced to meet high levels of demand. Flow production techniques are highly capital-intensive, often using a conveyor-belt system to move products through the production process. The workforce is often semi-skilled and involved in just a single task – usually operating machinery.

Almost all mass-consumer products, from cars to computers and toys to mobile phones, have been produced using some form of flow production. First developed by Henry Ford in the 1920s to make the 'Model T'. Flow production is now controlled by computer technology, this ensures precise planning and control of the capital equipment to maximise production levels.

5   Modern production techniques

The cost efficiency of flow production and its ability to meet mass-consumer demand ensured that it became the key to big business in the twentieth century. Yet traditional flow production brought problems of inefficiency and inflexibility that have led to new methods being sought. *Lean production* seeks to eliminate the waste that flow production can bring with it. It uses a range of techniques, including the reorganisation of production into 'cells'. These methods are explored in detail in Unit 36.

Using flow management to assemble car engines

Flow production

Advantages

- High levels of output – enable a business to meet high and continuous levels of demand. The ability to mass market the product allows the business to maximise profits through high sales volume.

- Reduced costs – the efficient use of capital equipment, the use of low-cost, semi-skilled, labour and the economies of scale gained from large-scale production combine to ensure low production costs per unit.

- Standardised products – the fact that every product is identical can be an advantage, not a drawback. Quality is standardised and parts are interchangeable. The customer knows exactly what to expect – part of the global appeal of mass-produced food, such as McDonald's.

Disadvantages

- Expensive to set-up and maintain – the massive investment required to provide the machinery and technology make this an option only for larger businesses. Unless demand remains high over a long period of time, the investment will not prove profitable.

- Poor worker motivation – the repetitive nature of the work, which is largely unskilled and unrewarding, could lead to a lack of job satisfaction. If workers become demotivated, productivity and quality could both suffer.

- Lack of flexibility – the product is standardised and mass-produced – individual customer requirements cannot be met. A change in tastes or fashions could mean large quantities of finished products cannot be sold.

- Errors or breakdowns are costly – if a mistake is made in the production process, a huge quantity of products may have to be scrapped or recalled from customers. The continuous flow of production means a breakdown at any one stage will stop the whole production line. The loss of production could be huge and costly.

For example ...

Yamaha tunes its assembly lines

The Yamaha Corporation of Japan, founded in 1887, has grown to become the world's largest manufacturer of musical instruments. It also produces a whole variety of other goods, from semi-conductors and robots through to sporting goods and furniture. Yamaha was one of the first piano manufacturers to make upmarket grand pianos using flow production techniques. The picture shows grand pianos being manufactured on an assembly line in much the same way as a car is produced.

Traditionally, grand pianos (as opposed to the less expensive and better selling upright pianos) were made using job production methods that relied on craft skills. The main advantage was that skilled workers could accommodate individual variations in the often inconsistent materials from which pianos are made. Each individual piano could be constructed to make a product unique in its tone and tuning.

Not so with Yamaha who turned the art of making a grand piano into the art of mass production. The result? Some of the highest quality pianos in the world, emphasising not just richness of tone, but also consistency and reliability!

Source: Slack et al., *Operations Management* FT/Pitman Publishing (1998), page 222

1 Why were grand pianos originally produced using job production techniques?   **[3]**
2 What benefits would Yamaha have gained from using flow production methods?   **[4]**

3 Explain the potential drawbacks of using flow production to manufacture grand pianos.   **[4]**
Total 11 marks

Want to know more?
www.yamaha-music.co.uk

6 Factors affecting the choice of method

In deciding which of the three production methods to use, or whether to combine them using modern technology, a business needs to consider:

- **The scale of demand** – if there is a mass market for a product, only flow production will be able to meet the demand. If demand is low or uncertain, the investment in capital required for flow production cannot be justified.

- **Customer needs** – if the customer requires a unique product, then job production is essential. If the market demands a cheap, standardised product then flow production techniques will be essential.

- **The nature of the product** – often the nature of the good or service dictates the choice. For example, a one-off project, such as designing a new building, or a service, such as hairdressing, cannot use flow production techniques.

- **The relative costs of labour and capital** – the expense of skilled labour may make labour-intensive job production unprofitable. On the other hand, the initial investment needed for flow production may make it unrealistic for a small business.

- **The goals of the firm** – if the aim of the business is to maximise profitability, it may seek to expand production through using batch and then flow production methods. If there is a commitment to personal service, quality and staying small, job production may remain the chosen method.

Activity

Which method of production would be most suitable to make:
- paracetamol tablets
- a piece of pottery
- a collector's bottle of wine
- a Formula 1 racing car
- a lightbulb?
In each case, explain why.

Methods of production: summary

KEY TERMS

Labour-intensive – the use of a high proportion of labour (people) compared to capital (machinery) in the production process.

Capital-intensive – the use of a high proportion of capital (machinery) compared to labour (people) in the production process.

Job production – the method used to produce a single good or service to meet the specific needs of a customer.

Batch production – the production of a group (batch) of identical items at a time. The batch is moved from one stage of production to the next until all processes are completed.

Flow or mass production – the continuous movement of items through each stage of production, enabling large quantities of an identical product to be produced.

Summary questions

1 Explain the difference between labour-intensive and capital-intensive production.
2 Identify **three** features of job production.
3 For what type of products is job production most suitable? Why?
4 Identify **three** features of batch production.
5 What are the benefits and drawbacks of switching from job to batch production?
6 Identify **three** features of flow production.
7 What are the advantages and disadvantages of using flow production?
8 Explain the factors that will determine the choice of production method?

Production methods at Raleigh

In 1888, Sir Frank Bowden bought a small bicycle business on Raleigh Street in Nottingham and the Raleigh Bicycle Company was formed. Its early success was based on quality bicycles raced by international cycling champions. These bicycles were built using job production methods. Highly skilled workers would build a quality bicycle from start to finish, to meet the specific needs of individual cyclists.

Bowden recognised the potential of the bicycle market and realised that production methods would have to meet high consumer demand. Batch production methods were used, with parts being moved in groups through the stages of manufacture and assembly. Bowden built the Nottingham plant into the largest cycle factory in the world, employing 7,000 people.

But recent times have been hard for the UK cycle industry, with cheap foreign imports and falling demand leading to job cuts. By the 1990s, Raleigh employed just 470 permanent workers in its Nottingham factory. In 1999, Raleigh bicycles sold off its bike-making machinery in a bid to cut costs. This made the Nottingham factory an assembly plant only, putting together mass-produced parts imported from the Far East. The assembly process still used batch production methods – making up to 600 bikes of a particular model at any one time. A total of half a million bikes were produced each year, almost all to the UK market. Despite a £28m investment into new machinery in the factory, production remained labour-intensive.

The costs of labour and of meeting high environmental standards in the UK, however, meant that Raleigh could not compete on a price-only basis with rivals in China and Taiwan. New initiatives in 2001 sought to build a competitive advantage for Raleigh away from the battleground of price. Developing its after-sales advice was one way of trying to meet customer needs. Another was to return to its origins of job production and build customised bikes to order. These moves, though, were not enough and it was to decided to shut the factory by the end of 2002, with all production of Raleigh bicycles to be carried out abroad. The decision marked the end of more than a century of bicycle production in Nottingham.

Source: http://news.bbc.co.uk

Exam practice

1 Using examples, explain the terms:
   a job production   **[3]**
   b labour-intensive. **[3]**
2 Why did Raleigh originally develop batch production techniques in its Nottingham factory? **[6]**
3 Consider the merits and drawbacks of Raleigh's strategy to return to the use of job production techniques in producing customised bikes. **[9]**
4 Raleigh's Far East rivals used mass production techniques to manufacture bicycles. Evaluate the strengths and weaknesses of Raleigh in competing with these foreign rivals. **[9]**
   Total 30 marks

Want to know more?

www.raleigh.co.uk

34 Stock control

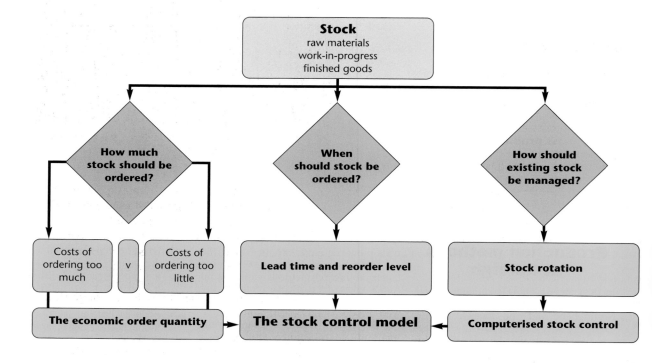

1 What is stock?

Stock is any type of stored materials within a business, but usually refers to materials at one of three stages in the production process:

- **Raw materials and components** – bought from outside suppliers and waiting to be used.

- **Work-in-progress** – unfinished products currently going through the production process.

- **Finished products** – completed products that have not yet been sold.

All organisations hold at least some stock of one type or another. A manufacturing business is likely to be holding component parts, semi-finished products and goods waiting to be sold. Retailers stock will be the goods ready for sale to customers – on shelves or in warehouses. Even service industries, such as the restaurant and hotel trade, hold stocks – food and drink being the most obvious examples.

2 Why businesses hold stock

Stocks are unavoidable whenever the amounts demanded and the amounts supplied are not evenly matched. If there is no stock, customer demand cannot be satisfied instantly. This will occur because:

- The purchase and supply of raw materials and components needed for production is not instant. If a business needs to expand production to meet demand, it cannot instantly acquire the extra inputs. To avoid hold-ups to production, a buffer (safety) stock may be held so that spare materials are available if needed.

- The production process is not instant. At any one time there will be stocks of unfinished products being worked on. The greater the volume of output and the longer the production time, the more work-in-progress there will be.

- Demand is unpredictable. A business may want to hold stocks of finished goods in case demand unexpectedly increases. Without stock the sales would be lost. However, when demand is lower than expected, finished goods remain unsold and stocks build up.

 STOP & THINK

How can a business try to minimise the imbalance between supply and demand? How will this help minimise stock?

Some warehouses can hold vast quantities of stock, requiring an army of staff to control its storage and movement

3   Ordering stock

The traditional response of businesses to this problem has been to seek the best level of stock to hold – one that balances the costs of holding stock against the costs of having none. This has led to the development of a system of stock control that plans:

- how much stock to order

- when to order stock

- how to manage stock.

How much stock should be ordered?

The amount and frequency of stock ordering will determine how much stock is held at any one time. When deciding how much stock should be ordered, an organisation must first weigh up the conflicting costs of holding and ordering stock.

Holding costs are the costs incurred in holding and storing stock, which will rise when more stock is ordered and stored. By ordering and storing large quantities of stock, a business will find its costs rise for a number of reasons:

- **Storage.** The space taken by storing stocks is costly, and could be used more productively. The business may have bought or rented storage space. There are also other costs associated with storing stock, such as warehouse staff wages, electricity, refrigeration and insurance against any loss of stock.

- **Wastage.** The more stock ordered and stored, the greater risk that stock will be wasted. High

stock levels mean that each item may be stored for a longer time. During this time, the product's quality may worsen – particularly if it is a perishable item, such as food. It is also more likely that stock may be damaged or stolen. Additionally, should fashions or tastes change quickly – such as for clothes – there will be wastage of stock because there isn't enough time to sell it off before demand falls.

- **Opportunity cost.** The money spent on ordering stock could have been used in other ways, such as investing in machinery or developing a new product. These alternative uses would have brought benefits that have had to be foregone (given up). What has been foregone is known as the opportunity cost. Another **opportunity cost** is when money to pay for stock is borrowed. This adds the further cost of interest payment on the overdraft or loan.

- **Liquidity.** Cash spent ordering stock, may leave the business short of cash to pay for other essentials such as wages or overheads. Storing stock ties up working capital, leaving the business short of liquid assets. This could cause dangerous cash-flow problems that leave the business unable to pay creditors.

- **Inefficiency.** Holding high stock levels makes it difficult for a business to see clearly where its operations are inefficient. There is little incentive for each stage in the production process to work swiftly to supply the next stage, because there are always stocks waiting. The effect is to hide, or even to encourage, inefficiency.

Ordering costs, in contrast, are the costs a business incurs by ordering only small quantities of stock and holding very low stock levels:

- **Administration.** Ordering small quantities means that the business must order much more frequently. Each order involves staff time in organising the purchase of stock, deliveries must be arranged, arriving stock must be checked and payment must be made to the supplier. Numerous small orders are, therefore, more costly than less frequent, larger ones.

- **Loss of price discounts.** Many suppliers charge a higher unit cost per item supplied if items are ordered individually or in small batches. Larger orders usually receive bulk-buying discounts.

- **Stock-out costs.** A business operating with very low stock levels risks stocks running out. This may happen when:

    - a supplier fails to deliver on time and production cannot start
    - a production bottleneck slows the rate of work-in-progress reaching the next stage
    - demand increases unexpectedly and finished products stocks are unable to meet customer orders.

As a result of these problems, output falls and costs per unit rise because the lack of stock has caused delays. Workers and machinery may stand idle because there isn't enough stock to continue production If the business cannot meet demand, customers may turn instead to competitors, and

sales will be lost. Consumers may view the business as slow and unreliable, risking the loss of its reputation and customer loyalty.

Figure 34.1 shows how these two types of cost change as order levels increase. Ordering costs fall as order levels increase while holding costs rise. The best balance between the two costs levels needs to be found. The optimum (ideal) point is shown on the diagram, where the combined total costs are at a minimum. This ideal order level is known as the *economic order quantity*.

 4   When stock should be ordered

A stock control system must establish how often and when stock should be ordered. The business decides its:

- **minimum (buffer) stock level** – the lowest level of stock it wishes to keep, to prevent the stock-out costs discussed

- **desired order quantity** – the ideal order quantity that minimises the overall costs of ordering and holding stock (economic order quantity)

- **maximum stock level** – determined by the space available for storage or the maximum stock the business wishes to hold, given the costs discussed.

To calculate how often, and when, stock should be ordered, the business must know:

- **how quickly stock will be used** – this is determined by the demand for the final product, and the production process rate of output

- **how long it will take for stock to be delivered** – this is known as the **lead time** and depends on the ability of the supplier to process and deliver the required stock.

The key is for the business to ensure that an order will be delivered before the minimum stock level is reached. This is illustrated in 34.2, which shows that:

- an economic order quantity of 300 units has been established

- the minimum buffer stock is set at 100 units

- the maximum stock level is, therefore, 400 units

- the lead time for delivery is one week

- each week 100 units of stock are used.

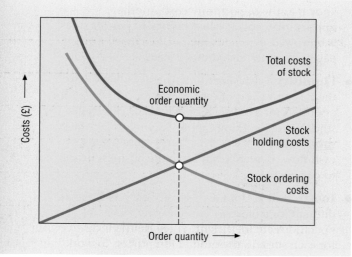

Figure 34.1 Ordering costs versus holding costs

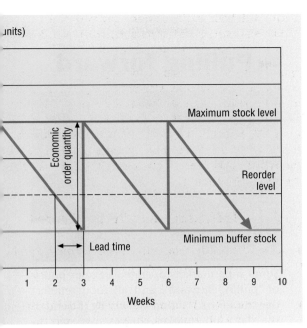

Figure 34.2 The stock control model

Using this information, the business calculates when, and how often, to order. To ensure the order is delivered before stock levels fall below the minimum of 100, a **reorder level** has to be set at 200 units. This means that when stocks fall to 200 units, a new order is triggered. By the time the new order arrives – a week later – stock levels will have reached their minimum of 100 units.

If demand and output continue at the same rate of 100 units per week, stock will be reordered every three weeks. However, if demand increases stock must be reordered more frequently. It is unlikely that sales and output will be as regular as that represented in Figure 34.2. The business must ensure its re-ordering system can cope with unexpected fluctuations in demand.

5   How stock should be managed

Consideration must be given to managing both the ordering of stock and its control.

Managing the ordering of stock

Avoiding the problems of too much or too little stock requires an effective system to manage stock ordering. The system need not be complex – many of the most effective systems are also the simplest.

Regular stock checks allow a business to assess how much of different types of stock need to be re-ordered. A two-bin system, on the other hand, provides a simple method of triggering a reorder. Two bins are filled with component parts or work-in-progress, ready for the next stage of production. When one has been used up, stock is ordered to refill it. One bin acts as a buffer stock, available to keep production going.

The use of computerised stock control systems has enabled firms to manage their stock more efficiently and accurately. Electronic point of sales (EPOS) systems combine barcode reading at retail checkouts with a computer database of all existing stock. This database is constantly updated when products are sold, triggering the system to automatically order new stock once the preset reorder level is reached. Manufacturers can use the same technology both to track components in the production process and work-in-progress.

Links with suppliers have also been improved through the use of IT. Using electronic data interchange (EDI), orders can be placed electronically with suppliers, reducing the administration. By reducing administrative costs, frequent orders of

Activity

1 Copy and complete the stock control diagram shown in Figure 35.3. Make sure you fully label the diagram.
2 Identify the following (stating the relevant figures):
   a re-order level
   b buffer stock level
   c weekly demand
   d re-order quantity
   e lead time
3 Sketch a fully labelled stock diagram to represent what might happen if demand increased sharply during the first three weeks.

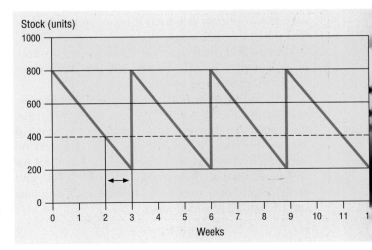

Figure 34.3 A stock control diagram

smaller quantities become more cost efficient. In addition, computerised stock control allows retailers, manufacturers and suppliers to monitor and analyse their sales and stock levels more closely. This helps them to anticipate trends in demand and future stock needs. This has been crucial in enabling the growth of just-in-time methods of stock control (see Unit 35).

Managing the use of stock

Maximising efficiency in production involves minimising waste, therefore, ensuring minimum **stock wastage** is essential. Stock wastage may occur due to:

- perishable products held in stock too long may become unsaleable because they have passed their sell-by date, or they may no longer be in demand

- damage or theft of items being held in stock

- inefficient production methods not making the best use of raw materials; for example, throwing away wood off-cuts when making furniture

- poor quality production, leading to items having to be reworked or thrown away.

Keeping stock levels low is one way of minimising this wastage. Accurate records of stock and well-organised storage are also essential.

Stock rotation is a technique used to minimise the stock wasted through becoming out-of-date. It simply involves methods of ensuring the oldest stock is used first – the so-called first-in-first-out (FIFO) principle. The most obvious use for this method is with perishable products, such as food. Fresh stock may not be put on sale until older stock has been sold. If it is put on sale then it is put to the back so that the older stock is sold first.

Unit 36 deals with a more recent approach to stock management – *just-in-time* systems that keep stock levels to a minimum.

Stock management, like most aspects of business, involves balancing conflicting factors. In this case, the costs of holding too much stock must be weighed against the costs of holding too little. There is no ideal stock level that fits all businesses. The ideal for any one business depends on the level and predictability of demand, the reliability of suppliers and the nature of the product.

For example ...

Pulling forward

Some supermarkets operate a regular policy of 'pulling forward', and all food retailers operate a food rotation system. By the end of the day, supermarket shelves can start to look a little untidy and, so the theory goes, customers are less likely to make impulse purchases if products are not presented properly. Staff 'pull' goods to the front of shelves and line items up in a neat and presentable fashion. In order to avoid stock wastage, they will usually rotate the stock at the same time.

1 Explain the term stock rotation. [2]
2 What is meant by stock wastage? Support your answer with a relevant example. [3]
3 Explain why supermarkets are keen to avoid stock wastage. [4]
4 State **two** ways in which stock wastage might occur within a clothing store? [2]
5 With reference to supermarkets, explain how the concept of 'opportunity cost' relates to stock management. [4]

Total 15 marks

Stock control: summary

KEY TERMS

Stock – any type of stored materials within a business, but typically raw material and components, work-in-progress or finished goods waiting to be sold.

Work-in-progress – consists of partly finished goods going through the production process.

Buffer stock – the stock of raw materials and components kept in order that production could be increased to meet an unexpected rise in demand.

Opportunity cost – the cost of what is foregone (given up) when a decision is made.

Stock-out costs – the costs of lost production, lost sales and customer dissatisfaction that occur if a business runs out of stock.

Lead time – the time taken for the supplier to process and deliver an order.

Reorder level – the stock level that triggers new stock to be ordered and arrive before the minimum stock level is reached.

Stock wastage – the loss of stock caused by inefficient management of the stock control system.

Stock rotation –methods used to minimise the wastage caused through stock becoming out-of-date, ensuring that the oldest stock is used first.

Summary questions

1 What are the **three** different types of stock?
2 Why is holding some stock unavoidable?
3 Explain why businesses experience costs when holding stock.
4 What costs arise from holding low levels of stock?
5 What is an economic order quantity?
6 Explain the terms:
   a buffer stock
   b lead time
   c re-order level
7 How have developments in IT affected stock control?
8 What is meant by the term stock wastage?
9 What is the purpose of stock rotation?

Exam practice

Spare parts shortage

MG Rover, the largest UK-owned carmaker, had to halt production for a week, in 2002, to resolve a spare parts supply crisis. The business shut down its production line for a full week to divert parts to the MG Rover dealer network. Individual dealerships were suffering parts shortages and were unable to provide basic repair or car servicing facilities. Suppliers were unable to increase production quickly enough to meet MG Rover's immediate needs, and drastic action was needed. The shortfall of 3,500 vehicles (that would have been produced during that week) was made up later in the year.

In the future, to overcome such difficulties, dealers are likely to keep larger buffer stocks of essential spare parts.

Source: *Financial Times*, 13 June 2002

Want to know more?

www.mg-rover.com

1 What is meant by the term 'buffer stock'? **[2]**
2 Outline **two** disadvantages of holding too much stock. **[4]**
3 Briefly examine the implications for dealerships of having too little stock. **[5]**
4 Sketch a fully labelled stock control graph to represent what might have happened to stock levels in an individual dealership both prior to and following the closure? **[5]**
5 Evaluate the importance of close supplier relationships to companies such as MG Rover. **[10]**
   Total 26 marks

35 Maximising quality

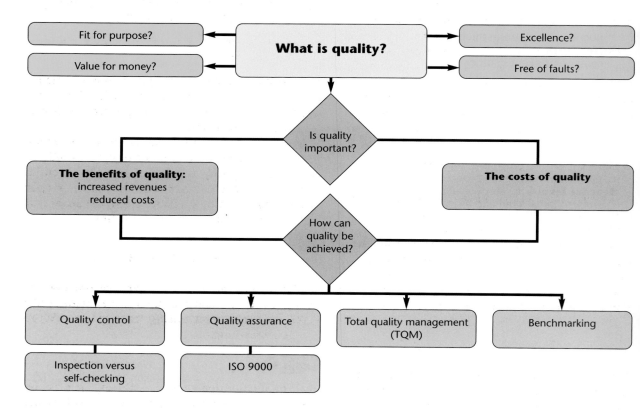

1 What is quality?

Think of a 'quality' product that you have bought. What features lead you to rate it as good quality? The following factors may have helped you to form your decision:

- Fit for purpose – it did exactly what it was intended to do.

- Excellence – in its function, appearance or overall image.

- Free of faults or errors.

- Durable – long lasting, without the need for repair or replacement.

- Value for money – a reasonable price for the standard of the product.

Quality doesn't have to mean 'top of the range', but any definition of quality must include the idea of satisfying the needs and expectations of different customers. For example, a watch that is technically excellent but not very attractive may not be considered a quality product if what customers value most is appearance. The challenge to business is to understand the expectations of customers and then meet differing needs from different types of customer.

> ### Activity
> List the features of quality that you would consider essential in a:
> - computer
> - house
> - haircut
> - train journey
> - pair of jeans

2 Is quality important?

By satisfying customer needs, a business can gain a competitive edge. To maintain customer loyalty, quality needs to be *consistent*. Individual incidents – such as the re-call of a faulty product – may destroy a reputation for quality that has taken many years to build.

In recent decades, consumers have become increasingly well informed about product quality. Information from groups, such as the Consumers Association, from the internet and from labelling – now required by law – have all enabled consumers to make comparisons of quality more easily. Consumers have also become more familiar with complaining about quality issues and seeking compensation. All these factors make quality crucially important.

3 The benefits of achieving quality

Achieving quality helps to increase revenues and cut costs, raising profitability. The ways in which this is achieved are summarised in Figure 35.1. While costs of scrapped products or customer compensation are easy to identify, others are hidden. In particular, the impact of poor quality on image, reputation and customer loyalty need to be appreciated to understand the full importance of achieving quality.

4 The costs of achieving quality

The different ways in which quality can be achieved are considered later in the unit. Whatever approach is taken, though, will create some costs, such as:

- **Checking product quality** – staff time is needed to inspect products to check for quality.
- **Cost of scrapped products** – throwing away faulty products wastes the cost of production, and the potential sale.
- **Costs of reworking products** – time and materials are needed to improve on poor quality.
- **Investment in equipment** – new machinery may be needed to improve quality.
- **Training costs** – employees may need training to raise quality.

The traditional approach to quality was to balance these costs against the benefits of quality. The result was a compromise that saw 100 per cent quality as too expensive to guarantee.

However, some of the costs of quality systems – such as scrapping or reworking products – will be eliminated if quality is achieved first time around. Given this and the massive hidden costs of poor quality, many organisations now seek to ensure that 100 per cent quality is achieved first time.

5 How can quality be achieved?

Quality can be achieved through the processes of quality control, quality assurance, maintaining ISO 9000 standards, total quality management (TQM) and benchmarking.

Quality control

The traditional approach to achieving quality has been through **quality control**. This involves the inspection of products to check they meet the

Increased revenues	Reduced costs
Customer satisfaction	Less wastage of scrapped products
Improved image and reputation	Less time and materials taken to rework faulty products
New customers attracted	Less time needed to deal with customer complaints
Existing customers retained	Fewer claims on warranties
Positive brand image helping to add value	Less compensation given to customers
Higher prices may be accepted by customers	Less needs for quality control or inspection when more certain of original product quality
Word-of-mouth helping to promote product	
Retailers encouraged to stock product	

Figure 35.1 Achieving quality to increase revenues and cut costs

necessary standards. The quality control process follows the stages shown in Figure 35.2. Checks on product quality can be made at the start, during or at the end of the production process.

Checking finished products has been the focus of many organisations' quality control – in seeking to ensure that faulty products did not reach the customer. Only a *sample* of products is checked because it would be too time-consuming and costly to inspect every product. An acceptable number of faults per batch may be identified, and a whole batch may be scrapped if faults exceed this level.

However, relying on this method to ensure quality is risky, faulty products may slip through untested. It assumes that there is an acceptable level of faults and, even though this may be low, it may still have a negative impact on the business. This method also creates an impression that ensuring quality is the job of quality inspectors and not of the production workers themselves.

For example ...

Developing the X5

BMW calls the X5 the world's first sports activity vehicle. BMW believed that cutting-edge technology and a commitment to quality would set it in a class of its own. Their commitment was to create a product that would give customers 'the utmost in driving pleasure'.

In 2000, the X5 outperformed all its main rivals in safety tests. BMW used 3-D computer-aided design tests to determine everything from the vehicle's heating and air conditioning efficiency to the ability of the car to withstand a crash.

'It goes without saying that quality and safety are interrelated,' affirms Eduard Walek, BMW's X5 project leader. 'If you can't guarantee that each vehicle coming off the production lines is of a high-quality standard, you can't ensure a high standard of safety either. Safety must not be left to chance. It must be planned.'

Source: www.qualitydigest.com

Car recalls surge to an all-time high

There has been a staggering tenfold increase in the number of cars being recalled by manufacturers. A survey by the Consumers' Association revealed that the number of cars recalled had risen dramatically from 150,000 to more than 1.5 million.

This week, German manufacturer BMW said it was recalling 56,000 X5 sport-utility vehicles after it discovered a problem with the brake pedal. At the same time, it announced it had to recover 38,700 Minis worldwide to fix a gearbox defect.

Perhaps the most worrying aspect of these failures is that defects are sometimes noticed years after production begins; in these cases, manufacturers find it impossible to trace all the vehicles, and some slip through the recall net.

Some industry experts believe carmakers need to spend longer on development before putting new models on the production line.

Source: BBC News Online

1 What does quality mean to BMW?   **[4]**
2 What are the costs of poor quality to BMW?   **[5]**
3 Why do you think faults occur in products even when manufacturers are committed to quality?   **[5]**
Total 14 marks

Want to know more?

www.which.net

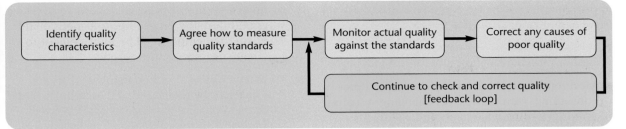

Figure 35.2 The stages of quality control

Quality assurance

Quality assurance differs from quality control in that it:

- Emphasises customer needs rather than just meeting technical standards

- Ensures that quality is built-in to a product rather than faults being inspected-out

- Develops systems to ensure quality in all aspects of the business, not just production

- Shifts away from checking by inspectors and towards self-checking, with workers taking responsibility for checking the quality of their own work.

Quality assurance brings additional costs:

- **Equipment** – needed for quality monitoring during the production process.

- **Market research costs** – to identify customer expectations about a product.

- **Training** – all staff to achieve quality outputs.

- **Time and disruption** – caused by re-organising business procedures.

However, the potential gains are considerable in comparison to more limited forms of quality control:

- Faults can be eliminated, or minimised – cutting the costs of scrapped or reworked products.

- It reduces the chance of faulty products reaching the customer. The business is not relying on sampling and inspection to prevent this. Customer satisfaction should increase.

- All aspects of customer expectations are considered, including service, and in the long-term this will produce customer loyalty and increased sales.

- Ways of improving quality can be identified helping to improve efficiency.

ISO 9000

ISO 9000 is an international standard for quality assurance. Most countries have their own national standards (such as BS5750 in the UK), but the purpose of ISO 9000 is to have a quality assurance system recognised throughout the world.

The ISO 9000 standard ensures that a business maintains quality at a consistent level. To achieve ISO 9000 an organisation must:

- design and document the procedures for controlling and supporting quality

- choose an independent organisation, such as the British Standards Institution (BSI) to inspect and confirm that the standards have been met

- act on any problems identified and be reinspected twice a year.

Registering for an accreditation such as ISO 9000 brings two types of benefits:

1 The benefits of following the quality procedures:

   - ISO 9000 guidelines, and support from an external organisation such as the BSI, can help improve existing procedures.
   - Provides an incentive to stick to the procedures because of the external, independent check.
   - The causes of quality problems can be identified and the costs of poor quality reduced.

2 The benefits of gaining the ISO 9000 certificate:

   - Customers can see the organisation takes quality seriously and has quality assurance systems in place at all stages of production.
   - Some customers may insist on ISO 9000 certification – particularly when they are buying components for their own production process.
   - Sales, image and reputation all gain.

Not all organisations choose to register for ISO 9000 certification, however, believing it will make little improvement to existing procedures. It could also cause a number of problems, such as:

- A focus on systems and paperwork may make the business too bureaucratic and inward-looking.

- Meeting the standards can be costly and time-consuming, with the costs of changing systems, training, writing documents and paying for ISO 9000 registration.

- Alternative approaches to achieving quality, such as continuous improvement, that may be more suitable for some organisations, are not included in the ISO 9000.

STOP & THINK

What type of businesses will gain most from ISO 9000 certification? Which businesses would gain little benefit?

Total quality management (TQM)

Total quality managment is an extension of the move from quality control to quality assurance. Its goals are:

- to create a culture of quality

- to involve all employees, whatever their role within the business

- to seek continuous improvement in quality

- to see quality from the customer's point of view.

The message of TQM emerged from the ideas of Dr W Edwards Deming and Joseph M Juran. From the 1950s onwards, many Japanese manufacturers put their ideas into practice – helping to establish Japan as leaders in the global market.

The key features of TQM are:

- **A focus on the customer** – understanding customer needs and using this to ensure the business meets their expectations. Market research is crucial in monitoring quality standards and seeking ways to improve.

- **The involvement of all** – workers at every level must be involved in the achievement of quality. The talents and ideas of each worker must be brought together. Teamwork is particularly useful in sharing ideas and motivating employees to improve quality. *Quality circles* are an example of this. Groups

of employees meet on a regular basis to consider ways of improving procedures to benefit quality. They are then empowered by management to put their suggestions into practice.

- **Quality chains** – because many workers are remote from the final customer, each link in the production process is viewed as a link between supplier and customer. So the next stage in the production process is seen as an internal customer. It is the responsibility of each worker to ensure that this customer's requirements are met. In this way, quality is built-in at every stage and problems are immediately identified.

- **Getting it right first time** – TQM aims to achieve **zero defects** by ensuring quality is built in at every stage of production, and in every other function of the business. All costs of poor quality should be eliminated and, in theory, there should be no need for quality inspection at the end of the production process.

- **Leadership on quality from the top** – a commitment to quality needs to be established through clear leadership and management.

- **Monitoring quality** – the use of sophisticated quality control techniques (known as **statistical process control**) to ensure any variation in key quality standards is kept to a minimum.

- **Continuous improvement** – a *kaizen* approach (see Unit 36), with a constant search for further ways to improve quality.

TQM's total approach to quality has been the foundation for the success of many businesses, including Motorola and Hewlett-Packard. Many others who have tried to implement TQM, however, have experienced little benefit. Figure 35.3 summarises the potential costs and benefits of TQM.

Whether it is successful for any one organisation depends on whether or not:

- there is clear leadership from the top

- the workforce is genuinely and fully involved

- training, time and support are provided to reinforce the policy

- quality is considered broadly enough to include all aspects of business performance

- procedures are adapted to meet the specific needs of an organisation.

Benefits	Costs
All aspects of quality in the business considered	May become just another set of procedures to be followed, making the business slow and bureaucratic
Costs of poor quality eliminated by getting it right first time	May be seen as an end in itself with all the focus on processes not on the final product
Clear focus on customer needs helps to make the business more competitive	Too much responsibility may be given to workers, who could lack proper leadership
Provides a positive and motivating working environment	May place too much stress on workers in demanding constant improvement, which could be demotivating
Makes the best use of the talents of the workforce	The disruption of change and the costs of training could outweigh the benefits

Figure 35.3 The costs and benefits of total quality management

Guru's views

You do not have to do this; survival is not compulsory.

Deming

Benchmarking

Benchmarking is a way of improving quality by comparing an aspect of the business against best practice of competitors, leading firms from other industries or even within other parts of the organisation. The aims of benchmarking are to:

- Find out how well one aspect of your own business is performing in comparison to other organisations.

- Set a standard for your own business to match or exceed the best of the rest.

- To find new ideas and ways of doing things that can be put into practice in your own business.

Xerox pioneered the use of benchmarking to help restore its reputation in the photocopier market. It benchmarked the way its photocopiers were built, the cost of each stage of production and the quality of the servicing it offered against its competitors and other businesses.

The benchmarking process follows the stages identified in Figure 35.4.

Benchmarking can bring a number of benefits:

- By identifying areas for improvement and observing how other organisations work, a business can learn a great deal about improving their own quality or efficiency.

- It can save time and money compared to working in isolation and only learning by trial and error.

- The focus of benchmarking is on how to be the best in each area examined. It helps to set clear targets that drive a business forward rather than just making do with current performance.

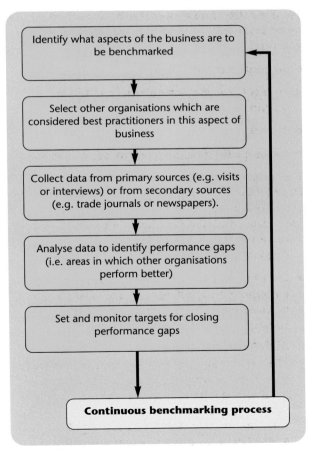

Figure 35.4 Stages in the benchmarking process

For example ...

The Document Company Xerox – copying the best

Xerox's initial control of the market for photocopier technology came under serious threat in the late 1970s as competitors moved in and beat it on price, quality and other important measures. Its solution was to benchmark:

- the way its photocopiers were built
- the cost of each stage of production
- the quality of the servicing it offered
- other aspects of its business against its competitors and other businesses.

Whenever it found something that someone else did better, it made this the new standard for it its own business.

Benchmarking has now become an everyday activity for all departments in Xerox. A recent example of its use came with a study of storage and distribution. Xerox compared their distribution against others such as 3M in Dusseldorf, Ford in Cologne, and Sainsbury's regional depot in Hertfordshire. Xerox discovered that:

- it had an extra, wasteful level of stock that could be removed
- its flow of information from HQ to individual depots was a day slower than the best (showing that its own systems needed to be updated)
- warehouses became efficient not through a high level of automation but through efficient manual routines.

Xerox then set about putting these lessons to work, upgrading their operations to be at least as good as the best they had found.

Not only has Xerox improved its financial position and stabilised its market share, but it has also increased customer satisfaction by 40 per cent in the past four years.

1 Why did Xerox decide to use benchmarking?   **[4]**
2 Using examples from the case study, explain the steps involved in benchmarking?   **[6]**
3 Why might benchmarking have worked for Xerox and yet not for other businesses?   **[5]**

Want to know more?

www.xerox.com

Although Xerox used benchmarking to improve its financial position, stabilise its market share and increase customer satisfaction, benchmarking does have problems and limitations:

- Rivals may not allow access to crucial information, and organisations from other industries may not prove similar enough to be a useful comparison.

- If benchmarking means that an organisation merely copies what others are already doing

rather than striving to lead, it will never be better than its rivals – or the first to innovate.

- Benchmarking could become no more than a paperwork exercise, identifying relevant information but not doing anything with it. Unless turned into a strategy for improvement benchmarking is pointless.

Maximising quality: summary

KEY TERMS

Quality control – the inspection of products to check they meet the necessary standards.

Quality assurance – ensuring that quality is guaranteed throughout an organisation and that both the final product and service will meet customer expectations.

Total quality management (TQM) – an approach to business that emphasises the involvement of everyone in an organisation in getting the product and service right first time.

Quality chains – a feature of TQM that views each link in the production process as a link between supplier and customer, so that it is the responsibility of each worker to ensure that customers' requirements are met.

Zero defects – a goal of TQM, to make no errors in production so that product quality is achieved first time around.

Statistical process control – a sophisticated quality control technique that monitors production to ensure any variation in key quality standards is kept to a minimum.

Benchmarking – a way of improving quality by comparing one aspect of the business against the best practice of competitors, leading companies from other industries or other parts within the organisation.

Summary questions

1 What are the key features of a definition of quality?
2 Explain how achieving quality can increase revenues and help reduce costs.
3 Why are there costs in achieving quality?
4 How does quality assurance differ from quality control?
5 What are the costs and the benefits of using a quality assurance system?
6 What is ISO 9000 and how might a business benefit from it?
7 Explain the features of total quality management (TQM).
8 What are the benefits of TQM?
9 Why might TQM not prove successful?
10 What are the benefits and problems of using benchmarking?

Exam practice

Black & Decker UK

Black & Decker's approach to quality today is greatly changed from that of the 1980s. Then, the definition of quality was meeting a minimum technical standard. Now that is seen as too narrow, limiting quality to just design and manufacture. All aspects of packaging, appearance and after-sales service are also of crucial importance. Black & Decker decided it had to change to a total quality management (TQM) culture in which everyone was working together to achieve quality and put the customer's needs at the heart of the business.

The workforce was involved in this initiative at every stage. Because workers had little direct contact with the end customer, their efforts were focused on meeting the expectations of their internal customers – the next people in the plant to receive the products of their work. Teams of workers were given direct control over quality, checking their own work and seeking ways to continually improve its quality.

Self-management has led to the removal of layers of management. The number of supervisors has been reduced from 68 to 20 and their jobs have been enlarged as business managers, with responsibility for skills and employee relations, capital assets and customer services. The reductions in costs have been significant, but Robin Mair does not emphasise this aspect: 'Cost is not the sole motivation. Quality as perceived by the customer is what we are aiming at.'

Source: *The Times* 100 case studies

1 How did Black and Decker's view of quality change over time? **[4]**
2 Why are 'the full costs of poor quality' often higher than is realised? **[5]**
3 Explain the features of TQM evident in Black and Decker's new approach. **[6]**
4 What benefits has Black and Decker gained from introducing TQM? **[6]**
5 Discuss the view that the success of TQM depends upon 'bringing all parts of the business together'. **[9]**

Total 30 marks

Want to know more?

www.blackanddecker.co.uk

36 Lean production

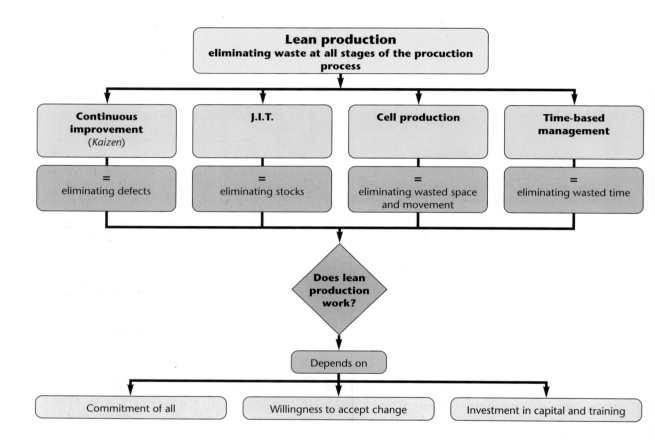

1 What is lean production?

Lean production aims to eliminate waste within the production process. It brings together a variety of approaches to production that seek to produce more using less, while maximising quality of output.

Many of its elements were inspired by the success of the Toyota Motor Company in becoming one of the world's leading car producers. The new techniques of Toyota contrasted with the more traditional mass-manufacturing techniques of US manufacturers, such as General Motors. While Toyota could produce a car in just 18 assembly hours, GM took 40.7; and while GM experienced defects at the rate of 130 per 100 cars, Toyota experienced just 45 per 100.

Figure 36.1 contrasts traditional, mass-manufacturing techniques with those of lean production.

Lean production involves four key concepts:

- Continuous improvement

- Just-in-time stock control

- Cell production

- Time-based management

	Mass manufacturing	Lean manufacturing
Type of production	Flow production	Small batch production
Machine set-ups	Slow and infrequent	Fast and often
Product design	Linear process through departments	Simultaneous development through project teams
Stock levels	High	Low
Stock deliveries	Occasional	Frequent
Quality	Quality control	Total quality assurance
Workers	Specialised, repetitive work	Flexible and multi-skilled
Management style	Autocratic	Consultative

Figure 36.1 A comparison of mass manufacturing and lean manufacturing production

2 Continuous improvement

The concept of continuous improvement – known by its Japanese name of *kaizen* – involves all workers in constant, ongoing improvements to quality. Unlike traditional methods of quality control, it focuses on getting the product right first time. If 'zero defects' can be achieved, there will be no wastage of materials, no need for quality control teams and no need for reworking faulty products. The result is savings of time and money.

Lean producers recognise the talents of their workforce allowing them to maximise quality at minimum cost, therefore they seek to release those talents by creating a culture of quality and involvement. At Toyota, for example, 740,000 suggestions for improving quality are made in a typical year and 99 per cent of these are accepted. Rewards for suggestions range from £2.50 to £1000!

3 Just-in-time production

Just-in-time (JIT) production techniques aim to minimise stocks of raw materials, work-in-progress and finished products. JIT production requires the conventional approach to manufacturing to be turned on its ahead. Stocks are 'pulled' into the production process when they are needed – 'just-in-time' – rather than the traditional approach of being 'pushed' in '**just-in-case**' they are needed.

The problems of the just-in-case approach

Traditionally, products would *first* be manufactured and *then* the business would try to sell them. Components would be ordered infrequently in bulk, in order to gain from bulk-buying discounts. Even if sales were falling, production may have continued in order to make full use of capacity.

This approach brings a number of problems:

- bulk ordering of component parts requires the business to have significant – and costly – warehousing space for storage

- the amount of stock of all types ties up large amounts of working capital that could be used more productively elsewhere

- holding sizeable buffer stocks disguises inefficiencies, delays and bottlenecks in the production process

- finished products may remain unsold and, therefore, wasted because they have been manufactured without any guarantee of being sold.

The JIT approach

The JIT system reverses this traditional approach because production is made to order. All finished products have already been sold and go straight to customers. The customer order generates the 'pull' effect that goes right back through every stage of production to the original suppliers of component parts. Suppliers must be able to respond swiftly and reliably to the stock demands of the manufacturer, delivering small quantities of specific items in time for them to be used on the production line. One such process at Nissan is illustrated in Figure 36.2.

The Japanese developed a *kanban* system to drive the whole JIT approach to manufacturing. The *kanban* is a card that accompanies each item through

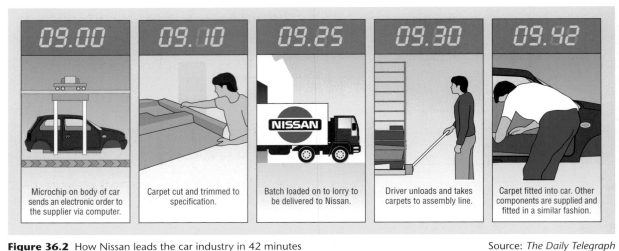

09.00	09.10	09.25	09.30	09.42
Microchip on body of car sends an electronic order to the supplier via computer.	Carpet cut and trimmed to specification.	Batch loaded on to lorry to be delivered to Nissan.	Driver unloads and takes carpets to assembly line.	Carpet fitted into car. Other components are supplied and fitted in a similar fashion.

Figure 36.2 How Nissan leads the car industry in 42 minutes

Source: *The Daily Telegraph*

the production process. The *kanban* authorises the next stage of manufacturing, triggering the production of more parts to be delivered to that workstation.

The kanban system allows the factory to hold little stock — empty bins are replaced by full ones by an external company

The benefits of the JIT approach

The JIT system brings a range of benefits and helps to eliminate waste in a number of ways:

- Reduction of stock levels reduces storage costs and eliminates the associated waste of factory and warehousing space.

- Working capital is freed up by reducing stocks, and can be used more productively elsewhere.

- Unsaleable products are not overproduced as products are made to order.

- Production can be very responsive to customer needs, making products that meet their requirements and cutting the time taken to manufacture and deliver.

- There is an incentive to achieve both quality and efficiency as there is no stock 'safety net' to cover errors or bottlenecks.

The implementation of JIT at Stoves, manufacturing cookers and ovens, helped to reduce their stock to almost zero. Stoves now make cookers only to customer order, but can make any combination of size, shape or colour. The production time for one cooker made to order is just two hours, meaning that the company can respond with impressive speed and flexibility to customer demand.

Oven production at Stoves

The problems of JIT

JIT is not a universal solution that can be applied successfully to all businesses. It may prove of little benefit and it can bring its own problems:

- The system depends on the reliability of suppliers and their ability to make frequent deliveries. The costs of stockholding are, in fact, just being moved from the manufacturer to the supplier. Many suppliers will, therefore, be unable or unwilling to act as a JIT supplier.

- JIT requires a fundamental change in all aspects of a firm's approach to business. This requires the willing involvement of everyone – management and workforce alike – to be successful. This cultural change can bring its own costs and difficulties that often undermine the success of JIT.

- Without buffer stocks of finished products, a JIT manufacturer may be unable to respond quickly enough to a surge in customer demand.

The conditions for successful JIT

If JIT is to be successful, the whole business approach to manufacturing and selling needs to change. It is certainly not as simple as just a change in the method of stock control.

- **Sources of uncertainty need to be removed** if the business is to be confident in its holding of zero stock. Accurate sales forecasting and reliable suppliers will all be essential in reducing uncertainty.

- **A flexible and committed workforce is required.** To avoid bottlenecks in production workers will need to be able to switch from one task to another. A philosophy of continuous improvement will be required to ensure each stage of production is seeking ways to improve its efficiency.

- **Good communication** is essential to the success of JIT. From communicating with customers, through communication between

cells to links with suppliers, the JIT system depends on precise and accurate understanding of the needs of other groups. Without this, the smooth flow of components, work-in-progress and finished products to satisfy a customer's needs cannot occur.

4   Cell production

In a traditional manufacturing layout, workers are lined up besides an assembly line. Each performs a single function on a unit of work, before that unit moves to another part of the production process. This method of production brings a number of problems:

- Performing a single, repetitive task and never seeing the whole process or finished product may demotivate workers.

- There can be a lack of flexibility among workers trained to perform just one task. The result may be production bottlenecks that cannot be solved by switching workers to different areas.

- Quality may be ignored as it may be seen as the responsibility of others, such as a separate inspection department.

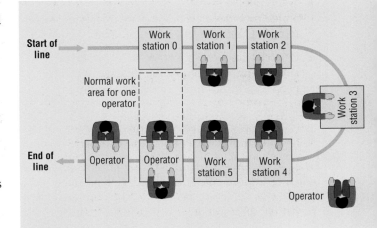

Figure 36.3 The U-shaped arrangement required for cell production

- At any one time, there may be considerable work-in-progress spread across the production line. This can tie up resources and make the business slow to respond to customer needs.

- Time may be wasted moving components and work-in-progress around a factory floor, adding to the cost but not the value of the product.

Cell production, however, organises groups of workers into small, self-contained units designed to complete a product or process. Each member of the team is multiskilled, which means that they can switch tasks to help other workers. Cells are organised in a U-shaped layout such as that shown in Figure 36.3.

Small quantities of components are delivered to the start of the cell layout as and when the team request them. Work does not start unless it can be completed, with the team controlling their work schedule and how to achieve it. Work flows around the U-shaped cell from one worker to the next, with each worker performing a different operation until the product is complete. Finished work leaves the cell at the point where it entered. The benefits of cell production are:

- Teamwork can improve motivation, while seeing the product from start to finish can add to job satisfaction. Productivity may improve as a result.

- Multiskilled workers make cells more flexible as they can be moved to ease production bottlenecks. Production in the cell can, therefore, be smoother and swifter.

- As there is almost zero work-in-progress at any moment, the business can operate a JIT system.

- The cell takes responsibility for its own quality, which provides a greater incentive for each worker to ensure 'zero defects' in the production process.

- Physical closeness of workers in a U-shaped layout aids communication, saving time by keeping people and stock movements to a minimum.

- The time taken to produce one unit of a product is drastically reduced, therefore the business can respond more swiftly to customer orders.

The Canon Group, manufacturing photographic and copying equipment, introduced cell production in 1998 with dramatic effects. Labour productivity increased, 25 warehousing units were abolished, the costs of factory-floor space were cut drastically and key product manufacturing lead time was cut from 13 hours to just ten minutes.

> **Guru's views**
> 'Factories should be like swift-flowing rivers, their current powered by their people, their water kept pure by Quality.'
> *PFU Manufacturing Division (Fujitsu Group)*

5   Time-based management

Time-based management focuses on eliminating time wastage in design and manufacturing. Time is a competitive weapon in business because:

- 'time means money' so reducing wasted time reduces costs

- time is vital in maximising a product's sales during its lifecycle – it is estimated that sales can be doubled by being first rather than second to launch a new product

- timing is essential when responding swiftly to changing customer needs, and in meeting orders without delay.

By analysing how time is used – and wasted – a business may be able to identify a number of ways in which time is used unproductively.

Examples of time usage include:

- unnecessary movement of workers or products

- reworking of poor quality products

- machinery set-up times

- production bottlenecks causing delays

- over-production of products that can't be sold.

Lean producers focus on time wasted in both the design process and the manufacturing operation.

Lean design

A traditional approach to new product development involves each different department carrying out its functions in a *linear sequence* (that is, one function after the other). One department waits for another to complete its work before it begins, as shown in Figure 36.4.

While this may seem logical, the effect is that different experts work in isolation from each other. If a department finds problems from a previous stage, the work-in-progress must be sent back and redone. The outcome is delay.

The lean design response is to form project teams

Figure 36.4 Linear design: separate departments carry out tasks one after another

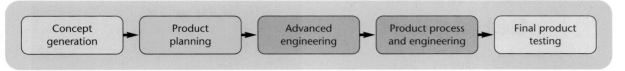

Figure 36.5 Simultaneous development involves the project team working on a variety of tasks at the same time

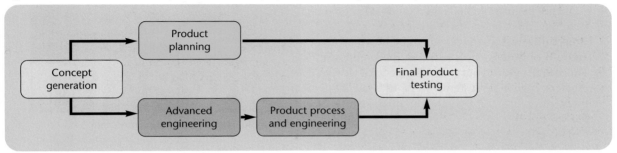

that draw experts from all departments. This allows **simultaneous development** – carrying out many design processes at the same time (see Figure 36.5). By working as a team, different views are brought together at an early stage, and potential problems resolved before time is wasted. Improved communication helps to improve final product quality, and dramatically reduces total product development time.

Lean manufacturing

Lean producers also seek to eliminate wasted time in the manufacturing process by:

- Producing in small batches rather than on a mass scale, allowing them to make to order and respond more swiftly to customer demand.

- Investing capital in equipment able to make a wider variety of products. This added flexibility helps reduce time wasted resetting machinery in order to produce a different batch of products.

- Training the workforce to be multiskilled, enabling workers to speed up by switching between areas of production, as well as being able to produce different types of products.

- Seeking to get quality right first time, eliminating the need to rework poor quality products.

The benefits of time-based management

The benefits of the lean approach to design and manufacturing all stem from cutting the time taken to develop, make and sell new products.

- **Cutting new product design and launch time** means a better chance of beating competitors to market (first mover advantage). The resulting brand image and customer loyalty can be hugely profitable.

- **Increased ability to respond swiftly to different customer needs** allows the business to differentiate its marketing strategy and target different market segments with a wider range of products .

- **Cost efficiencies** are considerable. Product development costs can be cut and worker productivity increased.

 ## How successful are lean production techniques?

The individual elements of lean production link to, and to some extent depend on, each other. Where they form part of a genuine change in the culture of a business there can be real benefits to productivity, quality and marketing. Lean production has been at the heart of the success of many manufacturers such as Toyota, Rolls-Royce and Ford.

Lean production needs a number of crucial foundations to succeed. It requires:

- The complete commitment of management and workforce for continuous improvement to become a reality and not just buzzwords.

- The willingness of all to accept change, and to be to be flexible in their work practices. The problem

For example ...

Get big fast

At Amazon.com customer service is everything. Trying to reduce the lead time between a customer ordering a book and receiving it was a key goal in Amazon's early years.

In the beginning, delivery time was four days that has now been cut to twenty-four hours. Everything was streamlined, right down to the amount of walking people did in the warehouse. The warehouse layout was changed for greater efficiency and IT systems were introduced to track stock and replace the manual keying of ISBN numbers.

This efficiency drive was set against Amazon's drive to 'get big fast'. Amazon spent much of its early business years adding capacity and significantly increasing the scale of its operations, building brand awareness and creating economies of scale. This get big fast policy was pursued at the expense of profits, Amazon spent vast amounts of money to get big and did not make any profits for many years.

Jeff Bezos, founder and CEO of Amazon.com

Source: Robert Spector, *Amazon.com*, Random House Business Books, London (2000)

1 Define 'lead time'. [2]
2 Explain **two** benefits of shorter lead times for online retailers such as Amazon. [6]

3 Discuss the case for and against Amazon's policy of 'getting big fast'. [10]

Total 18 marks

Want to know more?
www.amazon.co.uk

for some is that flexibility has become associated with redundancy, low pay and short-term contracts. The workforce is bound to resist any change that threatens their basic needs for job security and a fair wage. Similarly, management may resist change where they see employee involvement as threatening their authority to make decisions.

● A necessary investment in capital and training to develop the flexibility on which lean production depends.

Lean production: summary

KEY TERMS

Lean production – an approach to production that aims to eliminate waste at all stages of the production process.

Just-in-time production – a method of organising production to minimise stocks of raw materials, work-in-progress and finished products by 'pulling' parts into the process as and when required.

Just-in-case production – the traditional approach to manufacturing where products would be manufactured for stock, with parts being 'pushed' into the production process regardless of whether they are needed.

Cell production – organising groups of workers into small, self-contained units designed to complete an entire product or process.

Time-based management – an approach to business that focuses on eliminating time-wastage in design and manufacturing.

Simultaneous development – using project teams to carry out many design processes at the same time when developing a new product.

Summary questions

1 What is lean production?
2 How does lean production differ from traditional mass manufacturing methods?
3 What is 'kaizen'?
4 Explain the difference between a 'just-in-case' and a 'just-in-time' approach to production.
5 What are the potential **a** benefits and **b** drawbacks of JIT?
6 How does cell production work?
7 What problems of an assembly line does cell production attempt to overcome?
8 Why is saving time so important to business success?
9 Explain how **a** lean design and **b** lean manufacturing seek to save time.
10 On what factors does the success of lean production depend?

Exam practice

Leaning towards commonality

DEVOTEES of classic cars say that modern vehicles all look the same. However fair this view, if Ford's new commonality strategy works they could all start to look much more similar.

Traditionally, cars have been designed by dedicated teams working on different models. The result is often a large number of almost identical parts, often produced by the same supplier, being fitted to different models. Ford Europe, for instance, at one time used over a hundred different petrol caps on its petrol tanks, and over forty different headlight switches.

In order to realise some of the huge cost savings that could be made if parts were standardised, Ford appointed Nick Scheele as

'commonality guru'. In conjunction with manufacturers and car designers, Mr Scheele aims, for instance, to reduce the number of petrol caps used down to just two. Across the huge range of car parts that the customer never sees or that add little value to a car's identity, the costs savings are potentially huge. Economies of scale will also allow for the use of higher quality parts.

New models will get to market faster, since not every part has to be reengineered. Stock-holding costs will be significantly reduced.

The potential cost savings are all the more significant if this lean production strategy is applied across Ford's numerous brands (including Jaguar and Aston Martin).

Source: *The Times* 5 March 2002

1 Define 'lean production'. **[2]**
2 Define economies of scale'. **[2]**
3 Explain briefly how economies of scale might 'allow for the use of higher quality parts'. **[2]**
4 Explain **two** possible benefits Ford might gain from reducing the amount of parts held as stock. **[6]**
5 Commonality schemes such as this often rely on single supplier agreements. Evaluate the benefits and drawbacks of such an arrangement for Ford. **[8]**
6 To what extent will the advantages offered by the commonality strategy improve Ford's market competitiveness? **[10]**
Total 30 marks

Getting the grade: Operations Management

MANY students find operations management less exciting than some of the other topics. Indeed, many managers would rather avoid 'getting their hands dirty' and shy away from operations roles. Because operations management lacks the glamour of functions such as marketing, its importance is often overlooked. Yet good operations management is fundamental to getting the right product to the customer, in the right quantity, at the right time, and so on – in this sense, it is an integral part *of* marketing! Operations may also cost the business significant sums of money and controlling these costs may contribute more to a business's bottom line than introducing an exciting new product.

Key operations management issues include:

Trade offs

Successful operations management relies on balancing the different demands on operational resources. High productivity (and high volumes) may be achieved at the expense of variety (such as in McDonald's). Meeting customer demand is a trade off between the cost of storage, lead times and anticipated demand. Business strategy will shape (and be shaped by) these trade offs. McDonald's competitive advantage came initially from trading variety for uniformity and volume (and hence speed of service). No single approach is right, what matters is getting the balance right. You need to consider what gives a business its operational advantage (if any). How might operational changes affect this advantage?

The bigger the better?

'Economies of scale' is a student favourite. More production = economies of scale = lower unit cost = business success. Unfortunately things are not always that simple! Businesses may forgo economies of scale if the cost of increasing capacity is too great, or demand uncertain. Economies of scale is a concept to be employed wisely – consider its real benefit, and the cost of achieving those economies to the business as a whole.

Is more always better?

Increasing productivity is also considered by many students to be the Holy Grail of operations management. Higher productivity, after all, leads to lower unit costs and increased profitability. For many businesses this is true, and productivity *is* an important concept. However, you must consider the extent to which productivity affects the business in question. Job production, for instance, may not lend itself to productivity improvements. Skilled craftspeople may resent attempts to improve their productivity. Quality may be more important than cost.

It may also be necessary to examine the components of productivity.

- Will productivity improvement come from people or operations management?
- Better training or better machinery?

Consider which is *most* relevant.

Quality

The importance of quality was discussed in unit 35. Consider the extent to which quality is important in the industry in question, and specifically to the company you are looking at. Remember that many companies are successful because they offer cheap products that are 'fit for purpose', but may not be described as high quality. Many others are successful because of their quality (Mercedes, for instance). The extent to which quality is important will depend on corporate strategy, the type of product, customers' perceptions and the industry itself.

Business on a diet

You will need to be aware of the business implications of lean production. You should consider both the benefits and the problems. Lean production often results in rationalisation.

- Consider the impact on motivation and morale?
- What about the financial impact of redundancy payments?
- What will large redundancies do to corporate image?
- How will staff cope with production changes?

These and many other issues will affect the successful introduction of lean production.

Competitive advantage can be gained thorough operations management, or may shape operational strategy. Innovative production was at the heart of Dyson's successful entry into the vacuum cleaner market. To retain this competitive advantage (that is, innovation) Dyson's operations department now need to invest heavily in research and development. You must be able to link operations theory to these bigger issues – how will operational changes affect the whole business?

Section 6

External influences

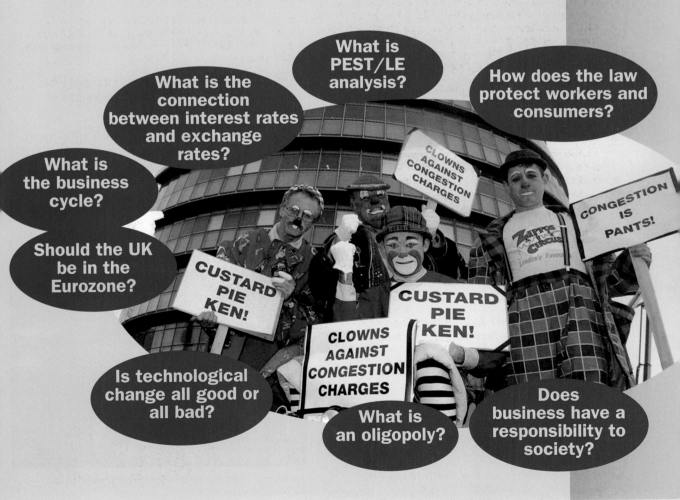

What is PEST/LE analysis?

What is the connection between interest rates and exchange rates?

How does the law protect workers and consumers?

What is the business cycle?

Should the UK be in the Eurozone?

Is technological change all good or all bad?

What is an oligopoly?

Does business have a responsibility to society?

37 Government impact on business

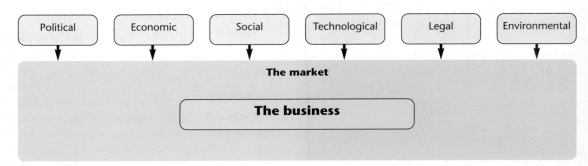

External environment

| Political | Economic | Social | Technological | Legal | Environmental |

The market

The business

1 The PEST/LE analysis

Good financial management, good marketing campaigns, good people and good operations management are not enough to guarantee business success. Success depends not only on internal excellence, but also on how effectively the business manages its external environment.

The external environment represents those factors that impact on a business, but are beyond its direct control. These can be summed up using a **PEST/LE** analysis (also called SLEEPT).

P is for 'political'. Government can affect business activities through taxation, legislation and so on.

E is for 'economic'. The current or forecast economic climate may impact on a business (for instance, changes in consumer income might affect sales).

S is for 'social'. Social trends and lifestyle changes may affect business activities. For instance, many businesses have started supplying products and services to the increasing numbers of over-50-year-olds in the UK.

T is for 'technological'. New technologies may present businesses with opportunities or threaten them. A business may need to embrace new production methods quickly to remain competitive.

L is for 'legal'. Changes in legislation often have a direct impact on businesses. For example, new health and safety laws can often be very expensive to implement.

E is for 'environmental'. The social shift towards environmentally friendly products has encouraged businesses to analyse the impact of their operations on the environment.

Tony Blair addresses the House of Commons ahead of a debate on Iraq

Almost by definition, external influences are very hard for a business to control. Some will be beyond its control entirely. External influences include unforeseen events such as natural disasters – things that cannot be planned for in advance. Even when a business can exercise some degree of control over its external environment, this may be limited. A business may successfully lobby the government to limit the impact of new laws, but will struggle to block the law entirely.

The uncertainty of external influences and the lack of direct control are what make the business environment so challenging and dynamic. Consideration of PEST/LE factors and the study of 'what-if' scenarios can help a business contemplate and prepare for all eventualities. Businesses that react effectively to changes in the external environment are often the most successful.

Activity

Put yourself in the shoes of the managing director of Aston Martin, manufacturers of high-end sports cars, made famous through the James Bond movies. Conduct a PEST/LE analysis of the external influences that Aston Martin might face over the next few years. Try to think of at least two or three influences under each heading, and evaluate the impact that each might have on the business.

Want to know more?

www.astonmartin.co.uk

2   Types of economy

Businesses do not exist in a vacuum. The type of economy that a business operates in will affect its chances of success, or even of survival. The kind of economy exists within a country is determined largely by its political system and the degree of political intervention in markets.

In **market economies** (also known as free-market economies), there is little government intervention in business. Businesses are free to run as they wish and can sell what they like and charge what they like. The forces of supply and demand will determine resource allocation.

In **planned economies**, the government decides what is produced, by whom, in what quantities and at what price goods are sold. In some cases, the amount of a good that a consumer can purchase is also controlled.

In reality, neither planned nor free-market economies exist in true form. Most economies are a combination of both systems. These are known as **mixed economies** – the UK is an example. In mixed-market economies, businesses and consumers are largely left to manage their own affairs, but markets are regulated and controlled by the government. For instance, a government will implement legislation to ensure fair prices and fair competition, and will ensure that essential services, such as health care, are provided. The government may also make provision for people unable to work, through unemployment benefits, for instance.

3   Government involvement in markets

The level of government intervention in markets will determine how far an economy leans towards a free or planned approach.

The greater the extent of intervention by a government, the closer the economy will be to a 'planned economy'. Where the government takes an **interventionist** approach, there will be strong market regulation. The government will have strict laws regulating business, and extensive consumer protection laws to prevent businesses harming consumers financially or physically. Many interventionists argue that a government should control key industries, such as rail, power companies and education, to prevent exploitation.

A **laissez-faire** approach is closer to the free-market system. Rules and regulations exist, but only where absolutely necessary, and the government keeps market interference to a minimum. The laissez-faire approach relies on competition ultimately providing the best deal for consumers and the most effective allocation of resources. Key industries, such as health care and education, would be largely privatised (see Unit 1).

STOP & THINK

Consider the interventionist versus laissez-faire approach. Is the one more likely to succeed than the other? Will everyone be adequately provided for by the different approaches?

For a business, the extent to which an interventionist or laissez-faire approach is preferred will depend upon the nature of the business. Some businesses will be affected to a much greater extent by legislation and government policy than others. Some businesses may also enjoy protected status under interventionist governments.

 4   Government influence

Governments can influence business activity in a wide variety of ways, ranging from regulation and legislation to foreign policy.

- **Regulation.** The government regulates certain markets through industry watchdogs. For example, OFGAS, OFWAT and OFTEL were set up to regulate the gas, water and telecommunications markets, respectively. To ensure consumer safety and encourage competition, the watchdogs have powers to set performance standards, to regulate prices and to open up markets. For instance, BT is required to allow other telephone operators access to its telephone lines, to give consumers a choice of telecommunications provider.

- **Legislation.** The government sets many laws that affect businesses. These may be employment laws (such as setting a minimum wage), competition laws, consumer protection laws and so on (see Unit 39).

- **Economic policy.** Government policy with regard to unemployment, regional aid and so on can all affect businesses. For instance, the government offers training grants to businesses that employ people who have been unemployed for a long time.

- **Taxation.** The government can alter the level of corporation tax and income tax. Corporation tax is a direct tax on the profits of business. Income tax is a tax on individuals' earnings. The higher the level of income tax, the less money people have to spend on goods and services. The government also controls the level of value added tax (VAT), directly affecting the retail price of goods (see Unit 43).

For example ...

Global disasters

Lloyd's, the insurance underwriter, maintains a list of realistic disaster scenarios likely to affect businesses. The two worst scenarios are an American windstorm and a Los Angeles earthquake, each with an insured loss running to a potential £34 billion. Others include a Japanese earthquake, with a $10 million insured loss, a marine collision, a major European storm and an aviation collision. For evidence that such events do happen, one need only keep an eye on the news – oils spills, explosions and industrial accidents are all too common occurrences. Even if the businesses themselves do not plan for such eventualities, Lloyd's has already put a price on them.

Source: *The Times*, 18 May 2002

1 Give **two** examples of external influences that might affect a business.   [4]
2 Explain **three** ways in which a business might be affected by external influences.   [6]
3 What problems can business face in trying to manage external influences?   [6]

Total 16 marks

Guru's views

'In this world nothing is certain but death and taxes.'

Benjamin Franklin

- **Government spending.** The way that a government spends and allocates its budget has a major impact on business. For example, the investment in education in recent years has been a major boost for suppliers of educational products. The government might also spend money on providing grants and benefits – education grants to underprivileged children, for instance – which again benefits education suppliers.

- **Foreign policy.** Government's attitude to foreign trade and relationships with other countries can directly affect business. The

decision on whether or not to adopt the euro is an example of a policy that can have significant impact on business.

These effects and others are considered in more detail in Units 39–44.

5   Impact of political change

Whereas individual governments can affect business activity, changes in government can potentially have a much greater effect on business. The election of Labour in 1997, after 18 years of Conservative government, marked a change in government policy towards business. The years of deregulation and privatisation by the Conservatives were replaced by, what many businesses saw as, excessive intervention by 'new' Labour, in the form of an array of new business laws and regulations. In the USA, many argue that Microsoft benefited directly in its anti-trust (competition law) case when George Bush was elected to power. The Bush administration is much less interventionist in business than the Clinton administration, which it replaced.

A change in political party may have a significant effect on the way government impacts on business. The attitudes of new political leaders towards intervention may determine how much each of the factors discussed in this unit impacts on the external environment of business.

In 1997, German shops displayed prices in marks and euros in the run up for the currency changeover to euros.

Government impact on business: summary

KEY TERMS

PEST/LE – an analysis framework used to consider the external environment (political, economic, social, technical, legal, environmental).

Market economies – economies subject to minimal government interference.

Planned economies – economies closely controlled and regulated by government.

Mixed economies – economies in which the government regulates business activity, provides essential services and legislates to protect consumers and society, but also allows market forces to operate – a combination of the market and planned approaches.

Interventionist – an approach that favours government involvement in markets.

Laissez-faire – an approach that favours businesses being left alone, on the prinicple that the government should not interfere in markets.

Summary questions

1 What does the acronym PEST/LE stand for?
2 What is the purpose of a PEST/LE analysis?
3 Give **two** example of how a nightclub might be affected by each of the elements of PEST/LE.
4 What is a planned economy?
5 What is a mixed economy?
6 Distinguish between an interventionist and laissez-faire approach to government involvement in markets.
7 State and explain **two** influences that government can have on business.
8 What impact can political change have on business?

Exam practice

The economy at a glance

Consumer spending, now in excess of £600 billion per annum, has been the key driver of economic activity in the UK since the mid 1990s. Retailing claims around 35 per cent of this total. The £30 billion spent on clothes makes clothing the second-largest item of retail spending after food, and it has been one of the sectors that has seen a substantial growth in sales in recent years.

Low inflation has had a significant impact on clothing retailing. Spending on clothes (inflation adjusted) has been rising by at least 8 per cent a year since 1999. Sales values, on the other hand, have risen at about only half this rate, which explains why retailers have not been able to convert volume growth into profit. With clothing prices falling by over 10 per cent in three years, retailers have had to sell more to achieve the same profits.

The competitive pressures on retailers have intensified, as retail capacity has increased by 6 per cent in recent years as a result of new stores opening. Shifts in spending patterns, consumer preferences and the age struc-ture are all having a profound effect on the shape of clothing retailing. These shifts are being underpinned by the UK's demographic profile. By 2006, for example, more than 21 per cent of the population will be over 60, while the number of under-16s will fall by 3 per cent. At the same time, there will be an 8 per cent decline in the fashion-conscious 25–39-year-old group.

Retailers also face increasing pressure from changes to EU law in a number of important areas. The euro is another significant issue for UK retailers, with far- reaching consequences. New 'green' laws are being proposed that will affect all UK businesses, and those businesses operating in developing countries, which include many retailers, are facing increasing pressure to be accountable for conditions in their overseas factories.

There will, therefore, be little respite for clothing retailers in the coming years. Adjusting to the demands of a fast-changing market place will have to be managed at a time when growth in demand is at best modest.

Source: *HSBC Economic Review*, April 2002

1 Study the article with its statistics and identify at least **five** key terms that relate to the external influences topic. Give brief definitions of each of these terms. **[10]**
2 Using the information in the article, and your own knowledge of the retail market, conduct a PEST/LE analysis of the external influences faced by UK retailers. Examine each of the issues raised and consider the impact that each one might have on different clothing retailers. **[20]**
Total 30 marks

38 Markets and competition

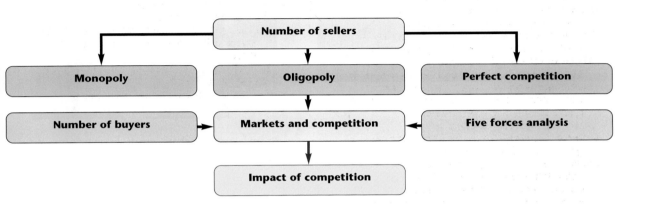

1 Buyers and sellers

A market is defined as 'an arrangement of buyers and sellers'. In most markets there are many buyers and many sellers. Think of a crowded high street on a Saturday – many buyers and many sellers! However, sometimes there might be more buyers or more sellers in a market. The numbers of buyers and sellers in a market, among other things, determines how competitive that market is. The competitiveness of a market has a significant impact on prices and overall business strategy. Hence, an understanding of competitive models is an essential piece of Business Studies knowledge.

> **Guru's views**
> 'There are more fools among buyers than among sellers.'
>
> *French proverb*

2 Supply and demand

Basic supply and demand was introduced in Unit 10. Buyers are willing to purchase more (demand more) as the price falls, and producers are willing to sell more (supply more) at higher prices. The point where the demand (D) and supply (S) curves meet is known

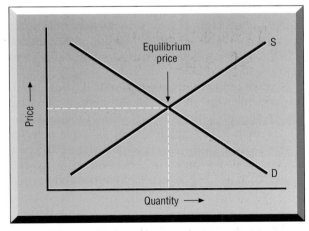

Figure 38.1 Equilibrium price

as the **equilibrium price** (see Figure 38.1). At this point, buyers and sellers are in agreement about price and quantity.

A market that demands more quantities than supplied, or has more supplies than demands, is said to be 'in disequilibrium'. The market may display **excess demand** or **excess supply** (see Figure 38.2).

Excess supply and demand

Where demand is greater than supply, excess demand occurs. The UK property boom of the last few years has been fuelled by excess demand. Excess demand tends

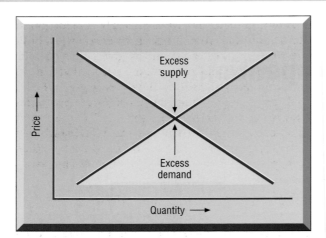

Figure 38.2 Market disequilibrium

to force prices up, as customers are willing to pay more to get their hands on 'scarce' goods. Excess demand is often caused by restricted supply. For example, when Playstation 2 was launched, the limited numbers produced encouraged people to pay more than double the retail price. Some businesses successfully restrict supply of products, creating excess demand and thus keeping prices high. The car manufacturer Mazda, for instance, produces a limited edition MX5 model, which it is able to sell at a considerably higher price than the standard MX5.

Excess supply occurs where supply is greater than demand; there are not enough customers to purchase the number of goods currently being produced. The UK car market has suffered from excess supply for many years, resulting in airfields full of unsold cars. A business may be forced to reduce its prices to sell excess stock – as supermarkets do at the end of each day – or it may cut production.

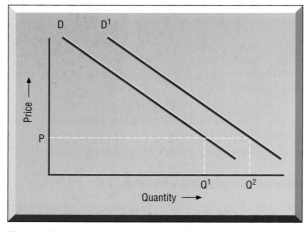

Figure 38.3 Graph representing a shift in demand

For example …

Football crazy

From supermarkets and boardrooms to schools and racecourses, football fans were able to catch every minute of World Cup action in 2002, thanks to scores of giant television screens erected around the country.

Demand for screens soared during the summer of 2002, as companies and councils invested in the technology to ensure that everybody could have a front row seat. Demand outstretched supply by more than 30 per cent. Screen-hire firms reported triple the usual number of rentals, forcing them to turn away millions of pounds of business as stocks ran out.

Source: *The Times*, 11 May 2002

1 Explain what you understand by the term 'excess demand'. **[3]**
2 Draw a fully labelled supply and demand diagram to represent the market for large screens during the summer of 2002. **[4]**
3 Examine both the long-term and short-term business implications of the situation as described in the story. **[7]**

Total 14 marks

Changes in supply and demand

Changes in market conditions can cause shifts in supply or demand. For instance, if consumer incomes rise, demand for cars may increase at any given price – more cars at every price point would be required. This would cause the demand curve to shift to the right, as shown in Figure 38.3.

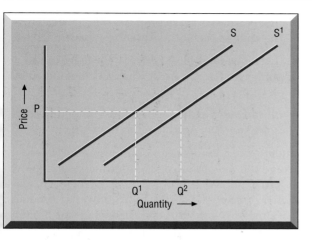

Figure 38.4 Graph representing a shift in supply

A shift in supply might be caused by a reduction in the cost of production. This might encourage a business to supply more goods at any given price – profits can still be maintained if more are sold at lower prices. The resulting supply shift is shown in Figure 38.4.

Shifts in supply and demand affect the equilibrium price. For instance, if a shift in demand in not matched by a shift in supply, excess demand may occur and prices may rise. An increase in supply may cause prices to fall if demand does not also increase.

3 Models of competition

The models of market competition range from **monopoly** – where there is only one major supplier – to what is known as 'perfect competition'.

Monopoly

A 'pure monopoly' occurs when one business is the only seller in a market. A 'legal monopoly' is where one business controls more than 25 per cent of the market. Being the only seller of a product means that monopolies can charge, within reason, whatever price they like. They are known as **price makers**. For instance, Microsoft has a monopoly in the operating

---

Activity

Figure 38.5 represents the possible changes to the prices and quantity of tickets sold at a cinema. Which of the graphs (A–D) represents the following:
- a reduction in demand for tickets
- an increase in ticket price, reducing demand
- an increase in demand for tickets
- a reduction in ticket prices, increasing demand?

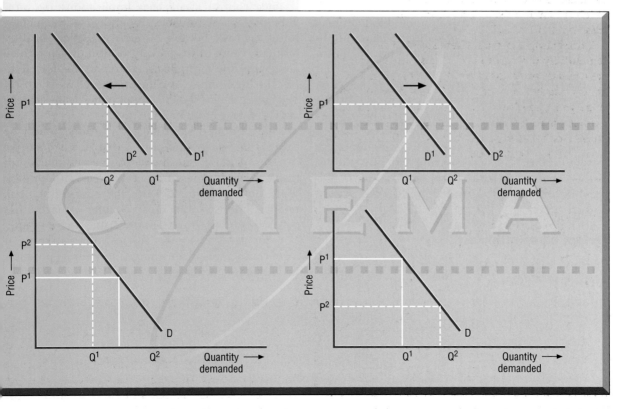

Figure 38.5 Ticket pricing – supply and demand

systems market (Windows XP, for example). Consumers have a restricted choice, so Microsoft can charge high prices. Demand will be price-inelastic because consumers have limited alternatives.

Oligopoly

An **oligopoly** is where a 'few' firms dominate the market. For example, the UK coffee market is dominated by Nescafé, Kenco and Maxwell House.

Under oligopoly, a product's brand image is very important and firms will compete fiercely for market leadership. Differentiation will be key in generating brand loyalty, allowing some price control. However, firms tend to focus on non-price competition – through customer service, image and so on. Price wars will be avoided, with individual businesses tending to set prices based on the 'going rate'.

Monopolistic competition

The characteristics of **monopolistic competition** are:

- many small sellers
- differentiated products
- few barriers to market entry.

Any one firm is too small for its actions to be noticed by others in the market. And although products may be similar, they are sufficiently differentiated not to be regarded as substitutes for one another. Each firm therefore has a 'monopoly' in its particular field, but is indirectly competing with all other businesses in the market. Some degree of price control is possible, and demand for the product may be relatively price-inelastic.

Hairdressing is an example of monopolistic competition. Hairdressers compete with one another in a way, but brand loyalty, and locality, ensure that each business has some degree of 'monopoly' over its customers.

Perfect competition

The model of **perfect competition** is based on several assumptions:

- that businesses make products that are exactly the same as each other (homogeneous)
- that consumers have perfect knowledge of the market and are aware of what is being offered by all firms
- that a large number of firms are competing and it is easy for new firms to enter the market.

Under perfect competition, businesses are 'forced' to accept the market price. Such businesses are known as **price takers**. If any of them were to charge a higher price, nobody would buy its products. Customers would shop elsewhere since all products are the same.

There are no true examples of perfect competition, but the online book-retailing market does display many of the characteristics, as seen in Figure 38.6.

 Impact of competition

The more competitive a market is, the less the control over price that any one individual firm will have. Hence, in perfect competition, firms have to take the market price whereas in monopolies firms can set the price.

Price control clearly has implications for profitability. A monopoly may not always set the highest price, but will be able to earn extremely healthy profits because of its market position. Because there are few substitute products, customers are 'forced' to pay the high prices. As companies such as Microsoft and Intel have shown, monopolies can achieve above-average profitability.

That is not to say that good profits cannot be earned where competition is fierce. Competitive markets demand successful business strategies to insulate the business from the effects of competition. Amazon.com is not the cheapest online book retailer, but it is the most popular. Amazon has developed a very strong brand name and a reputation for good customers service, differentiating it from rivals. Thus it can charge more for its products and increase profitability.

Perfect competition model	Online book retailing
Homogenous products	Books are identical regardless of where purchased.
Perfect knowledge	It is easy to compare book prices online (there are even comparison sites).
Large numbers of buyers and sellers	There are lots of online book retailers and it is easy for new ones to set up.

Figure 38.6 Perfect competition and online book retailing

Figure 38.7 Porter's 'five forces'

Unfair competition

Firms that attempt to obstruct market forces within a market may be guilty of unfair competition. This may involve colluding over prices (agreeing with other firms to charge certain amounts), restricting supply (forcing prices up) or market sharing (agreeing to sell in different geographical areas). The aim of unfair competition is to increase profitability at the expense of consumers.

For the most part, such practices are illegal. As discussed in Unit 39, the Office of Fair Trading investigates allegations of unfair competition and decides if the law has been breached and if consumers are being unfairly exploited.

 Market analysis

To analyse the competitiveness of a market, Michael Porter suggested that five major forces act upon a market (see Figure 38.7).

1 **Threat of new entrants.** The easier it is for new businesses to enter a market, increasing the number of sellers, the more competitive that market is likely to be. Where there are barriers to entry, such as high start-up costs, fewer firms are likely to be able to enter the market and competitive rivalry will be lower.

2 **Threat of substitutes.** If there is a wide range of similar products that consumers can easily switch to, competition will be intense. The easier it is to 'poach' customers, the more that businesses are likely to try. Hence, businesses spend large sums of money attempting to differentiate their products and develop brand loyalty.

3 **Bargaining power of customers.** The power of customers is determined by:

– the number of customers (for example, many suppliers to Marks & Spencer supply M&S only,

giving M&S a lot of power to control prices)
– whether customers can easily switch to alternative suppliers
– the degree of collaboration between buyers
– the importance of individual customers (even if M&S is not a clothing retailer's only customer, they will still exercise a degree of power due to their size).

4 **Bargaining power of suppliers.** Suppliers will determine raw material costs and thus affect price flexibility. Supplier power will be high when:

– there are a small number of suppliers
– the cost of switching suppliers is prohibitively high (for example, because machinery would have to be completely changed)
– suppliers have a powerful brand (a retailer might not be able to do without a particular brand).

5 **Competitive rivalry.** The extent of competitive rivalry is determined by the balance of the other four forces. A market with few barriers to entry, lots of substitutes and powerful customers is likely to be very competitive. In addition, rivalry is based on:

– the number of sellers in a market
– the degree of differentiation between products
– market size and market growth (a larger market may give individual firms more scope to compete).

Five forces analysis can be used to gain an insight into markets and to develop business strategies. For instance, it may be decided that a particular market is unattractive for entry, or that a strong brand name is needed to ensure effective differentiation. A business can use the model to identify where it may have a competitive advantage that cannot easily be replicated and presents a strategic opportunity.

Activity

Consider the market for window cleaning services in your local area. Investigate how competitive the market is. Comment on the following:

- Do your findings suggest that the market is very competitive?
- What impact do these market conditions have on consumers?

Barriers to entry and exit

How easy is it for new window cleaners to set up? How easy is it for current window cleaners to leave the market?

Availability of substitutes

How many window cleaners offer their services in your area? (A 'guesstimate' will do.)

Power of buyers

Do people have to have their windows cleaned? Can they stop using the service if it is too expensive?

Consumer knowledge

How aware are people of alternative window cleaners?

Product

Do all the window cleaners offer a similar level of service?

Markets and competition: summary

KEY TERMS

Equilibrium price – the price at which buyers and sellers are in agreement about demand and supply.

Excess demand – demand in a market that outstrips supply, forcing prices up.

Excess supply – supply in a market that outstrips demand, causing prices to fall or production to be cut.

Monopoly – situation where one firm supplies the entire market (pure monopoly) or controls over 25 per cent of market share (legal monopoly).

Oligopoly – situation where a few firms dominate the market.

Monopolistic competition – market with many sellers each with a differentiated product.

Perfect competition – situation where many sellers, homogenous (identical) products, low barriers to entry and perfect buyer knowledge combine to create a highly competitive market.

Price takers – businesses with limited ability to control prices.

Price makers – businesses with a high degree of control over prices.

Summary questions

1 Define 'market'.
2 List **three** factors that determine the degree of competition in a market.
3 Explain what is happening when a market is in equilibrium.
4 What is excess supply?
5 What factors might cause a business to reduce the supply of its products?
6 What impact might excess demand have on consumers?
7 What is a price maker?
8 What market conditions exist under perfect competition?
9 What is an oligopoly?
10 How might consumers be affected by a highly competitive market?
11 Discuss the impacts on mobile phone retailers of operating in a highly competitive market.
12 State and explain **two** examples of business actions that might be seen as unfair competition.
13 What are 'barriers to entry'? Give an example.
14 Whar factors might determine competitive rivalry within a market?

Exam practice

Mad about motors

Britain was on track for another record year of car sales in 2002, as consumers continued to cash in on low prices and cheap financing costs. In March 2002 the numbers of cars sold reached 423,727– the best March sales ever. First-quarter sales showed a 7.1 per cent increase to an all-time high of 722,718.

Sales were boosted by pent-up consumer demand and deep cuts in manufacturers' prices. There were calls that, in order to maintain these healthy figures, the current franchised dealer system, considered by some to amount to unfair competition and under investigation by the EU Competition Commission, would have to be maintained. Many industry insiders argue that if dealers were allowed to sell cars of any manufacturer, consumer confidence would be eroded – buying a Ford from a Ford dealer provides consumers with a level of assurance considered necessary in such high-value purchases.

Many see the price cuts as a short-term measure to reduce excess supply in the market.

Source: *The Guardian*, 6 April 2002

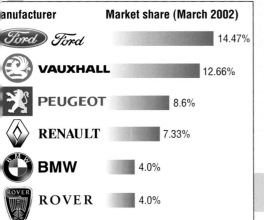

Manufacturer	Market share (March 2002)
Ford	14.47%
VAUXHALL	12.66%
PEUGEOT	8.6%
RENAULT	7.33%
BMW	4.0%
ROVER	4.0%

1 What is unfair competition? **[2]**
2 What is meant by 'excess supply'? **[2]**
3 Identify and explain **two** factors that might determine the level of demand for cars. **[4]**
4 Examine the factors that might determine how much control car manufacturers have over pricing decisions. **[8]**
5 Discuss which model of competition best describes the car market. Justify your answer. **[9]**
6 Evaluate the implications for car manufacturers of operating in highly competitive markets. **[10]**
   Total 35 marks

39 Business and the law

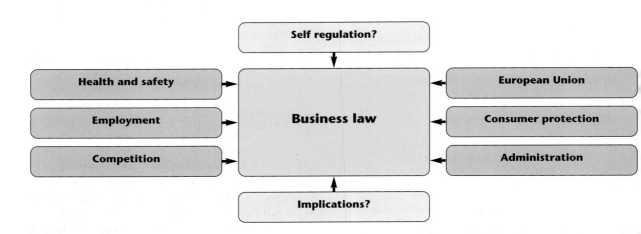

1 Laws as a framework

Law is essential in governing the way that individuals and businesses behave. Even though some businesses – and individuals – may adhere to stricter rules than those enforced by law, laws do provide a basic framework for business behaviour. A business must conform to the law if it is to maintain its reputation and its customers and avoid legal penalties.

> ### Guru's views
> 'Only one thing is impossible for God: to find any sense in any copyright law on the planet.'
>
> *Mark Twain*

You are not required to memorise all the different laws that affect businesses. But it is important that you understand what implications laws have for business, and can analyse and evaluate the significance of changes in the legal environment.

2 Administration law

Administration law governs the way that businesses are set up and managed. The legal process of incorporation, standard accounting practices and insolvency laws all affect the way that a business is run. Conformance to administration law means ensuring that all policies are followed correctly and that all relevant documentation is accurately produced – which often involves employing solicitors and accountants. Limited companies have to consider a much wider range of administration law than sole traders or partnerships.

3 Consumer protection law

The aim of consumer protection law is to save consumers from unfair or dangerous business practices. It includes a number of Acts of Parliament.

- **Fair Trading Act (1973)** – established the **Office of Fair Trading (OFT)**, with responsibilities for reviewing consumer affairs, monitoring unfair trading practices and taking action against businesses that breach consumer protection law.

- **Consumer Credit Act (1974)** – ensures that credit agreements are fair and protects consumers against exorbitant (very high) interest rates.

- **Sale of Goods Act (1979)** – states that products must be of merchantable quality, fit for the purpose for which they were purchased and not falsely described.

- **Weights and Measures Act (1985)** – controls product weights and volumes, making it illegal to sell goods below their stated weight.

- **Trade Descriptions Act (1968)** – protects consumers against false and misleading claims about products and services.

- **Consumer Protection Act (1987)** – makes it a criminal offence to sell harmful or defective goods (especially with reference to children's toys and electrical goods).

In reality, most businesses aim to provide products and services that exceed the quality standards required by law. Therefore the impact of consumer protection laws for many businesses is minimal. However, conforming to consumer protection law does have cost implications (such as changing packaging to display metric weights) and can affect promotional messages (firms must avoid making false claims about a product).

Activity

OFFICE OF FAIR TRADING

Go to www.oft.gov.uk and investigate the work of the Office of Fair Trading. What do they do? What current cases are they investigating? What impact might these investigations have on the businesses concerned?

Want to know more?

www.compactlaw.co.uk

4   Competition law

The basic aim of competition law is to ensure that fair competition exists in markets; that firms do not exploit 'unfair' advantages (such as monopoly power); and that the best interests of consumers are served.

- **Competition Act (1980, 1998)** – brought the UK into line with European Union (EU) law, by replacing the Monopolies and Mergers Commission with the **Competition Commission**, with powers to investigate unfair business dealings; to investigate and prohibit proposed mergers; and to prohibit **cartels** or other agreements that act against consumer

interests (for example, the Commission investigated and rejected the proposed merger of Lloyds Bank and Abbey National).

- **Restrictive Practices Act (1976)** – monitors and regulates **restrictive practices**, such as supplying only approved dealers.

- **Resale Prices Act (1976)** – prohibits firms from setting a minimum price at which goods must be sold. Some goods, such as pharmaceuticals, are exempt from this act.

Competition law can have a major impact on business activity. A proposed merger or takeover may be blocked and a business may be forced to change its practices. For instance, Birds Eye Wall's was forced to allow other ice cream manufacturers to have selling space in the freezers it provided to small retailers. Being forced to sell parts of a business, or being denied entry into certain markets to avoid monopoly power, can have a significant impact on a business's ability to grow and compete. Pricing strategies might also be affected and barriers to market entry may have to be removed – for instance, BT having to give other companies access to its telephone lines to enable competition.

Activity

Find out more about the Competition Commission by checking out their website:
www.competition-commission.org.uk

5   Health and safety law

The HASWA (Health and Safety At Work Act, 1974) and subsequent amendments seek to make workplaces as safe as is 'reasonably practicable'. Employers must ensure safe working environments, provide proper safety equipment and training, implement safe working systems and publish health and safety policies.

Health and safety law has a very direct and significant impact on business. Failure to comply can result in substantial fines and even business closure. The cost of meeting health and safety laws is often considerable.

Activity

Find out about the Health and Safety Executive by going to their website: www.hse.gov.uk.

Employment law

Employment law exists to protect the interests of workers. Employers are bound by law to safeguard certain employee rights. These rights are laid out in various pieces of legislation.

- **Equal Pay Act (1970)** – requires employers to offer equal pay and conditions for equal work .

- **Sex Discrimination Acts (1975, 1986)** – prohibits discrimination on the basis of gender in relation to recruitment, promotion and conditions of service.

- **Race Relation Act (1976)** – prohibits discrimination on the basis of race.

- **Working Time Directive (1998)** – an EU directive on working time (implemented by the UK in 1998) providing employees with the following rights:

    – four weeks' annual paid leave
    – 48-hour maximum working week
    – 11 hours rest between working shifts
    – at least one rest day a week (two for adolescents)
    – statutory rest breaks at work.

- **National Minimum Wage Act (1999)** – aims to provide employees with decent minimum standards and fairness in the workplace, applying to nearly all workers and setting hourly rates below which pay must not fall (see Figure 39.1).

- **Employment Rights Act (1996)** – requires that staff be provided with a **contract of employment** within two months of appointment. The contract sets out the terms and conditions of employment and gives basic information about the requirements of the job. The contract should include details of:

    – *pay*: how much and the method of payment
    – *the job*: nature of the job, its requirements and responsibilities

    – *number of hours*: statutory minimum number of hours and any overtime expected as well as the number and length of breaks
    – *benefits*: any fringe benefits that the employee may be entitled to
    – *dismissal/notice*: dismissal process and the length of any notice period (minimum notice periods are set by law and depend on length of employment, but many firms require notice periods longer than the legal minimum)
    – *grievances*: procedure for the employee to complain against treatment at work
    – *absence*: details of holiday entitlements, and any maternity or paternity leave entitlements above those required by law.

- The **Employment Rights Act (1996)** – sets out the law regarding redundancy (where a worker is no longer required, but there are no grounds for dismissal). Employees with more than two years service (and over 18) are entitled to redundancy pay. The amount payable is linked to length of service.

Having a contract of employment makes it unlawful to breach its terms and conditions. This applies equally to both employee and employer. An employee could take an employer to court for paying a salary below that stated on the contract, for instance. Employees have a responsibility to fulfil their contractual terms. They must complete tasks assigned to them (within the terms of the contract) effectively, provide a minimum notice to terminate employment and abide by any conditions set out in the contract (such as not revealing trade secrets).

Employment law can have a significant impact on business. Clearly, having to pay a minimum wage has a direct cost impact, but may benefit motivation. Firms must ensure that all employment policies (such as maternity leave and holiday pay) conform to relevant legislation. Legal action can be taken against firms that are in breach of the law. The impact of the **Working Time Directive** was also significant. Many firms found that shift patterns had to be changed, daily rotas altered and additional leave allowed – a time-consuming, costly and disruptive process, but with potentially positive effects on staff morale.

Main (adult) rate for workers aged 22 and over	Development rate for workers aged 18–21 inclusive
£4.20 per hour	£3.60 per hour
Source: www.dti.gov.uk – The National Minimum Wage Regulations 1999 (Amendment) Regulations 2002	

Figure 39.1 National minimum wage rates

For example ...

Part of the law

The Part-Time Workers (Prevention of Less Favourable Treatment) Regulations came into force on 1 July 2000. Broadly, the Regulations make it unlawful for part-time workers to be treated less favourably than full-time workers. Some of the main provisions require that part-time workers:

- receive the same hourly rate as full-timers

- receive the same hourly rate for overtime as full-timers

- should not be excluded from training opportunities

- should be entitled to pensions, perks, fringe benefits and sick pay on a pro rata basis

- have the same entitlement as full-timers to maternity/parental leave and annual leave on a pro rata basis.

1   What is meant by 'pro rata'?   [2]
2   What are 'fringe benefits'? Give two examples.   [4]
3   Why might some employers have resisted the introduction of this law?   [6]
4   How might businesses benefit from the introduction of this law?   [8]
Total 20 marks

Want to know more?
www.dti.gov.uk

6   European Union law

Businesses are subject to EU legislation as well as UK law. The EU **Social Chapter** (signed by the UK in 1997) covers health and safety, working conditions and industrial relations issues. EU laws such as those involving free trade also affect UK businesses – increasing market size, but also potentially increasing competition. EU competition policy also affects UK businesses, especially those that trade with other EU countries.

Ultimately, EU law overrides much UK law. An individual or business could appeal to the European courts if they felt that they had been unfairly treated under UK law.

For example ...

Hamming it up

Lovers of all things Italian may need travel no farther than their nearest ASDA to secure their favourite home-sliced Parma ham. The supermarket chain won a victory in its legal battle with Italian ham producers when an advisor to the EU's highest court said ASDA could sell *prosciutto* (Italian-style ham) under the name 'Parma ham' – even if the product were sliced and packaged outside the Parma region.

Lower courts in the UK had previously dismissed the Italian ham producers' claims that producing outside the Parma region but using the name breached EU law. The case then progressed to the European Court of Justice, which was asked to interpret EU law on this matter.

Source: *Financial Times*, 26 April 2002

1   Suggest **one** reason why ASDA might want to process Parma ham outside of the Parma region.   [2]
2   Suggest and explain **two** reasons why ham producers in the Parma region may be reluctant to allow production outside of the region.   [4]
3   Consider why some British companies resent being bound by laws set by the EU, as opposed to being set by the UK.   [6]
Total 12 marks

Want to know more?
www.asda.co.uk
www.europa.eu.int/index-en.htm

Implications of the law

How much a business will be affected by the law depends a great deal on the nature the business. For example, a chemical plant will find that health and safety laws impact more on its business than they would on, say, a small florist. Business size is also significant. Smaller businesses may find the costs of implementing new laws, such as offering stakeholder pensions, particularly burdensome .

Clearly, the most significant implication of business law is cost. New laws or changes to current laws often require a business to change its practices in some way. These changes may prove costly – whether in terms of lost production or lost sales, or by altering a product to conform to new laws (for instance, sales of some sports cars suffered after emissions laws forced changes to engine performance).

However, the cost of conforming to laws must be balanced against the cost of non-conformance. If a staff member or a customer were to be injured and the business found to be in breach of the law, the financial cost and damage to its reputation could be serious. Meeting the requirements of laws may even be beneficial: sales may improve and money might be saved if, in the long term, conformance results in fewer customer complaints.

Adhering to business law might also have a positive impact on staff. A workforce that feels well protected may be more productive. If a firm has a reputation for good employment policies, it may find it can recruit and retain staff more easily.

Yet, does conformance to the law really mean good performance? Laws represent basic standards. Truly excellent businesses will implement policies that are superior to those required by law.

 ## Self-regulation

Many businesses seek to avoid legislation and adopt self-regulatory procedures. For example, the advertising industry is largely self-regulated, through the British Code of Advertising Practice. With self-regulation, standards are set and maintained by independent bodies, so that formal legal constraints are considered unnecessary.

> **STOP & THINK**
>
> Does self-regulation work? Do you believe the advantages outweigh the disadvantages or vice versa? Is formal legislation always better?

Self regulation

Advantages	Disadvantages
• Industry knowledge allows for sensible/achievable regulations to be set.	• Some firms may choose to ignore regulations.
• Cost is borne by industry and not government.	• Industry may itself set lenient standards.
• More stringent regulations may be set than those imposed by government through laws.	• Many argue that regulators in self-regulating industries are not independent
• Industry repercussions – such as refusal to supply, or negative publicity – may be more damaging than fines imposed by law.	• Self-regulation is often criticised for being 'toothless' – regulators have little real power.

Business and the law: summary

KEY TERMS

Cartel – collusion among businesses to control prices or output.

Competition Commission – formerly the Monopolies and Mergers Commission, a government body set up to ensure fair competition in markets, with powers to investigate proposed mergers and takeovers and to halt them if considered to be against the public interest.

Contract of employment – legal document setting out the terms and conditions of employment.

Office of Fair Trading (OFT) – government body responsible for reviewing consumer affairs, monitoring unfair trading practices and acting against businesses that breach consumer protection law.

Restrictive practices – attempts by producers to manipulate a market by restricting competition or manipulating prices.

Social Chapter – a set of measures aiming to bring into line social legislation within the EU.

Working Time Directive – a set of measures detailing working time regulations, such as working hours and holiday entitlement.

Summary questions

1 What does the Competition Act 1998 aim to do?
2 Briefly outline the role of the Competition Commission.
3 What is a cartel?
4 Give **two** examples of restrictive practices that a business might engage in.
5 Give **two** examples of consumer protection law, and for each outline the main principles of the law.
6 State and explain **two** negative implications for businesses of having to conform to competition law.
7 State and explain **two** positive implications for businesses of having to conform to health and safety law.
8 How are UK businesses affected by EU law? Support your answer with examples.
9 What is self-regulation? What are the arguments for and against it?

Exam practice

Bob the Builder
– can they fix it?

Prices of some of the nation's favourite toys may have been fixed, and millions of parents ripped off. Hasbro, whose range includes Action Man, Bob the Builder and Harry Potter trading cards, is accused of rigging prices in collusion with high-street retailers Argos and Littlewoods.

If found guilty, Hasbro could be fined more than £20 million. The original complaint is believed to have come from a number of small retailers. The investigation has concentrated on whether Hasbro insisted on, rather than recommended, prices. Industry sources suggest that toy manufacturers are keen to control the prices of toys sold through the Argos chain, as they act as a benchmark for the rest of the industry. There is also concern that some shops are given exclusive rights to sell particular products.

The Office of Fair Trading can fine companies found guilty of price fixing the equivalent of 10 per cent of the last three years of turnover.

Source: *The Times*, 2 May 2002

1 Explain how Hasbro might have engaged in restrictive practices. **[4]**
2 Outline the function of the Office of Fair Trading. **[2]**
3 Examine the implications for Hasbro of failing to comply with business law. **[8]**
4 Argue the case for and against business self-regulation. **[11]**
Total 25 marks

40 Impact of the economy

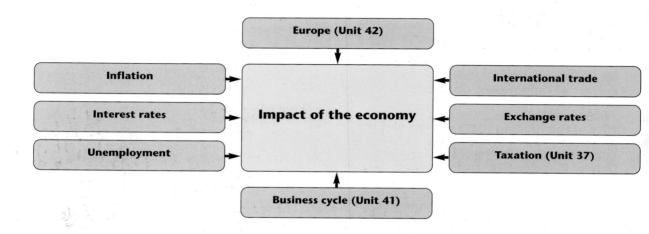

1 Managing the economy

Economic conditions and government economic management can have far-reaching consequences for businesses. Some of the economic impacts include:

- inflation
- interest rates
- unemployment
- exchange rates
- international trade
- taxation
- trade cycles.

To control the economy, the government uses a range of policies, including **monetary policy**, **fiscal policy** and **supply-side policies**. These are explained in Figure 40.1.

2 Inflation

Inflation is the general increase in prices over time in an economy. In the UK, **inflation** is measured through the **retail price index (RPI)**. The RPI is calculated by measuring the prices of a typical monthly 'basket' of goods representing spending patterns (see Figure 40.2).

Policy	Explanation
Monetary policy	Control of interest rates (through the Bank of England) and of the money supply (controlling lending by banks and government spending)
Fiscal policy	Uses of taxes and government spending to regulate demand in the economy
Supply-side polices	Range of polices aiming to promote business activity (for example, a reduction in business red tape to encourage more business activity)

Figure 40.1 Policies used to control the economy

The Retail Price Index (RPI)

Food and drink

IN: salmon fillets; organic fruit and vegetables; mayonnaise; French stick/baguette; chilled desserts; herbal/fruit tea bags; cereal snacks; spirit-based drinks; lager 'stubbies'/large multipacks

OUT: rainbow trout; leeks; salad cream; streaky bacon; delivered milk; sterilised milk

Household services

IN: bank overdraft charges; home removals; catering for a function; foreign exchange commission

OUT: bank custody of a sealed envelope

Household goods

IN: home office computer desks; cutlery sets; crockery sets; laminate flooring; greetings cards

OUT: nest of tables; table knife; bread bin

Clothing and footwear

IN: women's vests/strappy tops; women's evening dress; baseball caps

OUT: women's ski pants

Price comparisons over 50 years

	1947	1997
Dress	£15.10 (£15/1/11d + 7 coupons)	£69.00
Women's suit	£23.15 (£23/3/0d + 12 coupons)	£203.99
Women's cardigan/jumper	£4.16 (£4/3/2d + 6 coupons)	£35.00
Cold cream/cleansing cream	11p (2/2d)	£2.65
Pint of beer	7p (1/4d)	£1.65
Bar of chocolate (half pound [c. 225g] bar)	7p (1/4d)	79p
Road tax	£1.00 (£1/0/0d)	£145.00
Family saloon car	£416.03 (Austin A40) (£325.00 + £91/0/6d purchase tax)	(Ford Escort) £12,280
Over to you by Roald Dahl	38p (7/6d)	£5.99
Six-bedroom house, Wimbledon	£7,250	£775,000
Two weeks in Lucerne	£57.75 (£57/15/0d)	£815.00
Headache tablets	7p (1/4d)	£1.85
Man's wristwatch	£6.40 (£6/8/0d)	£29.50
The Observer	1p (2d)	£1.00
Daily Hansard	3p (6d)	£5.00
Music recording	24p (3/11½d) (12″ classical record)	£15.99 (Spice Girls' album)

Figure 40.2 What's in and what's out of the RPI basket

Source: *Daily Telegraph*, 20 March 2001

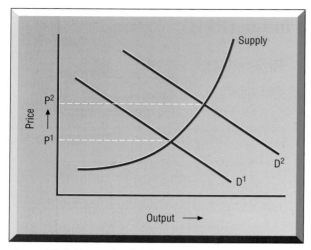

Figure 40.3 Demand-pull inflation

When an increase in production costs leads to an increase in consumer prices, this is called **cost-push inflation**. Increases in the cost of production could be caused by:

● increasing labour costs

● increasing raw material costs

● increasing fuel/energy costs.

Where excess demand is present in a market (see Unit 38), prices will be 'pulled' upwards. This is called **demand-pull inflation**. Figure 40.3 illustrates this concept: As demand increases from D1 to D2, price moves from P1 to P2.

3   Impact of inflation

Inflation impacts on businesses in a number of ways.

● **Increased costs.** The prices that a business pays for its raw materials, services and other costs may increase.

● **Wage costs.** As the price of goods increases, employees are likely to demand higher wages. Paying higher wages will push up business costs, contribute further to cost-push inflation (this is known as a 'wage–price spiral').

● **Menu costs.** Where prices are regularly changing, price-lists and menus have to be changed frequently, further increasing business costs.

● **Uncertainty.** A key impact of inflation is that it contributes to uncertainty. Businesses may find it difficult to plan, if future costs and prices cannot be forecast with any degree of accuracy.

● **International trade.** If UK inflation is higher than the inflation of trading partners, UK products will appear to be relatively expensive. This can limit the opportunities for UK firms to export goods, thus reducing demand.

Still more important to business may be how the government and the Bank of England respond to inflation. The government has a target for inflation of 1.5–2.5 per cent. As Figure 40.4 shows, since 1998 inflation in the UK has remained relatively static. This has the advantage of creating a more certain environment for business and reduces the likelihood that measures will be taken to control inflation.

If inflation exceeds – or looks likely to exceed – the government's target, the Bank of England is likely to increase interest rates. The government may also reduce its own spending, thus reducing employment prospects and putting downward pressure on demand.

> **Guru's views**
> 'Having a little inflation is like being a little bit pregnant.'
>
> *Leon Henderson*

4   Interest rates

The **interest rate** is essentially the price of borrowed money (or the return for depositing money in a bank). In the UK, the interest rate is controlled by the Bank of England's **Monetary Policy Committee (MPC)**. The MPC sets the base rate, and individual banks use this rate as a guide to setting their own rates.

To meet the government's inflationary target of between 1.5 and 2.5 per cent, the MPC uses interest rates to control consumer spending, and to slow business growth by increasing business costs. Figure 40.5 highlights this process:

Not all businesses or consumers will be affected to the same extent by interest rates. Businesses with low gearing (few loans) will be relatively unaffected. A business that operates solely within the UK may see little of the impact that the interest rate has on exchange rates. Sales of products that are very income-elastic may be affected much more than sales of essential products with low income-elasticity.

The long-term benefit of interest rates, hence inflationary, control for businesses is stability. In the UK, the interest rate stood at 4 per cent for more than

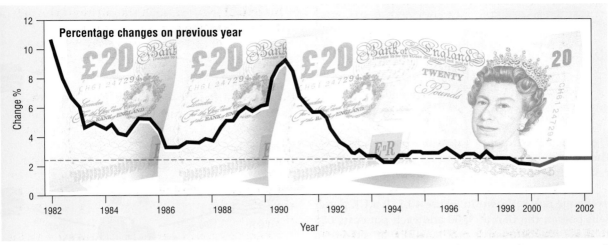

Figure 40.4 RPI movement 1982–2002   Source: www.hm-treasury.gov.uk

14 months and inflation has remained relatively stable (see Figure 40.4). Such stability makes it easier for businesses, as well as consumers, to plan, and ensures that growth is sustainable.

 Exchange rates

The **exchange rate** is the price of one currency against another – for example, the value of the pound against the euro. In essence, exchange rates are deter- mined by the forces of supply and demand. As demand for a currency rises, so does its value against other currencies.

A key factor in demand for a country's currency is that country's interest rate. For example, if UK interest rates rise, this will attract investors into the currency and into UK banks, because they will benefit from good returns on any deposits. This, in turn, increases demand for the currency and hence its price against other currencies. This is shown in

Economic condition/aim	Interest rate change	Impact on business	Impact on consumer
Low inflation **Aim** – stimulate economic growth and encourage increase in demand	• Decrease interest rate	• Reduction in cost of borrowing/loans • Fall in exchange rate, aiding UK exports • Increase in consumer demand	• Fall in cost of servicing mortgages and other debts, • increasing ability to spend • Increase in consumer confidence and in willingness to take on more debt, increasing demand for products
High Inflation **Aim** – reduce inflationary pressure by controlling demand	• Increase interest rate	• Increase in cost of borrowing • UK exports less attractive due to strong pound • Fall in consumer demand	• Rise in mortgage costs, reducing ability to spend • Delay/cancellation of large purchases by consumers because of high credit costs • Probable saving by consumers, rather than spending

Figure 40.5 Effects of interest rate changes

Figure 40.6. As interest rates increase, demand for the pound moves from D1 to D2 and the value (V) relative to other currencies increases from V1 to V2.

How prices are affected by changes in the exchange rate is shown in Figure 40.7. If a UK potter sells pots in the USA at $100 and each pot costs £25 to make, the company's profits will be affected by a rising or falling exchange rate as follows:

Revenue		Profit	
$100 ÷ 2 = £50		£50 – £25	= **£25**
$100 ÷ 1.5 = £66.67		£66.67 – £25	= **£41.67**
$100 ÷ 2.5 = £40		£40 – £25	= **£15**

Changes in interest rates, and hence in demand for the pound, can have a variety of effects on businesses importing and exporting goods, as shown in Figure 40.8. However, if a strong pound is forcing prices up, an exporter may choose to focus on non-price factors, thus maintaining sales. Importers may be able to source from other suppliers or use surplus stocks until such a time as the exchange rate changes in their favour.

Not all businesses will be affected by exchange rate changes to the same extent. If a business is both an importer and an exporter, the two effects may cancel each other out. Businesses with little connection to overseas trade, or in industries with few competing imports, may see little of the effect of exchange rate changes.

Exchange rates and the euro are considered in Unit 42.

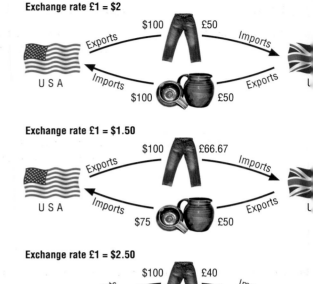

Figure 40.7 Effect of changes in exchange rate on prices

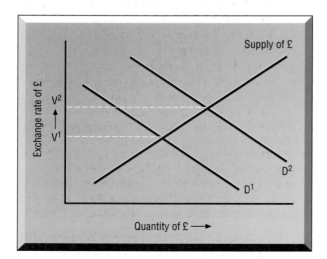

Figure 40.6 Effect of changes in interest rates on exchange rate

Change	Effect on £	Effect on business
Fall in demand for the £	• Fall in value of the £ against other currencies ('weak pound').	• **Importers** will find that they now have to pay more for goods. This may lead to price increases or a fall in profitability. • **Exporters** may enjoy healthy sales, as UK products now appear relatively cheaper abroad.
Increase in demand for the £	• Rise in the value of the £ against other currencies ('strong pound').	• **Importers** will benefit from the increased purchasing power of the £ and will find that their costs fall, leading to increased profitability. • **Exporters** may suffer a fall in sales as UK goods now appear to be relatively expensive abroad.

Figure 40.8 Effects of changes in demand for the £ on business

For example ...

Dollar strikes another three-year low

The dollar hit a three-year low against the euro during the early part of 2003, after reports that empty chemical weapons warheads had been found in Iraq. The finding increased the likelihood that the USA would soon be at war.

The threat of conflict in Iraq had been weighing on the dollar for months. Its value, which had been trying to regain its footing against the euro, swiftly fell to $1.0625 – its lowest level since October 1999.

Source: *Financial Times*, 17 January 2003

Want to know more?

www.ft.com

1 What is an exchange rate?   **[2]**
2 Consider the possible impact on US exporters of the falling value of the dollar.   **[4]**
3 Discuss the extent to which a US manufacturer might be affected by the weak dollar.   **[12]**
                                               Total 18 marks

6   Unemployment

The term 'unemployment' refers to the number of people of working age that are currently out of work within an economy. Because **unemployment** has many causes, there will always be some unemployment within an economy. But, broadly speaking, government policy will attempt to ensure that unemployment is as low as possible.

There are many types of unemployment, with many different causes.

● **Structural.** Significant changes in the economy cause structural unemployment. For example, the decline of secondary industries – employment in manufacturing fell from 20.9 per cent in 1988 to 15.6 per cent in 2000 – has accompanied a significant shift towards tertiary sector employment. Changes in demand, such as increased demand for technological products, can also cause structural decline in other industries. These changes cause unemployment if workers are not able to retrain in order to find employment within the 'new' industries.

● **Seasonal.** Employment patterns can be affected by seasonal changes in demand, producing seasonal unemployment. For example, theme parks, such as Alton Towers, close during the winter months and operate with minimal staff.

● **Cyclical.** Unemployment patterns coincide with shifts in economic activity – in a recession unemployment is likely to increase (see Unit 41).

The JobCentre may be the first port of call when seeking employment

- **Frictional.** People who move between jobs may be unemployed for a very short time. This is called frictional unemployment.

- **Search.** Where people are actively seeking a job but, perhaps due to lack of skills or lack of employment opportunities, they may be unemployed for a period of time.

7   Impact of unemployment

Unemployment affects different businesses in different ways. Fundamentally, business wants low unemployment, though some companies – those selling inferior goods – may benefit from high unemployment. By contrast, businesses selling essential goods may be little affected by unemployment.

Unemployment can impact in a variety of ways.

- **Demand.** The fewer the people that have jobs, the fewer the people that have money to spend, and the lower the demand for income-elastic products.

- **Economic growth.** Low unemployment is closely linked with economic growth. As the economy grows, business benefit from increased possibilities for expansion (see Unit 41).

- **Recruitment costs.** If unemployment is low, businesses may find it difficult to find suitable staff. The cost of recruitment may increase (Cisco Systems, for instance, were forced to recruit

engineers from overseas to meet UK demand). Salary and benefit packages may have to be increased to attract the best staff and to retain current employees. These increasing wage costs can contribute to cost-push inflation. Businesses may then be faced with the inflationary issues discussed earlier in the unit.

- **Headcount issues.** Bill Gates claims that the biggest constraint on Microsoft's growth has been the difficulty in recruiting suitable numbers of well-qualified staff. He claims that significant opportunities have been missed because Microsoft simply did not have the staff to pursue them.

8   Government policy and unemployment

To reduce unemployment, the government may adopt a number of measures:

- control of benefits policies – an attempt to reduce any incentive to stay out of work

- supply-side policies – making it easier for businesses to recruit employees, by reducing legislation and employment costs (reducing employers' National Insurance contributions)

- training – a wide variety of government-funded training initiatives designed to ensure that people have the necessary skills to find, and stay in, work

- government spending – increases in government spending, such as on education, help to create employment opportunities. The low unemployment levels experienced during 2002 were, in part, a result of public sector recruitment.

Ideally, businesses prefer an unemployment rate that supports healthy demand, but does not put too much pressure on recruitment and wage costs. Government policies to reduce unemployment are largely beneficial to business. The downside of low unemployment is increasing costs and potential inflationary pressure.

Activity

Investigate the current unemployment level. What are the implications for business?

For example ...

A 27-year low

Unemployment in December 2002 stood at 928,300, or 3.1 per cent of the workforce – a 27-year low. Since 1997, unemployment had more than halved. Forecasts for 2003 suggested further falls due to public sector recruitment, but with the possibility of increases if a slow-down in consumer spending resulted in significant job cuts in the private sector.

1 Analyse and evaluate the implications for a business of operating in a low unemployment environment.

Total 15 marks

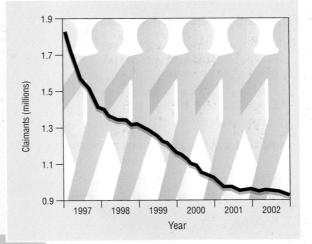

Figure 40.9 Unemployment in UK 1997–2002

9 International trade

Businesses engage in international trade – the buying and selling of goods between different countries – for a number of reasons.

- **Higher profits.** By selling products to a much wider market, the potential to earn higher profits is increased.

- **Diversification.** By trading in many countries, a business guards against the possibility that demand will dry up in any one country.

- **Economies of scale.** Businesses such as McDonald's can significantly reduce unit costs by benefiting from the economies of scale that result from selling to wider markets.

- **Market saturation.** Where a domestic market is saturated, it may be necessary to trade internationally in order to meet growth and profit targets. Orange, for instance, faced with a saturated UK mobile phone market, has over recent years attempted to increase its presence in Asian markets.

Activity

Use the internet to investigate what is meant by 'globalisation'. Give examples of companies that operate on a global scale. What are the negative implications of globalisation?

10 International competitiveness

A variety of factors can have an effect on international competitiveness.

- **Exchange rates.** The price of goods in different countries can be directly affected by exchange rates. How great is the effect on a business's competitiveness will depend on price elasticity.

- **Cost of production.** The lower the unit profit margin of a product, the more price-flexible a firm will be. Price flexibility may allow for price cuts so as to account for exchange rate fluctuations, or to ensure the product can compete with locally produced goods.

- **Product.** The type of product may determine its success. A unique product, which cannot be produced locally, may well enjoy healthy sales.

Quality will also be important: if local products are of higher quality, then sales will suffer.

- **Brand.** How well a brand name or image travels will affect its prospects of international success. Businesses that can adapt their product to local needs are likely to enjoy much higher sales (for example, McDonald's sells slightly different products in many of its different markets).

- **Trading relations.** Political relations between countries can affect how successful international trade is likely to be. Trade between European Union member states is made easier because of the removal of political and bureaucratic barriers to trade.

Even where a business has a competitive advantage, there are many potential problems with international trade. These are represented in Figure 40.10.

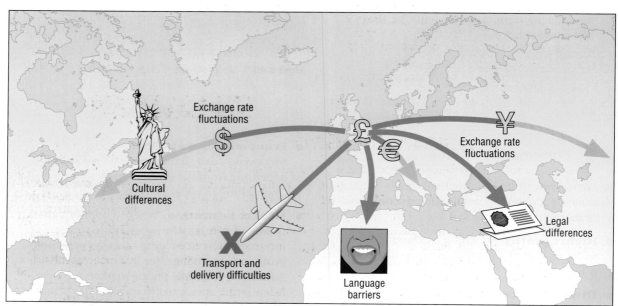

Figure 40.10 Possible problems in international trade

Impact of the economy: summary

KEY TERMS

Inflation – the general increase in prices over time in an economy.

Retail price index (RPI) – key measure of inflation, calculated by measuring the prices of a typical monthly 'basket' of goods representing consumer spending patterns.

Cost-push inflation – an increase in consumer prices caused by an increase in production costs.

Demand-pull inflation – prices 'pulled' upwards by excess demand.

Interest rate – the price of borrowed money.

Monetary policy – control of interest rates (through the Bank of England) and of the money supply.

Monetary Policy Committee (MPC) – Bank of England's committee responsible for setting interest rates.

Exchange rate – the price of one currency against another (for example, the value of the pound against the US dollar).

Fiscal policy – the uses of taxes and government spending to manage the economy.

Supply-side policies – range of polices that aim to promote business activity (for example, a reduction in employer National Insurance contributions to encourage more recruitment).

Unemployment – the number of people of working age currently out of work within an economy.

Exam practice continues ➤

Impact of the economy: summary (continued)

Summary questions

1 What is fiscal policy?
2 Give **one** example of a supply-side policy.
3 What is inflation?
4 How is inflation measured?
5 Contrast cost-push and demand-pull inflationary pressures.
6 Examine **three** affects that inflation has on business activity.
7 Discuss **two** impacts of interest rates on business.
8 Using a suitable diagram, illustrate and explain the links between interest rates and exchange rates.
9 Provide a numerical example of how business profitability might be affected by exchange rate changes.
10 Identify and explain **two** different types of unemployment.
11 Contrast the benefits and drawbacks of low unemployment for business.
12 Suggest and explain **three** benefits of international trade.
13 State **three** problems that a business may face when attempting to trade internationally.
14 Discuss **two** factors that affect a firm's international competitiveness.

Exam practice

Making a leap

Even if the Bank of England are 100 per cent sure that interest rates need to start rising, it is probably too late. The decision to begin tightening monetary policy usually requires a leap of faith, and in many cases nerves of steel. The problem is that there is a time lag between a change in interest rates and an effect on economic activity, but no one knows how long that lag is. For example, the Bank of England has to assume that the consequences of past interest rate cuts will continue to affect the economy for some time, before any change in rates will have any effect (the effect of interest rate rises on mortgage repayment is shown in Figure 40.11).

The Bank could wait until the economy is firing on all cylinders before raising rates. But this risks condemning the economy to inflationary pressure while it waits for monetary tightening to take hold.

Source: *Financial Times*, 28 May 2002

1 What is meant by 'inflationary pressure'? **[3]**
2 How else can monetary policy be tightened other than by interest rate changes? **[2]**
3 Explain the relationship between interest rates and exchange rates. **[5]**
4 Evaluate the effects on businesses and consumers of a rise in interest rates. **[15]**

Total 25 marks

How interest rate increases can affect you

Interest rate	£50 000 mortgage (monthly payments)	£100 000 mortgage (monthly payments)
5.75%	£314.55	£629.11
6.25%	£329.83	£659.67
6.75%	£345.46	£690.91
7.25%	£361.40	£722.81
7.75%	£377.66	£755.33

Source: London & Country   Assume 25-year repayment mortgage

Figure 40.11 Effects of interest rate rises on mortgage repayments

41 Growth and the business cycle

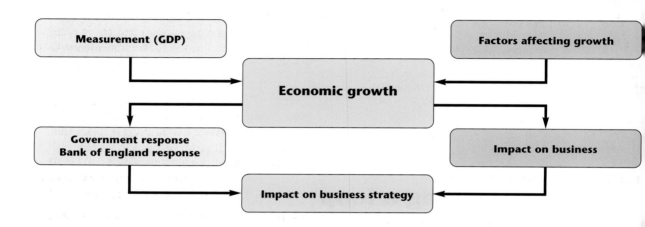

1 The media and the economy

Most newspapers in the UK carry almost daily reports about the state of the economy. Talk of recession, recovery, boom or bust is never far away. The reason for the intense media coverage is the importance of the economy for business growth, which in turn has implications for unemployment and consumer spending – things that affect us all.

Markets fear global meltdown

Panic grips global markets

Share prices soar

FTSE reaches record heights

2 Economic growth

At the heart of the media coverage is the interest in **economic growth**. A country's economic growth is measured by its **gross domestic product (GDP)**. GDP is the value of all goods and services produced by an economy and hence is a measure of economic activity. To ensure fair comparison between different years, the effects of **inflation** – rising prices (see Unit 40) – are removed from GDP calculations.

An increase in GDP represents an increase in economic activity, and thus economic growth. Figure 41.1 shows UK economic growth since 1992.

Economic growth can be measured relative to the performance of other countries, as shown in Figure 41.2.

STOP & THINK

Looking at Figure 41.2, what factors might account for the differing growth levels? Why is it useful to compare countries in this way?

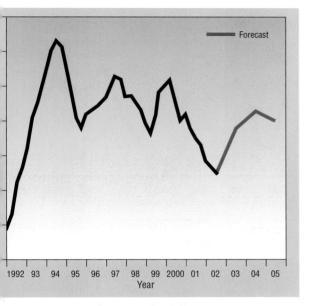

Figure 41.1 Actual and forecast UK economic growth 1992–2005

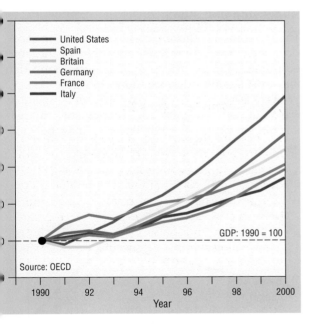

Figure 41.2 UK's economic growth compared to other countries

Economic growth is important because growth represents potentially favourable trading conditions for businesses – buoyant sales, low unemployment (though this does have its downside), expansion possibilities and high levels of confidence . But an economy may not always be growing. At times, economic growth may be relatively static or even negative. The rate of growth can be affected by a number o factors.

- **Technology.** New technologies can increase the production capacity of businesses and may generate new business in itself (such as the increased sale of mobile phones). The dot.com 'boom' was driven by the business possibilities of the internet.

- **Investment.** The willingness of firms to invest funds to ensure long-term business growth has an impact on economic growth: the more firms that invest, the higher economic growth. Investment is affected by business confidence.

- **Confidence.** The confidence that a business has in the future state of the economy affects its willingness to invest. If a business believes that the economy will grow, suggesting healthy demand in the future, it is more likely to invest in expansion or new products. Conversely, a lack of confidence reduces willingness to invest.

- **Labour.** The size and skills of a country's labour force affects economic growth: the larger the working population, the greater the potential for growth; the more skilled workers a country has, the greater the potential for businesses to succeed and grow.

> *For example ...*
>
> ## Setting a record
>
> By the end of 2002, the UK economy had enjoyed 12 consecutive years of economic growth. Despite doubts over consumer spending, threats of a housing market collapse and the bursting of the dotcom bubble, the economy had sustained this growth, even through difficult economic conditions in recent years. The economic upturn, having started in 1992, is the longest period of uninterrupted growth on record.
>
> Source: *Sunday Times*, 5 January 2003
>
> 1 What is economic growth?   [1]
> 2 How is economic growth measured?   [3]
> 3 Suggest and explain **three** factors that may have contributed to the continued economic growth of the UK.   [6]
> **Total 10 marks**

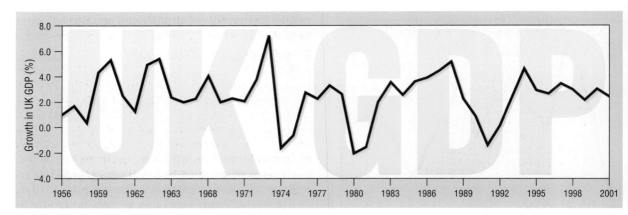

Figure 41.3 UK economic growth (GDP %) 1956–2001

Source: www.hm-treasury.gov.uk

- **International trade.** If a country can export more goods than it imports, then it is likely to enjoy economic growth.

- **Government impact.** By means of taxation, government spending and business regulation, the government can affect the ability of an economy to grow (see Units 37–40).

3   Business cycle

As stated earlier, economic growth is not always positive. The way that economic growth fluctuates over time is known as the **business cycle** (or **trade cycle**). Figure 41.3 shows that these fluctuations, which

although not occurring at regular time intervals or for defined time periods, do display a pattern.

The economic conditions represented by this pattern of **slump**, **recovery**, **boom** and **recession** have been simplified in Figure 41.4.

Recession and slump

The economy is officially considered to be in recession after two consecutive quarters of negative economic growth. The economic conditions that may exist in a recession are shown in Figure 41.4.

In some cases, a business may attempt to 'spend its way out of recession'. If investment in new machinery cuts costs, the business may be more likely to survive the recession and be in a stronger

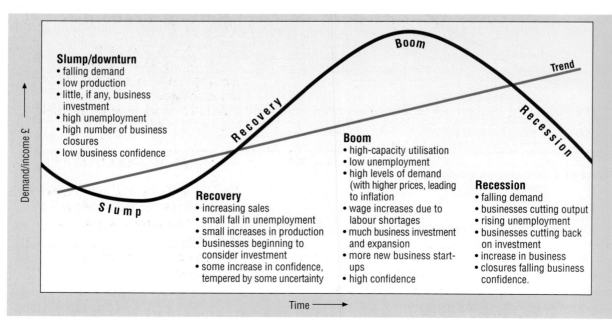

Figure 41.4 The business cycle

Strategies for surviving a recession

- **Stimulate demand**
  cut prices
  increase promotion
  introduce special offers.

- **Minimise costs**
  find cheaper raw materials
  reduce staffing levels
  introduce flexible working
  increase productivity
  cut unnecessary expenditure
  freeze hiring staff.

- **Production**
  reduce spare capacity (sell assets)
  stop overtime/reduce working week
  find cheaper production methods.

- **Investment**
  cancel investment plans.

position when the economy recovers. Moreover, good deals may be available during a recession, as suppliers discount products to stimulate demand.

A slump, or **downturn**, represents the lowest point of economic activity before recovery begins. Figure 41.4 gives details of its characteristics.

Recovery and boom

Business uncertainty can prolong the period of recovery and add to economic worries. Businesses may be reluctant to invest in new products or assets or take on new staff if the economic outlook is uncertain. The economic conditions that may exist in a recovery are shown in Figure 41.4.

Eventually, a recovery may result in an economic boom – a period of significant economic growth. Boom characteristics are shown in Figure 41.4.

A downside of booms is overconfidence and the potential for a subsequent downswing in economic growth. The dot.com boom is a classic example of overconfidence. During booms, businesses will often overstretch themselves, borrowing heavily to finance growth and taking perhaps unnecessary risks. Any change in economic outlook can have a significant impact on such firms. Investors will be quick to recall loans, and suppliers are likely to offer less-favourable credit terms. A minor dip in confidence can snowball into a recession, as overstretched businesses are suddenly faced with economic realities previously masked by high confidence (as was the case for Marconi and Enron).

 Impact of growth on business

What effect economic growth has on a business depends very much on the nature of the business. Different businesses are affected in different ways at different stages of the trade cycle. Some of the possible impacts are represented in Figure 41.5.

In general, most businesses will enjoy healthy sales in times of economic growth. Recoveries and booms can present opportunities to make healthy

Stage of trade cycle	Negative impacts	Positive impacts
Recession	• Luxury goods producers may find demand falls.	• Accounting firms (dealing with receivership), businesses selling inferior goods and pawnbrokers may benefit from an increase in demand.
Slump/Downturn	• Construction businesses may suffer as demand for new buildings falls.	• Pharmaceutical companies are likely to be relatively unaffected.
Recovery	• Discount retailers may experience a fall in demand.	• Demand for a wide range of products will be high. • Recruitment agencies may see an increase in demand for temporary workers, as businesses cautiously seek to increase production.
Boom	• Businesses reliant on a small pool of skilled labour may find it difficult and expensive to recruit.	• Luxury goods producers will enjoy healthy sales.

Figure 41.5 Effects of trade cycle on different businesses

The 'human' face of AOL

profits, to expand product lines and to make strategic acquisitions (takeovers) or conduct mergers, for example the merger of Time Warner and AOL.

The UK, over recent years, has increasingly displayed what is known as a **two-speed economy** (see Figure 41.6). Since 1996, retail sales have shown healthy growth while manufacturing has remained relatively static (and has even fallen in recent years). This meanss that whereas retailers have benefited from recent economic conditions, manufacturers have not. Moreover, it would appear that manufacturing and retailing are experiencing increasingly different trade cycles.

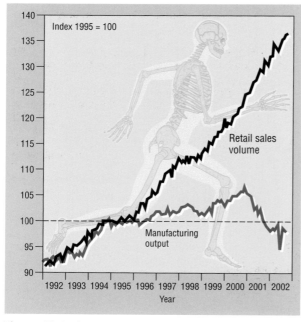

Figure 41.6 The UK's two-speed economy

Negative impacts of growth

Economic growth also has its downside, as explained in the discussion of boom. Overconfidence in markets can eventually lead to downswings and recession. Firms may overexpose themselves to risk, increasing the impact of any minor change in economic conditions and causing a more widespread decrease in confidence.

Economic growth can have a negative effect on the cost of labour to business. As unemployment is low, labour can be scarce and therefore expensive. Businesses may have to offer very generous salary and benefits packages to attract or retain staff, pushing up costs.

Economic growth can also lead to business inefficiency. When demand is growing and profitability is high, there may be little motivation to control costs. Management attention is often focused on external growth rather than internal efficiency. Those businesses that manage to exploit the opportunities for economic growth while avoiding the pitfalls, will enjoy long-term success. Businesses that survive recessions often find that the disciplines learned and the strategic decisions taken can lead to a 'fitter and leaner' company much more able to do business in changeable economic conditions.

Growth and inflation

Inflation is defined as a general rise in prices across the economy over time. Inflation and economic growth are closely linked. As economic growth increases, so does pressure on prices. Excess demand (see Unit 38) can lead to price increases, resulting in demand-pull inflationary pressure. To offset higher prices, employees may demand higher wages. Increasing costs of labour and raw materials can lead to cost-push inflationary pressure. Hence, businesses may not welcome strong economic growth because of its effect on costs.

In addition, the Bank of England's response to inflation may be to increase interest rates. This can add to business costs by increasing repayments on loans. Demand may also fall as consumer spending decreases, because of higher debt-servicing costs. For more detail on the impact of inflation see Unit 40.

5   The trade cycle and business strategy

To survive the changeable economic conditions, prudent businesses organise themselves in such a way as to ensure that, whatever happens, they are prepared. To achive this, they can employ a number of strategies.

- **Diversification.** A business with a range of products, or interests, across different markets may insulate itself from changeable conditions (especially if its range includes inferior, normal and luxury goods). Falling profits in one market may then be offset by healthy sales in another. Larger businesses may also benefit from geographic diversification – operating in a number of different countries (Unilever has a very diversified product range and operates globally).

- **Gearing.** Given the impact that interest rates can have on highly geared firms (see Unit 20), it may be prudent to maintain moderate gearing levels. Ideally, a business would ensure that even if it has 'geared-up' – increased loans – during a boom, it can quickly repay the loans at the first sign of cooling economic conditions, so that liquidity is maintained (see Units 15 and 20).

- **Flexible working practices.** Well-trained staff and flexible working practices will allow a business to react quickly to whatever surprises the economy has in store.

- **Lean operations.** Costs should be kept to a minimum at all times (see Unit 37).

A range of Unilever products

For example ...

2003 – A gloomy outlook...

The start of 2003 brought a gloomy outlook for the UK's businessmen and women. Gloom and uncertainty descended over business like winter snow. At what is often considered a time of new hope, the New Year brought wobbly stock markets, ominous economic surveys and the threat of a fall in consumer spending. Against a backdrop of worries about war, terrorist attacks and looming tax rises, many business prospects were, at best, uncertain. For some, talk of any recovery was quickly put aside as the prospect of further job cuts was threatened and market confidence took yet another hit.

Source: *Sunday Times*, 12 January 2003

1 What is meant by the term 'recovery'?   [2]
2 Discuss the relationship between confidence and the trade cycle.   [4]
3 Other news reports at the time suggested a more positive 2003. What impact might media reports have on the trade cycle?   [4]
4 How might a business respond to economic news such as that in the article?   [6]

Total 16 marks

Growth and the business cycle: summary

KEY TERMS

Boom – period of economic prosperity and economic growth, which may eventually lead to overheating and a subsequent downswing.

Business cycle (trade cycle) – the cyclical movement of economic growth characterised by recovery, boom, recession, slump.

Recession – period when the economy grows more slowly than before.

Economic growth – assessment of economic activity within a country, measured by GDP.

Gross domestic product (GDP) – a measure of the value of all goods and services produced by an economy.

Recovery – period when an economy starts to enjoy growth after a slump.

Slump (downturn) – economic conditions defined by falling demand, falling output and rising unemployment.

Two-speed economy – situation where one section of an economy (manufacturing) may be experiencing different economic conditions to that of another (retail).

Inflation – the general rise in prices over time measured by changes in inflation-adjusted GDP.

Summary questions

1   What is meant by 'economic growth'?
2   Describe how economic growth is measured?
3   Suggest possible reasons why the UK may have experienced lower economic growth than the USA.
4   What are the main stages of the business cycle?
5   Contrast recessions and booms.
6   What economic conditions exist in a recovery?
7   What might a business do to survive a recession?
8   Define inflation.
9   Explain the relationship between the trade cycle and inflation.
10 Why might a business prefer stable economic conditions?
11 Suggest and explain **two** strategies that a business might implement to minimise the effects of cyclical changes.
12 Define the term 'two-speed economy'.

Exam practice

Manufacturing – does it matter?

UK manufacturers have, over recent years, had a torrid time. As the chart shows, by comparison with America and Germany the UK has seen only negligible growth, followed by a two-year decline, caused as the American recession rippled across the world.

Manufacturing production in 2001 was only 2.7 per cent higher than in 1995. This is as compared to rises of more than 25 per cent for the services sector and 36 per cent in the financial services sector. As a result, manufacturing's share of the economy shrunk from 21.6 per cent of total output in 1995 to 19 per cent in 2001.

Does this matter? After all, 1995–2001 were successful years for the UK economy, with low inflation and sustained growth. Some argue that it does matter, particularly with regard to UK investment in research and development (R&D).

A viable and healthy manufacturing sector should allow the UK to benefit

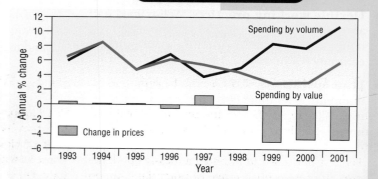

Figure 41.7 Spending on clothes in the UK

from technological breakthroughs, which in turn should drive productivity growth. Most research and development is conducted in manufacturing, and it is one of the main ways of spreading best practice across all UK businesses. This 'appliance of science' approach is a key strategy in the Department of Trade and Industry's (DTI) drive to improve the competitiveness of the UK manufacturing sector.

Source: *The Economist*, 9 April 2002

1   Define the term 'recession'.   **[3]**
2   What is meant by 'low inflation'?   **[2]**
3   Examine why innovation and R&D are important to the manufacturing sector.   **[8]**
4   To what extent might manufacturing businesses be able to isolate themselves from the effects of the trade cycle?   **[12]**
Total 25 marks

42 Business and Europe

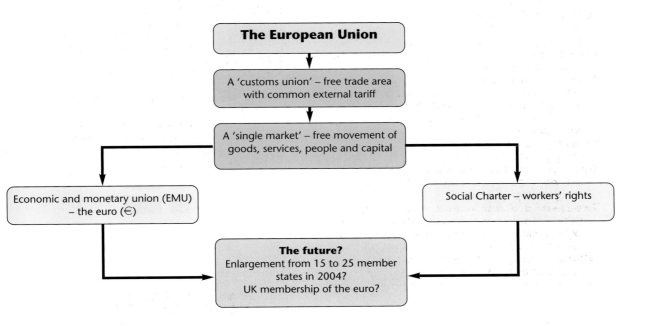

The European Union

↓

A 'customs union' – free trade area with common external tariff

↓

A 'single market' – free movement of goods, services, people and capital

Economic and monetary union (EMU) – the euro (€)

Social Charter – workers' rights

The future?
Enlargement from 15 to 25 member states in 2004?
UK membership of the euro?

1 Business across the world

Almost all larger UK businesses are directly or indirectly involved with relationships that extend into other countries.

The rest of the world provides a massive potential market, but also a huge range of potential competitors. The state of the world economy will affect demand and confidence in our own country. Trade with the USA and the Commonwealth is crucial to the success of many UK businesses.

In recent decades, however, it has been Europe that has come to have an increasingly important influence on UK business. This has been the result of the UK's geographical closeness to Europe, its membership of an expanding European Union (EU) and the closer integration between EU countries.

2 What is the European Union?

The European Union is a bloc of 15 European countries that have developed closer economic, social and political ties. It has grown out of the 1957 Treaty of Rome in which six countries – France, West Germany, Italy, Belgium, Holland and Luxembourg – agreed to set up the European Economic Community (EEC). The EEC was a free-trade area, known as a **customs union**, in which the member countries agreed to:

● get rid of any barriers to trade – such as taxes on trade, known as 'tariffs' – in order to encourage trade between them

● set up a **common external tariff** on trade with the rest of the world – that is, an agreed tax on any imports from countries outside of the EEC.

Businesses within the free trade area benefit from the growth in trading opportunities within the bloc, and

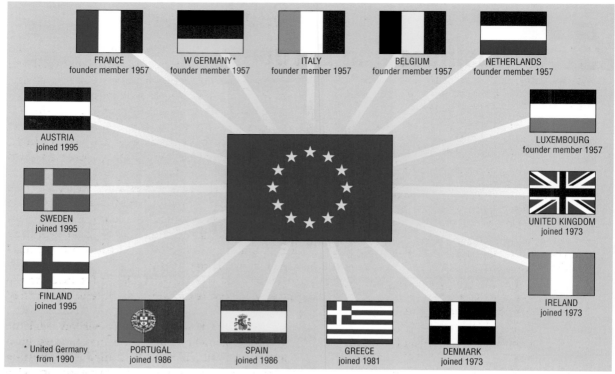

Figure 42.1 Member states of the European Union

from the external tariffs that make imports less price-competitive.

Attracted by the benefits to business and trade, other countries sought to join the EEC, and in 1973 the UK was admitted along with Ireland and Denmark. Figure 42.1 shows how, by 1995, membership had expanded to include 15 European countries.

Not only did membership expand, but the nature of the EEC was transformed and evolved into today's European Union (EU). This occurred through a number of key changes that included:

- the development of a **single market**

- the creation of a single European currency – the euro.

3 The single market

Taking away tariffs on trade between member countries undoubtedly helped to encourage trade between them. But many other 'hidden' barriers to trade remained:

- different laws on product standards or safety, which made it difficult to sell the same product in all member countries

- different tax rates (such as VAT) or subsidy levels,

which gave businesses in some countries unfair price advantages over others

- the paperwork and bureaucracy involved in moving products, people or finance from one member country to another.

The Single European Act of 1986 set a deadline of 1 January 1993 for these barriers to be removed and for a truly single market to be up and running. While reducing the barriers has proved an ongoing task, the single market in principle established four freedoms.

1 **Goods.** Companies can sell their products in any member country, with agreements on:

  a common product standards
  b common rules on many taxes and subsidies
  c reduced paperwork needed for trade.

2 **People.** Citizens of any member country can live or work in any other.

3 **Capital.** Finance can be moved freely from one member country to another.

4 **Services.** Professional services, such as insurance or banking, can be offered across all member countries.

UK membership of the single market

Advantages

- By removing barriers to trade, a single market of more than 360 million people has been opened up to UK businesses. The potential for sales growth and profits is huge.

- The expansion of sales could in turn lead to increased production, employment and economic growth across the UK.

- Operating on a larger scale may enable firms to benefit from economies of scale (see Unit 31). This means they may be able to reduce the costs of producing each unit of output through the benefits of growth.

- Costs have been cut as a result of simpler procedures and less paperwork involved in trading across Europe.

- The free movement of people enables business to recruit workers from across the EU, with a larger pool of workers potentially providing better quality applicants

- Free movement of capital enables business to access a wider range of sources of finance for investment purposes, or to invest in business ventures throughout Europe.

Disadvantages

- The single market opens up the whole European market to all European businesses. The increased competition that results could lead to UK firms losing sales and market share. Even UK businesses that do not themselves trade in Europe may find that European competitors are challenging for market share in the UK domestic market.

- The need to create common standards for products, employment or health and safety has led to an increasing volume of regulations and directives from the EU. Far from cutting business costs, these have led to increased bureaucracy and expensive changes in procedures for many businesses.

STOP & THINK

Which types of businesses will benefit most from the single market? Which have the most to lose? Which will be completely unaffected? Why?

4 The single currency

Perhaps the biggest barrier to trade between member countries of the European Union was that each had its own currency. Trading involved exchanging currencies, which was both costly and uncertain.

To remove this crucial barrier, 11 of the EU member states abandoned their national currencies at the beginning of 1999 and adopted a single, common currency – the euro. This process is known as **Economic and Monetary Union** (EMU). A European Central Bank was established to issue the currency and set a single interest rate for the whole **Eurozone**. Greece joined the euro in 2001, but Sweden, Denmark and the UK have so far kept their own currencies. Euro notes and coins became legal tender from 1 January 2002.

Having a single currency allows for **price transparency** – easy comparison of different countries' prices.

The fact that the UK has not itself adopted the euro does not mean that UK businesses have been unaffected by the change. UK companies exporting to Europe have had to price goods in euros and give price conversions in promotional materials. Many retailers in the UK have already converted tills to accommodate European customers wishing to pay in euros.

Pros and cons

Business in the UK is divided over whether the adoption of the euro would be advantageous. One car manufacturer has estimated that joining the euro would cut the company's costs by around £150 million a year. Staying out has already cost the UK new jobs. The Japanese car firm Honda will not make its new Micra in the UK because of the extra costs brought about by the UK's not belonging to the euro.

Yet, since the launch of the euro in 1999, inward investment to the UK has grown to record levels. Moreover, only 15 per cent of UK businesses trade with countries in the Eurozone, so only these would benefit form membership of the euro.

The costs and benefits of the UK adopting the euro would be unequally spread. Large businesses trading throughout Europe would benefit from the cost-savings of a single currency and can afford the initial costs of the changeover. Small businesses and those that do not trade with Europe are much more likely to suffer from the initial costs, without reaping the benefits.

UK's adoption of the euro

Advantages

- **No currency exchanges when trading with Europe.** Hence:

  - no commission costs involved in exchanging currencies
  - no uncertainty of fluctuations in exchange rates to threaten profitability.

- **Price transparency.** Easier to compare prices across countries when all are priced in one currency. This helps business to source the cheapest suppliers, and consumers to spot the cheapest products.

- **Easier exporting and importing.** Firms able to sell to a bigger market and benefit from increased sales and potential economies of scale.

- **Business investment in UK more likely.** Countries seeking to invest in Europe more likely to choose the UK if it is part of the single currency, bringing employment and economic growth.

- **Low and stable inflation rates** (see Unit 40). Made possible by a single interest rate, set by a European Central Bank, and no exchange rate fluctuations.

Disadvantages

- **High costs of changing over to new currency.** Tills, price lists, accounting systems and so on would all need to be changed. Staff may need to be retrained to cope with the new currency The British Retail Consortium says the changeover would cost shops £3.5 billion. The costs could cripple small businesses.

- **Price transparency.** Not beneficial to every business. Introduces new competitive pressures that could force some businesses to cut prices and profit margins or lose customers.

- **No new benefits.** Euro would make little difference to benefits from the single market and the economies of scale, which have already been realised.

- **UK already an attractive place to invest.** This is because of its low tax rates and flexible labour markets. The absence of the euro in the UK will not significantly change this.

- **Single interest rate bad for UK business.** If the UK economy is experiencing different problems from the rest of Europe, changes in interest rates may be inappropriate and harmful to business.

For example ...

One coin fits all?

Most smaller companies can see no benefit from the UK joining the single European currency, according to a Reuters survey.

Nearly 58 per cent of the companies with market capitalisation of £800 million or less that were surveyed said they could see no advantage to their businesses from being in the euro. More than 73 per cent believe that sales will remain the same, and 65 per cent believe that profits will stay the same. Some business managers argue that, even where sales increase, this may not result in increased profits. In contrast, over 60 per cent of large businesses are in favour of the UK belonging to the euro.

Source: *Financial Times*, 21 June 2001

1 Explain why it might be possible for sales to increase as a result of the euro, but for this not to result in increased profits. [4]
2 Why do you think small businesses might be against the UK joining the euro? [6]
3 Evaluate the arguments for and against the UK's membership of the single European currency from a large business perspective. [10]

Total 20 marks

5 Social Chapter

To keep pace with the growing economic integration of Europe, in 1991 the EU adopted the Social Chapter. This was an agreement to implement common rules and regulations across the EU that would protect workers' rights. The regulations introduced so far include:

- rights of parental leave for both mothers and fathers

- limits to the length of the working week and rights to rest breaks and paid holidays

- the establishment of works councils in larger businesses.

The UK initially opted out of this agreement, but signed up in 1997. The decision to opt out was taken by the Conservative government of the time, who argued that the costs to business of meeting the additional regulations would be too high. Higher costs, it was felt, would force businesses to raise prices, making them uncompetitive in world markets and leading to job losses. The Labour government in 1997 took the view that the benefits to workers of these guaranteed rights outweighed any additional costs to business. Indeed, business might itself benefit from improved productivity and efficiency if the additional rights were to produce a more motivated and cooperative workforce.

6 Enlargement of the European Union

The Copenhagen summit in December 2002 agreed that ten more countries should be allowed to join the EU in May 2004, if they had the support of their own

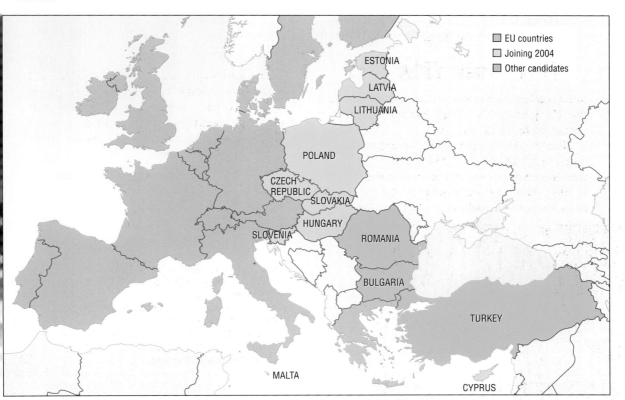

Figure 42.2 Future and possible future member states of the European Union

Source: www.bbc.co.uk/news

people in a referendum. This expansion will be the largest in the EU's history. The new members – mainly from the formerly Communist east – are shown in Figure 42.2. Bulgaria and Romania may be allowed to join from 2007, while Turkey has been told it must wait for at least two more years before talks on its entry can begin.

The massive enlargement of the EU brings increased opportunities for business. It will further boost the size of the single market and with it the potential for trade. New markets will be opened up to UK businesses, in countries that may previously been too difficult or unstable for trade. However, there are also likely to be costs of the enlargement and dangers. The poverty and economic problems of many of the new entrants will lead to increased costs for existing EU nations. It is estimated that this could amount to 67 billion euros between 2002 and 2006.

Adapting to the European market

The development and expansion of a single market may have opened up opportunities for UK business, but only with a carefully planned strategy will business be able to benefit to the full. This strategy will need to consider all aspects of the business operation.

- **Marketing.** Does the firm's marketing strategy need adapting for the European market? Different standards of living, cultures and languages in different countries may require promotional and pricing strategies to be varied.

- **Operations.** Where should production take place? Cost efficiency, reliability and quality all need to be considered when locating production or choosing suppliers.

- **Business size and organization.** Will expansion bring economies of scale or cause diseconomies? How best should the firm expand into the European market – through its own expansion or through franchising or licensing (see Unit 4)?

- **People.** Will the current size and skill levels of the workforce be sufficient to achieve success in the European market? How can recruitment and selection take advantage of the single market?

- **Finance**. Is expansion affordable and profitable? From where in the single market will the necessary finance for expansion be obtained?

While there may be no single best solution to the challenge of the European market, every business must decide how to adapt its strengths to meet the varied needs of consumers within the world's biggest single market.

Business and Europe: summary

Customs union – an agreement between a group of countries to get rid of barriers to trade between them and to set up a 'common external tariff' on trade with the rest of the world.

Common external tariff –a tax, imposed at the same rate by all countries within a customs union, on imports from the rest of the world.

Single market –the removal of all barriers to trade to establish the free movement of goods, services, people and capital.

Economic and Monetary Union (EMU) – the creation of a single currency (the euro) and a European Central Bank, which sets a single interest rate for all member countries.

Eurozone – the countries that have adopted the euro.

Price transparency – the ability to compare prices across Europe more easily, once they are all quoted in a single European currency.

Summary questions

1 Explain the concept of a 'customs union'.
2 How many member states does the EU currently have?
3 What 'freedoms' did the single market seek to establish?
4 Explain **two** opportunities and **two** threats to UK business resulting from being part of the European single market.
5 Why have UK businesses been affected by the euro despite the UK's decision not to adopt the single currency?
6 Explain **two** arguments in favour and **two** against the UK adopting the euro.
7 What is the Social Chapter?
8 Why did the UK government decide to opt out of the Social Chapter until 1997?
9 What will be the impact of the expansion of the EU to include ten more countries by 2004?
10 State **three** factors that a business will need to consider to adapt to the European market.

Exam practice

Rude awakening

Rude was set up three years ago by Rupert and Abi, who met at a graphic design company in London. They began putting original artwork of urban scenes onto T-shirts and canvasses, and started selling to places such as Selfridges in London.

When the designer brand business began to receive phone calls from over-seas stores that wanted to stock its T-shirts, the reaction in the office was 'Yeah! This is really exciting.' However, Rude soon found there was much more to exporting clothes than just putting them in a box with a freight sticker, which was its first approach.

Rude began to pitch up against problems – usually, unexpected rules and regulations. One concern involved bagging and tagging: EU laws require that every item be individually bagged and tagged. Another lesson came in the form of an invoice from a top German store, written in German, demanding payment for fabric safety tests (necessary before the store would stock the T-shirts).

The company already uses an export agent in Japan and is now considering using one for the increasing complex European market. Rude is, however, keen to expand, and exports will play an important role in terms of both revenue and brand awareness. Turnover was set to reach £600,000 by the financial year-end of 2003.

Source: *Financial Times*, 9 May 2002

1 Outline **two** difficulties British businesses might face when attempting to trade within the EU.   **[4]**
2 How would Rude be affected by the UK adopting the Euro?   **[8]**
3 How might Rude's marketing strategy differ when attempting to trade within the EU?   **[8]**
4 Evaluate the impact on UK businesses such as Rude of membership of the European single market   **[10]**
Total 30 marks

43 Society, ethics, environment

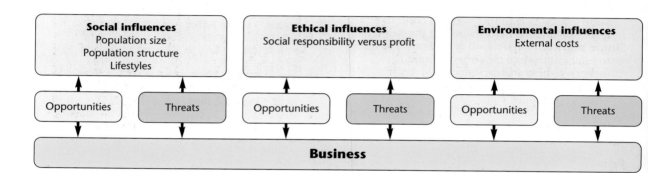

Social influences	Ethical influences	Environmental influences
Population size Population structure Lifestyles	Social responsibility versus profit	External costs

Opportunities — Threats — Opportunities — Threats — Opportunities — Threats

Business

1 A two-way relationship

No business can stand alone and isolated from the society around it. Society will present both *opportunities* and *threats*, which may determine the success or failure of the business. Business depends on society for its customers, its workforce and its resources. Society depends on business to meet the needs and wants of the population. Business will shape the wealth, choices and lives of the people in the society.

This unit considers three aspects of the relationship between business and society:

- social influences
- ethical influences
- environmental influences.

2 Social influences

Changes in the nature of the population and in the people's lifestyles will have a crucial effect on business. It is the people that are the consumers of a business's products, and they who provide the human resources needed for a business's workforce. The number and nature of consumers and workers will be shaped by three key **demographic factors**:

- population size

- population structure
- lifestyles.

Population size

The number of people in the UK – and indeed in the world as a whole – will affect:

- the number of consumers, and therefore the potential demand for a business's product
- the total workforce available to business
- the availability of land and other natural resources, given that business is competing for scarce resources.

Whether the UK population grows over time will depend on:

- the number of births compared to the number of deaths
- the level of immigration (number of people entering the country) compared to the level of emigration (number of people leaving the country).

Forecasts for the UK suggest that the population will rise gradually from the present figure of around 60 million to 65 million in 25 years' time. Having peaked at 66 million in 2040, population is expected

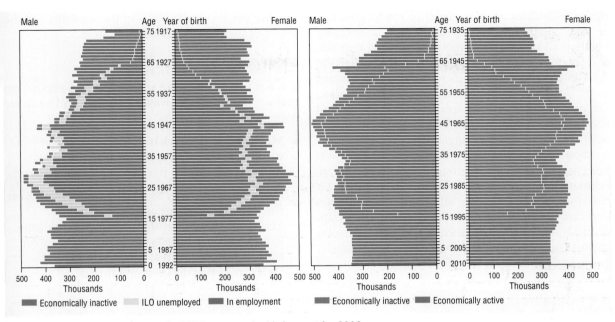

Figure 43.1 Population changes in 1992 compared with forecast for 2010

to decline thereafter. Longer life expectancy, which would increase population size, is largely offset by falling birth rates, as more women delay having children until they are older. Almost three-quarters of the predicted rise in UK population will be due to an expected increase in immigration, caused by the arrival of asylum seekers from Asia and Africa.

> ### STOP & THINK
>
> **What effects will these predicted population changes have on UK business?**

Population structure

Population characteristics such as age, gender and ethnicity are called **population structure**. Figure 43.1 shows how the age and gender structure of the UK population is changing over time, looking back to 1992 and ahead to 2010.

Although the structure of the population may be slow to change, Figure 43.1 begins to show the impact of falling birth rates and longer life expectancy. The combined effect is to create an ageing population and a growing **dependency ratio**:

- **Ageing population.** By 2014, the number of people aged over 65 will be greater than the number of under-16s. This will influence the types of products demanded by consumers, with a growing market for products aimed at older

people, such as specialist housing or specialist leisure activities. Firms may find younger workers in short supply, but a greater pool of older workers.

- **Growing dependency ratio.** The number of non-working people that each working person has to support is called the dependency ratio. Figure 43.2 shows the growth of the dependency ratio in the UK in recent decades and into the future. This places an increasing burden on the government and the taxpayer to ensure that the living standards of older people are maintained. It is this trend that has prompted the government to end compulsory retirement at 65 and to reform the provision of pensions.

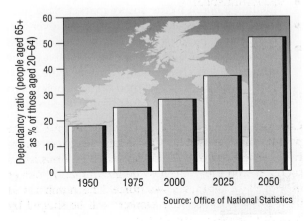

Source: Office of National Statistics

Figure 43.2 The UK's increasing dependency ratio, with future projections

Figure 43.1 illustrates the changing gender structure of the population. With female life expectancy higher than that for men, there are growing numbers of women over the age of 80. The trend seen in recent decades towards more women entering and staying in the workforce is set to continue. This will affect not only the labour force available to business, but also the number of financially independent women at whom businesses may target their products.

About one person in 14 in the UK in 2002 was from an ethnic minority group. People with Indian, Pakistani or Bangladeshi backgrounds number 1.9 million, while 1.3 million others are from families that came from Africa or the Caribbean. The multi-cultural nature of UK society has created new business opportunities in product areas such as food, music and clothing. It has also led many businesses to place equal opportunities in the workplace at the centre of their human resource strategies.

Lifestyles

It is not just the size and structure of the population that are changing; the way people live and work are undergoing changes too.

- **More flexible working**. Increases in part-time work, in flexible hours and in working from home have changed the nature of labour markets.

- **More leisure time.** More paid holidays per year, rising living standards and increased life expectancy have contributed to a growth in the leisure market. This has fuelled expenditure on consumer items, such as music systems and DVDs, as well as on sport and fitness.

For example ...

'A grand old age'

Many British businesses, including Sainsbury's and W.H. Smith's, are tapping into the skills of mature workers, particularly in well-off areas where there are difficulties in attracting part-time staff. Older workers are seen as more reliable, not wasting time and taking fewer days off sick. Professor Alan Walker of Sheffield University comments: 'The labour market is geared to a high turnover of recruitment and retirement, and that cannot go on. Employers will have to concentrate on retraining workers rather than getting rid of them and employing younger people.'

The future will not just bring more work and no play. The growing elderly population are fuelling a boom in the leisure market. Saga holidays, which specialises in trips for the over-50s, has been expanding into elephant trekking in Nepal and scuba-diving in the Maldives. The affluent elderly have their own magazine, *Good Times*, which sells more than 80,000 copies. Susi Rogol, its editor, says: 'Most of our readers have money to spend and time on their hands, and they are huge travellers, with 70 per cent taking more than two holidays each year. Older people also buy more cars than most younger people and are heavy users of computers, especially the internet. Sixty-year-olds are doing things now that 40-year-olds would have done twenty years ago.'

Popular culture will change. With over half the population over 50, it will no longer be dominated by obsession with youth. With most crimes committed by young people, and the elderly far more law-abiding, the crime rate is expected to steadily fall. There will be less of a need for police and prisons.

Source: *Observer*, 12 May 2002

1 Explain the statement: 'The labour market is geared to a high turnover of recruitment and retirement'. **[3]**
2 Weigh up the benefits and the drawbacks to firms of employing an older workforce. **[8]**
3 What marketing opportunities and what threats does an ageing population give rise to? **[6]**
Total 17 marks

- **Ease of travel and communication.**
Expenditure on foreign holidays has risen by 70
per cent in the last ten years, mainly as a result of
cheap air travel. Communication has become
instant, constant and global, thanks to the
internet and mobile phone revolution.

- **Fewer and later marriages and more
divorces.** The combined effect of these changes
has been to increase the number of single-person
households (see Figure 43.3). This has led to an
increased demand for housing and a growth in
the market for singles holidays and dating
agencies.

STOP & THINK

How do you think lifestyles will change in the
future? What impact will this have on business?

3   Ethical influences

Ethics are a set of moral principles that identify what is
believed to be the right thing to do. Businesses often
have to make 'ethical' decisions about how to act.

- Should they close branches to cut costs even at
the expense of mass redundancies?

- Should they find ways of reducing their pollution
even if these are expensive?

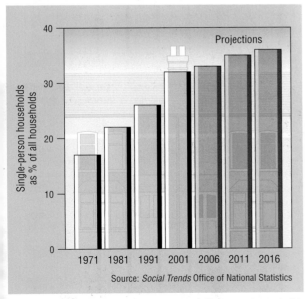

Figure 43.3 Increasing proportion of single-person households
in Great Britain, with future projections

- Should they turn down trade with countries
whose governments abuse human rights?

Stakeholders and shareholders

In making such decisions, businesses must consider
the interests of the various 'stakeholder' groups (see
Unit 3). These are the different groups that are
affected by the actions of a business, including shareholders, employees, the local community and
suppliers.

In deciding how to act, a business must decide to
whom it is ultimately responsible – that is, in whose
interests it is acting and whose needs it should be
placing first. There are two opposing views of what
this responsibility means.

- **The 'shareholder view'.** The most important
priority of business is to make a profit for its
shareholders. Shareholders have risked their
money by investing in the company and so it is
the duty of the business to reward them. The
'right' course of action is therefore, within the
law, to maximise profits.

Guru's views
'There is only one social responsibility of
business – to use its resources and engage in
activities designed to increase its profits...To
serve some general social interest is to spend
someone else's money.'

Milton Friedman

- **The 'stakeholder view'.** Business has a much
wider responsibility than just to its shareholders
(who are only one group of stakeholders). The
'right' course of action is the one that balances
the needs of many different groups. The needs of
employees, consumers and the community must
all be considered.

Guru's views
'We care about humanising the business
community: we will continue to show that
success and profits can go hand in hand with
ideals and values. We will demonstrate our
care for the world in which we live, by
respecting fellow human beings, by not
harming animals, by working to conserve our
planet.'

The Body Shop Charter

Social responsibility

There is clearly a potential conflict between social responsibility and making a profit. Shareholders' profits might be reduced if:

- costs rise in order to minimise pollution or improve working conditions

- sales opportunities are turned down because they are considered socially unacceptable

- charitable donations are taken out of business profits.

Nevertheless, many businesses today – such as The Body Shop and the Co-op – are committed to the stakeholder view. Why?

- **Legal regulation.** Laws and regulations in the areas of health and safety, consumer protection and the environment all require business to meet high standards. Meeting the needs of stakeholders is therefore part of staying within the law.

- **Self-interest**. By acquiring a reputation for ethical behaviour, a firm can improve its image and gain a marketing advantage. It will also reduce potential conflict with 'pressure groups' – groups that campaign on a range of social causes and try to influence business behaviour. A firm's employees may be more motivated and productive if their needs are being met by the business (see Unit 24).

- **Moral code.** The religious or ethical views of the owners of a business may be crucial in encouraging social responsibility among smaller businesses.

Guru's views
'Love your neighbour is not merely sound Christianity; it is good business.'

David Lloyd George

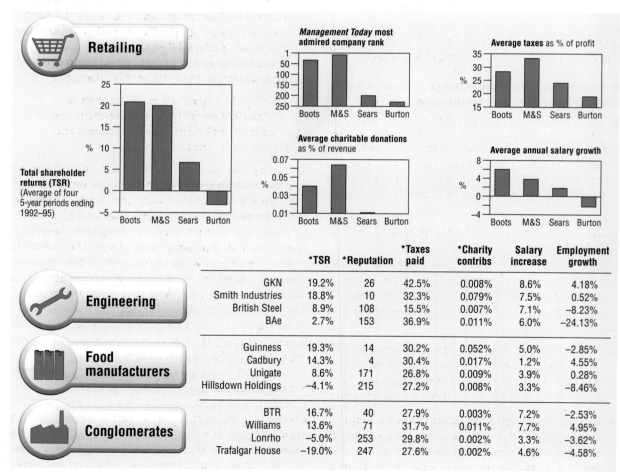

			*TSR	*Reputation	*Taxes paid	*Charity contribs	Salary increase	Employment growth
Engineering		GKN	19.2%	26	42.5%	0.008%	8.6%	4.18%
		Smith Industries	18.8%	10	32.3%	0.079%	7.5%	0.52%
		British Steel	8.9%	108	15.5%	0.007%	7.1%	−8.23%
		BAe	2.7%	153	36.9%	0.011%	6.0%	−24.13%
Food manufacturers		Guinness	19.3%	14	30.2%	0.052%	5.0%	−2.85%
		Cadbury	14.3%	4	30.4%	0.017%	1.2%	4.55%
		Unigate	8.6%	171	26.8%	0.009%	3.9%	0.28%
		Hillsdown Holdings	−4.1%	215	27.2%	0.008%	3.3%	−8.46%
Conglomerates		BTR	16.7%	40	27.9%	0.003%	7.2%	−2.53%
		Williams	13.6%	71	31.7%	0.011%	7.7%	4.95%
		Lonrho	−5.0%	253	29.8%	0.002%	3.3%	−3.62%
		Trafalgar House	−19.0%	247	27.6%	0.002%	4.6%	−4.58%

Figure 43.4 Profits and social responsibility

Consider the following business situations and decide to what extent you believe each to be 'right' or 'wrong'. Use a scale of 1 to 5 where 1 means 'wholly right – no concerns' and 5 means 'completely wrong – unacceptable'. Record your result and explain the reasons behind each decision.
- A fast food chain sponsors children's TV programmes to target the 3–8 year-old market.
- A UK arms manufacturer agrees a deal to send weapons to the government of a country engaged in civil war.
- A drinks company develops a new alcoholic drink that will appeal to young people.
- A clothing manufacturer moves its production to South-east Asia, where it can pay workers very low wages and so cut its production costs.
- A loan company offers to lend money to those already heavily in debt, but only at high monthly rates of interest.

Research in the 1990s showed that there was a strong link between how well a company serves shareholders and how it serves its other stakeholders. Figure 43.4 shows that the companies in each sector that returned most to shareholders were also those that rewarded their workers the best, contributed the most to charity and were the most respected. The conclusion drawn was that, while there may be a short-term conflict between profits and 'ethical' behaviour, in the longer term there is not. By considering the needs of workers, customers and the community, a business can build a reputation and culture that generate greater profitability.

 Environmental influences

Some businesses, in addition to the costs incurred by production, may also generate external costs to society as a whole. These are costs representing the negative effects that a business may have on the environment.

- **Pollution.** Emissions from factories may reduce air quality or contribute to problems of global warming. Oil or toxic waste may pollute seas or rivers. Noise pollution may disturb local residents.

- **Congestion.** Customer traffic visiting a major store, or fleets of distribution vehicles, will add to the problem of congestion on the roads. The result is delays for everyone using the roads, and increased air pollution associated with traffic.

- **Abuse of natural resources.** The destruction of rainforests, the overfishing of the North Sea and the loss of the countryside for development are all examples of how business has failed to consider its impact on the world's natural resources.

Whereas, in the past, business may have ignored the external costs of its actions, increasing public concern about the environment has forced companies to consider the issue very carefully. Harming the environment has become costly to business in several ways.

- **Increased regulation.** The passing of new laws such as the Environmental Protection Act has set limits on pollution levels. Fines and compensation may now be more costly than avoiding pollution in the first place. Similarly, a landfill tax now charges business for dumping waste in landfill sites. The aim is that, increasing the costs of dumping waste will encourage businesses to reuse or recycle waste materials.

- **Increased pressure group activity.** Pressure groups, like Greenpeace and Friends of the Earth, have launched high-profile campaigns against big companies, such as BP, whom they accuse of damaging the environment. These campaigns can cause disastrous publicity and be disruptive.

- **Damage to reputation.** Being seen as irresponsible towards the environment can damage the public image of a business and directly harm sales and profits.

Changing production methods or equipment to minimise any negative impact on the environment will raise a business's short-term costs. However, many businesses now believe that caring for the environment is in their own long-term interests. Some, such as The Body Shop, base much of their marketing appeal on their concern for the environment. So-called 'green marketing' has caught on to the extent that many businesses and new products seek to set out their environmentally friendly credentials. Figure 43.5 summarises some of the actions taken by the UK's largest companies to show their concern for the environment.

To establish the 'proof' that the business is caring for the environment, some organisations have introduced environmental audits. These are independent checks on all aspects of a firm's impact on its surroundings. The results are published as part of the annual report to shareholders, helping to build the positive image that the business seeks. The audit may also identify genuine opportunities for improvement,

1 Reducing environmental damage

- Shell: steps to reduce emissions
- ICI: development of environmentally-friendly fertilizers
- Corus: environmental control facilities in new plants

2 Waste reduction

- Reckitt &Colman: improved energy management and increased recycling
- Tesco: use of recycled paper for all internal stationery
- Safeway: promoting recycling of plastic bags and bottles

3 Raising environmental awareness

- BP: supporting the chemical industry's 'responsible care' initiative
- British Airways: environmental suggestion scheme for staff

- Tesco: 'Tesco cares' programme, giving identity to environmental policies

4 Supporting environmental protection charities

- Boots: substantial charitable donations
- Tate & Lyle: matches all employee contributions to rainforest conservation programme
- Marks &Spencer: support for Tidy Britain Group

5 Local community initiatives

- Bass: funded tree planting schemes in Birmingham
- Allied Lyons: 12,000 tress to surround one of the company's new factories
- Pilkington: supporting urban regeneration programmes

Figure 43.5 UK companies' environmental awareness activities

such as a way for the business to cut down on waste, for example.

For business to consider its impact on the environment is now standard practice. Most businesses know that showing environmental concern is vital to a business's positive image and, ultimately, to its long-term profitability. The question that business and many governments do not address, however, is whether the whole system of business and profit is sustainable given its effects on the environment and the world's resources.

Activity

Use the internet to investigate how different businesses seek to protect the environment. You might look at Coca-Cola, BP, McDonald's, The Body Shop and Unilever.

Society, ethics, environment: summary

KEY TERMS

Demographic factors – the size and structure of the population.

Population structure – the characteristics of the population, such as age, gender and ethnicity.

Dependency ratio – the number of non-working people that each working person has to support.

Ethics – a set of moral principles that identify what is believed to be the right thing to do.

Social responsibility – the duty of a business to meet the needs of a variety of stakeholders, including consumers and the community.

Pressure groups – groups of individuals seeking to persuade those in business or in government to promote a cause or the interests of a specific section of society.

Environmental audits – independent checks on all aspects of a firm's impact on its surroundings.

Exam practice continues ➤

Society, ethics, environment: summary (continued)

Summary questions

1 Why does business depend on society?
2 What is meant by the term 'demographic factors'?
3 How is business affected by a growing population?
4 What will be the effects on business of an ageing population?
5 State **two** trends in lifestyles and explain how they affect business.
6 Why do businesses face 'ethical' decisions?
7 Contrast the 'stakeholder' view of business responsibility with the 'shareholder' view.

8 Explain **two** reasons why socially responsible firms may experience:
  a lower profits in the short-term
  b higher profits in the long-term.
9 In what ways might a business impose 'external costs' on the environment?
10 Why have firms increasingly taken seriously their responsibility to the environment?
11 What is the purpose of an environmental audit?

Exam practice

Flashback ...

The Guardian, 28 October 1996

Change the rules

The pressure group Christian Aid has launched a 'Change the Rules' campaign, urging shoppers to lobby supermarkets to stop them stocking produce from developing countries where workers suffer unacceptably low wages or work in dangerous conditions.

The campaign could eventually lead to boycotts of particular products, if consumers felt the shops were not doing enough to safeguard the rights of foreign workers. Christian Aid has already singled out apples from South Africa, asparagus from Peru and tiger prawns from Thailand.

Christian Aid will first be calling on its 250,000 supporters to put pressure on their local stores. They will be asked to write messages to supermarket managers on the back of their till receipts, to underline the economic muscle behind their concern.

The four-year campaign seeks to persuade supermarkets to:
- adopt a set of ethical principles for buying from poorer countries
- implement a code of conduct
- introduce independent monitoring.

1 Define the terms:
  a pressure group [2]
  b ethical principles. [2]
2 Why might some pressure group campaigns prove successful in changing business behaviour whereas others might not? [6]
3 Explain the costs and the benefits to supermarkets of adopting 'ethical trading'. [8]
4 Evaluate the view that a business's social responsibility should come before profits. [12]
  Total 30 marks

Sainsbury's Statement 2003

We have become more conscious of the need to take some share of the responsibility for social development, and for the welfare of employees who produce the goods we sell. Sainsbury's is a founder member of the Ethical Trading Initiative and has been actively involved with its activities. We also stock a number of Fairtrade products within our stores. This has increased from nine to over twenty products within the last year, reflecting the increase in customer demand for such products.

Source: www.sainsburys.co.uk

Christian Aid Statement 2003

Two years since the campaign's launch there has been much talk and much less concrete action. The burden is on industry to prove that the Ethical Trading Initiative (ETI) can become a fast track to ethical trade, rather than a bucket in which to dump and then forget about public concerns. We remain convinced that the High Street food giants could do more – and more quickly – to achieve ethical trading in the food production and retailing industry.

Christian Aid recognises that we live in a world of conflicting interests – but does not believe that the interests of the British shopper, the supermarkets and the Third World producer are completely incompatible. We do not have to choose between trade and ethics. A marginal shift away from profits for supermarkets to protection for Third World workers would not break the High Street food giants, but could make all the difference to producers overseas.

Source: www.christian-aid.org

Want to know more?

www.christian-aid.org.uk

44 Technological change

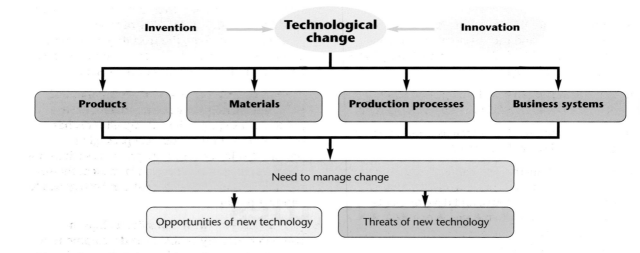

1 What is technological change?

No business can afford to ignore change. Any business that does will soon find that its products and its processes no longer meet its customers' needs. Knowledge and ideas are expanding all the time; materials are being discovered or created; new ways of doing things are being pioneered. This is what is known as 'technological change'.

Research by business, higher education or government is generating new ideas (**invention**), while the business world constantly seeks to develop these ideas into opportunities for profit (**innovation**). The pace of technological change is increasingly rapid – each new idea provides further opportunities for invention and innovation. Among the most significant technological developments in recent years has been the growth of the internet, mobile communications, digital technology and genetic advancements.

Not all technological change will be beneficial to a business. Changes in technology will affect what customers want, what competitors provide and how businesses operate. Broadly, the areas of change can be divided into four categories:

- products
- materials
- production processes
- business systems.

> ### Guru's views
> 'If you've always done it that way, it is probably wrong.'
>
> *Charles Kettering (inventor)*

2 Products

All the time, technological change is enabling the development of new goods and services. The invention of a new form technology makes a business want to be the first to use it to develop and launch a new product. Doing so, gives a 'first-mover advantage' (see Unit 8), which can boost the sales and profitability of the product over its lifecycle. Cutting new product development times (see Unit 36) is therefore very important.

The most significant areas of recent product developments include:

- digital technology – interactive digital television, digital radio services and the rapid growth of DVDs

- mobile communications – the global rise of the mobile phone and the development of new generation mobile technologies, including WAP and picture messaging

- hand-held computer technology – the ability to pack the power of a PC into a palm-top device

- internet-based services – such as internet banking or music sales via the internet

- medical and pharmaceutical products – the development of vaccines, such as the vaccine for one strain of meningitis, and developments in cloning technology, which have opened up opportunities to clone human body parts or even produce cloned babies.

STOP & THINK

In what areas of business do you think the next major product innovations will come? Will they bring real benefits to consumers?

3 Materials

Invention and innovation can give rise to new materials that transform the way products are made and packaged. New or adapted raw materials may provide ways to reduce costs, improve quality, increase productivity or even develop entirely new products.

- **Genetically modified (GM) food.** Trials of GM crops have shown their potential to increase both the quantity and quality of food production. However, the risks they pose to the natural environment have also been highlighted, and the GM issue remains controversial.

- **Packaging materials.** The development of polystyrene and strong plastics has enabled product packaging to be redesigned. This has often resulted in more durable packaging, produced at lower cost. New products such as hot coffee in a can have also been launched, thanks to materials and processes that can both generate and retain heat.

- **Silicon chips.** The use of silicon chips in computer circuitry enabled the development of personal computers, and, later, palm-top devices, using ever-smaller components, were developed.

4 Production processes

Computer technology has totally revolutionised production methods. In many manufacturing

DVDs double sales to 3.8m in revolution for retailers

SALES OF DVD players and discs have more than doubled in the past year.

The British Video Association reported sales of 3.8 million machines in 2002 compared with 1.9 million in 2001. Last month, consumers bought 1.2 million players.

Since it was launched in 1997, the DVD (Digital Versatile Disc) player has been bought by one in four consumers, making it the fastest-selling electrical entertainment product in retail history. The phenomenon is partly put down to the popularity of family films released on DVD in the past 12 months and the falling price of the player; which costs between £100 and £200 for a top-of-the-range machine. Sales of DVD discs

reached 80 million last year – a rise of 111 percent.

The British Video Association said yesterday that film companies had increased efforts to release films that would appeal to a wider market than the early DVD owners, who were film fans and devotees of digital innovation.

Lavinia Carey, director general, said: 'It is not just the early adopters of technology, such as single young men, but the whole family appreciating the advances of DVD.'

Industry experts forecast a similar rise in sales of the recordable DVD, once manufacturers have agreed on a universal format for re-recordable discs and reduced prices, currently starting at about £400.

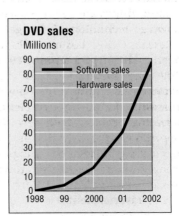

DVD sales
Millions

industries, computer technology is now integrated into every stage of the production process. This is called **computer integrated manufacture (CIM)**. It includes **manufacturing resource planning (MRPII)**, **electronic data interchange (EDI)**, **computer-aided design (CAD)** and **computer-aided manufacture (CAM)**.

- **Manufacturing resource planning (MRPII).** This software enables production managers to plan the production process and test the effects of different decisions, using MRPII's powerful 'What if?' facility. For example, it could show the effects that cutting the workforce or changing supplier would have on meeting customer orders.

- **Electronic data interchange (EDI).** The ability to link branches, factories, head office and suppliers through the internet allows an efficient and integrated production process. EDI can be used to trigger the reorder of parts from suppliers as they are needed, forming part of a just-in-time production system (see Unit 36).

- **Computer-aided design (CAD).** Most product design is now carried out using the 3-D capabilities of computer design, rather than by hand. CAD enables design drawings to be altered swiftly and easily, produced with maximum precision and computer-tested to ensure they match required specifications.

- **Computer-aided manufacture (CAM).** CAM involves the use of computer technology to plan and control the manufacturing process. It can link CAD-produced drawings to computer-controlled machines to automate production. CAM enables both precision accuracy and a flexible response to the needs of different customers.

5 Business systems

Technology has transformed the way that businesses are organised and run, and every business function has been affected by it.

- **Marketing.** The development of the internet has had a major impact on marketing strategies and techniques:

  - **Promotion.** Using the internet, businesses can communicate directly with customers across the world. Websites have been developed to promote products effectively. –

  - **Place.** Businesses can sell directly to consumers, without using the traditional middlemen – retailers, wholesalers or agents. Internet shopping has opened up new markets and helped businesses to cut costs.

  - **Price.** Consumers can compare prices from rival firms across the country or the world, forcing tougher price competition onto businesses.

  - **Products.** New products can be researched and launched more easily on the internet, including computer software, music and financial products.

- **Communication.** Cellular phone technology, together with rise of the internet, has helped bring about a communications revolution. No longer do organisations and their managers have to be tied to fixed locations to communicate.

  - 'Mobile office'. Laptops, internet, e-mail and mobile phones together allow work and communication to continue almost anywhere in the world. **Teleworking** – working from home – has become an increasingly popular trend in business, using communications technology to link with the organisation or with customers.

  - Instant communication. E-mail has enabled the swift transfer of documents and images across continents.

  - Video conferencing. Using the internet to transfer voice and images, so that people can see and hear each other, reduces the need to travel for face-to-face meetings.

- **Stock control and purchasing.** The use of **electronic point of sale (EPOS)** technology enables businesses to monitor sales and stock levels far more efficiently. EPOS involves laser scanning of barcode information at the point of purchase. This information passes to a database of stock information, automatically updating the level of stock and triggering reordering when it falls below a certain level.

- **Finance.** The use of spreadsheets in business to record and monitor financial data is now commonplace. Specialist accounting software

Technological change

Advantges

- **Lower costs.** Technology can increase business efficiency and so help to reduce costs. By speeding up product design or manufacture, wasted time can be eliminated. New production processes or materials may increase output without a need for additional inputs. Repetitive tasks may be carried out more cheaply using technology than by employing labour.

- **New markets.** Advanced technology creates new product opportunities, opening up new, potentially profitable markets. The internet has also opened up new selling opportunities, extending a business's market right across the world.

- **Better communication.** Improved communications technology has made business communication quicker, more mobile and more sophisticated, allowing the rapid exchange of information and ideas. The widespread access to information, and the ease with which ideas can be exchanged, has encouraged businesses to promote greater participation and empowerment of its employees.

- **Better quality and more choice.** Quality of products can be improved by the use of new materials and new production processes. New products bring greater choice for consumers, meeting their needs and helping to raise living standards.

- **Benefits to employees.** Boring and repetitive tasks can be automated, leaving workers to take responsibility for more creative or innovative aspects of a job. The workplace could be made safer, cleaner or quieter through the use of new technology. If reduced costs and new markets make a business more profitable, employees may benefit through increased wages or bonuses.

Disadvantages

- **Risk.** New products and processes bring increased risks, compared to tried and tested products or methods. The technology may not yet be proven or accepted by consumers. Recordable DVDs, for example, have a range of possible formats, with no single format so far accepted as the industry standard – for a business to commit itself to any particular format could prove a costly mistake. Switching to new technology can also be risky because of delays or breakdowns. Major organisations such as the Air Traffic Control Service and the Passport Agency have faced major problems in recent years when introducing new computer systems.

- **Cost.** New technology may offer improved efficiency in the long term, but the initial purchase and implementation can be expensive. Maintenance costs and staff training costs also have to be considered, as well as equipment replacement costs in the future. Given the speed of technological change, a business may find that its new products, processes or equipment are out of date within several years, or even months.

- **Overload.** Technology's ability of to speed up business communication and decision-making can cause problems. The volume of communication has increased so much, due to the use of mobile phones and e-mail, that many businesses suffer from 'communication overload'. The constant interruptions, the need to respond to messages and the amount of information communicated are making employees less productive and less effective.

- **Unemployment.** Technological change may lead to increased automation at the expense of jobs. The unemployment so caused may bring not only personal hardship, but also wider problems to communities and society. Job losses may also be a cause of conflict between management and the workforce, with the prospect of damaging industrial action.

- **Resistance to change.** Workers may fear technological change because it can undermine:
    - job security: taking away jobs
    - routine: taking away existing ways of doing things
    - status: challenging the traditional expertise of some workers
    - skills: rendering established skills useless.

Introducing technological change, such as air traffic control, can cause major problems

provides a sophisticated package that enables managers to analyse financial information, such as cash flow or budget variances.

- **Personnel.** Many businesses keep records of employees' personal details on a computer database. This enables a business to monitor aspects of human resource management, such as the skills and training of its workforce or the rate of labour turnover. A database can also be used to manage the payment of employees, calculating rates of pay and taxation and making payments directly into employees' bank accounts.

 ## 6   Managing technological change

Using Maslow's hierarchy of needs (see Unit 24) as a framework, it can be seen that technological change can undermine an individual's lower- and higher-order needs. The consequence is that employees may feel threatened by new technology and resist its introduction. This may be evident in:

- low morale
- lack of cooperation
- poor productivity
- high absenteeism or high labour turnover.

If the threats posed by new technology are to be kept to a minimum – and the opportunities maximised – change needs to be carefully managed (see Unit 29). Businesses must pay careful attention to:

- development and testing – before accepting the risks that adopting new equipment or processes can bring
- ongoing market research – to anticipate and meet the needs of its customers
- planning new technology's introduction – to ensure the minimum of disruption
- overcoming staff fears – making staff feel valued and involved in the process of change
- training and development – enabling the workforce to adapt successfully to the new processes or skills required.

Activity

A bank is thinking of introducing new technology into its branches. This would include new cash machines for use by customers, each machine keeping detailed records of customer accounts. The machines would give customers the flexibility to manage their accounts, without having to enter the bank or talk to a cashier. Consider the benefits and drawbacks of such a scheme from the bank's point of view, using a table like the one below. Examples have been given to start you off.

Benefits of new machines	Drawbacks of new machines
Fewer branch staff needed	Cost of staff training

For example …

Technology takeover

Terms such as CAD, EPOS and EDI have been familiar to most business men and women for some time now. They have slowly become an integral part of business. The usage of such technologies is, however, dwarfed by the use of e-mail. In a few short years, e-mail grew from a novelty to something that few businesses can now survive without. Hundreds of thousands of e-mails are sent each day, vastly speeding up both internal and external business communications.

Just as quickly, however, e-mail became one of the prime causes of unofficial 'lost time' in the workplace. Traditionally, businesses 'lost time' due to unofficial cigarette breaks. Now, more time is lost through the use of e-mail to organise social lives or share the latest joke. Stories abound that, in some offices, people e-mail colleagues on desks just a few metres away, rather than get up and talk to them!

1 Define the term 'CAD'. [2]
2 Define the term 'EPOS' [2]
3 Explain why some staff might fear the introduction of new ICT systems. [6]
4 What are the advantages of increased use of e-mail within the workplace? [6]

Total 16 marks

Technological change: summary

KEY TERMS

Invention – generating new ideas or creating new products.

Innovation – developing new ideas into profitable products.

Computer integrated manufacturing (CIM) – computer technology that integrates every stage of the production process.

Manufacturing resource planning (MRPII) – computer software that enables managers to plan the production process and test the effects of possible decisions.

Computer-aided design (CAD) – the use of computer-generated images to design and test new products.

Computer-aided manufacturing (CAM) – the use of computer technology to plan and control the manufacturing process.

Automation – the replacement of people with machines in the production process.

Electronic data interchange (EDI) – the use of the internet to link computers in branches, factories, head office or suppliers, for the exchange of information.

Electronic point of sale (EPOS) – laser scanning of bar code information at the point of purchase in order to update records of sales and stock.

Teleworking – working at home, using technology to provide communication with an organisation or customers.

Summary questions

1 What is meant by 'technological change'?
2 What is the difference between 'invention' and 'innovation'?
3 Give **two** recent examples of your own of new technology leading to new product launches.
4 Why is there an incentive for a business to be the first to launch a new type of product?
5 Explain the benefits of CAD and CAM technology.
6 How can businesses make use of EDI?
7 How has marketing been affected by the growth of the internet?
8 Explain how technology has affected stock control.
9 Explain **three** opportunities that new technology presents to business.
10 Explain **two** reasons why some staff might resent the introduction of new technology.
11 How can business manage technological change successfully?

Exam practice

Ring of confidence

Many of the country's increasing number of call centres are labelled 'modern high-tech sweatshops'; this is largely due to the high labour turnover, high absenteeism and low staff morale that are often prevalent. These call centres are usually customers' first line of contact with a business and are being used increasingly by banks and online retailers. Customers can ring the centres and, in the case of banks, receive automated balance information, or talk to a customer service representative about their account. Often, customers are passed through complex automated navigation systems, allowing them to choose from a variety of options using touch-tone telephones. (A customer requiring just an account balance would select one option whereas a customer wishing to discuss a credit limit would choose another option.)

Many call centres are considered 'state of the art'. The technology they use is often far superior to that used by manufacturing businesses. There is even a case of a food manufacturer benchmarking itself against a call centre to help solve its quality problems.

One criticism frequently levelled at call centres is that of management. The centres are often managed by the IT department (given their high-tech nature), but this can be a mistake, as the people in call centres are perhaps more important than the technology. Whoever manages the centres, human resources should take a keen interest. This is essential if the problems associated with call centres are to be avoided or solved. After all, the call centre might be the only personal contact a customer has with a business.

Source: *Financial Times, FT Creative Business Supplement,* May 2002

1 Identify **one** reason why call centres are becoming increasingly popular. **[2]**
2 Outline **two** benefits that a call centre might gain from introducing an automated navigation system to its telephone answering systems. **[4]**
3 Why is it important that human resources 'takes a keen interest' in call centre operations? **[6]**
4 How might the introduction of technology into the manufacturing process solve a food manufacturer's quality problems? **[10]**
5 'ICT creates as many communication problems as it solves.' Discuss this statement. **[8]**

Total 30 marks

Getting the grade: External influences

EXTERNAL influences impact on business activities in many ways. At first some students may find the breadth of the topic quite daunting. It is important to remember, though, that in Business Studies (as opposed to Economics) it is the *impact on business* that is important and not necessarily the economic theory itself. Understanding the *impact* of exchange rates is far more important than understanding how exchange rates are determined. Understanding how exchange rates may have *different* impacts on *different* firms will gain you more marks than being able to link together the multitude of economic theories.

With this in mind, you should take the following key points into account when revising external influences:

Get used to data

It is quite likely in your exam that you will be presented with information about the state of the economy, in numerical or graphical form. You need to be comfortable about interpreting and using this data. Don't make the mistake of ignoring it. Unfortunately, if you do not find using data easy, there is only one way to get better – practice! Use newspaper articles, online resources, past examination papers and the questions in this book to develop your skills. Little mathematical ability is required, having a 'feel' for the data will often be enough – remember it is how the data will *affect* business that is important not the data itself.

One key point to remember – a slowdown in economic growth does not mean that the economy is shrinking, just that it is growing more slowly (perhaps 1 per cent growth instead of 2 per cent).

To what extent

Very often you will be asked to consider the likely extent to which economic changes will affect a firm. Remember, not all firms are affected to the same extent. A business selling luxury goods will be more significantly affected by a fall in real incomes than a business selling essential goods. You must decide how significant the economic changes will be for the *particular* firm in question.

You are not a lawyer (yet)

Even if you are intending to pursue a career in law, for your AS Business Studies you do not need a detailed knowledge of business law. Outline knowledge of some of the key laws, and the ability to consider the impact of the law on a firm, is far more important.

External and internal

It is very easy to get 'bogged down' in external influences and to forget the internal dimension. The ability of a firm to react to economic changes, and the extent of any impact, will be determined by internal factors. Interest rates may have less of an impact on firms with low gearing. A business with numerical and functional workforce flexibility will be better placed to react to shifts in the economic climate. Both the internal and external context will be important in shaping your answers.

Business strategy

Reaction to economic changes is of course only half of the equation. Truly great businesses will proactively implement business strategies to help isolate them, to the greatest possible extent, from external influences. You need to understand and be able to discuss the strategies that may make this possible. For instance, where demand is very income elastic, what capacity management policies or marketing strategies might be used to minimise the effects of shifting demand?

The best way to develop an understanding of the external environment is to keep your eye on the news.

Consider, for instance:

● What is the interest rate at the moment?

● Why?

● Was its last movement up or down?

● Why?

You will find the answers to these questions, and detailed analysis of the impact on business in general, covered in the media almost every week. Pick a company (or even several) that you are familiar with and, for every piece of economic news you hear, consider the impact (if any) on that firm. If you do this regularly, you should be in an excellent position to analyse and evaluate the economic challenges facing the company used in your examination case study.

Index

The page numbers in **bold** are where the Key Term definition for that word or phrase can be found.